International Management

A review of strategies and operations

Third edition

Michael Z Brooke

Stanley Thornes (Publishers) Ltd

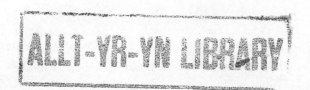

First published 1986 by Hutchinson Education

Third edition published in 1996 by
Stanley Thornes Publishers Ltd
Ellenborough House
Wellington Street
Cheltenham
Glos. GL50 1YW
UK

96 97 98 99 00 / 10 9 8 7 6 5 4 3 2 1

A catalogue record for this book is available from The British Library

ISBN 0 7487 2245 9

Typeset by Columns Design Ltd, Reading
Printed and bound in Great Britain at Redwood Books, Trowbridge, Wiltshire

Contents

Part 1

1.1 The nature and scope of international management • 1.2 Aims and objectives • 1.3 A career in international management • 1.4 Outline • 1.5 Conclusion

2.1 Trade • 2.2 Investment • 2.3 Organization • 2.4 International investment • 2.5 Exercises, questions and further reading

3.1 From explorers to competitors (motives for operating internationally) • 3.2 Expansion strategies • 3.3 Strategies for servicing foreign markets • 3.4 Analysing the strategies • 3.5 The transfer of knowhow: managerial and technical • 3.6 Conclusion • 3.7 Cases, questions and further reading

Part 2

4.1 Pre-export • 4.2 Market selection • 4.3 Significant obstacles • 4.4 The options • 4.5 The foreign agent or distributor • 4.6 Organization and staffing • 4.7 Documentation • 4.8 Conclusion • 4.9 Cases, questions and further reading

5.1 Selling knowledge abroad • 5.2 Licensing agreements • 5.3 Franchising agreements • 5.4 Management contracts • 5.5 Other contractual arrangements • 5.6 The selection and control of contract partners • 5.7 Organization • 5.8 Conclusion • 5.9 Cases, questions and further reading

Part 3

Acknowledgements

The need for a reasonably brief but comprehensive book on international management, written from a non-American standpoint, has long been obvious and a number of people have encouraged me to write it. I owe a great debt to numerous colleagues, students and friends, both in commerce and in education, for their advice and assistance. The difficulty has been to steer a course between those who advocate brevity and those who urge comprehensiveness.

Some topics are summarized, some discussed in greater depth. The selection has been according to a number of criteria – above all the need to put into the hands of the reader as thorough, up-to-date and research-based a review of a fascinating and topical subject as is possible in a confined space. Material that has had to be left out can be found in references; the lack of availability of accessible sources for reference was one of the criteria for inclusion. One whole chapter has been omitted – that on the history of international business; perhaps this will form the subject of a separate book later.

Numerous executives, academics and students from at least 16 countries have helped in some way with this book or with the research and teaching that underlies much of its content. My special thanks go to Professor Bjorn Alarik (of the University of Goteborg), Dr Alan Mitton (of Manchester Polytechnic) and Dr Quy (of the European Business School), each of whom has read the whole manuscript and offered valuable suggestions which have been incorporated into the final draft. I also have to thank students at the City University Business School, the European Business School and Henley Management College who used the book in manuscript form and made many helpful comments.

Others who offered advice were Professor Peter Buckley (Bradford University Management Centre), Mr Roy Earnshaw (formerly of Turner and Newall plc), Mr John Hutton (Henley Management College), Mr Peter Lawrence of Loughborough University, Professor Sylvain Plasschaert (Antwerp University), Professor Lee Remmers (Institut Européen d'Administration des Affaires, Fontainebleau), and Mr Freddie Saelens (NV Philips, Eindhoven).

Naturally, in thanking so many generous helpers, I must emphasize that I take full responsibility for the final result; the shortcomings are all mine.

I would also thank my long-suffering family, who have now had to live through 24 books in 25 years, and my secretary, Elizabeth Hickson, who has keyed (and rekeyed many times) the whole manuscript and designed most of the figures and tables. Her perseverance and hard work have kept us to our deadlines in spite of my inability to allow enough time.

Acknowledgements to this edition

The acknowledgements of the first two editions still stand, although sadly one of those who offered advice (David Liston) has since died. Many users of the book have since offered helpful suggestions; queries have been received from business schools in North America about the use of the case examples. The author is always glad to help, but in the European context it hardly seems feasible to publish a separate teacher's manual.

Preface to this new edition

This book was designed to identify the main elements of international management for the student of the subject. This subject was seen as a body of knowledge rather than as a bundle of theories (although those are also identified). The first two editions were published in 1986 and 1992; the second edition did set out a mixture of substantial truths with more ephemeral matter. This edition re-emphasizes the long-term truths, while replacing the more perishable elements. Inevitably much has changed, this is a dynamic subject, but much has stayed the same. Cases and examples remain when they illustrate companies wrestling with problems that are not dependent on short-term economic or political phenomena. The chapter headings and subheadings have been retained for the benefit of students on distance learning courses who are using this book as a textbook. If you are in this position, please be reassured, the cross-references from your course notes are still valid!

The keyboard analogy

At the end of Chapters 3, 4, 5 and 6 there is a diagram entitled a 'keyboard analogy' comparing corporate decision-making to playing a piano. Many of the notes have to be played at once, while the combinations and sequences are all important. This analogy is as exact as an analogy can be and, hopefully, illuminating. Unfortunately, as has been pointed out by more than one correspondent, it does not illuminate those who are unfamiliar with music. The author can only invite them to take on trust the statement about sequences and combinations. A glance at a keyboard instrument will usually demonstrate the truthfulness of the diagrams. See the further note at the end of Chapter 3.

How to use this book

International Management is designed for students aiming at a career in world business and for upwardly mobile executives. Within these target groups, there are:
executives who want to supplement and broaden their hard won experience;
students (full-time or part-time, in a college or on a distance learning course) who need a course book that is comprehensive but compact;
participants on management courses (in-house or external).

The book was tested on several groups before publication, and amended in the light of their comments. It is designed to provide a basic working knowledge of the management of international business whatever the specialization of the reader. Finance, marketing, production, personnel or research and development specialists, as well as those in general management, should expect to acquire a better understanding of the realities of international decision-making from these pages.

To keep within a reasonable compass, some issues are treated briefly or in summary form; there are plenty of signposts for further reading. The aim is to give you the flavour of a fascinating subject.

Executives should start with Chapters 1 and 3 and then follow with the chapters or sections which match their needs. The book has been kept to a size suitable for reading while commuting.

Students of internatonal business should read the book through; it follows a well-tried syllabus on the subject. You will note how the focus of interest broadens from management to the environment and finally to the future. Those in related specializations will use the book selectively.

Seminar participants will read the relevant passages, although they should also skim through Chapter 1. Any of the other chapters could provide background reading for a whole seminar.

All readers will have special interests and priorities and the subject index is designed to help you locate them.

Each chapter, after the first, is arranged as follows:
brief summary at the beginning,
then division into major topics,
finally, suggestions for exercises (including cases, role playing, and computer simulations), discussion questions and further reading.

The chapters are self-contained, so that readers can' change the order to suit their purposes. The plan is:

Introduction, background	Chapters 1–3 (and Appendix 1)
Management	Chapters 4–12
Environment	Chapters 13–16
The future	Chapter 17

'Management' comes before 'environment' in the belief that this is the natural learning order.

In the notes, which are to be found at the end of the book and in the reading list at the end of each chapter, references to books in the Bibliography are given by author and date only. Full references appear in the *Bibliography*.

A service to our readers

Every effort has been made to ensure that this book is as informative and reader friendly as possible, but much of it is necessarily compressed and some background knowledge and experience has been assumed.

Chapter 1 is intended as a general guide to help readers to find their way around, but any assistance the author can provide will be gladly given.

If you have questions to ask or comments to make, do not hesitate to contact me. Write (c/o the publisher) or phone direct (0161–746 8140 or, from outside the United Kingdom, +44 161 746 8140); FAX: 0161 746 8132, or +44 161 746 8132. Electronic mail can also be used, directed to: urmston@brooke.u-net.com.

International Management should be regarded as part of a wider information service on a vital topic. Advice and notes for future editions are always welcome.

PART ONE THEORY AND STRATEGY

This part introduces the subject of international management and examines some of the underlying thinking behind international business studies. The following chapter headings summarize the main themes of the book.

1 International management
2 Trade and investment
3 Corporate strategy

1 International management

Much zeal and effort are concentrated on international management. The trader is an ancient character, the villain of some stories and the hero of others. His goods may be food supplies or medicines; they may also be heroin or slaves. His products have led to enrichment, and a higher standard of living for many of those who produced them; they have also meant exploitation and misery. The economies of nations are boosted by international commerce; they are also undermined by it. That paradox suggests one division of the subject, the first of several to be proposed in this book, that between an activity – buying, selling, moving goods, moving funds and supplying services across frontiers – and a control of that activity to ensure the benefits and minimize the dangers by means of laws, regulations, codes and customs, as well as the ethics and skills of management.

A necessarily prosaic study need not ignore the challenge, the excitement, the hard bargaining and the risks incurred in staking resources and committing careers to the management of business affairs in economies, cultures and political systems that must always be full of unknowns, even to the most expert. The junior export clerk has his imagination stretched by out-of-the way places and almost unintelligible regulations which make his work more testing than that of colleagues of similar rank in other departments; while the junior analyst for the international investor is involved in regular international conferences, by phone or in person, to appraise the potential of a variety of businesses in situations of great uncertainty. At senior levels, a daunting complexity must be reckoned with and accepted while constant travel is the rule. In addition, the activity has to be undertaken against a mixture of praise and blame which are both inescapable. There is no formula which can enable the international executive to earn praise from his company and from interested parties in foreign countries, all at the same time. He can earn respect for his skill, but he must tread nimbly through conflicts which no amount of optimism can remove. The ambition of this book is to provide the basic knowledge and understanding which practical experience will ultimately transform into that nimble tread.

Like every other aspect of management, the international one has a long history, developing from the most ancient of human wanderings and informed by a growing body of expertise. The knowledge required has changed in kind as well as in quantity. If modern science could be applied to ancient trade, no doubt meteorology would be more regarded than economics, tide tables than bills of lading. The old-time investor worried about security in transit rather than exchange controls. One historical process has been the transition from trade to investment with its gradual spread from the colonial nations to the United States, to Japan, and now to the newly industrializing countries of Latin America and South East Asia, and now from large to smaller firms. In the process a number of social, political, ethical and other issues have emerged in addition to those inherent in trade like logistics, currency exchange and frontier crossings.

The emergent issues include relations with governments and with employees – both organized and unorganized – along with the exploitation of new techno- logies. A growing number of interest groups, worried about the rise of the international investor (the multinational firm), have begun to articulate their con- cerns. These include the consumer, the trade union and the political, in which there is a right-wing as well as a left-wing opposition to the multinational. The consumer interest embraces movements for consumer protection but also users of medical drugs, foods, cars, machinery and other industry sectors now domin- ated by multinationals. Social concern is reflected, too, by interest on the part of religious bodies like the World Council of Churches.[1] This widespread concern is recorded in some of the later chapters as are the differing interests of various kinds of countries, East and West, North and South. Meanwhile this introductory chapter sets out to provide an understanding of international management in terms of conceptual approaches and relevant disciplines.

1.1 The nature and scope of international management

International management conjures up a number of contrasting images. Are we to examine the controversies over trade theory or are we to record travellers' tales on how to sell ice to the Eskimos? Is the emphasis to be on logistics – the move- ment of products and components through a global maze of conflicting regulations, taxes and national aspirations? Or is the focus to be on the underly- ing economic, psychological and sociological pressures? Are we to trace out the patterns of operation or to concentrate on the issues that produce those patterns? The answer to these questions is that the subject brings together a number of skills as well as a wealth of theory and practice, that have to be reduced to a coherent body of knowledge. The knowledge outlined on these pages can be approached in a variety of ways and through the insights of a number of discip- lines. Figure 1.1 identifies three approaches – observation, experience and theory.

Observation

The observation approach comes from the outside and is detached. It brings together information of all kinds – fact, opinion, anecdote, the fruits of casual conversations and of systematic researches – and analyzes them into a coherent system. A number of phenomena pose questions that give the subject its urgency. International trade is controversial, a shift in its balance can destabilize a govern- ment or bring starvation to a people. To those in authority, imports are vices and exports virtuous.[2] Since one country's imports are another's exports it is difficult to reconcile such political morality, and it is hardly surprising that much time is spent by statesmen and their advisers, as well as by a small army of lobbyists and consultants, trying to sort out the problems of virtues turning to vices when they encounter a boundary post set up as a result of wars long past.

In the light of this and other problems, it must be said that one of the character- istics of international trade – and one that certainly calls for a theoretical explanation – is its resilience. In the early 1970s inherited and accepted wisdom affirmed that floating exchange rates would destroy trade. In fact, since 1972, 20 years of floating exchange rates, import duties, unpredictable controls, inflation and world slump have accompanied a steady increase in trade flows in real terms.

APPROACH	DESCRIPTION	METHOD	EXAMPLE
OBSERVATION	Observing facts and phenomena which stimulate questions and provide data for answers	Systematic assembly of data (including statistical tables) and checking on hunches	Company finds exports to country X declining while market increasing
EXPERIENCE	A bundle of activities which together constitute the functions of the international manager	Recording, comparing and interpreting experience (including case studies)	Decision process on whether to withdraw or to manufacture locally (and if so whether by licensing or direct investment)
THEORY	Considerations which together build a body of knowledge and elements of theory	Employing relevant concepts, methods and theories to understand the phenomena and activities and to predict change	Examine theories of comparative advantage, imperfect markets and corporate expansion

Figure 1.1 International management: approaches to the subject

Some figures to illustrate what must surely be regarded as one of the most remarkable success stories of recent history are shown in Table 1.1. In spite of this success, there still exists strong pressure to stabilize exchange rates, as has been shown by the determination to stand by the Exchange Rate Mechanism (ERM) within the European Union, by most of its member states, in spite of the difficulties.

Table 1.1 also shows that trade has increased more rapidly (even after allowing for inflation) than other economic indicators during a period when so many discouragements were offered to the trader. Although large numbers of companies do not conduct business outside their national frontiers, there are many compelling motives for entering trade and these are discussed in a later chapter. It used to be said that every company could profitably go international apart from the corner shop and the local bus service; in fact many a local shopkeeper also runs an export–import business and some bus companies (whether privatized or not) offer tours abroad.

Table 1.1 Trade and inflation (index figures for 1993, 1990 = 100)

(a) Three years of growth

	Exports	Consumer prices
Canada	127.629	109.2
France	216.588	107.9
Germany	410.104	112.0
Japan	287.581	106.4
Sweden	57.540	117.0
United Kingdom	185.172	111.5
United States	393.592	110.6

Sources: *International Financial Statistics* (I.F.S. 1994)
During a ten-year period (1983–91): world exports increased by 47% (in real terms), consumer prices by 20%. Since 1981, the exports of Asia and the developing countries have kept well ahead of inflation. So have those of the United States, although the exports of the other industrialized countries have lagged in real terms.

(b) Annual increase in selected years (per cent)

	1988	1991	1995 (estimate)
World output	4.5	0.3	3.0
World trade	7.3	4.6	6.5

Investment across frontiers is also increasing and in a number of different directions such as both ways across the Atlantic, within the countries of Europe (both the European Union and the European Free Trade Area) and now out of as well as into some developing countries. As with trade, investment flows have shown a tendency to increase in the face of discouragement, a phenomenon which is also discussed later. The international investor has become an even more controversial figure, while international investment has more supporters in the present climate of opinion.

Many of the reasons why international firms have become the object of increasing controversy are intangible and hard to identify. Even if they did not bring disadvantages as well as benefits, their size and pervasiveness would no doubt cause controversy. The pervasiveness can be simply illustrated by listing the possessions of an ordinary household, an exercise which usually demonstrates a high proportion of goods manufactured by subsidiaries of international firms. The typical larder in Europe, for instance, is stocked with such products even where the products themselves appear national, like wines in Italy or marmalades in Britain, some of which are produced locally by American-owned companies, along with canned foods and fruit juices in most countries. This example shows that international companies are involved in much else besides high-technology products. Indeed food companies are now changing hands so quickly that it is hard to keep track of their current owners and to which national company they do belong. Nationality is ceasing to be relevant to a company that sources in one country, packages in another and sells in several others.

A few of the largest companies have sales that exceed the expenditures of smaller countries, including some that are industrialized. Under these circumstances a finance director can be handling more money than some finance ministers. The political problems that arise from the perception that governments are faced with rival centres of power should not be underestimated.

Experience

The experience approach comes from the inside and takes us into decision-making and the examination of strategies illustrated by case studies. In this, it contrasts with the previous approach which was marked by a mixture of speculation and fact, as well as insights designed to lay bare deeper issues. Most chapters will contain some of this illustrative material, and the tables and case examples are designed to stimulate interest and analysis. In addition, many of the chapters contain the results of analysis and records of actual incidents. The collection and exposition of relevant experience are essential elements in the discussion of international management. Much of the research behind this book is, therefore, of a clinical nature, based on the experiences of international managers, providing a description of problems encountered and solutions laboriously worked out.

Theory

At the heart of the subject of international management lies a body of knowledge assembled from a number of disciplines and reframed to provide analytical tools and theories capable of interpreting the phenomena into a coherent intellectual scheme with a facility for prediction as well as interpretation. The scheme is not to be seen as a unified theory, but rather as a fragmented collection of theories held together by some unifying ideas and hypotheses, developed and tested through methods widely used in management studies.

Conclusion

The thought process was illustrated in Figure 1.1. The first approach was that of observation – surveys, perceptions, memories, reports, documents and similar sources. These are assimilated through analysis and experience into practice. The analysis and the assimilation can be conducted by instinct but can be made more systematic and more reliable by relating them to a body of theory for which they, in turn, will provide support or amendment. Intellectual challenge is to be found in all three approaches, but the theory will be unrealistic and ill-informed if it is not checked against the experience and the observations.

An attempt is made in each chapter to weave together insights in order to help the reader make the transition from observations to in-depth thought and back again. Thus insights from different disciplines have been incorporated where relevant. A more detailed review of the concepts is to be found in the conclusion to this chapter where they are related to the disciplines available for understanding international business in a series of diagrams (Figure 1.3, A to E). This book is designed to take you through the body of knowledge on a relatively informal but guided tour.

1.2 Aims and objectives

This book is offered as an aid to managers and to students of management to help them form a basis for a thorough in-depth understanding of the subject. Experienced managers will, it is hoped, be able to relate their experiences to the material provided here while for others the book will provide an introduction to a subject that is both full of intellectual challenge and a route to a career.

An advantage of studying international management is that a fruitful source of material can be found in the financial columns of the daily papers and in weeklies like *The Economist*. Regular reading of journalistic as well as academic sources enables the student to develop an increasing grasp of a subject that is rooted in everyday experience. The *Financial Times*, the *Neue Zürcher Zeitung*, and the *Wall Street Journal* (among many other business papers) are as much essential reading as any of the publications recommended in the bibliography. To this should be added at least one newspaper from the rapidly growing economies of South East Asia. There are many English language papers in the region, in case you cannot cope with other languages, an example is *The New Straits Times* of Malaysia which includes regional as well as local business news; incidentally it is also interesting because it sheds a different light on European news from that to which you may be accustomed.

Each chapter in this book contains an outline of its topic – designed as an introduction, not as an encyclopaedia – and advice intended to stimulate further study. In addition to references and suggestions for further reading,[3] there are questions and exercises. The questions are intended for discussion or written work. On principle they cannot be answered simply by reading this book. At least some supplementary reading is assumed, along with an attempt to grasp the day-by-day implications of commercial policies. The book is not to be regarded as a substitute for courses and seminars, but as an aid.

Among the exercises are case examples, printed in full, as well as references to relevant case studies. The distinction between the case example and the case study is one of size and comprehensiveness of information. The case study usually provides comprehensive information on a known company, though the identity is sometimes concealed. In the case example, on the other hand, the company is normally anonymous, and only brief details are given. There are two reasons for the anonymity. One is that some companies have only been willing to allow the facts to be printed on this condition (sometimes after further disguises have been demanded as well); the other is that the issues are typical and timeless, and identification with a company could divert attention to particular characteristics for which the company is known.

The case example is modelled on the kind of short briefing that the junior executive is often faced with. Most of the cases listed are designed to concentrate attention on broad decisions rather than specific issues. These are not printed here because they can usually be obtained readily from their compilers or from a case clearing house.

Exercises

The case examples themselves are designed as teaching aids which emphasize self-help on the part of the student. They are based on actual incidents which someone has had to solve, and most have been tested with students and on post-experience courses. In solving the problems, bear in mind that imagination is required as well as knowledge. Work out what must have been involved to cause the situation to arise and use information collected from other sources, including newspapers and reference books.

The information provided is the minimum required to identify the problem and you are advised to work systematically through the following six stages:
1 Examine the problem in greater depth, list all the issues that might be at stake and prepare a brief for further investigation. Carry out your own personal brain-storming session.
2 Search out relevant facts about the environment – economic, legal, social, political and other conditions which might affect the solution.
3 Use imagination and experience to produce a set of operating figures about the company (the scanning of company reports may stimulate the imagination). Sales, capital committed, profits and potential profits, market share and other factors need to be worked out and be consistent with one another.
4 List all the possible solutions together with costings and (where relevant) cash flow projections.
5 Select a preferred option or coherent group of options and explain the reasons for the selection. Usually there will be more than one solution and it will be advisable to make short-term as well as longer-term proposals. It is perhaps also worth reminding you to include 'do nothing' among the options; it may be that the company is already pursuing a correct course of action and needs to persevere through the difficulties that have arisen.
6 Conclusion – to answer the question: what has been learnt of wider application from this case?

Some of the case examples are specifically designed to provide role-playing exercises; these can be used with small groups, each of which should be asked to make a presentation to their colleagues. One advantage of this particular method of learning is that it can be used at any depth required or for whatever time is available – from a brief research to a major project. Clearly, some back-up materials are required in the form of a library or information centre. As a minimum a selection of company reports, country surveys and reference books on international business must be available. For readers working at home, either on their own or on a distance learning course, advice should be sought on how to obtain the information required.

A computer with a spreadsheet program is helpful for preparing the operating figures. Some of the chapters also have suggestions for computer simulation exercises. These can be carried out on any computer which can run electronic spreadsheet and database programs. (The author first ran them on an Apple IIe with 128K of memory. Nowadays, he uses an IBM compatible Tandon with 640K using Multiplan, Lotus 123, dBase III and Paradox software. Less memory and simpler programs would be adequate.)

1.3 A career in international management[4]

Most users of this book will not be treating international management as an abstract subject to be studied in its own right. Unless teaching the subject, they will have careers in view, probably in a specialized branch of management with international responsibilities. Many will, at some stage, find themselves in a line position managing across frontiers. The following notes are distilled from comments made by a number of executives in companies or in employment agencies with experience of international placements.

The first problem is to know how to get onto the international circuit. Industrialists are prone to sound off about the 'absolute necessity' of overseas experience, but many of these statements seem to be aimed at governments or trade unions rather than at themselves. Companies can be all too unwilling to back such statements with money or manpower, and you may well wish to seek out those that do give priority to their foreign business. A check on the backgrounds of executives and a study of company reports will at least help to eliminate those that do not give such priority.

The following list notes some appointments where international expertise is especially valuable.

1 Posts in an export department, international division or other unit specializing in international trade (a licensing department, for instance). The usual backgrounds for these posts will be accountancy and marketing with some from general management. A technical background is sometimes needed for the licensing manager.
2 Finance departments dealing with control and financing issues.
3 Marketing departments, including:
   (a) business development managers,
   (b) foreign trade and country analysts,
   (c) contracts managers,
   (d) sales teams.
4 Corporate planning departments (similar titles to the marketing department).
5 Research and development (R&D) departments.
6 Production, production engineering and other technical departments.

A panel of recruitment experts recently (1995) said that most initial foreign postings were likely to be for the short-term only. One of the experts said that most international posts these days were based in the home country with responsibilities abroad. Obviously a domestic track record is required for these. On the other hand, some recruitment agencies are themselves international and look for people eligible from any country in which they operate for posts in any other.

Rare skills

Skills in special demand include the following:
1 the ability to negotiate, to go abroad and fix a complex deal, especially when there are several companies involved;
2 technological skills are much in demand at the present time, particularly in Third World countries and especially for those with some management knowledge as well;

3 knowledge of franchising, licensing, distributorships, agencies, intra-company trading and other contractual arrangements;

4 marketing, with the ability to mastermind the entry into new markets and to understand the requirements of selling at the same time;

5 financial managers, with an understanding of money markets around the world, used to have one of the most sought after skills of all; there are now more suitable candidates available and the demand is fluctuating.

United States companies are frequently looking for Europeans to conduct a feasibility study with a view to setting up a subsidiary in Europe, and then to operate the subsidiary if it comes into existence. The reverse is less likely as European companies usually enter the United States by buying a going concern, keeping the American management in place.

Opportunities to work abroad still exist, indeed they have been increasing of late after a steep decline some 20 years ago. A glance through the relevant career advertisements will show what is available. It will also show that many of the jobs are specialized, but if you have the necessary expertise, some additional knowledge of international business will put you ahead of other candidates who are equally qualified. Internal promotions from one country to another are also possible within foreign multinationals, mostly at two levels – junior staff and senior line managers. There is the further possibility of transfer to a head office abroad.

Postings are available for people with some experience but normally in the early stages of their careers. A short period abroad (some say two years as a maximum, others suggest longer) is usually a help later, but only for those who are under 30 or at the most 35, unless an expatriate career is looked for. For others, a long period abroad is regarded as a handicap because the manager will have become out of touch with changing conditions at home, let alone the political scene within his company. There are also personal difficulties, like that of readjusting to a lower standard of living and narrower responsibilities on the return.

It is still possible to make a permanent career abroad, although this is less common than it once was. For most people the advice is to make sure of a job back home before agreeing to a posting overseas and not to change jobs while away. A knowledge of at least one foreign language is an advantage and is increasingly specified in advertisements. However, this obvious qualification is often not demanded when an appointment is actually made, and is certainly no substitute for business experience – except for Europeans with languages in special demand like Japanese, Arabic or Chinese.

Naturally the availability of jobs varies according to economic conditions as well as other factors which affect both supply and demand. However a slump at home, which means that more qualified people are available, also means that companies are forced to pay more attention to their foreign business. There will usually be openings for qualified people with the necessary skill and enthusiasm; informed advice and sound instincts also help.

In summary, most recruits for international management, whether home- or foreign-based, have some specialist background. This may be in almost any specialization – financial, marketing, technical and so on. They will also have taken the trouble to equip themselves with an understanding of the demands of the international exercise and probably have joined a professional institute with an international orientation. This book sets out to provide the necessary equipment.

1.4 Outline

To match its objectives, and to suit the requirements of teachers and practitioners, the book covers three main areas of study.

I Theory and strategy

The first three chapters introduce the subject and summarize some theories that are useful in building up a coherent pattern of thought and body of knowledge, followed by an outline of strategies available to the international company. Chapter 3 concludes the introduction and develops the main theme, that of strategic thinking about global management.

2 Management

The core of the book studies international management directly, beginning with export (Chapter 4), licensing (Chapter 5) and investment (Chapter 6), followed by four chapters (7 to 10) on how various departments operate internationally, while Chapter 11 discusses organization in a framework of decision-making. The issues covered in these chapters are restated under 'corporate planning' in Chapter 12 which also focuses attention on the third main subject area, the business environment.

3 The business environment and the future

Since this is a book about management, the section on the business environment is limited to those aspects which most closely affect the manager's role. In most publications, the environment is discussed first, its logical place, but the author considers the present arrangement more suitable for learning purposes. The reader grasps environmental questions more quickly after realizing how they affect decision-making. These questions include economic (Chapter 13), cultural (Chapter 14) and political influences (Chapter 15). International organizations (including the United Nations, the European Union, the Association of South East Asian Nations and many others) are the subject of Chapter 16. A final chapter summarizes the book in the process of identifying some directions into the future.

Bibliography

Each chapter contains some suggestions for further reading as do the notes. The bibliography at the end of the book contains a selective list of relatively recent or seminal texts which the author believes to be a useful contribution to an understanding of international business. This is a proposal for a personal library and each publication is recommended, not just listed, from a vast collection. References elsewhere in the book to this bibliography are given by author and date. Older publications and journal articles are referenced in full in the notes, and not included in the bibliography.

Since the chapters are self-contained, readers are at liberty to change the order, if they wish, by reading, for instance, Chapters 13 to 16 first and Chapters 2 to 3 last. Figure 1.2 summarizes the outline of the book.

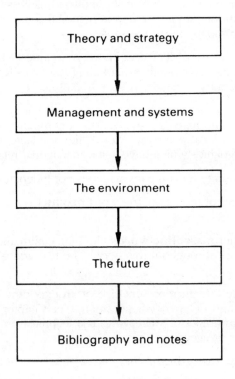

Figure 1.2 International management – the scheme of the book

Definitions

The **international company** is any firm that conducts business across frontiers, from the smallest of export orders to the multi-million pound investment. All sizes of company are considered in these pages.

The **multinational company** is used to refer to a subset of the international company – any firm which performs its main activity and owns facilities, whether in manufacturing or service industries, in at least two countries.

Other definitions and other words (like transnational, used in United Nations documents) are not employed in this text except in quotations.

Countries are classified by the following (International Monetary Fund) criteria:
1 industrial market economies;
2 countries in transition;
3 fuel exporting developing countries;

4 higher income developing countries;
5 low income and least developed developing countries.

The classification is explained in Chapter 15.

Home country is the country of origin of a particular company while **host country** is a foreign country in which it conducts business. **Head office** refers to the principal centre of authority in an international company; words like headquarters or parent company mean the same.

Strategic alliance: a group of two or more companies which have made an arrangement for sharing technology or marketing resources for their mutual profit in more than one country.

Subsidiary refers to an independently incorporated company which is owned (in whole or in part) and managed by the parent company. A foreign subsidiary is sometimes called a local company. Words like associate or affiliate are used more loosely of companies which have some managerial relationship.

Branch is used of a unit of a company which is not independently incorporated.

To avoid another kind of repetition, the word **product** is used of both manufactures and services.

Note that he and other **masculine words** like him, chairman, salesman are used solely for convenience throughout this book. The text and subject matter apply equally to both sexes.[5]

Agent is used of the foreign representative of an exporting company and may include distributors and independent salesmen, (see Chapter 4), while **licensee** is used of the foreign holder of a licence to use technical property. **Principal** is used of the exporter or licensor.

Normally a company is described as 'it'.

The word **environment** is used of the business, social, political and other circumstances within which the international company has to operate, not (unless stated) of the physical environment.

Commercial and **non-commercial** are used to distinguish between considerations that directly influence the profit and loss account and those whose influence is less direct. In particular, the non-commercial environment is used of legal, political and social influences on company decision-making. As with other seemingly obvious distinctions, the contrast between commercial and non-commercial is less watertight than at first appears. If a company acquires a bad reputation (a non-commercial factor), this may bring government restrictions which affect its ability to conduct business (a commercial consideration) along with others in the same industry sector.

Abbreviations

Since this book is designed to be read in non-English-speaking (as well as English-speaking) countries, abbreviations are kept to a minimum. Some long names like the Organisation for Economic Cooperation and Development (OECD, OCDE in French) and the General Agreement on Tariffs and Trade (GATT), but not its successor (the World Trade Organization, WTO) are abbreviated when used frequently. Where this does occur the abbreviation is separately entered in the index. In sums of money m is used for million (000,000) and bn for billion (000,000,000). Some standard abbreviations (like ch. for chapter and p. for page) are used in the notes but never in the text unless they occur in quotations.

1.5 Conclusion

This chapter began with a review which referred to the many and varied elements that make up our subject. Figure 1.1 illustrated different levels of approach – observation, experience and theory – while stressing that there were intellectual challenges at each level. A concluding series of charts (Figure 1.3) attempts to bring together a number of skills and disciplines that have been taken for granted in drafting this book. These are expressed in terms of five stages (A to E). In each of the first four charts, the following stage is to be found in a centre circle with the intention of gradually concentrating attention from the basic disciplines and the business environment towards the specific issues faced by the international manager. The five stages are explained below.

Figure 1.3A   Portrays the basic disciplines which contribute to an understanding of an international firm. The disciplines are expressed in bold print. The natural sciences are included to express a suspicion that the collaboration of some natural scientists might help to explain some phenomena; that (for instance) genetic factors in influential characters are important for the development of world trade and investment. There is little documentary evidence for this and the subject is not discussed here. Some reference has been made to the other disciplines listed in the chart.

Figure 1.3B   The environmental influences are interpreted in the light of the basic disciplines and in their turn provide a framework within which the manager has to work.

Figure 1.3C   The management process – the core of the book – is outlined in the form of an organization chart for ease of reading. The chart is *not* to be interpreted in a static sense but rather as representing a constant process of interaction between its various elements. Some pressures to change are found in Figure 1.3E, but first come the characteristics.

Figure 1.3D   The characteristics, such as the reasons for trade and investment, are specified and their influences illustrated in Figure 1.3E.

Figure 1.3E   The pressures to change from within the organization are outlined including its response to competition. In Chapter 11 these pressures are examined in terms of conflicts between different groups of managers and with outside interest groups.

The diagrams are illustrative only and include some cross-references to chapters where the subject is discussed further. Where there are no specific references, the ideas underlie much of the book, especially Chapters 2, 3 and 17.

A. *The disciplines*

Figure 1.3 The study of international management

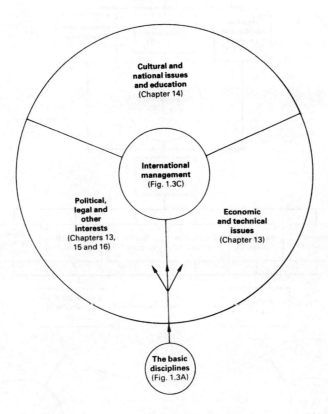

B. *The environmental influences*

Figure 1.3 continued

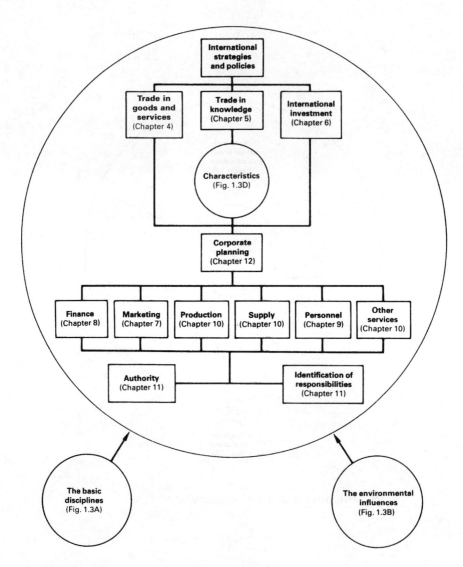

C. *The management process*

Figure 1.3 continued

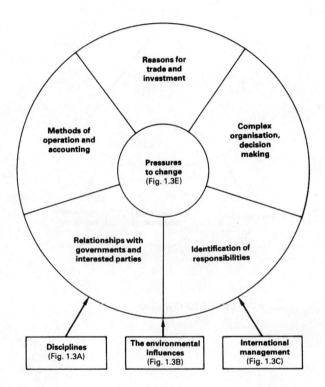

D. *Characteristics*

Figure 1.3 continued

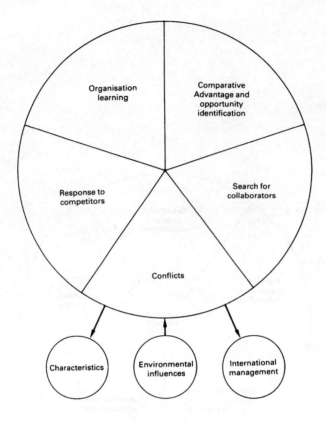

E. *Pressures to change*

Figure 1.3 continued

2 Trade and investment

This chapter offers a summary of theories that are relevant to the study of the international firm. These are culled from economic insights on trade and investment and from socio-psychological writings on the complex organization. Together they provide a standpoint, a framework and a set of criteria which are taken for granted in the following chapters. The notes and suggestions for further reading provide the reader with guidelines for pursuing topics introduced in this review. Direct investment is explained further in Chapter 6.

Feeling one's way is a phrase that suggests itself when discussing international trade. The phenomena that make up the subject, and the arena in which the international manager operates, have been examined by experts in most of the disciplines listed in the previous chapter (see Figure 1.3A). Adequate explanations have proved elusive partly, no doubt, because no discipline by itself can look at the issues whole. However, a number of elements of theory are emerging by means of which it is possible to comprehend a sometimes bewildering array of information. Some of the theoretical insights are pieced together in this chapter and assumed in the rest of the book.

On the subject of theory, it should be said that two opposing views appear among writers on multinationals. One laments the lack of a general theory and suggests that this somehow casts a shadow on the whole subject, while the other believes that the search for such a theory is illusory and that the correct approach is to seek a body of knowledge constructed from many elements and concepts. One problem is the use of words; some proponents of the general theory outlook appear to confuse the word *theory* with *opinion* and would have us fit the multinational firm into their world view. Others would turn the word into a straitjacket, fitting the complex and many-sided realities of multinational business into a simplified formula or slick expression. The aim of this chapter is to identify relevant insights and organize them into a body of knowledge. One preliminary question is how to find a framework within which theorizing can legitimately take place. For this, refer back to the scheme proposed in the last chapter.

Economic theory is concerned with costs and benefits, advantages and disadvantages, to both companies and countries. A benefit to one can be a cost to the other or, a possibility not to be overlooked, a benefit to both. A particular company may have an identity of interest with a host country government, but the reverse can also be true. A cost-benefit analysis is likely to identify a mixture of common interests and conflicts. Indeed, it beggars belief to suppose that corporate policies can always pursue the best interests of a company (shareholders as well as employees) in each of several countries, and the national interests of those countries at the same time; nevertheless foreign business brings some benefits. The opposite view – that multinationals are involved in a conspiracy to destroy their own customers – also beggars belief; nevertheless there are some costs.

21

There is scope for numerous conflicting interests and some policies are bound to be controversial. For the organization theorist, too, the reality (and many-sidedness) of the conflicts in which the manager is necessarily involved can be seen to change according to the framework chosen for analysis. The multinational is a coalition of interest groups and its subsidiaries are corporate citizens in many countries.

For the reader, no doubt, the most interesting aspect of theory is as a guide to the international business scene, a set of direction indicators for making sense of what is and predicting what is to be. To understand why business has developed from a transaction at the cottage door or trading post to a global search for materials, markets, finance, technologies and the other elements of world business, is to begin to see the routes likely to be taken in the future.

Questions arise like:
What are the advantages that make all the effort worthwhile?
How can those advantages be pursued and what problems arise in the pursuit?
How are the methods of pursuit changing and how are they likely to change further? In particular, how are they influenced by both commercial and non-commercial considerations?

In this chapter the main theoretical ideas that have relevance to these questions are listed with suggestions for further reading. The ideas between them add up to a body of theory designed to stimulate thought and to provide at least a suitable viewing stand, if not a complete framework, for the body of knowledge presented in the following chapters.

2.1 Trade

This section considers the elements of an understanding of international trade. It is couched in terms of advantage (absolute where a product is only available in a particular place, or comparative where it is more economically produced in one place rather than another) including the relative costs of factors like labour and capital. The increasing mobility of these factors has led to a rethinking of earlier theories. Managerial issues involved in exporting and licensing are considered in Chapters 4 and 5, and the economic environment in Chapter 13.

A keyword under this heading is *advantage*, the ability to produce in one area for sale in another on terms with which the latter area finds it difficult to compete. The advantage may be absolute, like the mineral which can only be mined where it is found or the fruit that can only be grown in a certain climate, or it may be relative. Where a high proportion of the cost of a product is, say, labour, it is likely to be produced where suitable labour is also inexpensive. That is straightforward, a first lesson in geography or economics. When it comes to applying it to world trade as it exists today a number of complications have to be accounted for.

Some of the complications are familiar. These include: technology, which can provide substitutes to remove absolute advantages; large-scale production which can reduce costs; or skilled marketing that can render customer demand less sensitive to price. Also some of the factor costs involved in production are not as straightforward as they may appear. For instance, it was recognized over 150 years ago that low wages did not by themselves mean low labour costs. It has been argued, for example, that slavery was abolished because the cost of supporting a slave had risen above the cost of supporting a free labourer. A dramatic instance of this was the discovery in a survey of the 1830s that coal mined in Wales and transported 3,000 miles by sea was being sold more cheaply in the Black Sea port of Odessa than coal mined by serfs in the nearby Donetz Valley.[1] Another instance is when a government intervenes to change the balance of advantage in favour of its country. Some of the forms the intervention takes – like tariff and non-tariff barriers, import controls and subsidies – are discussed in Chapter 15 as are the international treaties designed to minimize the effects in the following chapter. Corporate decisions about location of facilities also produce changes in advantage as well as being influenced by existing advantages.

A problem posed by simple propositions about relative advantage is that the various factors can operate in contradictory ways, or at least ways that are subject to such rapid change as to appear contradictory. An example of the contradiction is the ability to make a product acceptable even when a cheaper version is available. While an example of rapid change occurs when interest rates affect the price. This is particularly the case with heavy or bulky products where the costs of distribution are high and require a large amount of working capital on which high interest has to be paid. A sudden rise in the rate can mean the loss of a market. The same applies to exchange-rate fluctuations. Countries as different as Britain and Nigeria both suffered losses in their exports in the early 1980s which were put down to over-valued currencies.

The world view also has to take account of the trade in services. This has grown steeply in absolute terms but not in proportion to trade in goods. In the United States, for instance, during a period of rapid growth in the service industries at home, their share in foreign trade hardly changed. Between 1972 and 1982, the proportion of employees in services rose to 67 per cent but the export of services declined from 16 per cent to 12 per cent as a proportion of total civilian earnings from abroad. In 1992 the export of goods still accounted for 60 per cent of American trade.[2] In Britain, during the same period, receipts from invisible exports increased by four and a half times and provided a surplus over payments in every year, as opposed to trade in goods which was in deficit in eight years out of the ten. But these figures, while demonstrating the importance of services to the economy, are balances that also reflect large imports of goods. The proportions of products and services in international trade would be more closely balanced if the service elements in manufacturing companies were isolated in the statistics.

The combination of service and manufacturing activities is an important factor in trading success. A working agreement between a manufacturer, a banker and an insurance company to provide credit terms that are satisfactory to the customer can win contracts. This relationship is formalized in Japanese trading groups which have such services in-house.[3]

A formula which attempts to take account of many of the less measurable, as well as the more easily quantifiable, factors in the calculation of the costs and benefits of exporting, is shown in Table 2.1. On the left-hand side of the table are hidden costs, while the benefits include some (like *acquiring experience*) which are notional. In the formula, the items are grouped appropriately to provide a fair view in spite of difficulties about items that are not always comparable. The consequences of the ready availability of capital and skilled advice are hard to account for (but see point e in the table), although they may in the end be crucial to success.

Table 2.1　A formula for calculating trading costs and benefits to a company

Costs	Benefits
1. Management:	
a　proportion of senior management time devoted to project	d　acquiring experience of operating in different economies
b　proportion of head office staff time (including planning, personnel, research and development)	e　making use of spare management capacity and the availability of skilled advice
c　costs of administering exports	f　greater payback for research
2. Production (or provision of service):	
g　interest on fixed and current assets used for export	k　materials
h　design	l　labour (wages, benefits, training and employment costs)
i　depreciation	m　balancing figure for spare capacity
j　running costs	
3. Marketing:	
p　market research and competition research (assessing and allowing for the reactions of competitors)	t　costs of offices, warehouses and other facilities abroad
q　promotion and selling	u　exchange losses (± hedging costs or gains)
r　distribution (transport, insurance, warehousing, frontier charges, taxes tariffs, interest on working capital)	v　income from sales
	w　income from sale of spares and servicing
s　fees for agents, distributors and foreign salesmen	x　acquiring of goodwill
	y　preventing competition
	z　exchange gains (± hedging gains or losses).

$$\text{INCOME} = [v-(p+q+r)]+[x]+[w-t]-[g+h+i+k+l-m]-[(a+b+c)-(d+e+f)]\pm[z-u]$$

Trade theories

Theories of trade start from explanations of the locations of business centres and the flows of goods and money. The explanations are couched in terms of advantage and scarcity. Business will move from high cost areas, where particular factors of production (like materials, labour or finance) are scarce and costly, to those where they are more plentiful. There are counter-pressures, partly because the costs will go up as business moves in, and partly because there are ways of overcoming the disadvantages of scarcity through technical innovation and increased productivity. In spite of the shortcomings, earlier theories have assisted later writers to analyze the phenomena of international trade and examine their component parts, as well as suggesting criteria for assessing restraints on trade. As a result attempts have been made to assess the costs involved in trying to regulate a market.

An attempt at setting out the influences that trade may have on government policies can be found in Table 2.2. This table considers only the costs of a product in use in a country. Care should be taken in interpreting it in view of the evidence that export promotion is more beneficial to an economy than import substitution. These policies, like other issues considered in this chapter, are subject to change as a result of the rapid growth of international investment.

Table 2.2 A formula for calculating trading costs and benefits to the country

Direct benefits or costs		Indirect costs	
A.1	Cost of providing (A.1p) product A locally less cost of importing product A (A.1i)	a.1	Unemployment caused by imports
		a.2	Switch to other industries made necessary by imports
A.2	Effect on A.1 of fluctuations in exchange rates	a.3	Consumers refusing imports
A.3	Consequences for balance of payments	a.4	Economic cutbacks cause adverse consequences for balance of payments
Similar considerations for products B, C, D and so on.			

National benefit = positive products − negative products

One of the weaknesses of traditional trade theory, as has often been pointed out,[4] is that it treats each country as an independent unit with its own limited stock of resources. The movement of a factor of production, like capital, is only allowed for in a limited sense. The multinational company, as well as the international portfolio investor, has brought a new element to the discussions. When capital (and labour) is transferred relatively easily, the world becomes increasingly a single market and theory must take account of this. This change is brought about by investment, the subject of the next section.

2.2 Investment

This section considers theoretical explanations of foreign direct investment; managerial issues are considered in Chapter 6 and the following chapters; the reactions of governments in Chapters 15 and 16.

International investment played a limited part in theoretical discussions until an attempt was made to integrate it into trade theory by claiming its benefits for the costs, and availability, of various factors of production. It was held that investment had changed the terms of trade after itself developing as a result of advantages that came to light when location and scale of activity altered.[5] This insight overcame the weaknesses in earlier theories that had not taken sufficient account of the significance of investment, and adapted those theories to circumstances in which it was gradually changing the directions of trade.

Doubt was later cast on how comparative advantages actually influenced location by a series of studies which showed that United States foreign investment was not apparently determined by the degree of labour intensity against capital content as existing theories predicted.[6] These studies have, in their turn, been criticized in that they did not differentiate between types of labour cost – whether skilled or unskilled, for instance – but even so the case presented was sufficiently impressive to set off a series of investigations into the reasons for foreign invest-ment. The following are the best known among the economic theories that the investigations have produced.

Product cycle

A theory based on a product-cycle model has been applied to industry sectors, service as well as manufacturing, in several countries.[7] It originated in the United States but has been tested elsewhere too. The theory began with a reassessment of the reasons for American investment abroad, starting from the presupposition that market conditions in the United States – with its size, wealth and relative sophistication – made it suitable for the introduction of new products. The high cost of labour provided a further pressure to technical innovation which was labour-saving. A number of other reasons were suggested for initial production in that country, or in any industrialized country in which an innovative product had been developed. A company would favour production close to headquarters and the product would not be too price-sensitive at first; effectively it had a monopoly, albeit a temporary one. If the product succeeded, an export market would build up which would eventually change the pressures. The product then became more price-sensitive as competition set in and local demand in export markets developed sufficiently to justify local manufacture. Once the product matured, the innovator's skills and knowledge began to carry less advantage and local manufacture became more probable. At the final stage, the advantages gained by reducing cost factors, like labour and transport, would become all-important and production would move elsewhere, while the country of origin became a net importer. Finally, the effects of the growth of trade between related parties – two subsidiaries of a company, for instance, rather than two separate companies – was pointed out. These effects were likely to unsettle predictions, which would be unsettled further when they produced a reaction from government (in any of the countries involved), an issue that became more central in the internalization theory mentioned later.

Portfolio theory

An approach which sees the multinational company in the role of banker using its funds to best advantage, both for making profits and for hedging against losses, is called portfolio theory – interpreting direct investment by analogy with portfolio investment.[8] A company can be expected to allocate its resources, domestically or internationally, according to the level of return and risk available both in the long- and the short-term. This theory corresponds with the views of many managers, but the practice is usually constrained by other factors includ-ing an assessment of the risks involved. More is likely to be heard of this approach as risk analysis becomes more sophisticated.[9]

Internalization

This theory stems from a distinction between the *internal* market, where goods and services are bought and sold within the company, and the external in which the suppliers and customers are *external*, independent companies. The view is taken that investment follows when conditions make the internal market more profitable than the external. The reverse is also held to be true; where the external market can provide goods or services more cheaply, the company will opt for a non-investment method.[10] The theory applies particularly where some form of vertical integration brings the supplier–customer relationship within the company. From this can stem a number of benefits including the long-term supply of raw materials or of a monopoly component. Transfer prices can be used to secure advantages like reduced tariffs.

One advantage of this theory is that it makes explicit the imperfections in the market, which are implicit in other theories. When control of the market can be advantageous to the company or when external influences can be fruitfully manipulated, there is a likelihood of internalization. Where neither of these considerations apply, an external relationship like licensing may be preferred. An additional advantage is to safeguard supplies and markets where trade is controlled by competitors who have themselves internalized.

The eclectic theory

An attempt to modify the internalization approach and to cover the different pressures that apply in different conditions has been called the eclectic theory.[11] This rests on bringing together three kinds of advantage:
1 ownership-specific (ranging from size and established position through proprietary knowledge to government support);
2 incentives for internalization (from ability to reduce costs associated with market dealings, to control of supplies and conditions of sale);
3 location-specific (input prices, transport costs, infrastructure and so on).

The eclectic theory takes account of non-commercial as well as commercial considerations. One of the categories listed among the 'location-specific' advantages, for instance, is 'psychic distance'. This refers to the linguistic, cultural and other differences which influence corporate decision-making. Such psycho-sociological issues are considered in the next section which examines organization theories.

2.3 Organization

The conflict theory of the international firm states that changes in a company's aims and methods derive from conflicts that are built into the organization and its relations with outside interests. This is derived from earlier behavioural theories of the complex organization. These do not deny the economic theories, but help to explain how underlying pressures are translated into corporate policies through the interaction of interest groups. The ideas contained in this section underlie much of the argument in Chapter 3 and some of the following chapters, especially Chapter 11 in which company organization is discussed in detail.

International trade and investment are increasingly dominated by large organizations which do not respond to stimuli in the same way as simpler entrepreneurial concerns. Decision-making is influenced by internal company politics (and external political influences) as well as straightforward commercial considerations. Opportunities for profit along with the threat of bankruptcy operate as boundary marks within which inter-group and inter-personal relationships play a part, complicated by national and cultural differences. Behavioural theories have explained these in terms of a process of *organization learning* that is stimulated by disagreements and conflicts between management groupings. The most obvious of these are represented by titles like *marketing, finance* and *production*.[12] The conflicts are never completely resolved because the groups represent different elements in the decision-making which are often contradictory. In governments, there is a similar and equally well-known tension between (for instance) the treasury, dedicated to conserving financial resources and allocating them in line with government priorities, and spending ministries like education, health, transport and defence which are meant to promote their departmental interests.

In the case of an international company, conflicts over the allocation of resources are complicated by the fact that a third dimension – the geographical – is added to the normal two-dimensional decisions that have to be made between functional specializations (like marketing and production) and product divisions. Also complicated is the exercise of power and authority through a matrix of pressures operating both inside and outside a company.

The conflict theory has been developed to interpret and generalize about these pressures and to build on earlier behavioural theories.[13] The theory states that changes in organizations occur as a result of conflicts of opinion and of interest that are built into the organization itself and are influenced by its commercial environment. In the case of international companies this means that the company is exposed to a network of unavoidable conflicts between interest groups, some of which are internal to the company and some between the company (or particular units) and outside interests.

Strategies and organizations derive from the means used to resolve these conflicts which, in their turn, arise from the complex interplay of factors identified by both economic and behavioural analyses.

Figure 2.1 is an attempt to illustrate this statement diagrammatically and shows how conflicts between formal groups (like domestic and international divisions) or informal groups (like those which support foreign investment and those that oppose it) influence the organization and its strategies.

The figure also shows how the outcome of these internal conflicts will be affected by pressures from outside the company where there are also conflicting views. One of these conflicts is between those who are anti-business and those who are pro-business. Another is between the *cosmopolitans* (who emphasize foreign business) and the *nationals* (who do not). In the case of a country, these terms are used to describe an orientation either for or against a world view. The *cosmopolitans*, for instance, are likely to favour export promotion rather than import substitution. Similar conflicts are played out in a company and within its subsidiaries, where the distinction between *cosmopolitans* and *locals* is between those who see their careers within the company world-wide and those who see themselves permanently employed in their own country.

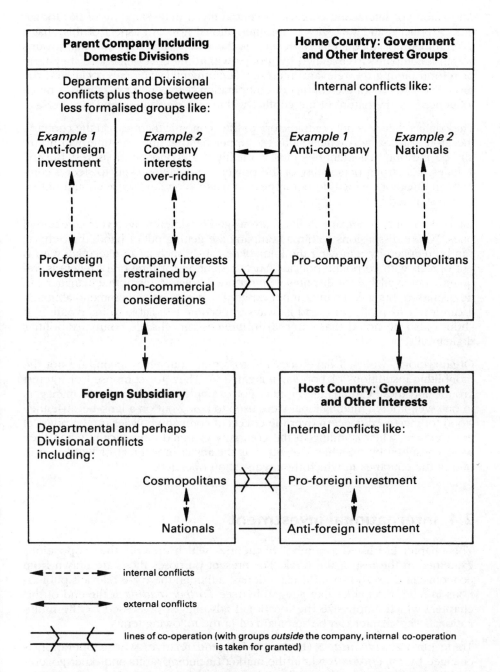

Figure 2.1 The conflict theory of the international firm

An analogy of interacting conflicts is central to an understanding of the formation of policies and strategies in an international firm. An aspect of this, that a diagram cannot adequately represent, is the way formal and informal groups within a company are matched by groups within the environment as they form or reform among the relevant interests (departmental, national, social and the rest). The intensity of the conflict or co-operation between organizations is much influenced by the nature of the conflict within an organization and vice versa.

The conflict theory is not contradictory to the economic theories; on the contrary, the group or coalition which gains the upper hand at any one time will normally be the one that identifies most correctly the economic pressures. But the abilities of a strong personality or the power of marketing skills to steer a company in directions which do not appear to make economic sense should not be underestimated.[14]

Internal conflicts (company politics) are waged by different means from external ones. Where dissensions within a company are getting out of hand, their effects can be reduced by removing the immediate cause, such as an executive who is out of step with corporate policies. Such a solution (or temporary relief) is frequently not available for disputes with outside bodies. A disruptive manager can be dismissed, but a company cannot rid itself of a national government, although it can lower its profile or mend its ways to become less liable to intervention. It should also be noted that external influences can change company politics dramatically.

Organizations, we shall have occasion to remind ourselves again, are not the monolithic institutions of popular imagination. They are composed of interest groups and these can change rapidly. For example, a small group of managers in one well-known multinational were used to being out on a limb because they stood for increased concern over the effects of company policies on the physical environment. Their standing in the company changed dramatically when they were consulted by the chief executive as the result of a threat of legislation in one of the countries in which the organization operated.

2.4 International investment

This chapter has listed a number of theories which underlie the propositions examined in the rest of the book. For present purposes these are drawn from economic and psycho-sociological writings, although there are relevant publications in other disciplines like geography (see *Further reading* at the end of this chapter) which emphasize the locational advantages possessed by the multinational. The chapter can be summarized in the following terms.

Trade pursues *advantages* (both absolute and relative) whose operation is changed by *imperfections* within the market (including tariffs and other government measures) and by *investment* which is partly caused by constraints on trade, but also pursues other advantages – including those where the imperfections in the market are most readily met by bringing purchasing and selling transactions inside the firm. The whole process influences, and is influenced by, a changing network of pressures and counter-pressures through which are formulated the strategies outlined in the next chapter.

2.5 Exercises, questions and further reading

Exercises

Computer simulation – trading risks

The purpose of this exercise is to help the reader to understand the risks that face an international firm both in its trade and in its investment abroad. The figures are given in US$, but you should translate them into the currency of your own country on the day of the exercise. A newspaper which gives exchange rates is essential for this exercise (unless you have a computer with an on-line link, in which case a business data base should serve the purpose).

Technical Enterprises is a manufacturer of sophisticated machinery which is assembled in four countries and sold in another eight. It has net assets of $1.1bn and annual sales of $2.5bn. Its home country is country A, the home country of the reader who should enter the names of the other countries before starting the exercise. The following is the position:

In country B	Assets of $50m	Income of $10m to be brought home in six months' time
In country C	Assets of $150m	To be sold and capital repatriated within 12 months
In country D	Assets of $40m	Only 10 per cent of income of $3m to be repatriated each three months
In country E	Assets of $90m	Income of $4.5m to be repatriated in six months

Assume exports to each of the other eight countries yielding $30m every six months.

Work out anticipated income and asset values over the next two years on each of the following assumptions:
1 that exchange rates remain the same,
2 that the domestic currency depreciates by 2 per cent after each six months,
3 that the domestic currency appreciates by 2 per cent after each six months,
4 by making your own assumptions about likely changes in parities.

If you do have an on-line computer link, you can also work out the actual figures for the last two years.

Questions

1 Discuss the view that a comparative neglect of non-price factors in markets for industrial goods can lead to a company's decline.

2 Analyze the costs and benefits of inward direct investment for a particular country of your choice. Suggest policies that would increase the benefits.

3 Critically discuss the product cycle model as a guide to the reasons for foreign investment.

4 Examine the internalization of markets approach to the growth of foreign direct investment, and explain what the examination tells us about the types of markets likely to be internalized.

5 Evaluate the contribution made by economic theory towards the understanding of the resilience and success of multinational firms.

6 Consider the economic issues associated with the development of labour-intensive manufacturing facilities inside developing countries as part of the vertical manufacturing arrangements of multinational companies.

7 Explain and evaluate the view that assets are not exposed to exchange risks if planning periods are long enough.

8 Evaluate critically the contribution made by any single economic theory towards an understanding of the desire of a firm to locate a subsidiary overseas and its ability to do so.

9 Do you consider that behavioural theories make a worthwhile contribution to our understanding of international direct investment? Give detailed reasons for your answer.

Further reading

Buckley and Casson, 1976.
Casson, 1983.
Caves, 1983.
Dunning, 1981.
Hood and Young, 1979.
Robock and Simmonds, 1983, ch. 1–3.
Rugman, Alan M, *Inside the Multinationals*, Croom Helm 1981 (a detailed study of internalization theory).
Vernon and Wells, 1981, ch. 1.
Walter and Murray, 1982, ch. 1.
Woodland, A.D. *International Trade and Resource Allocation*, North Holland, 1982.

3 Corporate stragegy

This chapter considers the decision to move abroad, the result of an analysis of the company's strengths and weaknesses when that analysis offers the message 'Go international'. The message is set in a context of expansion strategies any of which can lead abroad under suitable conditions. The chapter also considers how the options for operating abroad – exporting, licensing and direct investment – are evaluated. Consequential developments are explored in the next three chapters while the planning process itself is discussed in Chapter 12, which includes a section on information.

Strategy means determining a sense of direction, a set of objectives, for a company and appropriate routes in order to achieve the objectives. These do not have to be articulated or committed to a carefully thought-out document. On the contrary, the sense of direction may only exist in someone's head. Often strategic decisions are hardly taken at all – companies drift into international operations by following opportunities that arise by chance. There are also some which follow the international route as part of a well-thought-out strategy. One example (from some years ago) was Crown Cork and Seal in Philadelphia.[1]

This company was the subject of a radical reorganization about 30 years ago when a new chief executive was appointed with a brief to reorient the firm. The company was in a critical position, that of a middle-sized company in a market dominated by two major organizations – Continental Can and American Can. The brief was implemented by means of three strategies, all of which had international implications:

1 The first strategy was to change the financial structure, to increase the value of the equity by buying in shares and by ceasing to pay dividends. When this was applied rigorously in the British subsidiary there was uproar among local shareholders.

2 The second strategy was to build facilities close to the customers' plants and to dedicate entire production lines to a particular customer. This action made foreign manufacture almost inevitable.

3 The third strategy was aimed specifically at foreign markets. It recognized that international diversification was the natural route for a company of this relative size in its chosen role as a low technology, bulk supplier to the drinks industry. The company took abroad its manufacturing methods, its ideal of customer service and a financial structure designed for rapid expansion.

These strategies led to rapid and sustained growth in a competitive sector; Crown Cork followed its customers.

A company which moved abroad on the strength of its technology was Wilmot Breeden, a small British car components' manufacturer which had a world lead in its car locking mechanism. In an industry which, in the late 1950s, appeared to have the capacity for unlimited expansion, the pull abroad was very strong and the company soon achieved export markets in Europe and elsewhere. At the same time, it became clear that facilities nearer to the customer were necessary to retain some of these markets. Large-scale manufacturers were unlikely to remain permanently dependent for a vital component on a sole supplier in another country but the resources required were costly for a small firm. Eventually, it was decided to set up manufacture in France by purchasing a local company and by moving it to an area of high unemployment (in the Vosges mountains in the East) where government and local authority grants would be available. The factory would bring a substantial return to Wilmot Breeden by manufacturing its products but without making too great a demand on its staff as the French management would remain in charge.

The commitment of parent company finance was limited thanks to a long-term loan from a Swiss Bank in addition to the French sources of funds. This Swiss loan, which was to prove vital later, was fortuitous at the time. Exchange-control regulations, which were then in force, limited the amount of money that could be taken out of Britain which implied that sources of finance had to be found elsewhere. In the short-term, most of the plans led to disaster, and disaster on grounds that have since become familiar. The costs of the move proved higher than the grants, the French management did not switch smoothly to the new products and the English accountants – unfamiliar with the French accounting system – failed to anticipate an approaching crisis. As a result of bank guarantees, the huge losses in France nearly bankrupted the parent company. In fact, salvation came from the Swiss bank which provided the extra funds required to survive the crisis.

After some years of heavy losses abroad, resulting in passed dividends at home, profitability was at last restored and some years later it was the French subsidiary that was making money at a time when the home (British) market was in recession.

Eventually the company was taken over by an international car components group.

These two examples from the past show how two middle-sized companies elbowed their way into the world of international giants by adopting follow-the-customer strategies. The world into which they moved was full of companies that had explored business opportunities outside their home countries in order to reap the benefits of easier profits where competition was less. In recent years, these competition-avoiders have been replaced by competitors, a change which forms the subject of the next section.

3.1 From explorers to competitors

Yesterday's companies were *explorers*. They scanned the globe for profitable business opportunities but above all they sought to boost their income by escaping from competition. Given this expansionist outlook, there also existed a relatively easy-going atmosphere in which subsidiaries were established and left to manage their own affairs with minimum interference. 'Set up a subsidiary, appoint a trusted executive to take charge and leave it to that executive with the minimum necessary supervision and oversight' is a saying that identifies the explorer.

The *explorers* still exist, but increasingly international firms are becoming *competitors*. They seek to match the competition, not to avoid it. Their strategies are determined in the light of this principle – assess the plans of the competition and match them. Success is not judged by making easy profits from lax margins, but by making even larger profits out of narrow differences between costs and revenues.

The *explorers* looked for growth – this was regarded as a great virtue. The *competitors* look for market share; growth is welcome when profitable, but not for its own sake. The need to operate within intense competition leads to tighter controls and company-wide policies. 'Every subsidiary is under constant review and will be closed or sold if it does not produce satisfactory results, we cannot afford to support loss-making operations that may never become viable' is an explorer saying; a similar saying identifies the competitor.

The search to establish where an organization's advantages lie is a continuous process. At some stage it is likely to take a company abroad. The first moves are often casual, to be followed by a series of developments, and perhaps withdrawals, during which time a set of policies emerge which derive from the dominant strategy.

The basic strategies will concern issues like the nature of the business, the required return on investment and other performance indicators, the market segment aimed at and so on. The pursuit of any of these objectives may immediately lead the company abroad, as may any strategy for expansion. Other motives for operating abroad are listed in the following section, after which (in Section 3.2) the main routes to business growth are discussed, along with some estimate of their popularity and likelihood of success.

Motives for operating internationally

Raising the corporate sights from local to national and then to international markets may seem such a natural progression as to render the search for motives superfluous. However, only a minority of companies are into world business, and many of them are casual exporters. In virtually every exporting country figures can be quoted in the form of '80 companies (a minority) account for 60 per cent of the country's exports'. The common experience that a minority of companies account for a majority of exports needs explaining. No doubt part of the explanation is in the attitudes of senior executives; some think internationally, some do not.[2] There are also various pushes and pulls in national and world markets. The underlying factors have been identified in the last two chapters; the following list is of those most often mentioned by managers. They are summarized and classified in Figure 3.1.

1 *A saleable idea.* Various phrases – like 'saleable idea' (in the centre of the figure) or 'unique product' – give expression to the view that once a successful package has been put together, there will be pressures to offer it outside the domestic market. Naturally the package may need adaptation, but scope for profitable expansion is the most straightforward and usual motive for the move abroad, whatever other factors may underlie its achievement. Take, for instance, the retailing industry where companies as diverse as Woolworths,

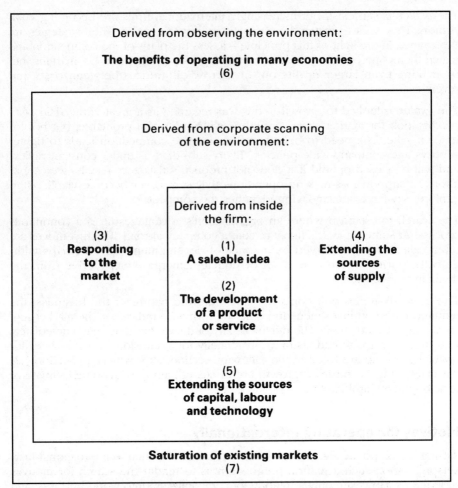

The numbers on this diagram correspond with the numbers in the text.

Figure 3.1 The motives for operating internationally

C & A, IKEA, Marks and Spencer and Hertz have developed retailing methods and corporate images which have been promoted (either by direct investment or franchise) in numerous countries. If a company has spare resources, surplus management expertise for instance, this will help to make the saleable idea an even stronger motive.

2 *The development of a product or service* (also to be found in the middle of the figure). A product's life cycle can often be extended by international diversification. The point at which profitability ceases at home, or at which new techniques or changing fashions render the product obsolete, may yet be followed by many years of profitable sales abroad. This applies to household goods, but also to machinery where the home market may require labour-saving equipment which is not so necessary in countries where wages are low. Soap powders, for instance, made obsolete by the development of automatic

washing machines, can continue to be sold in parts of the world where washing by hand is still usual.

3 *Responding to the market* (to the left of Figure 3.1). Responding to new market opportunities is naturally the principal route to business abroad; it is also one that contains some notorious traps. If the company's expansion into new markets is to be guided by approaches from those markets, then resources may be wasted or deflected from more valuable uses. The ability to seize profitable opportunities implies developing plans and criteria for sifting them. A different situation arises when the approaches come from existing customers. Banks, insurance companies and other service industries expand abroad to provide a world-wide deal for their customers. Some firms that manufacture components do the same.

4 *Extending the sources of supply.* Purchasing is frequently the most international of functions. Even the company whose eyes are concentrated on the domestic market has to buy materials and components abroad which are unobtainable at home. The search for higher quality and more reliable sources as well as for the lowering of costs is a normal route to the vertical integration mentioned earlier. Engineering firms, dependent on metals of special quality, have an obvious motive for buying into their suppliers.

5 *Extending the sources of capital, labour and technology.* The search for cost reduction in all the factors of production has already been mentioned. As with sources of materials and components, the search has its problems – these are considered in later chapters.

6 *The benefits of operating in many economies.* A powerful motive for generating international growth is to gain an advantage from operating in more than one economy. This has benefits for most industry sectors, but especially those affected by cyclical and seasonal factors. Industries most affected by the economic cycle, from building materials to domestic appliances, are especially subject to the possibility of smoothing the flow of sales; the peaks and troughs of different economies occur at different times. Figure 3.2 illustrates the fluctuations in manufacturing production in a few economies in recent years. These fluctuations, even though less varied in times of world recession than in boom times, demonstrate the advantages of a spread of operations over different economies. Products with seasonal variations, such as clothing or gifts, can also find steady sales throughout the year if they are marketed in areas with different climates or different religions.

7 *Saturation of existing markets.* Another reason for operating abroad is when market conditions make further expansion at home impossible or unduly expensive. The costs of further penetration in the domestic market necessitate development abroad under a number of conditions which partly depend on the size of the firm. For instance, a large firm in an oligopolistic situation (competition between a few similarly sized companies) might find it impossible to make permanent gains in market share, while small firms might be unable to break out of the niche they have established for themselves. If factors such as these make organic expansion unduly costly, there is still the take-over option. In this case, the possibility of buying firms abroad will be looked at alongside that of buying them at home, especially if domestic take-overs are likely to activate monopoly legislation. The opportunity for introducing foreign managers may be seen as an attractive result of the

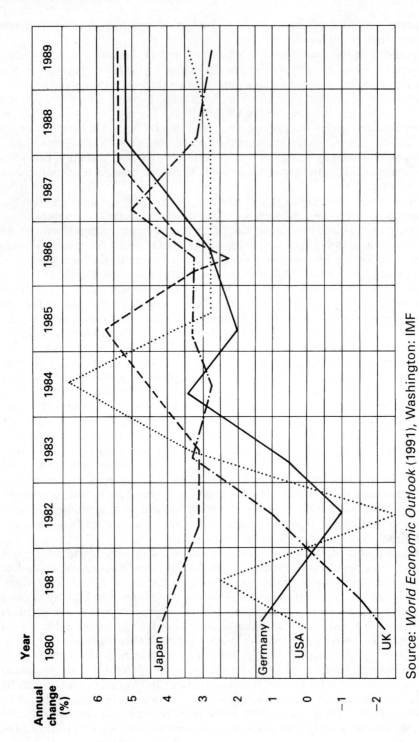

Source: *World Economic Outlook* (1991), Washington: IMF

Figure 3.2 Industrial production: international comparisons (base: 1967 = 100)

take-over. The saturation of existing markets accounts for international expansion on the part of firms without the advantage of high-technology products. Food-processing is an industry which has expanded internationally for this reason.

In practice, few British small firms have investments abroad; 4 per cent is the figure in a recent British Chamber of Commerce survey which gives 'cost' as the main reason why more small firms do not invest abroad in spite of perceived advantages in reliability and quality.

3.2 Expansion strategies

Examine the following statements.

'We are manufacturers of building components. As soon as a recession begins to bite our business slumps. So it makes sense to operate in various countries, hoping that they will not all be in recession at the same time.'

'Our bank has moved into this country to service our existing customers who are investing here; once established we hope to acquire local customers as well, particularly those who wish to invest in our country.'

'In the toy business, trade is seasonal. Our peak selling period is the early autumn when the shops are stocking up for Christmas. Other countries have different peaks, so operating internationally helps us to maintain a steady income and production flow.'

'Our traditional business is in heavy machinery, but this is high risk since there are limited numbers of large contracts available. The competition ensures that margins are very narrow even when you do win an order. So we have moved into light engineering products which are nearer the customer and where margins are higher.'

'Ours is a business with high margins but little scope for expansion. This has brought us a surplus of funds and we are looking for acquisitions in almost any fast moving consumer goods businesses where we can use our marketing skills.'

All these statements have been made to the author; they reflect five common motives for international business, namely:
1 a search for business in different countries to smooth over the effects of the trade cycle,
2 a similar search to reduce the impact of buying seasons,
3 a search for products with higher margins to support a lower-margin business,
4 an opportunity to service international customers,
5 a money-rich company in a static industry sector looking for other uses for its money.

There are numerous reasons for diversification, but underlying most of them is the desire to move into businesses which will stave off threats to a company's current position. For this purpose eight main routes to expansion have been identified of which only one is specifically international, but all can lead to foreign operations. Growth without diversification is listed first.

1 Organic growth

The most usual method of growth, by expanding the core business, will lead to international operations when certain conditions arise. These include the emergence of opportunities abroad, market saturation at home, the need to operate in different markets in order to meet performance targets and other motives already listed. Although market saturation is an obvious and common reason, in general a move abroad solely designed to escape from problems at home is not recommended.

2 International diversification

This differs from the previous category in that the international operations are integral to the business plan: perhaps as a result of a strategy which declares that a proportion of the corporate investment will be placed abroad; perhaps to ensure that the company is less subject to seasonal variations or changes in the economic climate.

International diversification may also arise from the nature of the business. Air and sea transport, for instance, are bound to operate internationally while mining and oil firms are likely to do so. Trading companies also come into this category.

3 Horizontal integration

The purchase of companies in the same line of business is one of the most common and most successful means of expansion.[3] It can result in a domestic company becoming international without any intervening stage. This happened when Derbyshire Stone, a domestic British quarrying and road building firm, took over Neuchâtel Asphalte which had subsidiaries on three continents. The combined operation was later taken over by Tarmac.

4 Vertical integration

Acquiring suppliers or customers is a strategy which gains in popularity in times of boom when companies find a need to concentrate on safeguarding supplies. The sale of these acquisitions in times of slump is sometimes used to provide extra finance for the core businesses when the company is hit by recession or high interest rates. As suggested by internalization theory, vertical integration can prove advantageous when the costs of the external market are high. This strategy leads to foreign investment when, for instance, it is preferred to licensing as well as when raw materials and components have to be sought abroad.

5 Concentric marketing

When a company decides to expand by buying into businesses that are unrelated except that similar marketing skills are required, the strategy is described as concentric marketing. Most of the examples that come to mind are, in fact, of companies that are already international – like tobacco companies diversifying into other high-volume consumer products. Where this policy is undertaken internationally, one problem is that the marketing skills are not relevant everywhere. The learning process often turns out to be more expensive than was anticipated when the strategy was determined.

6 Concentric technology

When a company decides to expand by buying into businesses that are related only by research skills, the strategy is described as concentric technology. Parallel to expansion along marketing lines is that along those of technological expertise. With the growing internationalization of technology, this strategy is likely to lead to foreign investment or at least to a licensing or consortium arrangement. In fact with the growing expense and expanding lead-times of technological innovation, the latter option is more likely.[4]

7 Conglomerate

Expansion by taking over businesses that have no vertical, horizontal, marketing or technical relationship could be called concentric finance or portfolio strategy. The firm taken over is usually chosen for its contribution to the parent company's spread of investments – bringing, for instance, experienced management or high profits in the short-term or capital gains in the more distant future – or simply because it is being sold at a price where a rapid increase in profitability is considered possible. Sometimes the purchase may be because the business appears singularly well managed. In spite of this, the number of failures incurred by this method has been large. Managers who are successful when independent do not always perform so effectively inside another organization. There have also been some marked successes. The modern conglomerate usually operates internationally, selling off units which do not fit a global financial policy.

8 Niche strategies

This chapter opened with an account of Crown Cork, a middle-sized company in an oligopolistic market (one dominated by a few similar-sized competitors), and how it found a niche in international trade. Research has identified a number of ways in which so-called 'non-dominant companies' find their niches. One outcome of the research has been the identification of four strategies used by non-dominant companies. These are:

1 extension to less competitive markets,
2 transfer of technology,
3 segmentation of primary markets,
4 reconfiguration of a traditional business.

The strategies, together with types of customer and examples, are listed in Table 3.1. Apart from the first, all involve defining or redefining a niche.[5] Even though only one of the strategies specifically includes foreign operations, companies have grown internationally along all these routes. The options for the business abroad and the most usually expressed methods of international growth are discussed next.

Table 3.1 Corporate strategy

No. in text	Name	Customer	Example
1.	Organic growth	Similar to existing	Any company or division increasing its sales, market share, return or investment
2.	International diversification	In foreign markets	Any company or division selling abroad
3.	Horizontal integration	Same type	An electrical manufacturer adding hi-fi equipment to a range of household appliances, or a bank moving into credit cards
4.	Vertical integration	The firm itself	An electrical manufacturer adding components manufacture or retailing to its hi-fi and household appliances
5.	Concentric marketing	Same type	A tobacco firm moving into drinks
6.	Concentric technology	Similar or new	A motor manufacturer moving into marine or aero engines
7.	Conglomerate	New	A food manufacturer moving into machinery manufacture
8.	Niche strategies	Similar or the same	A chemical manufacturer selling in small quantities moving into other chemicals

3.3 Strategies for servicing foreign markets

Some companies spring ready-armed, as it were, onto the international scene; most arrive there gradually, starting from insignificant export sales which develop until a more permanent presence is established. This process, known as *incremental,* has been well documented and corresponds with perceptions widely held among businessmen.[6] There is evidence, however, that it is by no means universal. What emerges from the incremental growth is a three-tier system of international policies – export, knowledge sales and investment. The three cover a wide variety of activities which will be considered in detail in the following chapters. Meanwhile the choice of method of operation needs to be taken for each product and for each market and reappraised at frequent intervals. The options are summarized in Figure 3.3.

The export of goods or services is likely, as already suggested, to be the first choice under most conditions. It uses any existing spare capacity to advantage and involves the minimum commitment of additional resources. In the case of services, there is a narrow dividing line between export and knowledge sales or investment, since most services require some presence in the market which can be met by agents when goods are being sold. The crucial question is – what is being sold? If the answer is know-how rather than a product, then a licensing agreement may ultimately be more profitable. The move to direct investment will usually be made when an established market comes under threat.

Knowledge sales cover a wide variety of agreements, some of which are listed in Figure 3.3 and discussed in Chapter 5. These have a number of characteristics in common – that the agreement as such does not involve the movement of goods (although there may be related agreements that do, such as sales to the licensee company or purchases from it) and that the principal does not have a substantial capital commitment abroad by virtue of the contract. An implication of this second characteristic is that extensive investment is needed at home in research and development, as well as in general product improvement, to retain an advantage in the particular skills that enabled the company to achieve the knowledge sales in the first place.

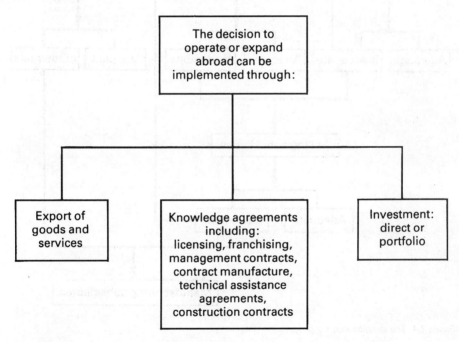

Figure 3.3 The international business options

Investment is of two kinds – direct investment (purchasing or establishing sub-sidiary companies abroad), and portfolio investment (where shares are bought for income or capital gains). Between the two lies the purchase of a minority holding in a foreign company, either because it is believed to provide a suitable return on spare funds or because it will help to safeguard a market or source of supply. The latter case resembles that of direct investment, the former portfolio investment.

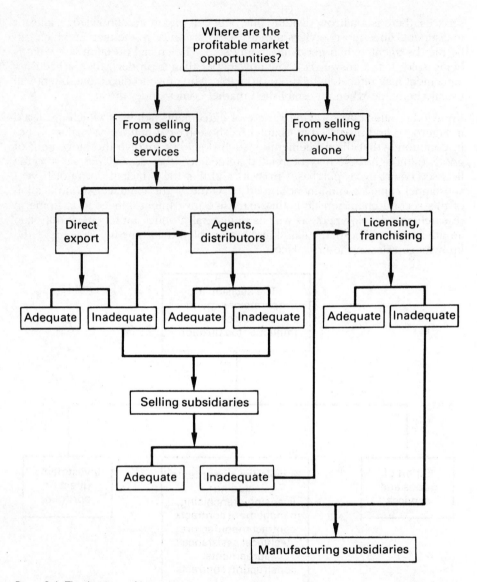

Figure 3.4 The decision-making process

Both forms of foreign investment are able to take advantage of the safeguards provided by operating in different economies at the same time (the opportunities suggested in Figure 3.2); both also carry risks of a different order from the risks incurred in the other two options. The investor has to provide for exchange rate fluctuations and the possibility of loss of assets through confiscation or some other disaster.

Figure 3.3 sets out the major options and sub-options available to a company at each stage of its progress abroad. Although an initial move into exports is normal, and companies that have once embarked on investment do not usually withdraw altogether, the ability to switch from any one option to any other is always available. This ability can be seen to depend on a company's planning procedures and its organization. Some systems have less built-in flexibility than others. The decision process is outlined in Figure 3.4 which assumes that most companies do not jump straight from domestic operations to foreign investment, but will try each method in turn after making an initial choice between selling products and selling know-how. (The choice may vary from product to product and market to market as with the other options.) For simplicity, Figure 3.4 gives 'inadequate' as the reason for moving to another option. Naturally this can have a number of emphases, including unprofitable or even over-successful, both of which can render existing arrangements inadequate.

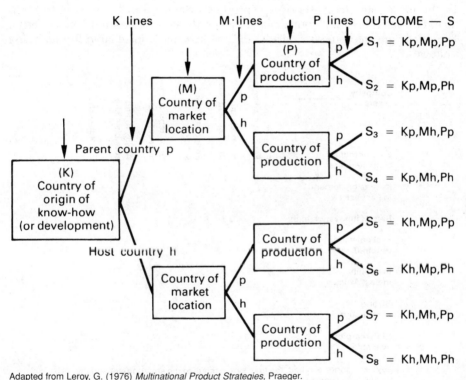

Adapted from Leroy, G. (1976) *Multinational Product Strategies*, Praeger.

Figure 3.5 Typology of basic states for a product

3.4 Analysing the strategies

The previous sections have taken a broad view of strategic options and how to choose the most appropriate for a whole company or for a particular business in a particular market. Behind this choice lies much hard analysis, wrestling with the massive uncertainties that beset a project in a foreign environment whose success depends on conditions years ahead. A number of schemes for analyzing the formation of international strategies have been proposed. One is outlined in Figure 3.5.[7] The figure starts from the country of origin of the product, whose development is represented by the letter K, while p (parent) represents the home country and h (host) the foreign country. Of the two lines on the left of the diagram (the K lines) the top one leads to a first marketing (M) in the home country, and the bottom one to the host. The four middle (M) lines show the options for the market; and the eight lines on the right (the P lines) show the possibilities for the country of production (where the host country may, of course, be different from the host country of market location). The eight P lines lead into the outcomes $(S_1, S_2, \ldots, S_8)$ which represent the eight options for cross-frontier strategies – with home or host countries being used for new product development and market and production facilities. Of these options S_1 (outcome 1), the most usual, consists of Kp (product originated in home country), Mp (market located in home country) and Pp (production located in home country). The others are interpreted similarly and the scheme is invaluable for analyzing strategies.

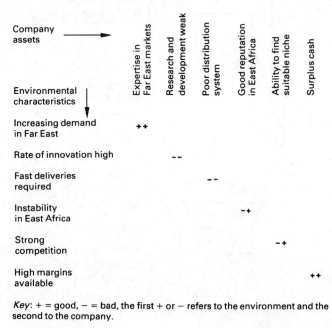

Company assets →

Environmental characteristics ↓

	Expertise in Far East markets	Research and development weak	Poor distribution system	Good reputation in East Africa	Ability to find suitable niche	Surplus cash
Increasing demand in Far East	++					
Rate of innovation high		--				
Fast deliveries required			--			
Instability in East Africa				-+		
Strong competition					-+	
High margins available						++

Key: + = good, − = bad, the first + or − refers to the environment and the second to the company.

Figure 3.6 A matrix scheme for identifying opportunities and dangers in strategy formulation

In one sample of large companies the most common moves were from S_1 to S_3, from S_1 to S_3 and S_4, or from S_8 to S_6. These particular findings may be biased by evidence drawn from mature multinationals which were operating a wide range of options, including innovation in the host country (S_8 and S_6) which is unusual. Examples of 18 states or progressions were recorded, interestingly these did not include any instances of the one that corresponds most closely with the product cycle model ($S_1 - S_3 - S_4 - S_2$). Different results would no doubt be found in an investigation of less mature companies but the *incremental model*, represented by S_1, proved the most common even in mature multinationals. According to this model operations overseas develop gradually, sometimes on the basis of experience gained in regional markets at home, and one method is added to another as the foreign business develops.

Research in Australia, Finland and Sweden has investigated incremental growth internationally and the learning process involved. Where, however, the market is small and open to competition, the process may be speeded up.[8]

Figure 3.5 offers a means of diagnosis; methods for prescription, after analyzing opportunities and dangers, are illustrated in the matrix scheme outlined in Figure 3.6. The issues are simplified and chosen at random to show how the scheme works. It enables a systematic evaluation of as many options as the analyst cares to insert. In Figure 3.6 the plus and minus signs are used to indicate a general view of strengths and weaknesses; the appraisal can be made more precise by inserting numbers.[9]

A similar scheme can be used to distinguish between the three major methods (export, knowledge agreements and investment).

3.5 The transfer of know-how: managerial and technical

The successful multinational is usually assumed to owe its success to superior management and technology. Its ability to transfer this know-how to its subsidiaries is regarded as its most important asset, the core of its strategic thinking. However, this transfer often proves more difficult than anticipated. Acquiring the expertise, on the other hand, is one of the benefits a country expects from foreign investment; but these benefits also prove difficult to realize. In both cases high expectations are hard to achieve, and the transfer of know-how easily becomes a problem area.

In the case of management, skills which succeed in one culture can fail in another; control systems are differently interpreted and marketing techniques prove ineffective. Yet sometimes the impact of a novel idea is singularly successful, while holding back valuable techniques out of sensitivity to supposed local prejudices can be even more resented than riding roughshod over local customs. Sometimes, on the other hand, local preferences will obstruct all efforts to promote methods that have succeeded elsewhere. And even when management skills are welcome, the fees charged may be criticized as unduly high, at the same time as they appear to companies to fall short of their costs.

A control system is a readily transferable technique and a particularly valuable one. The regular identification of revenues, expenditures, capital requirements, market share, production and productivity figures, sales per salesman and other items can be used almost anywhere to revive a flagging concern. The wording of the manuals in which the procedures are explained may cause difficulties, but the purpose is readily understood. Other parts of the management package sometimes need more adaptation and later chapters of this book review the skills of international marketing, finance, personnel and the rest. Different hopes and different problems accompany the transfer of technical know-how.

The transfer of technology[10] is not just a matter of selling patents and blueprints. The recipient – whether a licensee, a subsidiary or an independent operator – has to be taken through the processes of turning a saleable idea into a marketing and manufacturing programme. This includes the mobilization of finance, market research, product design, the selection of a manufacturing facility, the building and operating of that facility, the recruitment of suitable staff and suppliers, the cultivation of the market and the planning of future improvements in production and promotion as well as providing technical information, developing necessary skills and writing manuals.

From the company point of view, problems are caused when technology is transferred in an unimaginative way, without consideration for a recipient who has not been through the learning process and comes to the innovation cold. These problems may be made worse by a mutual recognition that relevant management skills are necessary for success. There is also the possibility of teething troubles at each of the stages listed in the previous paragraph. Yet another problem is timing; it is widely believed that the imitator, or at least the follower, does better than the innovator who incurs the expense of cultivating the market.

From the country's point of view, the technology may appear too expensive and the project too comprehensive. The same technology can seem too advanced to some, while others are suspicious that they are not getting the most up-to-date equipment. The expense appears even higher when the technology comes as part of a package which includes management and marketing.

No doubt many of the problems of transferring know-how are inescapable and have to be lived with – minor setbacks in a major thrust. Whatever the difficulties, strengths in management skills and in technology are usually regarded as critical to the formation of strategies. To minimize the difficulties, a company has to recognize that management is culture-bound and that some techniques reflect the values of the home country which are not necessarily those of the host, while governments and clients (whether joint venture partners or other collaborators like licensees) have to accept that management is a major cost to the company as well as a saleable skill, and that commercial success is inseparable from the specialized skills developed for a particular company or industry sector.

Technology is an asset whose price is higher than the immediately perceived value of a particular product or process; it carries expensive development costs which have to be recouped. Governments are concerned that technology is not neutral in its political and social effects, and that it needs to be appropriate and adapted to local conditions. Governments and clients are often reluctant to recognize that there are circumstances in which the elements of a technology package are inseparable. With simple technology, a sale of patents may be adequate, but more advanced technologies are likely to have been developed with their distinctive marketing programmes, training schemes and other management activities built in. A strategy for the international transfer of the technology is unlikely to succeed without the relevant programmes. Even if it could succeed, the supplier company is worried about the effect on its reputation if technology is supplied without the necessary training.

3.6 Conclusion

The strategic decision process begins with a number of familiar questions like:
  What kind of business are we in?
  What are our strengths and weaknesses?
  What opportunities is the market offering and what demands is it making?
  Where do we go from here?

In answering these questions an international company is influenced by the conflicting pressures of managers operating in each of the four dimensions: the functional, the product, the customer and the international. Typical answers can be classified into eight expansion routes any of which can lead a company abroad, although one specifies international growth as the main strategy. The conditions under which this is likely to be favoured have been discussed in terms of saleable ideas, product development, responding to a market, enlarging a supply base, acquiring fresh sources of capital or labour, the benefits of operating in different economies, the saturation of existing markets and the servicing of clients as they expand internationally.

For the move itself, three routes are seen to be available – exporting, knowledge sales and investment. Most companies consider the options in that order and, unless other routes are unavailable, do not enter their first foreign markets through investment. However, to experienced operators, all three options are available for most opportunities. The choice depends on the circumstances of the individual market and the amount of capital or managerial support a company wishes to place in that market.

A simple but realistic means of looking at the options for international business is by analogy with a piano keyboard. As in music, the sequences and the combinations (the chords) are all-important. This is illustrated in Figure 3.7 where the wide (white) keys list some methods of conducting the foreign business and the narrow (black) keys the methods of financing it. At the least Figure 3.7 illustrates the range of choices facing the strategist and the analogy will be used in a similar way in later chapters to illustrate the choices for export, knowledge agreements and investment. Too often companies are choosing from an unnecessarily narrow range.

Note: It has been pointed out that the keyboard analogy is only illuminating to those with an interest in music, but a glance at any conventional keyboard instrument like a piano or an organ will surely demonstrate the combination of white (broad) and black (narrow) notes sketched in Figure 3.7. Once that is grasped the significance of a sequence of notes (which produces a tune) or a combination (which produces harmony) is not hard to grasp. As with all analogies, this provides a limited but very clear idea of the subject illustrated – in this case the importance of sequences and combinations of strategies or activities for international managers.

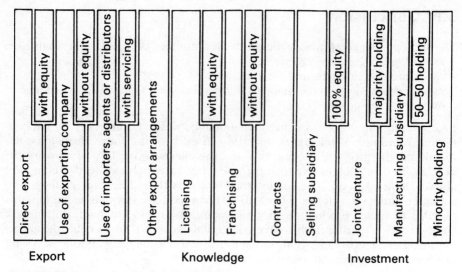

Figure 3.7 The keyboard analogy – international strategies

3.7 Cases, questions and further reading

Cases

Alfa-Laval Thermal, see Robock and Simmonds (1983) pp. 648–69.
Dexion-Overseas Ltd., see Robock and Simmonds (1983) pp. 692–704.
IBM World Trade Corporation, see Vernon and Wells (1981) pp. 326–52.
Yoshida-Kogya K.K. (Strategy of YKK by D.F. Channon) Case Clearing House
   no. 382–025–1.

Questions

1 Select an industry sector and examine the particular problems of developing an international strategy for that sector.

2 Examine the view that the process of internationalization is likely to develop through a series of clearly defined stages, each of which demands its own information needs and managerial strengths.

3 What factors influence the choice of methods of market servicing on the part of international firms? Analyze the choice between exporting, licensing and foreign investment in terms of penetrating and servicing markets.

4 Outline a strategy either for an expanding high technology company or for a restaurant chain with no experience abroad.

5 List the available routes to diversification and discuss one in some depth with examples.

6 It has been said that the main motive for a company to operate abroad is to defend itself against fluctuations in the domestic economy. Comment critically on this assertion.

7 Discuss the position of a company like Crown Cork – a middle-sized firm in a market dominated by two giants – trying to establish an international strategy.

8 A small, thrusting computer peripheral manufacturer has been offered the opportunity of a chain of licences in foreign markets. The Board has commissioned an outside adviser to report on whether to accept the offer or whether it would be wiser to develop abroad by other means. Write the adviser's report, making whatever assumptions about the company you consider to be necessary.

Further reading

Daniels and Radebaugh, 1995, ch. 14 and 15.

Fayerweather, 1982, ch. 1–5.

Hamel, G. and Prahalad, C.F., 'Do you really have a global strategy?', *Harvard Business Review*, July–August 1985, pp.139–48.

Henzler, H. and Rall, W., 'Facing up to the globalization challenge', *McKinsey Quarterly*, Winter 1986, pp.52–68.

Leontiades, J.C., *Multinational Corporate Strategy*, D.C. Heath, 1985.

Leroy, G., *Multinational Product Strategies*, Praeger, 1976.

Robock and Simmonds, 1983, ch. 13.

Vernon and Wells, 1981, ch.1.

Further reading

PART TWO   MANAGEMENT

This part covers most of the activities of the international manager summarized by the following chapter headings.

 4 Trade in goods and services
 5 Trade in knowledge and expertise
 6 Foreign investment
 7 International marketing management
 8 International financial management
 9 Personnel and industrial relations
10 Logistics, purchasing, distribution, production and research
11 Decision-making and organization
12 International corporate planning

4 Trade in goods and services

This chapter covers exporting (and to a less extent importing, which is also included under purchasing in Chapter 10). Figure 4.1 presents the issues together with cross-references to other chapters. Other aspects of international marketing are covered in Chapter 7.

The direct sale of goods and services is one option in a strategic approach. This chapter assumes that the decision has been taken that direct export has been selected as the correct method for a particular industry sector, company or product in the chosen market. The consequences of this choice are addressed in this chapter, and the answer takes account of a complicated time sequence rather than a simple instruction to start exporting.

The evidence assembled below suggests that the key to success in international trade is to be found in systematic preparation, not in a snap decision.[1] 'We'll spend a little time on it when we can' or 'Let's push out a few samples and see what happens', are phrases that can lead to expensive disillusionment. Indeed, disappointment arises when the foreign business is found to be less profitable than the domestic, to be abandoned when the home market improves. Naturally, there will be other reasons for failure like inadequate costing or pricing policies, or simply an unskilled approach.

One assumption that underlies this chapter is that, given skilful international management, planned and sustained exporting can be very profitable and is often a key to survival. Another assumption is that the exporter has to keep a weather eye on the political situation to steer a path through a labyrinth of incentives and constraints. Details of company–government relations are considered in Chapter 15, while this chapter considers the following subjects:

pre-export (4.1),
market selection (4.2),
significant obstacles (4.3),
the options (4.4),
the foreign agent or distributor (4.5),
organization and staffing (4.6),
documentation (4.7),

Relevant issues discussed in other chapters include: market research (Chapter 7), product policies (Chapter 7), pricing policies (Chapters 7 and 15), finance (Chapter 8) and insurance (Chapter 8).

Naturally a project involves reviewing the options, the possible collaborators, the organization, and the finance at the same time – and not necessarily in that order. Almost any order is in fact possible. An approach from a would-be agent can, for instance, set the process in motion. The list is restated in the form of a system in Figure 4.1 and it should be noted that there are other loops not shown in the figure. Rethinking of the whole scheme can be set off by problems at any stage in the process.

(The numbers in brackets refer to chapters or sections of chapters)

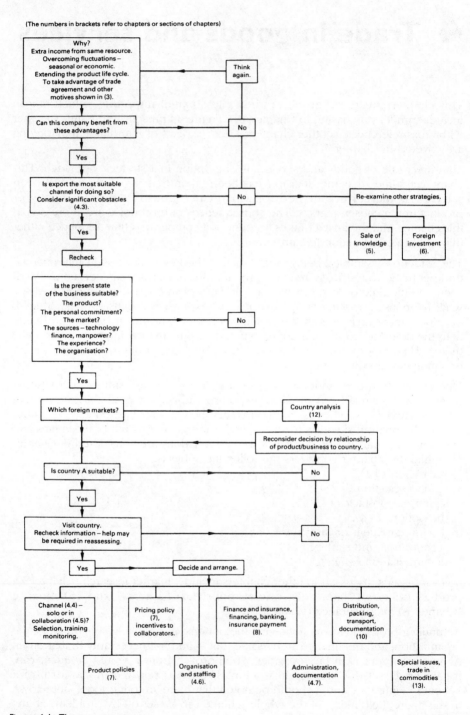

Figure 4.1 The export process

4.1 Pre-export

Exporting normally starts from a profitable domestic business. Success is to be taken abroad, not failure or incompetence; a management worried by difficulties at home is unlikely to succeed in a foreign market. This is the conventional wisdom, although there are circumstances in which declining sales, like spending cuts or increasing competition in the domestic market, may set off an export drive. Usually a proven track record is regarded as essential if a convincing sales drive is to be undertaken abroad. Given this record, the company also needs to be convinced that the home market is reasonably saturated.

Research mentioned in the last chapter demonstrated that most exporters began by expanding into various regions of their home country and learned to cope with local differences and distribution problems before embarking on other cultures and on cross-frontier logistics.[2] Geographical expansion at home develops management and thus makes the move abroad more viable. It is also likely to increase the range of a company's contacts. This research also emphasized the importance of attitudes in the decision, however strong the market pressures may be.

Another finding on pre-export is that many firms (60 per cent in one American survey of smaller-sized exporters)[3] are persuaded into exporting by external influences before they are sufficiently prepared. The influences include approaches from would-be customers, both export houses at home and importers abroad. The response to such approaches, as well as small-scale efforts like the sending abroad of samples, is regarded as an experiment – an experiment that is easily abandoned. In fact, one research (recorded in note 3, see the *Notes* section) found that 86 per cent of failed exporters in the sample had had some successes.

One result of abandoning an export effort is that a company accepts the view that exporting is either too expensive or irrelevant to its needs, whereas the true reason may have been inadequate preparation or an inappropriate method. This is a form of organization learning which can build up obstacles to rational development. The characters as well as the outlooks of the senior managers are a significant factor. The export thrust demands perseverance and understanding. A company led by people who dislike foreigners, are insensitive to cultural differences and are unwilling to travel is unlikely to succeed abroad. The opposite characteristics may predispose decision-makers to open up export markets – perhaps even prematurely. The firm's previous experience and its reaction to fresh opportunities will help to determine its suitability as an exporter. The research also demonstrated how operating in different regions of the home country could be a preliminary to exporting – an easy way to learn how to cope with local variations.

Given these preliminary conditions, the general motives for international trade already listed will operate. For instance, a company which finds itself especially sensitive to the trade cycles will be able to smooth over the consequences if it operates in more than one economy. Seasonal fluctuations can also be a reason. Another motive may be provided by a trade agreement, an international loan or a similar circumstance. Exports can help to spread sales while keeping the factory more continuously employed and the warehouse less full. There are sometimes opportunities to move abroad on the backs of other businesses – like tourism – or to provide components for large-scale manufacturers. The buying manual of an aeroplane manufacturer, for instance, contains items as different as jet engines and ash-trays.

Check-list: readiness for export

If any of the following questions are answered in the affirmative, there is some readiness for export; conversely if any are answered in the negative there is an obstacle.

1 Does this company have experience in selling out of more than one centre?
2 Does this company have experience of adapting products for more than one type of customer?
3 Does this company have the resources for adequate market research abroad?
4 Does this company have staff trained in export procedures (in particular are they members of an appropriate professional institute)? Can they speak any foreign languages?
5 Have the objectives of the export drive been adequately defined?

4.2 Market selection

An important concept in the export decision is that of the critical mass.[4] This derives from observations that small amounts of exports to many markets produce little or no profit. The minimum size of market required depends on the product and the company. But entering a country is a major project in its own right, and only when a company has sufficient sales in one particular country is the time right to enter another. Of course the critical market share will depend on the *exact* definition of the market in terms of segment, sector, niche or other considerations but failure to observe this maxim is a common cause of frustration and failure.

To be successful, the process can be expected to be sequential and limited to the resources available. There may be an advantage in developing the move abroad fast enough to enter a number of economies where the industry is one that is dependent on the trade cycle; there is no advantage in spreading the corporate effort around several markets none of which is being cultivated adequately. In Britain, a report on the need to concentrate on key markets was published as long ago as 1975.[5] This advocated the greatest possible penetration of a limited number of markets. The opposite is often practised. Successful sales in one market tempt a company to try others. This is a known route to disaster, but the temptation is not in doubt. The principles of market selection follow the attempt to relate corporate strengths to environmental opportunities already outlined (see Figure 3.6).

4.3 Significant obstacles

There are a number of difficulties that arise with exporting; some stem from within the company and some from outside influences.

Within the exporter company

The obstacles within the firm are of three kinds:
1 hostile or casual attitudes,
2 inadequate preparation,
3 lack of resources.

Given any of these, the costs of exports are likely to exceed the benefits at least by perception and probably by fact. The resulting disenchantment constitutes an obstacle to further effort. Lack of preparation produces other difficulties which are considered later in this chapter, including errors in documentation as well as inadequate knowledge of market and legal conditions in the foreign country.

Outside influences

A battery of regulations exists in most countries to control imports. These include:
1 tariff barriers,
2 health and safety regulations,
3 restrictions on certain classes of goods,
4 other conditions, like part manufacture locally.

With services, foreign companies are prohibited in some countries in sensitive sectors like insurance or banking. In addition to official controls, there may be buy-local policies especially on the part of governments and local authorities. Less official obstacles are the need to understand local customs and fashions which can make an apparently suitable product unsaleable.

4.4 The options

The channels can be classified according to the way the exports are handled – whether by the company itself, by an agent or by a co-operative agreement with other exporters. Some of the options are sketched out in Figure 4.2 and explained in the following notes.

1 Sales from the exporting company itself

In this case there are a number of sub-options.
(a) *Sales in the home country through responding to enquiries and orders received from foreign buyers.* This method does not require a sales drive, but it does incur the danger of developing exports before the company is ready. It is a normal starting-point for small firms in the consumer goods sector as well as other manufacturing companies. Some service industries, like management consultants and insurance firms, have also developed this way. Their reputation sells their service through international contacts acquired in the normal course of business. As a method of building up a substantial export trade, this option has problems. Selling expenses are low, but distribution costs are often high. There is also a need to establish expertise on shipping, on

documentation, on the adaptation of the goods to the relevant markets and on other related subjects, but the slow build up can mean that the expertise becomes under-employed. This responsive approach can be supplemented by a limited advertising and direct mail campaign, while a list of criteria is drawn up to determine which are the more profitable opportunities. Although expenses of promotion are low with this channel, the distribution costs are high, as are the hidden costs in executive time and frustration. Using other channels does not rule out a rapid response when appropriate, but does ensure a context of planning and policy formulation which reduces frustration. The next option involves a sales drive into foreign territory.

(b) *In a foreign country through travelling sales representatives.* The travelling sales team, often led by a company director, has been the traditional method used at least by European firms in the capital goods industry.[6] The sales teams took their intimate knowledge of the products, such as textile machinery or machine tools, into the market. This method had the advantage of keeping down overheads, since there were no expensive local facilities to maintain, and of eliminating the problems of supervision. Greater flexibility was also maintained where the number of potential orders in any one country was small. The travelling sales team was not only a feature of the capital goods industry, but of service industries like construction. Some consumer goods companies also used this method, in their case usually for supplementing sales from the home base. In any industry, such a method begins to appear inadequate when the competition becomes intense and the customer expects more sustained attention both before and after the sale. As firms from other regions (North America and the Far East) have developed their corporate presence in the market, European firms have been compelled to follow suit or to drop out. This has led either to direct investment or to the employment of agents and distributors.

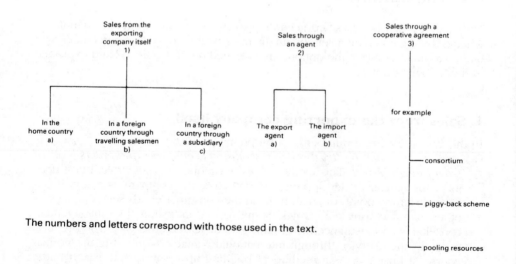

The numbers and letters correspond with those used in the text.

Figure 4.2 The export options

(c) *In a foreign country through a local presence.* A company is likely to move into a local office, a marketing subsidiary or a manufacturing operation when the market can no longer be serviced profitably by other means. While direct investment is the subject of another chapter, the advantages of a marketing subsidiary are that it overcomes the deficiencies of agents and travelling sales-men by ensuring a corporate presence in the market. If the potential is large enough to justify this move a number of consequences follow, including: a closer link between head office and the customer, a faster turnround of stocks and a more efficient after-sales service. The subsidiary can also be the centre for developing a regional business in a group of countries.

2 Sales through an agent

Another group of methods is to sell through an agent, an export firm in the home country, an import company abroad or by a co-operative arrangement.

(a) *The export agency,* sometimes known as an export-managing firm or an export-import house, is an arrangement under which the goods are sold in the home country to a firm that undertakes to sell them abroad. The agent can be used for all exports or for certain markets or for certain products. This option is especially relevant to the small company, since it avoids the need for expertise on transportation and documentation which is provided by the specialist exporter. It is also used by large companies, but mainly for more distant or difficult markets. The disadvantage is that the firm is subletting a function which is an important part of the learning process for developing foreign trade. If the principal has no contact with the market, more is being lost than knowledge of transport and documentation. The exporter will need to develop skills in international marketing before progress can be made and may, in any case, eventually find that the discounts which the intermediary requires could be used to build up the necessary knowledge internally.

(b) *The import agent or distributor,* a firm in a foreign territory which undertakes to represent exporters. This is the most common arrangement, apart from direct investment, but the exact services offered vary; some are listed in the next section (4.5).

3 Sales through a co-operative agreement

This heading covers many different arrangements with companies, trading organ-izations and export associations combining to establish sales facilities abroad. In the case of large companies and banks, some form of *consortium* is established commonly to sell the equipment, the expertise and the financing for a construc-tion project or a production system. It is generally recognized that, in large deals, the financing arrangements are as important a part of the sale as the product or the price.

In the case of a small company, there are special advantages in an arrangement which makes direct contact with the foreign market possible but minimizes the expenses, in particular making it unnecessary to set up a specialist export depart-ment. A variation is an arrangement under which an experienced operator provides export services for a new starter, *piggy-backing* as it is called. Such arrangements were pioneered in the United States by General Electric more than 50 years ago, and have been followed elsewhere with varying success. One difficulty, as with so many attempts to aid small businesses, has been an unwillingness on the part of clients to provide the necessary information and their fear of being overpowered by the larger partner. Nevertheless there have been successful arrangements helpful to both parties. The existing exporter, the company which provides the piggy-back, has found an additional use for existing facilities, while the client has moved into export trade by a relatively inexpensive route.

Yet another option is a group arrangement in which several small companies in different products agree to enter a market together; they then pool their resources to appoint a joint representative in that market.

4.5 The foreign agent or distributor

Companies that do not have their own branches or subsidiaries abroad usually find that an import agent is the most effective and profitable channel. At best, the agent is established within the foreign market, has a knowledge of local methods of conducting business and, if a thruster, has the ability to achieve a market share more rapidly than by any other method. However, this can also be an expensive channel which causes problems and disillusionment. Some of the problems arise from a straightforward conflict of interest or standpoint, when the agent's whole business is devoted to one among the markets that the principal is attempting to service. The agent is suspected of being content with too small a market share or failing to follow guidelines about market segment. The agent company, for its part, complains of irregular and undependable supplies and inadequate back-up services. Both parties worry about the agent's commission, although for different reasons.

For the new exporter, and the small company in particular, an agency agreement might be the first collaborative venture ever undertaken. This leads to personal difficulties when the management of collaborative arrangements is uncharted territory in which the rising entrepreneur lacks experience and for which it might be unsuited temperamentally. There are also commercial and legal problems that stem from the novelty of the venture. If, for instance, a small firm's legal and accounting advisers are unfamiliar with the law and conventions in the foreign country, costly errors can result. One implication is that the initial selection largely determines the later success. Selection by casual encounter ('I just happened to meet the ideal chap on an aeroplane') is a common reason for failure.

Selection of the foreign agent

Before the selection process begins, a framework is needed to decide upon the characteristics required in an agent. A profile of the ideal collaborator can be worked out under the following headings.

The types of agent

An agent can serve many different functions and agency agreements can be classified according to the functions served. One arrangement shades into another adding up to numerous possibilities, but there are three main types:

1 *a sales representative* – a freelance salesperson who takes orders for the principal in return for a commission and does not usually hold stocks;
2 *a distributor* who holds stocks and provides some services;
3 *an agent* who acts as a full representative of the principal (who may have some capital committed) and provides a full range of services including credit (the *del credere* agent). The classification here takes account of the common international usage. In Britain the fully representative agency is usually called the distributor; this usage confuses the phrase 'del credere agent'. Whichever words are used, and they are usually interchangeable, the fact of a series of closely related roles running from the freelance individual to the full company representative providing a corporate presence in the market, is crucial. Most agents are not individuals but companies.

1 and 3 should be regarded as the opposite ends of a long list in the course of which are added services like stock-holding, warehousing, after-sales service, market planning, the management of sub-distributors, limited assembly and processing, testing products and credit arrangements.

Agency law

In some countries a definition of the types of agency is included in the commercial law. In France, for example, there are 28 possible arrangements each with its own legal status – from the freelance salesperson to the *del credere* agent. French law, as well as that of most members of the European Union apart from Britain and Belgium, stipulates that an agent who takes on a comprehensive marketing engagement for a company cannot be dismissed without compensation, whatever the contract may say. The courts have been awarding two years' anticipated profits in cases of disputed dismissal, and more in some countries. This is to pay for the goodwill that the agent has brought to the business.

To overcome this problem, the company needs to decide what functions the agent will be called upon to perform. The decision might be for a simple agreement at first, with other duties added later. This avoids a common source of difficulties – making long-term agreements for what then turn out to be temporary situations. The most suitable arrangement will, in any case, be determined partly by the nature of the business. If an after-sales service is required, the agent is likely to be asked to provide it on the grounds that it increases the incentive to promote the goods and is likely to prove less confusing to the customer. However, in this case, a complicated agreement is required to cover the training of the agent's staff as well as facilities for stocking spares. There will probably be implications for other parts of the business as well.

The scope and duration of the agreement

The agent's contract will normally cover all the services it is expected to supply couched in terms that will be upheld by the country's law. In the past, it was common to attempt to use the law of the home country, but this is seldom advisable. What can be done, however, is to provide for recourse to some international body for arbitration in the event of a dispute.[7] There is a tendency to place restrictions on agents – demanding that they do not accept business from competitors, for instance, or trade outside a limited territory – restrictions that sometimes fall foul of competition laws. In the European Union many of the cases so far brought under its competition policy have been over restrictive agreements with agents.[8] In any case, there is always a trade-off between the desire to work with an experienced agent who, by definition, will have an existing business, and the wish to prevent the agent dealing with competitors. On the other hand – and also likely to fall foul of competition policies under some circumstances – are the agent company's efforts to acquire an exclusive right to the principal's products in its area.

Criteria for selecting an agent

The exporter usually wishes to stipulate the skills required by an agent. Less obvious is the question of size. Some match with the exporter is likely to be needed for a number of reasons, including the wish to achieve a relevant market share. The small company will look for a similar niche in the foreign market to that already attained at home, and will want an agent accustomed to operating on the appropriate scale. A large company might require a substantial market share to make established methods of supply viable and will need an agent capable of matching that requirement. In either case, the agent will need to demonstrate an ability to grow with the business and the lack of such an ability is a common source of problems. It will also need to show a willingness to keep up-to-date with changing technology or fashion. The agent's track record and financial stability can be checked by a third party such as a bank or consultant. The verification is usually conducted with a list which restates the requirements in terms of size and operating experience as well as profitability, indebtedness and other relevant considerations, along with the expected compatibility of the agent as a business partner.

The search for an agent

The search process is likely to follow a process of organization learning. The first appointment is sometimes by chance, the seizing of an opportunity; the most visible problem is the effective servicing of a growing market. Later appointments will usually be more cautious as the need to avoid difficulties with agents acquires priority. The criteria for the appointment will include the compatibility of the agent's company, size, track record and the other issues mentioned in the previous paragraphs. The search itself can be facilitated by a number of organizations – government departments, banks, consultants and others – which publish lists or arrange contacts.[9] Some operators, however, prefer direct enquiries in a market believing that, by the time a list is published, a successful agent will already have found sufficient business. The process needs to be systematic, not the casual appointment of a plausible character met in a chance encounter.

The following are the usual steps:
1 formulate the search process, requirements and desirable features listed in order of priority;
2 develop appropriate contacts and scan lists;
3 vet for reputation and financial stability;
4 make contact with short-listed agencies;
5 final selection.

IMPORTANT NOTE. The most significant need in selecting agents – as in selecting any collaborators – is to form a systematic selection procedure. Many disappointments and disasters arise from haphazard methods of selection. The following list provides a rough guidance for drawing up a check-list:
 track record,
 acceptability in local market,
 viability as a business,
 willingness to operate with principal's system.

Each of these headings can be turned into a list of questions to be used at an interview with an executive of a potential agent.

Managing the agent

Once the selection has been carried oùt, there is a need for continuing management. Strictly it is the *relationship*, rather than the activity, that is being managed as the agent is an independent company, but a common view is that the relationship should be as close as possible. A regular monitoring of the agent's business along the same lines as that of a subsidiary is considered to produce the most satisfactory results.[10] However, this is not always possible and some compromise has to be accepted. Similarly, the maximum information needs to pass from the principal to the agent, but in a form that can be understood, digested and used.

The key to the management of agents is that a business relationship has to be established and sustained. This is more important than the legal agreement, but the drafting of the agreement remains vital in order to clarify the interests of both parties, to ensure that responsibilities are allocated satisfactorily, and to provide an escape route if the relationship breaks down. To this end, the terms must be viable under the laws of the agent's country. Sustaining the relationship includes a two-way flow of information. It also includes regular visiting in order to co-ordinate plans, to sort out problems, to arrange for staff training and to organize any other activities that might be required, like the feeding back of information to research and development and to market planning departments.

4.6 Organization and staffing

A question like 'Which comes first?' is seldom presented in a more acute form than when discussing an export department. Some of the decisions clamouring for priority are:
 Who will take responsibility for exports?
 Is an export department needed at all?
 If so: Where will it fit into the company? To whom will the export manager report?
 Is it necessary to recruit specialist staff?

The employment of specialist staff is a risky commitment for a growing business, but growth will be delayed if specialists are not appointed. One difficulty is that problems that inhibit progress and increase costs arise at two different levels –

the management and the clerical. Companies are therefore unsure about which level to recruit. The manager needs a grounding in export marketing and he requires the status to impose order on the haphazard business, in all too many markets, which is likely to face him on his appointment. The clerk needs to be trained in detail to ensure that the documentation is completed, meticulously, and is available when and where required. Sufficient skill to establish a satisfactory relationship with shippers, insurers, customers and customs officers is also important. The compromise that one person has to be both clerk and manager leads to a downgrading of the function of export management; that this can continue even after the department grows is witnessed by the fact that the average salary often remains below that of other branches of management.[11]

It has been alleged that, as a result of the ambiguous position of the export department, documentation – the essential skill of the export clerk – takes precedence over the development of strategy. At the same time complaints are heard that the documentation is not carried out effectively because of lack of interest or lack of supervision. It is not easy to quantify the extent of these problems. They are mentioned in circumstances that suggest that improved organizations and training are required.

Before exporting begins, an executive director needs to be given responsibility for it.[12] This ensures that the company as a whole is committed and that exporting appears on the regular agenda of board or executive committee meetings. The staffing at lower levels can either depend on a calculation of income or of business handled, frequently a combination of the two. Assuming that a small export department (consisting of three people – manager, clerk and secretary) costs £75,000, a common rule of thumb suggests that foreign sales of £750,000 a year will justify the appointment of an export manager. This allows 10 per cent for the cost of the department, which is justified if there is growth potential.

The manager's duties will be to mastermind the thrust abroad, to keep in touch with customers, to maintain contact with foreign agents and distributors, to monitor their efforts, to represent the views of customers and agents to fellow managers, and to supervise the detailed work of delivering the products. The other means of calculating the manning levels is by number of consignments handled. It has been shown that the growth of a department from the appointment of its first clerk begins when the number of consignments exceeds 100, although some companies only employ '2 to 4' clerks when the number exceeds 5,000.

Another rule of thumb limits the number of markets entered to the ability of the staff to maintain adequate contact. An approach to further outlets then depends on the ability to appoint extra staff, when income justifies this. At the earlier stages, export will probably be a sub-department of either the central or a divisional marketing department. If the department is handling more than 30 per cent of a firm's business, there is a case for promoting it to a top-level function. The implications of setting up international and regional divisions are discussed in Chapter 11, while the objection that co-ordinated marketing may be difficult if domestic and foreign operations are separated is answered in two ways. One is that the costs of not employing specialists are easily underestimated. Losses are made, for instance, by sales managers who are too impatient to take advice and who make inappropriate payment arrangements, like unconfirmed letters of credit in an unstable market. The other reason for separating foreign business from domestic is that successful exporting requires just as much co-ordination with the production, finance and research departments as does home marketing. The international or export department is able to feed back more effectively information on problems that arise in the market as a result of product design, reliability, financing methods or other relevant policies.

Once a department grows, the functions are usually subdivided. A fully fledged export operation has a strategic staff to plan, promote and monitor the thrust abroad along with an administrative staff to handle the documentation and formal control system. Figure 4.3 presents a typical system for a large export department, whether the appointment of the manager is at board level or subordinate to marketing. In this example the overseas representatives report direct to the manager and the other departments provide them with a service. This arrangement enables high level representatives to be recruited, but may cause difficulties in relationships with agents.

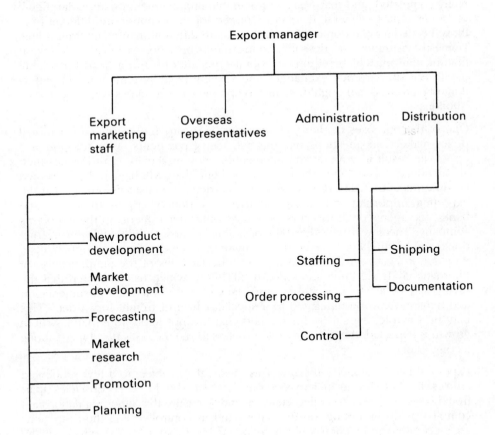

Figure 4.3 The export department

4.7 Documentation

The boundary between management and routine clerical work becomes blurred when documentation is considered. It is well-known that serious consequences – loss of profits and even of markets, not to mention prosecution – can result from incompetent documentation. Hence the need for careful supervision. As one authority described the epitaph of the untrained exporter: 'It was easy enough to sell, a pity we didn't get paid.'[13] It should be equally obvious that markets are not won by filling in forms. A system for the paperwork is required to avoid losses and frustration, but is subordinate to export development. Possible losses can include demurrage charges if, for instance, the unloading of a ship is delayed for lack of the necessary documents. For this reason, it is often thought wise to ensure that the documents are delivered to the local office or agent before the goods arrive, incurring a small additional expense which can save large sums.

One survey in Britain estimated that 30 per cent of export documents were incorrectly completed, and that was a considerable improvement on an earlier figure of 55 per cent. In general, the skills required for the exporter are different from those needed for the domestic marketer – more different than many firms admit. Domestic insurance and despatch arrangements bear no resemblance to export documentation, which requires elaborate precautions and a head for minute detail; nor do currency exchanges and varying legal systems normally affect domestic business, although there may be problems in countries with federal constitutions.

One of the purposes of the documentation is to provide statistics for national policy-makers on questions like the balance of payments. As a consequence errors can result in government intervention, not an activity most businessmen are anxious to encourage. The documents themselves will have to be presented to either the purchaser or his agent, the carriers, the customs officials (in the exporting, importing and transit countries), the port or airport authorities, the banks, the agents or distributors as well as other departments in the exporter's company. There will be either bills of lading or air-way bills, delivery instructions and certificates, credit notes, insurance certificates and much else. Preparation costs can be saved by using the facilities of the Simplification of International Trade Procedures Board (SITPRO), which has estimated that the saving may be as much as 50 per cent. Many of the problems of documentation and transport can be delegated to a specialist firm of freight forwarders. This may be suitable, especially for markets that are not likely to expand. Where growth is expected, the company often prefers to see the skills developed among its own staff.

Exporting is encouraged officially. This means that, subject to a few prohibited articles like heroin and military equipment, there should be no obstacles apart from border enquiries to collect statistics and to ensure that other regulations are complied with. Importing, on the other hand, is controlled and the restrictions are becoming more complex; this is occurring in spite of the efforts of the General Agreement on Tariffs and Trade now the World Trade Organization (WTO) (discussed in Chapter 16). Since every export must also be an import, most of the administrative problems are encountered in the foreign country (the country of import), a point not always understood by colleagues with no experience of international trade.

The requirements of the importing country, as well as of the countries of transit, have to be met. These will include documentation, currency exchange, import controls, regulations (such as health and safety laws and consumer protection) which affect the product and its mode of transport, tariffs and other taxes and, of course, the existence or non-existence of facilities for transport and security. The routines of exporting and importing are very traditional, in spite of efforts to modernize them through international organizations and official bodies like the Simplification of Trade Procedures Board (SITPRO).

Table 4.1 The exporter's dictionary

Incoterms   An internationally accepted list of terms used to define the point at which the goods change hands

Cost and freight	CFR**
Cost, insurance and freight	CIF
Carriage paid to	CPT
Carriage and insurance paid to	CIP
Delivered at frontier	DAF
Delivered duty paid	DDP
Delivered ex quay	DEQ
Delivered ex ship	DES
Delivered duty unpaid	DDU
Ex works	EXW
Free alongside ship	FAS
Free carrier	FCA
Free carrier (named point)	FRC
Free on board	FOB
Free on board aircraft	FOR*

* FOT is often used but is not a standard abbreviation
** C and R is often used but is not a standard abbreviation

SAD (Single Administrative Document) has been used in the European Community; in theory it became obsolete after 1992.

Aligned System of Documentation   A series of documents required at all stages of the sale, export, insurance and delivery of the goods. There may be 20–30 documents in all, including:

Bill of lading
Commercial invoice
Documentary letter of credit
Performance bond
TIR convention permits

Table 4.1 sets out some of the most common items in the dictionary of the exporter. One purpose of the documentation, demonstrated by this list, is that of determining where the title to the goods changes hands. The Incoterms are an internationally recognized list of abbreviations defined by the International Chamber of Commerce and used in trading contracts and other documents.[14] The aligned system of documentation is an easy way (it can be computerized) of assembling all the documents required in transit, for making insurance claims or for requesting payment.

4.8 Conclusion

This chapter has traced out most of the sequence of actions that follow once a decision to export has been taken – the sequence sketched in Figure 4.1. After examining the necessary preliminaries, the options for the exporter were identified. The keyboard analogy, introduced in the last chapter, is restated in Figure 4.4 to illustrate how the export options can be used in various combinations, or in sequences, to provide a convincing strategy. Agency and other collaborative agreements were discussed at some length, as they form a common method of operation that produces many problems. The stage beyond such agreements is to bring the agent within the company, and this is discussed in Chapter 6 on investment. One suggestion echoed in this chapter is the possibility of establishing a relationship with an agent company that is similar to that with a subsidiary.

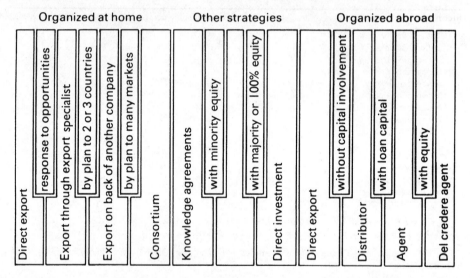

Figure 4.4　The keyboard analogy – export

The figure uses three sets of sequences.

Export organized at home

Under this heading there are four main sequences:
1 **direct export,** the exporter selling direct to a foreign customer;
2 **export through an export specialist,** the exporter sells to a specialist company in its own country;
3 **export on the back of another company,** the title used is 'piggy-back' system in which another company takes on the exporter's foreign sales;
4 **consortium,** the increasingly used method whereby a pair or group of companies, which do not compete with one another, join for business with a customer they all share.

Under these headings there are another three sequences, each of which can be combined with any of the four.

1 **response to opportunities** approaches from foreign companies or responses to market research may reveal opportunities for export;
2 **by plan to two or three countries,** an intensive thrust into few (preferably a *few*) countries identified as probable markets;
3 **by plan to many markets,** the same procedure but to many markets. This should only be undertaken by a company that already has large-scale exports.

Other strategies for foreign sales

Two methods, both discussed in Chapters 5 and 6, are for knowledge agreements and direct equity. Both can be combined with either a majority or 100 per cent equity, or little or no equity – the former is a direct investment.

Export organized abroad

Like export organized at home this can be combined with four major sequences: direct export or export through a distributor, agent or *del credere* agent. Each of these can, in turn, be undertaken without capital, with loan capital or with equity.

The need for specialization was emphasized in the section on organization and staffing. The beginnings of an export department can be planned as soon as substantial trade develops. While staff are brought into position when the business warrants it, they need to possess expertise that enables them to avoid expensive blunders. Financing and controlling the exports are also specialized skills. There is a need to restrict the amount of money, as well as of goods, in transit or lying idle, and to ensure that export credits are adequately safeguarded.

Finally, there was a note on the documentation without which the export effort would come to a standstill. Throughout the chapter different approaches have been indicated as relevant to companies of different sizes in seeking additional market share or using international sources of finance. The following provides a check-list for the exporter.

Check-list

1   The conditions for successful exporting:
profitable domestic business,
planned approach,
opportunities,
resources,
product: suitability and adaptability,
commitment,
experience.
2 The export decision:
(a) recheck resources, such as:
funds,
staff,

        production capacity,
        sales;
    (b) recheck policies on
        methods of entry and operation (direct sales or through collaborators),
        pricing,
        organization,
        documentation,
        handling collaborators,
        monitoring,
        communication,
        status of export within company;
    (c) recheck the market and reassess the possibility of gaining adequate mar-
        ket share;
    (d) finance (see Chapter 8);
    (e) distribution (see Chapter 10).

4.9   Cases, questions and further reading

Case example

R.O. Bury and Sons Ltd. – control of agents

R.O. Bury & Sons Ltd was a small family business manufacturing toys for young
children. Mr Rob Bury, grandson of the founder, has been successful at building
up an export trade through many tours abroad. His goods are sold at toy shops,
stationers and souvenir shops. So far, Mr Bury has sold mainly to individual shops
or small distributors. This has put enormous strains on his shipping office, and
has proved expensive in selling costs.

The one exception to this method of distribution was France. Some two years
earlier, on one of his travels, Mr Bury had met a Monsieur Vincent Oleur in a
bar in Paris. Monsieur Oleur ran an import-export agency and, in the course of
conversation, he offered to promote Bury's goods in France. Mr Bury asked his
lawyer, who was a personal friend and adviser but who had no knowledge of
French commercial law, to draft an agreement. In this Monsieur Oleur was
granted exclusive rights for the sale of Bury's products in France and certain
countries of North Africa. An immediate increase in orders followed. The success was maintained and France soon became the largest single foreign market
for the Bury products. Problems also began to emerge.

Monsieur Oleur began to demand an increased commission, and Mr Bury then
made some calculations which convinced him that sales in France were already
so expensive as to make a negligible addition to his income. This was going to
be an increasing problem if he had to bring fresh production capacity on stream
to meet these sales.

Monsieur Oleur was selling goods manufactured by one of Bury's competitors,
and this made the future uncertain.

Monsieur Oleur was complaining bitterly about irregularity of supplies, missed
deadlines and lack of adequate information about new products.

While contemplating how he could solve the problems without the risk of losing the market, Mr Bury learnt that one option appeared to be closed. Because of his lawyer's lack of understanding of French law, it seemed that the agreement could not be broken without paying Monsieur Oleur compensation which Bury regarded as prohibitive. Knowledge of European Union law was also lacking.

Case studies

The Bassett Case (1976) Sheffield City Polytechnic, CCH. 377–029–1.
Designer Jeans, Terpstra (1983) ch. 10.
Scientific Instruments Company Inc., Terpstra (1983) ch. 10.

Questions

1 Evaluate the main types of selling arrangement available to the exporter. Relate your conclusions to an industry sector of your choice.

2 Outline an organization suitable for an export department in a large company and discuss the options available.

3 Design a programme of training for an export manager in a small company which has never made such an appointment before.

4 Select and discuss some issues relevant to the decision whether or not to establish agents or distributors in West African countries for a British company in consumer goods with annual sales of £20m.

5 A company manufacturing industrial goods has won orders in Mexico, Poland and Japan. Provide advice on financing those orders.

6 Outline, with examples, the documentation required for an export order for consumer goods to the United States.

7 It has been said that the results obtained from foreign agents and distributors are directly related to the efforts put into their selection, stimulus and control. Discuss some implications of this statement.

8 Draw up a plan for the appointment of an agent/distributor.

Further reading

Introductory
BOTB Services to Exporters, a series of booklets, (London: British Overseas Trade Board).
United States Department of Commerce, International Trade Administration, *Annotated Bibliography of Selected Research on Export Behaviour*, Washington, D.C., 1980.
Whiting, D.P., *International Trade and Payments*, MacDonald and Evans, 1978.

Management
Brooke and Buckley, 1988, ch. 2.1 to 2.11.
Czinkota and others (1995).

Davies, G., *Managing Export Distribution*, Heinemann 1983.
McMillan, C. and Paulden, S., *Export Agents: A Complete Guide to their Selection and Control*, 2nd ed., Gower, 1974.
Robinson, 1984, ch. 2.
Terpstra, 1983, ch. 10.
Walsh, D., *International Marketing*, MacDonald and Evans, 1982.
Walter and Murray, 1982, ch.8 to 15 and 29.

Documentation
Watson, A. *Finance of International Trade*, Institute of Bankers, 1976.
Whitehead, G., *Elements of Overseas Trade*, Croner, 1976.

5 Trade in knowledge and expertise

This chapter is concerned with a range of business methods – licensing, franchising, technical assistance, management contracts and others. Many are similar but are known by different names; all have in common that know-how is being sold rather than goods or services. This know-how is drawn from an increasing variety of industry sectors as more companies come to realize the possibilities.[1]

There is a sense in which most sales are sales of knowledge. Some superiority, a comparative advantage rooted in invention or experience, usually underlies the ability to sell. This truth gains a greater significance when conducting business abroad; expertise is required to ensure that the product is profitable and can stand up to local and international competition. Superior knowledge, constantly updated, is a key to successful trading. It provides, at least temporarily, a form of monopoly advantage. A company which is selling advanced technology needs to develop new products to keep its advantage.[2]

A natural consequence is that, under some conditions, it may appear more profitable to sell the knowledge than the product; consultancy is an obvious example. More companies are realizing this, although exact figures are not available. In Britain, for instance, royalty receipts from independent companies increased by 42 per cent between 1975 and 1988. The agreements will be classified in this chapter into three major types – licensing, franchising and management contracts – and a few miscellaneous categories. They have in common the existence of a contract, written or assumed, between a principal or parent company and a foreign partner. Otherwise, there are considerable variations. Different industry sectors favour different types of agreement and use each for a number of purposes. Some common forms are listed in Figure 5.1.

Figure 5.1 shows the basic arrangements in the first column. The lines converging on the box in the middle represent the addition of management functions outside those included in the original concept. When these are brought together the agreement becomes a management contract in fact, although not necessarily in name. Indeed, names are a problem for the investigator of knowledge agreements. Sometimes 'licensing' is used of more than one activity while 'licensing' and 'franchising' are often used interchangeably. Sometimes different words are used of the same activity. (The 'technical assistance agreement' and the 'management contract' are often the same thing, the former being regarded as a phrase that is more acceptable to the client.)

Although increasing, knowledge sales remain a small proportion of international trade as a whole (not more than 10–11 per cent). The small proportion is partly due to unfamiliarity and this will change. Gaining the most profitable advantage out of knowledge sales is the subject of the first part of this chapter, which also includes the following sections:

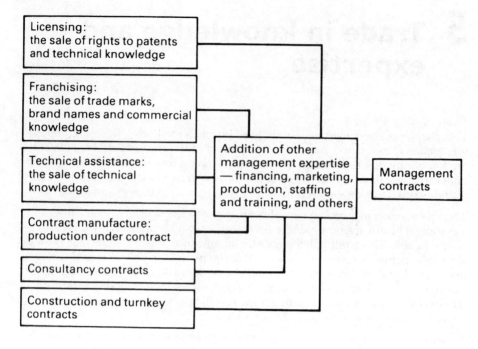

Figure 5.1 Knowledge agreements

1 selling knowledge abroad (the necessary preliminaries, the potential advantages and disadvantages, the legal issues),
2 licensing agreements (the special requirements for basic licensing agreements are outlined),
3 franchising agreements,
4 management contracts,
5 other contractual arrangements,
6 the selection and control of contract partners,
7 organization.

Note: the above distinctions are not rigid or clear-cut. For convenience, the word 'licensing' is sometimes used generically of all kinds of knowledge agreement as it is in some companies.

5.1 Selling knowledge abroad

The sale of knowledge abroad has a number of advantages, not least that the investment in the foreign operations is minimal, but there are certain essentials without which the advantages are unlikely to be realized. One obvious necessity is that the knowledge shall exist. The decision to embark on a policy of contractual arrangements leads to a fruitless as well as costly exercise unless there is an adequate basis of technical or commercial knowledge which is kept up-to-date. That said, a variety of skills and techniques are being sold across frontiers and by numerous methods, while many a saleable idea must be failing to realize its full potential because the possibility of foreign sales has not been considered.

Licensing, franchising or management contracts come on the agenda when a company decides that it possesses assets best suited to the knowledge business. A common transition is that from international licensing as a casual seizing of an opportunity to the strategic approach where this method is developed as a business in its own right. This development is subject to the following conditions.

1 The possession of a relevant saleable technology or technique.
2 An appraisal of the merits of the other options. Where the product or service can be more profitably supplied using the market, rather than internally, then licensing is probable.
3 The ability to keep the saleable knowledge up-to-date. This is a critical condition. The knowledge agreement may save on capital commitment abroad, but investment is required at home to ensure that the company remains competitive. A company that lives by licensing is also committed to a continuing investment in research and development.
4 Skilled advice on the legal and taxation regulations for each country in which operations are proposed. General attention is required regarding two issues:
   (a) *The form of contract.* All aspects of the proposed business relationship need to be discussed and the legal conditions in the host country understood. In some countries a lengthy and elaborate document will be required. Experience shows that it is impossible to foresee and provide for every eventuality, but it is essential to set a time limit with the possibility of renegotiation in case of problems.
   (b) *The means of getting the money out.* The arrangements for repatriating the money earned under the contract have to be determined before the contract is signed. There may be government restrictions. The tax position also needs clearing – the rate of withholding tax[3] (if applied) compared with that levied on other business methods.
5 Procedures are required for the resolution of disputes.
6 Control methods and communications' routes have to be agreed with the partner. Reports required will frequently be similar to those that would be asked of a subsidiary. Monthly figures on income and expenditure for the product, sales figures and general information about changes in the market are needed. In return, the partner needs to be provided with full information about the progress of the product elsewhere, expected changes and prospects.
7 In general, companies will consider which corporate strengths indicate knowledge agreements and which do not. The advantages discussed below provide some criteria for operating these agreements. Figure 5.2 provides a systematic way of appraising a proposal. As with all such decision models, it is intended as a general guide to more systematic thinking. Some of the factors are not capable of the sort of comparisons provided. For instance, if direct investment is impossible that particular option is not available and there is no comparison between (say) 10 which means impossible and 9 which means just possible. Nevertheless, Figure 5.2 provides guidance and has the advantage that it can be used either as a simple, rough guide or, on the other hand, that considerable sophistication can be built into it. Another advantage is that any

time horizon can be placed in the second column – how far ahead decisions have to be taken for a particular product. Naturally, the shortest viable time should be selected as the further ahead the greater the uncertainty. For a first attempt, each heading should be scored 1–10. In practice, weightings will have to be introduced to suit individual needs. Thus some companies might consider 'security of contract' a vital question and multiply it by some factor (say 2), while others might rate it low in the confidence that they can provide the required expertise. Naturally the figures will change if weightings are introduced.

When figures have been entered on the model for a particular product in a particular market, the conclusion is:

Score over 65 is virtually certain that licensing or other knowledge agreement is suitable. Proceed to more detailed evaluation.

Score 35–65 reconsider figures.

Score under 35. This is unlikely to be the correct channel.

	Today	*In 5 years' time**
(1) The difficulty of export (internal = resources available within company)		
(2) The difficulty of export (external = possibility of proposed channel in country)		
(3) The difficulty of direct investment (internal)		
(4) The difficulty of direct investment (external)	**Under each of the**	
(5) Net income from fees minus net income from export⁺	**two headings fill in**	
(6) Net income from fees minus net income from investment⁺	**appropriate numbers from 1 to 10****	
(7) Availability of suitable licensees		
(8) Security of contract		
(9) Suitability of products for licensing		
Total	———	———

*Any time limit can be inserted to suit a product.
⁺Can be answered by rough judgement or sophisticated calculations.
**For questions (1)–(4), 10 = impossible; with questions (5) and (6), 5 = 0 with + or − figures according to details of calculations; with (7), 10 = plenty to choose from; with (8), 10 = absolutely secure; with (9), 10 = totally suitable.

Figure 5.2 Scheme for determining whether to expand abroad by knowledge agreement

Advantages

The knowledge agreement is a means of making money abroad without substantial investment in the market. This is not to say that no financial support is required; it is often found necessary to spend money on developing the market and financing the collaborator, and to undertake the investment at home needed to keep the knowledge up-to-date. However, this support is different from that normally required for direct investment abroad. What is more, the know-how agreement offers the chance of an increased return on research and other expenditure on skills which then prove to be saleable.

One reason for expecting that knowledge agreements will increase is precisely because of a growing realization of the saleability of knowledge as such. Both principal and client are being offered a comparatively low-risk means of operating in a market.

The purpose of most agreements is to undertake foreign production at minimum expense or risk. It is not easy to judge when this is the correct decision; currently companies tend to move in this direction when other options are blocked. The blockage occurs under various circumstances including the loss of an export market. When exporting ceases to be viable, due to government import restrictions or to competition, the choice is between sale of know-how or direct investment.[4] This choice is likely to be influenced by the size of the company – investment may not be an option for a small firm – and by perceptions about the balance of advantage in dealing with an external rather than an internal market. The perception will be affected by the costs of setting up and managing a subsidiary or a collaborator against the anticipated income from each. Past experience will also count. The control that goes with owning the licensee will be balanced against the greater flexibility of non-ownership.

Investment means a commitment to a particular production centre; know-how agreements can more readily be adapted to changing conditions. Restrictions on foreign investment are also avoided by this method, and the costs of remittances may be reduced, especially when there are higher taxes on dividends than on royalties or fees. In a country undergoing balance-of-payments difficulties, permission to pay fees and royalties is often granted before permission to pay dividends. Know-how agreements have other advantages, like the safeguarding of technology or techniques and increased ability to tackle pirating. These advantages are shared with investment.

Disadvantages

The danger most frequently mentioned by managers is that of setting up a competitor. The nature of a know-how agreement is that valuable expertise is being transmitted and there may be little to prevent a licensee from ending the agreement and capturing a market. There are, of course, a number of legal safeguards in the form of copyright, trademark and patent laws, but these are usually difficult and expensive to invoke. In addition, there may be other reasons – such as loss of reputation – for being wary of invoking them. In some countries the legal system makes it difficult to enforce a company's normal practices in the way of protecting its commercial know-how. More effective is the continuing growth of the company's expertise but, in the end, there is no substitute for careful selection of the collaborator firm and the development of a close relationship. This will, in many product sectors, produce a safeguard against competition rather than a competitor.

Another disadvantage of knowledge agreements is the difficulty, from the principal's point of view, of obtaining an adequate price. This is matched by complaints of overcharging from licensees and governments. It is easier to agree to a price for a product or a service than for know-how, either technical or managerial. While some cases of overcharging have been established, companies have often brought the accusation upon themselves by undercharging in the first place and raising their prices later. There is a sequence of events in which a company begins by regarding licensing as providing a little extra income,[5] along with other anticipated spin-off effects, on a project that is already profitable. This leads to pricing expectations on the part of the collaborator which cannot be sustained when the volume of licensing becomes a significant part of the business and the side effects seem less valuable.

Another problem frequently encountered is that of quality control. This is related, also, to the question of the market segment into which the product is sold. The licensee can damage a product's image internationally by lowering the standard of quality control. There may also be problems if the standards are raised and the product is effectively moved into a higher market segment.

Legal issues

Other general issues of knowledge agreements are those of resolving disputes and of determining which country's legal system is to apply. The conventional wisdom used to be that the principal should insist on a legal system with which he was familiar, that of his own country. This is naturally unacceptable to the client, who will resist it if he has sufficient bargaining strength. It may also be unwise. There is little that the principal can do if foreign courts do not uphold the agreement. In some circumstances, the domestic legal system is more restrictive – when, for instance, the agreement is between a principal in an industrialized country and a client in a developing one and the dispute invokes competition law. Under most circumstances nowadays, the law of the client country is likely to be preferred, especially where competitors also take this view. Sometimes the law of a third country may be considered, at least for purposes of settling disputes, or the services of an international arbitrator.

Examples

The following are some typical examples of knowledge agreements.

Company A invents a rapid and safe equipment for hand-drying in public lavatories. The company is too small to meet the world demand that is expected, so the device is manufactured in several countries by local firms under *licence*.

Company B possesses a highly saleable package for managing hotels, but does not have the resources to build the hotels on many suitable sites; so would-be proprietors in other countries are *franchised* to adopt the package.

Company C has been dispossessed of its sugar plantations, but continues to manage them under *contract.*

Company D is an experienced shipping line and manages ships belonging to other lines under *contract.*

5.2 Licensing agreements

Arrangements for the licensing of patents are among the oldest and most common forms of know-how contract. Many companies use no other, and a rapid increase has taken place in recent years. For instance, in the United States receipts from miscellaneous services increased from $5,745 to $19,626 between 1982 and 1992,[6] much of that accounted for by licensing.

A basic international licensing agreement is a contract between two companies in different countries whereby one provides technical information, including the right to use patents and trademarks, to the other in return for a fee. The provider has no specific duties once the patents have been handed over, apart from any liabilities that may be written into the contract or are contained in the laws of the host country. Few arrangements are basic in this sense, and additional services may be provided from the start or added later in the light of experience. Two factors especially influence companies to provide these additional services – that the licensing agreement is often regarded as a means of servicing existing markets and that payment is usually per product.

The conditions for adopting licensing policies, with their advantages and disadvantages, are listed in Table 5.1. Under conditions **A**, it will be seen that the first six items are part of a preparation, a pre-licensing phase. This covers two activities – a process of determining that the company is prepared and that the market is ready. The selection of the licensee is considered later in this chapter (Section 5.6).

The advantages **B** are also of two kinds – those concerned with market protection (1–4), which are normally found to be uppermost in corporate thinking, and those concerned with market penetration (5–11). Although these latter are less often quoted, they demonstrate a variety of reasons for licensing. High-technology products, which also need to be manufactured near to the customer, are particularly likely to be eligible for licensing. The typical licensor possesses a patent for a product which has already established itself in the domestic market and for which a foreign demand has been proven. The proof can be either through export sales or through market research. Subject to the safeguards already mentioned, there is no reason why licensing should not provide a rapid and inexpensive route to world markets.

Problems are also listed in Table 5.1 (at **C**). While the fear of competition rates high among companies considering licensing, the problem most often reported by experienced operators is more immediate trouble with licensees. The essence of the deal is that the principal puts in the technical knowledge and the local collaborator handles the market, sources of finance and production. When the licensee proves inadequate, the licensor either has to alter the arrangement – by setting up a subsidiary, seeking another collaborator or withdrawing – or to inject some of the skills which the licensee lacks, making the project more costly than had been anticipated.

The advantages and disadvantages listed in Table 5.1 are mainly those for the licensor. The licensee company has a common interest in that it, too, will be looking for rapid entry to a market by what frequently proves the only available route.

The licensee's country, although not necessarily the licensee itself, may find a disadvantage if it incurs an over-dependence on foreign technology. This may frustrate local research and development initiatives.

Remuneration

The issue under this heading is to reach an agreement under which both parties may make a profit from exploiting the technology.

A relatively simple cost calculation should provide a view of what the licensee can afford while keeping within a market price. That calculation will fix a maximum fee; it will not determine the value of the know-how which can only be assessed in the light of experience and knowledge. In calculating its costs, the licensor will take account of:

1 The **opportunity costs** – the revenue the licensor would expect from selling the product rather than the know-how. If direct sales are impossible, the 'opportunity costs' reduces to zero.
2 The **real costs** of managing the project, these may be balanced by extra revenues from (for example) sales of supplies.
3 **Other value to the licensor** including the sale of supplies.
4 **Anticipated value to the licensee**, if the licensee has a large potential market the licence may be charged at a higher price.

The most common arrangement for payment is a lump sum plus a royalty. The royalty is usually a percentage of the licensee's income (5 per cent being a common figure), but there are numerous bases for the calculation. Taxation and transfer regulations, in both countries, will influence the formula, which is sometimes per product and sometimes a percentage of net receipts. In either case, a minimum annual payment is often negotiated while a proportion of the royalties may be commuted for a share of the equity. In some cases – where for instance, patents for equipment which is obsolete in the licensor's country are being sold – there is a lump sum only.

The remuneration agreement usually emerges from a process of bargaining which is likely to be influenced by the strengths of the two parties: how vital the arrangement is, what other options exist, the reputation of each party, the personalities involved and other factors which affect bargaining positions. The status of the licensee is another factor. Where the status is in doubt, the licensor will press for a higher lump sum and a lower royalty. The reverse is the case when the hopes for a successful product are particularly high and the licensor presses for maximum royalties. One ironical feature of licensing is that of problems generated by success. These partly arise from the difficulty of determining which

Table 5.1 Licensing: a summary

(A) Conditions for adopting licensing policies

1. The possession of patented devices and attractive trade marks, preferably in some novel or advanced technology, or special know-how that no one else has access to.
2. The ability to protect patents across different legal systems.
3. That trading conditions in the licensee country inhibit other means of conducting business.
4. That licensing is the most profitable option.
5. That a general appraisal of the investment required by the licensee, both in plant and in promotional activities, has been undertaken. The length of time required for establishing the facilities has also to be estimated.
6. That the results of market research are known suggesting at least adequate sales in the first and subsequent years, and confirming the breakeven and other calculations. The licensee's profits can then be estimated.
7. The type of licence has to be considered – whether it will confer exclusive or non-exclusive rights in the area, whether all or limited parts of the manufacture and sale of the product are included, and whether the right to sublet will be a part of the deal and if so on what terms.
8. It has been observed that companies with no foreign investment are more likely to enter licensing agreements than foreign direct investors.
9. An easy route to diversification for a company that finds itself saddled with a dangerously low growth in its core activity.

(B) Advantages of licensing

1. To increase the income on products developed as a result of expensive research.
2. To retain a market to which export is no longer possible or is likely to become unprofitable due to: import prohibitions, quotas or duties, transport costs, lack of production facilities at home or other related factors.
3. To protect patents, especially in countries which afford weak protection for products not produced locally.
4. To make local manufacture possible where this is favoured, for other reasons than those listed above. Examples are the need to adapt the product, the opportunity to cash in on local nationalism, the lack of use for the particular patent in the domestic market. This last advantage may well apply to low-technology products for which there is still a market in developing countries.
5. To make possible the rapid exploitation of new ideas on world markets before competitors get into the act.
6. The penetration of new markets – licensing agreements may open up parts of the world previously closed to a company, either in the licensee's own country or through exports from that country to others.
7. There may be a valuable spin-off if the licensor can sell other products or components to the licensee. If these are parts for products being manufactured locally or machinery there may also be some tariff concessions on their import.
8. A means of entering a market where the nature of the competition, a few dominant and highly competitive firms for example, makes any form of entry apart from licensing too expensive to be contemplated.
9. A means of entering markets that are less competitive than the domestic. This provides funds for extra research and development which then, in its turn, improves the chances of licensing where the competition is stronger.
10. One considerable advantage for the small firm with an appropriate product is that licensing can be a much more plausible means of expanding abroad than export. It is easier to handle a number of markets this way.
11. Licensing is a viable option where manufacture near to the customer's base is required.

(C) Disadvantages of licensing

1. The danger of fostering a competitor. This is strongly maintained when technical information is being provided; and there is no substitute for a satisfactory working arrangement to minimize the danger. The use of internationally promoted trade marks and brand names may also deter the licensee from setting up in opposition. To this end it is advisable that the parent company registers the trade marks in its own name.
2. The danger of a reducing return.
3. The fact that there is often a ceiling to licensing income per product, sometimes about 5% on the selling price. Innovating products, at least, might rate higher rewards if marketed in other ways.
4. The danger of the licensee running short of funds, especially if considerable plant expansion is involved or an injection of capital is required to sustain the project. This danger can be turned to advantage if the licensor has funds available by a general expansion of the business through a partnership.
5. The licensee may prove less competent than expected at marketing or other management activities; hence the licensor may find his commitment is greater than expected. He may even find costs grow faster than income.
6. Opposition is encountered in some less developed countries to royalty payments on the grounds that too high a price is being charged for the knowledge provided.
7. Negotiations with the licensee, and sometimes with the local government, are costly and often protracted.

partner has contributed most to the success: was it the technology or was it rather the marketing? Some agreements anticipate difficulties by stipulating payment on a sliding scale, but there is still scope for disagreement on how the income is shared. Another problem of success arises when the business outgrows a small licensee.

Problems can develop at a later stage as a result of expectations on the part of the licensor that were too low in the first place. When the income is regarded as a small extra return on a project that is already viable, there is a tendency to make too little demand in the original negotiations. A similar consideration may lead to the costs being underestimated. They include at least the licensor's promotion costs and perhaps trouble-shooting for which it is difficult to secure repayment. Equity participation, which is often requested by the licensee, is also helpful to the principal when it compensates for the problems just mentioned, but it involves a commitment the licensor may be trying to avoid.

Remuneration in goods, at least in part, has been a feature of licensing agreements. The subject of counter-trade is considered later (see Section 7.7). In licensing agreements, the licensor will sometimes have to accept payment in products of the machinery sold under licence. There may even be a reverse barter in which the licensor claims the right to some of the products as part payment. Yet another arrangement is for cross-licensing, where each party is offering a licence to the other. In this case there may be no money changing hands, or only a reduced fee. Although counter-trade used to be an increasing feature of agreements, licensors are learning to avoid them. Selling the products of machinery requires different skills from selling the machinery; the market also is different.

The final element in the fee calculation is that of other benefits derived from the licence. The licensor may receive some income from the sale of parts, materials or other services to the licensee. The value of these sales will probably have been an issue in the negotiations. Reciprocal rights and a full exchange of information can be of benefit to both parties. Feedback from the licensee also provides a valuable advantage, especially if the information leads to product modification, new products or new customers.

A number of issues are especially liable to lead to controversy. Among them are restrictions on the sales territories of the licensee. Such restrictions seem commonsense to the licensor; the purpose of granting the licence was to ensure coverage of a specific market, not to produce competition with other affiliates manufacturing the same product. To the licensee, on the other hand, restriction may appear an unwarranted limitation on the business – an attitude which is likely to be reinforced by its government. Such restrictions are major matters of controversy between companies and governments. As well as infringing national trading policies, they may fall foul of competition legislation.

A final difficult issue is that of safeguarding patents and trademarks and ensuring the security of technical and commercial secrets. The relevant laws vary from country to country, especially in sensitive sectors like pharmaceuticals. In any case, the licence will only be valid as long as the patent lasts, and that is for a limited period.

5.3 Franchising agreements

An agreement for the sale (franchise) of commercial information and trademarks is a rapidly increasing business technique. In contrast to licensing, franchising emphasizes marketing (or the total business idea) rather than technology, but the two are growing more alike. Examples of franchising include car rental firms, soft drinks suppliers, fast food restaurants, staff agencies and hotels. In these cases a package is put together which usually comprises:

1 the formulation of a business idea which the franchisee firm is permitted to use within its allotted area for a fee;
2 the provision of trademarks and other insignia which may add up to a total corporate image;
3 the provision of training programmes for the employees of the firm which holds the franchises. In some cases attendance at these programmes is compulsory.

Like other forms of knowledge agreement, franchising makes it possible to conduct business in a foreign country and derive income there, without a substantial capital commitment. A contract is negotiated for the use of trademarks and business methods. Since there are no patents involved, the policing of the agreement is more difficult. The franchising companies overcome this by their registered trademarks and their distinctive house styles, backed by heavy advertising to make piracy as complicated as possible.

Franchising includes a range of options. On the one hand is an undertaking whereby the local manager has equity participation in the business; for all other purposes he is an employee. At the other extreme, the franchisee is an independent businessman using some of the know-how of the parent company. Some franchisors, hotel chains for instance, place great emphasis on uniformity. The traveller is guaranteed an almost identical service under similar conditions everywhere in the world. Sometimes this causes problems: Holiday Inns in Germany, for instance, had to modify their policies to conform to local tastes. Usually the rules, including minor details, are enforced throughout the world as a condition of a franchise. Where the distinguishing marks and designs are protected by copyright, these may be easier to enforce than patents. Some advantages and disadvantages of franchising are listed in Tables 5.2 and 5.3.

Table 5.2 The advantages of franchising

Some of the general advantages of knowledge agreements apply to franchising, in particular it is:

1. A convenient method of making the greatest possible use of a business idea abroad. Commercial experience and knowledge can produce income with a minimum of capital and risk.

2. Goods and services can be sold abroad with only minor production and distribution problems.

3. Given the clear and striking public image of most franchising arrangements, progress abroad enhances progress at home. The image goes global to the advantage of all the parts.

The advantages of franchising are similar to those of licensing, but the protection of the business idea is more difficult. The hands-off arrangement of the basic licensing agreement, with a minimal involvement on the part of the principal in the licensee company, is seldom possible. The essence of the international franchise is an image and standard of service that is sustained in all the countries in which the business operates. This implies supervision, training and quality control. A well-known example is McDonald's which has a detailed and rigorous manual of aims and operating requirements, including twice-yearly quality inspections covering 100 points.

Quality (see Table 5.3, number 2) is the issue that often proves most difficult to handle. The franchisor is selling a world-wide image to clients, any of whom can affect the reputation of all the others.

Table 5.3 The disadvantages and problems associated with franchising

1. Immediate difficulties exist in market evaluation, franchisee recruitment, patent and trade mark concessions, banking and credit arrangements, taxation and legal considerations, and location of suitable sites. Skills have to be built up early in the progress of the operation to surmount these difficulties.

2. Quality control is particularly vital – the global image can easily be wrecked – and is often difficult to enforce. It is necessary to ensure that the threat of removal of the franchise is real and enforceable.

3. Supervision and appraisal are required across boundaries of language and culture.

4. Intense competition is encountered, especially in franchises for fast foods. Market entry can appear deceptively easy; maintaining a presence may be more difficult.

5. More specific problems that are encountered in international franchising include the following:
   (a) Legal or other restrictions imposed by governments, such as import controls and customs duties, may make the use of standard materials difficult. Competition laws may have the same effect.
   (b) Recruitment – there are sometimes difficulties in finding people who can cope with the franchising relationship.
   (c) Local finance.
   (d) Incentives for the foreign investor may make franchising appear less attractive than direct investment.
   (e) Control.
   (f) The need to design the franchise package to suit local conditions.
   (g) Trade marks, design, service marks and other insignia may prove difficult to protect.
   (h) Acceptability of the standard package to the foreign consumer.
   (i) Problems associated with the local tax structure, especially the need to adapt standard accounting procedures, deadlines and so on.
   (j) Lack of suitable sites, especially in thinly populated countries. Most international franchising operations depend on population or traffic density.
   (k) Legislation concerning labour and the protection of the employee may make some of the rules inapplicable in a particular country.

The necessary condition for an international franchise is a business idea that is saleable in various parts of the world without major modification. The package frequently includes marketing know-how, staffing and staff training expertise, buying policies, image and quality safeguards, as well as relevant technical knowledge and management techniques. The franchisor will be concerned to ensure that the franchisee uses the whole package. To this end training programmes (often in the home country) are a common condition. In general, franchising is a convenient and profitable way of making money out of a business idea that has already proved itself. A distinctive and well-publicized image helps to ensure that the franchise is not misused. The principal problems of this channel concern product acceptability, staffing and the general need to ensure that the objectives are achieved. The difficulties are often easier to manage than those associated with direct investment.

5.4 Management contracts

An arrangement whereby a company operates a foreign firm for a client who retains the ownership is known as a *management contract*. There are a number of variations, but a broad distinction between foreign management and local ownership is a characteristic feature, and the management typically extends to all functions. The relationship between the management contract and other knowledge agreements was demonstrated in Figure 5.1 where it was shown that there is an indefinable boundary between licensing and franchising arrangements, on the one hand, and management contracts on the other – they shade into one another. In the management contract, the principal operates a complete management system. This method of conducting business has only gradually emerged. It can be said to carry the divorce between ownership and management, that has been a feature of the business scene for many years, one stage further. Figure 5.3 illustrates the principle of the three-cornered relationship between contractor, client and contract venture.

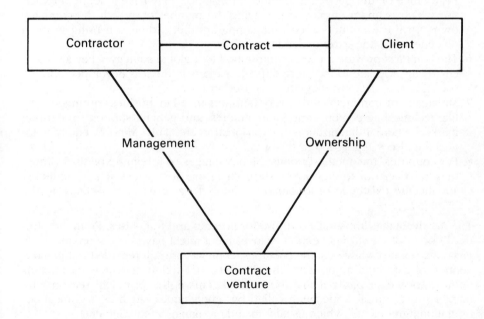

Figure 5.3 The basic management contract

In a basic management contract the local (host country) company holds all the equity, but in practice the contractor often takes a small amount. The holding of equity makes it easier to negotiate the other terms; the contractor company does not feel so impelled to provide for an increasing royalty in the event of success as it knows that it will share anyway. On the other hand, the holding of equity may bias the advice the contractor gives, especially when it is not managing all the functions.

Advantages and disadvantages

The reasons for developing management contracts as a policy are similar to those for licences and franchises with a number of additions which include the following.

1 Dissatisfaction with an existing licensing agreement where the licensee or franchisor does not show sufficient marketing, financial or other expertise to develop the business.

2 The expropriation or nationalization of a subsidiary where the parent company's commercial expertise is still required.

3 The development of a consultancy or technical aid contract into a total management contract.

4 Fees for management services may be easier to transfer, and subject to less tax, than royalties or dividends.

5 Under-employed skills and resources are a common factor in deciding to opt for management contracts. The licensing specialist may be in a position to negotiate the contracts and employ a number of the other experts available at head office on the project. An airline, for instance, may have a depth of expertise which is under-employed managing the number of aircraft the company owns. In these circumstances, managing another airline can bring in extra revenue with little extra expenditure.[7]

6 The contracts provide a useful contribution to a global strategy. They are particularly appropriate to the more difficult markets in the less developed and the socialist countries; but they are also used in Europe.

7 Management contracts can provide support to other business arrangements, like technical agreements and joint ventures, and general support for existing markets where indigenization or expropriation are likely. Minority equity holdings are also safeguarded in this way.

8 For countries, this method brings the advantages of foreign expertise without the drawbacks of foreign ownership. There are advantages when funding is sought; the existence of a contract is likely to give extra confidence to the bankers.

The disadvantages are similar to those for licences and franchises. From the principal's point of view, direct export or investment might have been more lucrative. From the point of view of some countries, contracts are still regarded as the intervention of a foreign authority – and the issue of foreign management remains delicate, however badly it may be needed. This is the principal reason why management contracts are often called by other names (such as 'technical co-operation agreements' which usually include a management element).

Industry sectors

The following kinds of company are likely to undertake management contracts.

1 *Publicly-owned industries in Europe, especially in transport and utilities.* Contracts can provide a profitable use for spare resources, and this can be particularly valuable in static or declining industries.

Contracts may also provide a channel for exports. Private manufacturing companies can enter a market in the wake of a state-owned contractor and sell the equipment, for instance mining machinery or electrical components.

2 *Service industries.* Hotels, hospitals and transport systems are frequently run under contract, especially in the Middle East and Africa.

3 *Tropical agriculture and foodprocessing.* Some firms in these industries came into management contracts when subsidiaries were taken into state or local ownership. Often they continued to manage the plantation or factory after the take-over. The management expertise was then marketed in other countries.

4 *Metal and timber.* Similar considerations apply to these industries as to tropical agriculture, but the path has been different. The politically sensitive industry of mineral extraction has still many examples of companies retaining some equity, and using the contract to protect their holding.

5 *Petrochemical and chemical industries.* These are also politically sensitive but the complexity of the technology and a need for many scarce skills have enabled companies to retain a strong contractual interest.

6 *General manufacture.* This is an ill-defined group, but consists of companies that usually treat the contract as a second-best arrangement where a majority equity holding is no longer permitted. The hope is that the terms of the contract will make it possible to retain control. The other objective is to create or to expand a market by exporting components and equipment to the contract company's plants.

The host country

Management contracts exist in every type of country. In developing countries they are controversial. The technology is welcome, and contracts are often encouraged because they bring know-how without the accompanying conditions of direct investment. However, the presence of a powerful international company is still resented and there remains the suspicion of exploitation, the feeling that the technology could be acquired elsewhere at a lower price. The management contract may change the terms of the company-to-country relationship, and this is one of its advantages, but all occasion for conflict is not thereby abolished.

In conclusion, the management contract provides a means of doing business without equity. The whole range of skills of the parent company can be profitably employed, and a project is managed without the problems that arise with licensing agreements or investment. A country receives the benefits without the strings that are attached to investment, and a company avoids risks and enters parts of the world where business would otherwise be impossible. A number of critical problems have to be resolved to get the best out of the contract, however. These include arrangements for paying, organizing, staffing and controlling. This means of conducting business is expected to expand rapidly in the future, along with some similar arrangements which are examined in the next section.

5.5 Other contractual arrangements

A number of other arrangements were shown on Figure 5.1 and these will be considered briefly, starting with the construction contract.

A construction contract

The total amount of international construction business is increasing, but the average size of each contract is growing smaller. Some of the characteristics of construction are more akin to direct manufacture than to other knowledge agreements. The total business of the company is committed, so the income cannot be regarded as an optional extra.

One characteristic is that sub-contractors will be involved, and so relationships have to be negotiated with two types of collaborator – the partner or client for the finished product, and the subcontractors who will carry out specialized parts of the building or its equipment. Another consideration is the size of many of the contracts, and the difficulty of selling a service which may not be required again in the same area. If a major project is out for tender, only one company can win. The unsuccessful rivals may have spent much labour and money (six-figure sums are not uncommon) in acquiring the necessary familiarity with the country, only to find that this familiarity is of no further use to them. One key consideration is the reducing of risk and increase in competitiveness. Both are provided by a consortium arrangement with a package that includes turnkey deals and management contracts. The successful large-scale contractor will develop a portfolio of knowledge agreements to achieve his aims, while some governments provide assistance with the tendering process. To win a construction contract, it is often necessary to offer to hand over the project in working order in a turnkey arrangement.

A turnkey arrangement

This exists when a foreign company operates a business for a limited period before transferring it to the owners in working order. In a construction project a contractor may undertake to build, equip and then operate a plant. In a turnkey contract the operating is for a limited period, say one year, with the intention of getting rid of any bugs before the project is handed over. Such arrangements have become more common as international competition has increased in this industry. They are to be regarded as part of the marketing formula and to be judged as such. The temporary operation of the plant may be an expense to the constructor, and one which is difficult to recoup in full, but without it the contract might have been lost. A contrary advantage of the turnkey, if the operator is also a manufacturer, is that equipment and materials can be supplied from the home base.

A consortium

A consortium is formed as the result of an agreement between a number of companies jointly to tender for a contract. Frequently, one is the principal and the others are subcontractors. Similarly, finance may be provided through a consortium of banks, any one of which would be too small to fund the project alone. Another form is the consortium licence whereby a company grants a licence to a group of companies (perhaps in different countries) for each to manufacture different stages of the product. The consortium is typically used for large construction contracts where the size of the project and the variety of skills required would make it an impossible undertaking for any one company. It is also used for high-technology ventures and major mining projects, and by banks needing to share large risks. Increasingly, consortium-type projects stretch across several frontiers, involving complex negotiations. Increasingly also, the number of participants is large, some of them operating in unfamiliar countries. These considerations demand special skills for the organizer of the consortium; there are many routes for the profits to leak away.

Contract manufacture

This is an arrangement in which the production function is operated by a foreign company – either within a market, or in a suitable position to supply a market. The most usual reasons are:
1 to service customers that cannot readily be supplied in any other way;
2 production facilities are overloaded at home;
3 tariff barriers or treaty obligations make supply difficult from other sources;
4 there is no suitable licensee available;
5 a better deal is obtainable through production under contract;
6 direct investment is too risky, too expensive in scarce capital, or undesirable because of insufficient volume for production.

Contract manufacture can be brought into action more rapidly than other options and with a minimum commitment of risk capital on the part of the parent company, so long as a suitable manufacturer can be found. Manufacturing problems, like the use of equipment where demand fluctuates, are avoided, as are labour problems. Valuable market knowledge can be gained and contacts made with additional customers or prospects, including government purchasing agencies. If the contract is for assembly, there is the additional advantage that a tied customer has come into existence. Other advantages include less expense in stopping production if market conditions make this necessary, and none of the problems of closing a plant. There are also cost savings that result from local production. Where this arrangement is successful, a closer relationship – such as the purchase of some of the foreign firm's equity, or a more comprehensive contract – may follow.

The difficulties of this procedure are those common to other knowledge agreements: quality control, the training of a competitor, and the fact that a greater commitment develops than was expected when the plans were laid. Careful planning can overcome these snags, and one of the additional advantages of this method is that it can readily be used as a temporary expedient while other, more profitable, methods are planned. Finally, contract manufacture is a viable response to laws, found especially in wealthier developing countries, that insist on assembly or part manufacture locally.

Technical assistance agreements

These are similar to licences but usually couched in more general terms. A fee is paid for the supply of the technical information required to manufacture a product locally. Management may also be included and a technical assistance agreement is often identical to a management contract combined with a licensing agreement.

5.6 The selection and control of contract partners

The appointment of contract partners is often haphazard, as it is with agents, and problems arise from this. The licensee complains about inadequate, fly-by-night principals with little back-up for their technology, while the licensor finds that clients have less business skills than expected. In fact, there is no shortage of offers. Names of possible licensees and other contract partners can be assembled from lists published by trade, banking, consultancy and government organizations. Many government agencies publish 'swop shop' lists of openings available and required. Newspaper advertisements also provide leads. A firm can compile its own list by consulting trade directories and company profiles, or enquiring from executives in non-competitive businesses. Many companies prefer to let it be known that they are seeking a licensee and then wait for referrals or applicants. Their view is that a firm that needs to get onto a printed list is unlikely to be of the calibre they require.

The main guidelines for selection are:
1 to ascertain the compatibility of the proposed licensee's business with that of the licensor;
2 to check on the financial status;
3 to check on the commercial standing in the local market and especially whether the image is suitable, the market sector is correct and the relationships with existing customers are satisfactory;
4 to check on the quality of staff in the proposed contract partner, and in particular their potential for parent company training schemes;
5 to check on the physical facilities available.

In addition to these issues there are also more elusive considerations, such as the likelihood of a collaborator being willing to observe the policies of the principal on product design, market segment, sales areas and the preservation of the company image. These are not matters on which the terms of the contract can have much influence. The most reliable safeguard is intensive discussions at more than one level between the two companies before the deal is finalized.

The degree of supervision that the principal will exert or the client accept is another issue; some approximation to the parent–subsidiary relationship is often recommended. If this is accepted, the licensee or contracting firm is asked for regular (monthly) accounts, at least for the product, and for market reports. In return for this, the foreign affiliate can be invited to take part in the corporate planning system, and be kept fully informed about the progress and plans of the parent company.

Naturally, the reporting system will also cover any other subjects that the parent company regards as critical. In the case of franchising, more marketing information will be required since that is the area of expertise. Part of the control system is an attempt to stimulate the collaborator to greater effort and to feed back more detailed information about the market.

5.7 Organization

The success of knowledge agreements will depend to some extent on effective organization at home. The principles will be similar to those for controlling agents. A structure is needed to ensure that the strategic implications of any development are monitored and that there is sufficient competence to supervise the licenses. The following questions have to be resolved.

1 *How many partners should be involved?* An agency agreement is usually one-for-one and this may be the case in the licensing or franchising contract as well. But often there are three or more collaborators – the parent company, the foreign partner and other companies set up to operate the licence or contract. In a consortium, there can be many more than three partners and the organization, once established, has to cope with multiple relationships that vary from country to country.

2 *What is the specialized knowledge required?* The organization must make possible a rapid communication of technical and other expertise to the foreign operations. An all-purpose unit can serve agents, but not licensees.

3 *What proportion of a company's business is this element?* For some companies the sale of knowledge abroad is a major part of their business. For most it will be a comparatively small part and will be controlled from a department with other priorities. This makes the fixing of responsibilities all the more urgent.

4 *Does the project requires skills of a high order: legal and negotiating?* In this case, there is little routine work.

5 *How much of the work should be done in-house?* The complexities of patenting legislation are such that most companies will require outside help. Each country has its own laws which provide firms with unexpected traps. Among national variations are: different periods for which products can be patented, different methods of drafting specifications, different systems for taxing royalties, different types of goods for which patents can or cannot be obtained.

The organization needs to contain at least one person with a knowledge of the questions to ask and the difficulties to expect. This is related to the general questions of organization that are explored in Chapter 11.

5.8 Conclusion

There is nothing mysterious about knowledge agreements. This discussion began with the statement that 'most sales are sales of knowledge,' that is a characteristic of international business in the 1990s. Licensing, management contracts, franchising and the other arrangements considered in this chapter result from isolating the element of expertise from the rest of a product package. Many advantages of such sales have been identified, such as increased income from an invention or technique with minimal risk. At the same time, in many parts of the world, there are less obstacles to this method of conducting business than there are to import and direct investment. Income is also likely to be taxed at a lower rate. The question that needs answering is why this method is not more used.

Management in some functions   Other strategies   Management in all functions

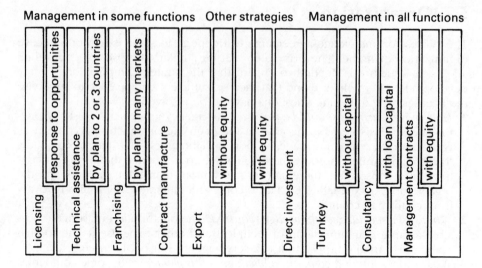

Figure 5.4 The keyboard analogy – know-how agreements

One answer refers back to the discussion on internalization in Chapter 2. Bringing the market within the company by investment is, or is perceived to be, less profitable than dealing with a third party. Another answer is the fear of establishing a competitor, and yet another is the preference for undivided control. This last may, as has been shown, rest upon assumptions about relationships with collaborators that are not necessarily correct.

The link between the knowledge and other strategies is shown in a revised version of the keyboard analogy in Figure 5.4. The knowledge agreement, in this context, is one part of a strategy for moving manufacture outside the home country. As such, it opens fresh horizons to the newcomer and the established operator alike. The licensing agreement may develop into an investment, and a form of contract that makes this development difficult is to be avoided. Direct investment is considered in the next chapter, meanwhile a steady increase in sales of knowledge can be expected.

The following check-list is suitable for appraising know-how agreements. Conditions requiring attention include:[8]

 1 technical assistance,
 2 managerial assistance: marketing, control and other key expertise,
 3 feedback,
 4 insurance against non-payment,
 5 sales territories,
 6 safeguarding patents and trademarks,
 7 time limits,
 8 security of secrets,
 9 conditions on pricing,
10 conditions on sales methods and market segment,
11 consequences for other agreements,
12 safeguarding agreements,

13 remuneration:
   (a) what the licensee will pay,
   (b) financial status of licensee,
   (c) expected success,
   (d) competition,
   (e) cost,
   (f) other payments by licensee,
   (g) barter,
   (h) reverse barter,
   (i) duration,
   (j) cross licensing,
   (k) equity,
   (l) royalties.

5.9 Cases, questions and further reading

Case examples

FEC SA: a licensing agreement

FEC SA was a French engineering company with production in other European countries and in Latin America. It had no business in the Far East until a licensing agreement was entered into with a Singapore firm for manufacture in that country for export to other parts of the Far East. The royalty was based on a per-product arrangement, since the patents registered in Singapore were for components of other products which the licensee also manufactured. There was a provision for the royalty percentage to increase as the quantity increased.

An elaborate agreement had been drawn up with the local licensee which: defined the countries within which the products could be sold, gave details of quality control and gave instructions on the protection of trademarks as well as of patents. The management of FEC had now become dissatisfied with the arrangements. In spite of the agreement, the goods were being sold in other countries in competition with their own exports. They also suspected that other components were being used in some of the products, and thought that a breach of patent might be occurring.

The problem was to know what to do. Legal action would be expensive and might turn out to be counter productive; besides, their licensee in Singapore was technically competent in contrast to others they had used. They doubted whether they had the financial resources or the management expertise to set up their own subsidiary in the South East Asia. But was there any other option open to them if they were to build up a satisfactory business? That was the question members of the executive committee were asking themselves.

ABC Corporation: the problems of a consortium

The ABC Corporation of Michigan was a manufacturer of building materials and a plant constructor. It had joined a consortium to tender for a large new plant complex in Thailand. Its main partners, both also from the United States, were a site preparation firm and an equipment manufacturer. The contract had been won against intense competition at a time when the construction industry in the States

was depressed. After some frustrating delays, the contract got under way, but ABC began to run into problems.
1 Its domestic business had picked up and it was having to turn down highly profitable work because so much of its resources were absorbed in this contract.
2 To relieve the pressure on its American plant, it could use its German factory as a supplier. But the strength of the D-Mark and rising costs in Germany made it difficult to see how this could be profitable.

The vice-president in charge of Far Eastern operations was asked to produce an immediate report setting out the options available and his recommendations.

Timberaid Ltd: establishing a competitor

Licensing and management contracts run the risk of establishing competitors. Timberaid Ltd licensed the manufacture of woodworking machinery in Kenya. The local company agreed to pay fees on each machine sold within the country. Nothing was said in the contract about sales outside the country; Timberaid assumed that the licence had only been granted for the home market. It soon became known, however, that the machines were being sold all over the world in competition with Timberaid's products. A law suit to stop the exporting failed.

Even if there had been a clause to prevent exports, the licensee might have found a way round it. Governments do not favour such restrictive clauses, nor do treaty organizations like the European Union. In any case, the patent would eventually have expired or the expertise gained would have been used to develop new products.

There were several ways of overcoming the problems including:
1 taking legal action in the countries to which the products were being exported, but this might not be successful and would be expensive and time-consuming;
2 fixing a fee for the licence at a level which would make the profits worthwhile even if competition did develop;
3 establishing a business relationship in which it would not be worth the licensee's while to offend the parent company – for example, an interruption in the flow of technical information from the home base would be damaging.

Discuss the most suitable method. This can be done through a role-playing exercise in which participants represent different standpoints.

Questions

1 Examine critically the statement that the export of goods is being replaced by the export of know-how.

2 Discuss the salient features of either licensing, or franchising, or management contracts and explain the circumstances under which your chosen channel is likely to be selected.

3 A Swedish engineering company, with sales of SKR 220m (a little over £20m) a year makes a simple but novel machine which is selling successfully in developing countries. A decision has been taken not to expand production at home but to investigate the

possibilities of manufacture in an area of expanding sales – West Africa. The company is looking for a local concern for a licensing or contractual arrangement. Explain the issues that should be considered and suggest some outcomes.

4 Discuss the merits and demerits of manufacturing high-technology products abroad through licensees.

5 Develop a strategy for a hotel chain wishing to expand internationally with minimum investment.

6 Discuss the following statement.
'Ensuring that the licensee does not cause problems for the company by poor quality is a common nightmare for licensors. Whatever the contract may say, the affiliate often wishes to cut prices at the expense of quality. Ironically the same problem can arise if standards are raised as well. For quality is also related to market segment and the aim is to keep the licensee in that part of the market which the company has chosen, where a suitable niche exists.'

7 A foreign affiliate often cannot be prevented from acting for competing principals, but this can give rise to difficulties. For instance, the story is told of a firm in Latin America which managed to obtain orders for contract manufacture from three rival American manufacturers of soaps and detergents. Write a consultant's report to a company that found itself in the position of one of those three.

Further reading

An interesting and up-to-date discussion can be found in:
Chaponniére, T.R. and Lautier, M., 'Breaking into the Korean Market – Invest or Licence?' *International Journal of Strategic Management*, Long Range Planning, 28.1 (1995) pp.104–111.

This article argues that companies are likely to invest in Korea, because it is a difficult country to invest in, *although* – it also argues – investment is the surest way to achieve market share. On licensing, the article stresses that the objective of the Korean government is to unbundle the foreign direct investment package by contracting out all of its components (technology through licensing, marketing through subcontracting arrangements).

Brooke, 1985.
Casson, 1979.
Daniels and Radebaugh, 1995, ch.15.
Golden Square Services, *The Successful Franchise – A Working Strategy*. Gower, 1985.
Terpstra, 1983, pp. 342–61.
Thunman, C.G., 'An approach to asymmetrical capabilities in international licence agreements' (Working paper, Department of Business Administration, Uppsala University 1982). This paper contains three case studies of licensing arrangements negotiated by small companies. The same author has written another paper in the same series entitled 'Swedish licensing in world markets.'

6 Foreign investment

This chapter traces the progress of foreign investment from the initial decision to operate abroad through the establishment of a selling subsidiary to a full-blown multinational operation. Some related decisions about ownership, whether or when to buy, to build or to disinvest, are then considered. There is also a note on portfolio investment. Chapters 7 to 10 consider the implications of the move abroad for marketing, finance and other departmental policies, while Chapter 11 outlines the decision-making systems and organization.

The landmarks of international investment are changing in unexpected ways. Take three examples – these are drawn from a few years ago, but all would have been considered science fiction before they occurred.

1 'Ikarus of Hungary, one of the world's largest bus manufacturers, plans to set up within months an assembly operation in Britain.'
2 A report from a Ford executive at the Turin motor show pointed out that 'Ford was already importing Escorts from its Brazilian subsidiary for sale in Norway, Sweden, Finland, Denmark and Switzerland.'
3 A 50–50 joint venture between a Sicilian entrepreneur and a Chinese enterprise to manufacture kitchen equipment in China.[1]

These are all examples of international *direct* investment, where the equity participation is accompanied by management. Investment is the other main route to international operations, after exporting and licensing, and represents a change in the corporate system that can be seismic in its ultimate effects. However, the effects are not necessarily registered at once, and companies bring problems upon themselves by continuing to employ a management system appropriate to a domestic firm after they have developed significant world responsibilities.[2]

Once thought of as a strategy for the large company based on an industrialized country, direct investment is now undertaken by small companies and increasingly by companies based on less developed countries. Naturally the conditions and the predicaments will vary according to the size of the firm, and the variety is such that only a few major issues can be detailed in this chapter. The first two sections look at the 'how' and the 'why' of direct investment.

6.1 First steps

Investment decisions are usually taken for a complex variety of reasons which are difficult to analyse in individual cases. *Process* seems a more appropriate word than *motive*, as a company can be seen to move abroad step by step, drawn by factors many of which are unplanned but appear convincing at the time. For instance, a limited amount of equity invested in an agent or licensee may lead inexorably to the ownership of a foreign subsidiary as the equity is increased. If other shareholders pull out, the exporter is left with the choice of buying the agent or losing the money already invested (and perhaps the market as well). The choice sometimes emerges gradually, almost imperceptibly, as more and more investment and business are committed to a project. Other foreign investment is dictated by the nature of the product. A mineral, for example, can only be mined where it exists. In the case of service industries, the process of international growth can appear even more inexorable. The bank, advertising agency, insurance company, consultant or other similar business is drawn abroad by its customers who seek a similar service world-wide.

The use of the word 'process' in international investment has now become controversial. Exceptions have been found that imply that, while the conventional wisdom suggests that there is a 'process' of gradual expansion using other means of operating abroad before eventually investing, research has demonstrated that many firms have not gone through this 'process'. A firm that becomes an international investor through a merger is unlikely to go through the 'process', while the concept was introduced to account for the methods that small and medium-sized firms use in expanding in many markets.[3]

In addition to buying into an existing business, the process can start with the establishment of an office abroad to which other responsibilities are gradually added. This is the most likely route for a service company, but is common among manufacturers as well. It may arise from the need to supervise agents rather than replace them. A regional office is used to co-ordinate and perhaps re-organize a network of collaborators who have been collected over the years. It can readily be upgraded into a marketing subsidiary which is the next landmark in the emergence of foreign investment. The process is set out in Figure 6.1 but, as the last paragraph explains, a particular company may leave out some of the steps.

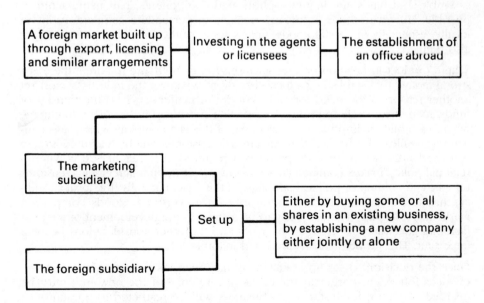

Figure 6.1 The emergence of foreign investment

The marketing subsidiary[4]

Several developments give rise to the marketing subsidiary, sometimes known as a 'selling subsidiary'. The first is when a company concludes that its own marketing skills are superior to those of its collaborators, or that a collaborator lacks the ability to expand, and the investment process is set in train. A related reason is when the business is seen to be static or declining in the face of competitors with a local presence. For both manufacturing and service industries, the ability to offer after-sales service is often considered the key to success. For the manufacturer, local warehousing and the provision of spare parts may be necessary. A marketing subsidiary is also in a position to co-ordinate and promote a product in a region or group of countries. The parent company is able to exercise more control over its operations in the market.

As against these advantages, there are certain drawbacks. The placing of an investment abroad exposes the company to fresh risks and absorbs funds which could be spent on new product development. Research and innovation at home may be more important to the export thrust than facilities abroad if a choice has to be made. Sometimes there is also a loss of flexibility. A subsidiary is a commitment which is harder to change than an agency agreement.

Certain product characteristics make a selling subsidiary more likely: some, but not all, of them also apply to manufacturing subsidiaries. For instance, a local corporate presence may be advisable in a capital goods industry where the products are of a one-off nature, where they take the form of complete systems, or where the amount of capital involved is low, either as a proportion of sales or as perceived by the supplier or customer. If the product is relatively simple to assemble, but has some highly sophisticated components, part manufacture is possible. However, these factors are unlikely to persuade a company to invest locally, especially in capital goods, unless some of the following conditions are also fulfilled.

Where product installation or after-sales service, or both, are required, there is a strong motive for establishing a local subsidiary, whatever the industry sector. Yet another reason is the need for close control in matters such as the transfer of funds, market research and sales. A marketing subsidiary is also likely to emerge where credibility is important. An example of this is a company which sells dangerous chemicals for further manufacture. The customer will be reassured if there is a local presence to provide back-up if required. Another reason is when a regional policy makes commercial sense in view of trading agreements, customs unions, and cultural or political affinities. In this case, naturally, the local subsidiary has to be granted regional authority. In a consumer goods company a marketing subsidiary is more likely to be a stage in the development of a manufacturing subsidiary as the market grows and the other considerations become important. The various reasons are listed in Table 6.1.

Once the decision to set up a subsidiary has been taken, a number of consequences follow. In particular the terms of reference of the new unit must be decided: whether, for instance, its business will be restricted to a country or extended to a region and, if the latter, how the region is defined. The relationship of the subsidiary to existing businesses will also have to be determined –

whether it will replace or supplement established means of supplying a market. This decision may have been pre-empted during the process by agreements entered into with suppliers or agents. Making long-term arrangements for short-term business requirements is a common error.

Table 6.1 Reasons for establishing a foreign selling subsidiary

1. Superior marketing skills in parent company cause dissatisfaction with agents, licensees and other collaborators.
2. Business static compared with competitors possessing a local presence.
3. Need to provide warehousing, product installation, after-sales service and other facilities locally.
4. Need for close control of finance and credit, market research, sales and other business activities.
5. Need for local presence to provide greater credibility with major customers.
6. Need to mastermind a regional strategy.

In sum, then, a marketing subsidiary is likely to come into existence by gradual changes, each one brought about by inadequacies in the current servicing of the market or situations which demand a stronger corporate presence. These latter arise either from the ambitions of a company or the activities of its competitors. The subsidiary may vary from a one-man office to a large company with distribution and servicing facilities. Whatever its scope, the risks of a loss of flexibility and a drain on resources have to be taken on board.

6.2 Motives for direct investment

Why go international? Why take on the risks and possible frustrations of owning property and managing businesses in foreign countries? An immediate answer to such questions lies in the process just described. The risks to an existing market, and the costs and frustrations inherent in current methods, are perceived to be greater than those likely to be incurred by investment. Underlying reasons were discussed in Chapter 2 where a number of economic and socio-psychological motives for corporate expansion were considered. These can be restated in managerial terms in a number of ways.

Table 6.2, based on enquiries from 120 experienced multinationals, nearly 80 per cent of whom said that market defence was the main reason for their foreign investment, provides a check-list for examining motives. The table is based on a classification of defensive and aggressive motives, with a third category to cover responses to approaches from outside. It was noticeable in the enquiry that approaches from other companies were mentioned more often than the influence of governments, although this influence features large in other publications. Companies are, on the whole, suspicious of government incentives which may not meet the extra costs of operating in a development area; usually incentives for investment are regarded as concessions to be negotiated after the decision has been taken rather than as factors in the decision.

Various countries have taken steps to lure foreign investors in recent years, if only by removing restrictions on investment in their growing markets. Thailand, for instance, which, in the early 1990s experienced a decline in foreign investment (by 28 per cent in 1993) has relaxed some restrictions; at the same time there are still industry sectors prohibited to foreign investors. Other rising South East Asia nations are similarly removing restrictions and opening up incentives to foreign as well as domestic companies.

Another means of classification is according to the factors that influence the decision: the market, investment conditions at home and abroad, the reduction of costs, the safeguarding of supplies and the response to outside approaches.[5] Yet another is to relate the take-over to the diversification strategy. One study of European take-overs of United States firms showed that 57 out of 77 led to horizontal and nine of the 77 to vertical integration.

Table 6.2 Reasons for establishing a foreign manufacturing subsidiary

The reasons	The frequency with which this reason was mentioned (symbols explained at foot of the table)
1. Defensive strategies, where a company is operating abroad to defend its existing business as result of:	
1.1 Government action in establishing or increasing:	
(a) tariff barriers,	A
(b) the subsequent lowering of tariff barriers,	B
(c) import controls,	D
(d) legislation (at home or abroad) against monopolies or trade agreements,	C
(e) legislation for import substitution, usually by enforcing part local manufacture or assembly;	D
1.2 Demands for local manufacture and other problems of nationalism in overseas markets;	C
1.3 Transport costs and delays;	A
1.4 Difficulties with agents and licensees;	A & B
1.5 Troubles with after-sales service and other technical difficulties abroad;	C
1.6 The need to protect patents;	C
1.7 The need to ensure supplies of raw materials and components;	C
1.8 The need to go international when competitors, suppliers or customers do so;	B
1.9 The need to protect shareholders at home from trade recessions by:	
(a) a geographical spread	C
(b) product group diversification (which may involve geographical as well).	D
2. Aggressive strategies, the search for:	
2.1 More profitable uses for under-employed resources at home in:	
(a) capital and equipment,	C
(b) personnel,	D
(c) know-how;	C
2.2 Lower factor costs, including those for:	
(a) capital (availability as well as cost),	C
(b) labour,	C
(c) supplies;	D
2.3 The more effective use of opportunities by the development of global plans and strategies for resources and markets;	C
2.4 Access to foreign knowledge or methods;	D
2.5 The need to expand, when this can only be abroad, and the possibility of escaping from constraints at home.	E

Table 6.2 continued

The reasons	The frequency with which this reason was mentioned (symbols explained at foot of the table)
3. Other pressures	
3.1 Influence of governments, for example:	
(a) by general encouragement to foreign investment,	D
(b) tax concessions,	D
(c) cheap loans,	D
(d) grants or guarantees,	D
(e) buildings;	E
3.2 Influence of other companies including approach for know-how;	C
3.3 Internal to company, such as pressure groups advocating overseas manufacture because of the expertise and insights of members.	C

Note on the frequency (col. 2): It has proved impossible to give a weighting to the different pressures in the form of:'2.2 was reported by 16 companies'. Over 100 companies have been questioned but the more inquiries that are made, the more acute becomes the problem of defining a company. If Company X is said to report a certain motive, who for this purpose is Company X? The chairman? The managing director? A majority of the board? The public relations officer? The official historian? Or who? In the end the answer lies in the judgement of the investigator, not in the number of people who can be persuaded into answering his questionnaires. Hence the letters have been used to represent as accurately as possible the weight given to the different motives.

A: This motive was mentioned by virtually everyone questioned or reported in every company to which it was applicable at all, for instance under heading 1.1 companies exporting manufactured goods and under 2.2 companies importing scarce raw materials.
B: Mentioned in some form or other by executives in over half the companies investigated or reported.
C: Mentioned by executives in less than half, but more than two of the firms.
D: Mentioned once or twice only.
E: Not mentioned at all in companies questioned, but referred to in the literature.

Judgement has also, of course, been applied in the numerous cases where contradictory opinions have been expressed in the same company.

Source: author's own research

6.3 Foreign subsidiaries for manufacture and services

The founding of a subsidiary for manufacture or for selling services is a major step even for the largest of companies. Before it is taken, the motives will be supplemented by pressures that build up in the company to provide the necessary impetus. While the subsidiary may emerge from a take-over, or be founded from scratch, the main consideration will be to ensure that the objectives are achieved. Steps taken to this end include the following.
1 Ensuring that the extra production will be sold profitably by an analysis of the revenue accounts of existing manufacturing units to compare costs.
2 Ensuring that adequate funds are available for the start-up period.
3 Ensuring that foreseeable risks are covered either by insurance or by other precautions such as hedging, the balancing of one risky area against another, or by insurance.

4 If the main purpose of a subsidiary is to offer services or supplies to customers that are already international, it is necessary to ensure that it is operating on a sufficient scale to service the customers efficiently. The objective is not attained simply by bringing the subsidiary into existence. The location must be correct and the resources adequate.

Some subsidiaries are set up as a source of supply for the parent company or its established markets. Countries around the world, from Ireland to Singapore, have concessions to encourage companies which will manufacture within a country but which only supply markets outside – the offshore companies considered later (see Figure 6.2). As with other government concessions, these may appear more attractive than they are. If a country has to take such measures to attract business, there must be costs and some companies have run into trouble by finding the costs higher than expected. Others have established viable and successful businesses with government help.

Incentives for foreign investment have become an increasingly vexed question. Originally offered to encourage companies to operate in countries whose location or other special circumstances involved higher costs, incentives have spread to most countries. They have become part of a significant international competition for foreign investors. This competition has been raised at the level of a number of international regulatory bodies and incorporated in the codes of conduct mentioned in a later chapter. Companies are nowadays more likely to use incentives as a bargaining counter after a decision to invest has been taken, rather than as a motive in taking the decision. They will play governments off against one another in seeking to raise concessions.

Other questions to be answered in starting a manufacturing subsidiary – the place of the new affiliate in the corporate system, the organization and control arrangements, staffing and labour affairs – are discussed in later chapters. Once manufacture abroad begins, a company is likely to encounter a chain of upheavals. The structure of the home base is proved inadequate as the demands of the subsidiaries grow on both the support and the disciplinary systems. A chain reaction starts at home for which the company needs to be prepared. Some of the problems that stem from this reaction can be minimized if the company is the sole shareholder in its foreign operations. However, there may be good commercial reasons for joint ownership, as is argued in the next section.

6.4 Ownership and the joint venture

Ownership is one of the most debated issues in establishing a foreign subsidiary. The potential advantages and disadvantages of various ownership policies are easily stated but whether the advantages will be realized in practice depends on the exercise of a number of personal and managerial skills, or the failure of those skills. The most frequently mentioned policies are the following.
1 *To own all the equity in their foreign subsidiaries.* This is a policy strongly held by some companies. In keeping with this principle there have been a limited number of withdrawals, some of them accompanied by much publicity. Most such closures were on the part of United States' companies operating in less

developed countries; in industrialized countries there are few restrictions. Among multinationals the 'drive to unambiguous control,' as it has been called, is still strong, but more are willing to compromise and accept partners when the need for investment is urgent.[6]

2 *To own all the equity in countries where this is permitted* and to accept local shareholders elsewhere. A few years ago it could be said dogmatically that this was the most common ownership policy. The situation is changing, but the practice remains common. What cannot be said so dogmatically is whether the advantages gained by 100 per cent ownership really outweighed the costs at any time. Some relevant arguments are listed below (under 'advantages' and 'disadvantages'); their force varies according to the other shareholders who may be companies or individuals. Control can be more easily exercised in the latter case, but excellent business relationships are often negotiated with a corporate co-proprietor.

3 *To decide each new foreign operation on its own merits.* This 'horses for courses' policy, as it has been called, examines the situation afresh in the case of each new investment and asks whether the skills and resources possessed by the company suggest a joint venture or not. The availability of a suitable partner, the need for finance, and the structure of the market are other relevant factors.

4 *To expand abroad through joint ventures as a normal rule*, only excepting operations for which suitable local investors cannot be found.

Any expansion through joint ventures raises questions about who the other shareholders will be. If the equity is sold on the local money markets, there will be no dilution of authority although some policies – dividend policies, for instance – may have to be modified to suit the local interests. In this case, the partners take no active part in the business. The other option, the joint venture proper, is when a proportion of the shares are allocated to two or more companies who will require a part in the decision-making, including seats on the subsidiary board. The dilution of authority may cause problems but compensations are expected, like the resources the partner will bring – knowledge of the local markets, finance, or other relevant expertise.

It has been demonstrated that certain types of company are particularly resistant to joint ventures. These are:

1 those in advanced technologies, where research and development is a relatively high proportion of expenditure;
2 aggressive consumer goods companies where a high proportion of expenditure is on advertising;
3 those where control of raw materials is important,
4 those where policy standardization rates a high priority.[7]

There are also national differences. United States' companies have usually been hostile to joint ventures. Of the nearly 3,000 American affiliates in Britain, for instance, even now only a limited number have quotations for the subsidiary on the British Stock Exchange. British companies have also preferred 100 per cent ownership, although the preference is now less than it was ten years ago. Other European countries show more flexibility, but also prefer total ownership.

Japanese companies, on the other hand, frequently develop abroad with local shareholders.

The advantages of joint ventures

Most of the advantages of joint ventures are found in the following list, to which should be added the speed of entry made possible if the venture is successful.

1 *Expansion with limited capital outlay.* This will be an even greater advantage if expansion is made possible into a number of high-profit and high-risk areas at once. Such simultaneous expansion ensures the benefits and insures against the risks. In any event, the risk is limited in a joint venture.

2 *A suitable partner will provide expertise* not already possessed by the parent company. Knowledge of market conditions in the host country is an example. The local partner may also provide an insurance against the dangers of expropriation. Some businessmen argue further that a locally quoted company is itself a good managerial discipline. 'You cannot get away with any mess in a publicly quoted company,' one said.

3 *Improved sales prospects*, especially to governments; sometimes joint ventures provide a captive market.

4 *There is no alternative in many instances.* In some countries, especially the less developed, joint ventures are compulsory, although the actual conditions may be more flexible than a reading of the law suggests. Within a general prohibition, exceptions up to 100 per cent ownership are occasionally negotiated. The insistence on local participation may be considered a reason for not investing but, if the investment is regarded as essential, the regulations determine the form it will take, whatever its disadvantages. There are a number of countries where local participation is usually required on either legal or commercial grounds including those which:

(a) insist on local shareholding in all circumstances, like India and the former Yugoslavia;

(b) allow 100 per cent foreign ownership for companies whose products are considered especially vital to the local economy, but not for others;

(c) allow 100 per cent foreign ownership with permission from the appropriate authority, but where to aim for 100 per cent may be undesirable for either or both of the following reasons: (i) permission will be hard to get otherwise and may be accompanied by a number of restrictions; (ii) the cultural and other differences make a partner essential.

A world trend to liberalization of capital movements has increased the possibility of joint ventures in the 1990s while the need to reduce risk has increased their attractiveness. The growing size of projects which involve new technology is another stimulus to joint operations when no single firm can marshal the resources to go it alone.

For this and numerous other reasons, practices over joint ventures have changed radically in recent years. A decline in traditional industries along with a surge in new (high-technology) sectors have combined to place some markets beyond the reach of many companies. These factors have combined to produce a rapid increase in joint ventures in which an increasing number of companies are taking part. Some companies used to resist pressures to joint ventures in free market economies, where such pressures are seen as restrictions, but bid for joint ventures in planned economies where they are regarded as concessions. This apparent double standard already cast doubt on the commercial objections to joint ventures. These are considered next.

The disadvantages of joint ventures

1 *Lack of adequate control.* Policies found to be profitable elsewhere may have to be modified to suit the partner, thus risking a lower profitability than might otherwise have been achieved. The risks of outside interference in decision-making are assumed to be minimized by 100 per cent ownership. On the other hand, a satisfactory business relationship can enable policies, particularly the company's normal controls, to be employed without modification.

2 *The partner may not have the requisite skills,* and the parent company can easily find itself providing services out of all proportion to its expectations. As one executive said: 'we put in 60 per cent of the equity and take out 60 per cent of the profits, but we take on 90 per cent of the work'. This can be overcome by providing for the payment of fees for management services when the venture is first formed.

3 *Rigidity.* Rapid changes of policy, rationalization across frontiers or even disinvestment are among the options made more difficult by a joint venture. In general, it is harder to mastermind global policies and optimize the use of resources across a group of companies not wholly-owned. On the other hand, if the partner does disinvest, a company may find itself left with a larger commitment than anticipated.

4 *Division of interest.* Policies that are to the advantage of a company as a whole may not be to the advantage of an individual subsidiary. A number of examples illustrate this.

   (a) Dividend policies. A company may want to use all its profits for expansion in a particular year or years. The other shareholders may want a regular dividend. The same consideration applies to other financial policies, like the prices at which goods are sold to the joint venture from other units of the company and vice versa, and the proportion of the capital held in loans.

   (b) Trading areas. A company may need to determine which subsidiary supplies which market. Not every concern feels impelled to do this and the decision is controversial on political as well as other grounds, but there are many reasons for limiting the trade of affiliates. In a joint venture, however, it can be difficult to regulate because the other shareholders will consider any restriction as a limit on their earning power. Similar considerations apply to other policies, including new product development and marketing.

   (c) Pricing policies. These frequently lead to disputes between the partners. When, for instance, a company's policy is to transfer materials or components from one unit to another at cost price plus a percentage addition (the most common method, see Chapter 7), the partner may argue for a lower percentage on incoming goods and a higher market-based price for outgoing – when trading within the company.

(d) Production policies. Some policies – like international standardization of products or parts, the rationalization of facilities or of supply routes – are difficult to accommodate to joint ventures.

(e) Competition. The sharing of competitive information, techniques and technologies may cause difficulties.

Special provisions

A number of arrangements can maximize the advantages and minimize the disadvantages.

1 A clear statement about the expectations of each partner – in terms of sales, market share, income and so on – to keep conflicts of interest to a minimum. This statement is likely to be followed by one on the distribution of earnings, the criteria for deciding how much is to be paid out in dividends and how much retained in the business.

2 A high-level board fully representative of the major shareholders which will monitor progress and problems regularly. This board will also be responsible for senior appointments which will include experienced representatives of the partners.

3 A control system acceptable to both sides which gives advanced warning of difficulties at regular intervals.

4 Pricing policies for sales from the parent company to the joint venture agreed with the partners beforehand.

5 Predetermined policies about increases in capital, if required, and whether any increases must safeguard the relative shares of the partners.

6 Agreed policies on framing the corporate strategies and the long-range plans of the joint venture; and how these will be integrated into the planning systems of the parent company and, if necessary, the other partners.

Conclusion

To share or not to share the ownership is a difficult decision. The sale of shares in the local subsidiary has traditionally been unpopular with western management, but practices have been changing for both political and commercial reasons. As more companies become accustomed to a divided ownership, they become less resistant to the idea. Special skills are certainly required, as well as foresight, to build up a business relation which will withstand the divisions of interest which are bound to exist.

For recent research into joint ventures see: Madhok, Anoop, 'Revisiting multinational firms' tolerance for joint ventures: a trust-based approach,' *Journal of International Business Studies*, 26.1, First Quarter 1995.

As with other investment issues, modern practice on joint venture has overtaken the conventional wisdom. The sheer scale of many projects and the size of the risks involved have impelled companies to seek partners at almost any price. Of course the risks of the joint venture have to be minimized, but this consideration now ranks below the need to enlist partners.

Joint ventures in the 1990s

The foregoing text outlines current knowledge on joint ventures, but practice has moved on past many of the traditional outlooks although they are still relevant.

The market, the technology and the financing requirements of an increasing number of industry sectors dictate that the joint venture is the only viable way forward.

The question now is *not* to examine the advantages and disadvantages, but to find ways of making joint ventures work and solve problems that arise. It is these problem-solving procedures that demand attention and a focus (as mentioned before) on a high level board that can solve the inevitable clash of cultures between the partners. Contrasting control styles has been mentioned as an example of how conflict can be generated.

6.5 The parent company and the subsidiary

The move abroad will alter the management system of the parent company. Whether the changes come gradually or in sudden bursts will depend on previous experience and the problems that currently face the company. Naturally a severe loss in a foreign subsidiary will lead to more careful monitoring. Complaints about lack of support for the foreign operators are another frequent cause of change. There is no simple formula that makes it possible to predict when changes will take place. The timing will vary according to the industry sector, the size of company, the countries of operation and other factors. Nevertheless, by the time 20 per cent of total investment is abroad, the management system is likely to be geared to cope with the foreign operations; changes can be expected as efforts are made to cope more effectively. The whole management system will need to change (Chapters 7–11 outline the changes). The risks can be minimized by operating in a number of markets, by keeping a minimal commitment in high-risk regions, and by investment insurance.

The need for change in the relationship between head office and the foreign subsidiary becomes clear to head office, either gradually or through a traumatic experience. The offsetting of the financial risks is usually the first issue to require attention, followed by the need to improve communications. Meanwhile, a subsidiary comes into existence, or is re-organized, as a result of two further decisions.

The means of establishment

This may be either by purchasing an existing company, or by founding a new one. The purchase of an existing company used to be the preferred method under most circumstances. A take-over provided a going concern and avoided the problems of starting up from scratch in a little-known environment. More importantly, the purchase brought with it an existing order book, a distribution network and a sales team already in the market. Starting up afresh was the prerogative of an experienced operator, large enough not to worry about the teething troubles of a new venture. Nowadays, many companies find such troubles less of a worry than integrating an established firm, with its personalities and traditions, into an existing system. There are political conditions attached to take-overs

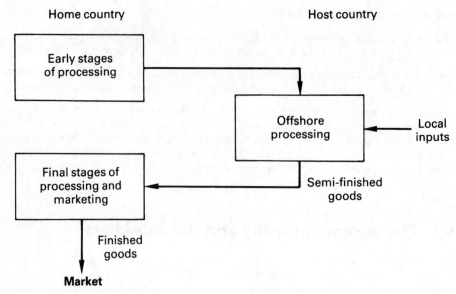

Figure 6.2 The offshore production process

in a number of countries, and for many companies these alone have tipped the balance in favour of a new venture. Small firms, untroubled by political worries because of their low visibility but looking for experienced local management, continue to prefer buying a going concern. Their first move is frequently the purchase of an agent or licensee.

On the other hand, a firm with a technological advantage is likely to favour starting from scratch: *greenfield* entry as it is sometimes called. By using this method, a firm finds itself less committed to existing staff and techniques and with more freedom in choosing a site. As against this, the advantages of buying a skilled management team are often cited, in spite of difficulties in integrating and motivating it, especially at a time of rapid technological innovation. Where questions of knowledge and location outweigh other considerations and indicate a greenfield policy, this is likely to be pursued. Otherwise, a take-over will be the first choice. One survey of a few years ago showed that 54 per cent of new foreign direct investment in the United States was of the greenfield type.[8]

A sub-division of the *greenfield* venture is the *offshore* subsidiary. Originally devised by newly industrializing nations as a means of attracting foreign manufacturers, this arrangement has spread and is now used by industrialized as well as less developed countries. The basic arrangement is that a country sets aside an area that is held to be extra-territorial in terms of customs and other import regulations. This is the force of the word 'offshore'. The products or components are not held to have been imported, although the facility may be inland. Figure 6.2 illustrates the system.[9]

The government is assuming that the offshore subsidiary will provide employment and revenue for the country through personal spending and income taxes. Customs duties are remitted altogether, when there is no home market, while national and local taxes are also remitted or reduced for a number of years. Since these facilities first started there have been forecasts that increasing wage rates, together with transportation difficulties, would make them uneconomic. This has not happened yet and duty-free areas have, in fact, spread to countries with higher wages. It is, however, likely that factories that do not serve a home market will be more subject to rationalization than others, but this also has still to be proved.

The legal framework

The regulatory framework varies from country to country but the wholly-owned foreign firm, or the kind of joint venture which does not include a public quotation, will generally take the form of a private limited company. This will enable the firm to meet its obligations with the minimum of formality. In some countries, a private company is not required to disclose any information to the general public, although many multinationals do make information available for the sake of public relations. Where there are to be local shares sold on the local money market, a public company will be needed. The requirements of the money market will have to be met as well as the law of the land.

It has been assumed so far that the foreign venture will take the form of a subsidiary – that it will be registered as a company under the law of the host country – and there are advantages in this arrangement. The legal theory is that a subsidiary is an independent company; the role of the parent company is that of a shareholder. The latter is not, therefore, liable for the debts of its affiliate. There may also be tax advantages when profits are transferred. In spite of these considerations a number of companies do operate through branches, even where substantial manufacturing facilities exist. In such cases, agreements are negotiated with both countries to apportion the taxes. For small sales offices, the branch arrangements are more common. The European Union (EU) has regulations designed to make branches of firms operating between the member states feasible, and they are likely to come back into fashion in Europe. This trend needs to be taken into account when formulating plans for expansion within the EU. The advantages, where branches are possible, are simpler and less expensive formalities both in establishment and in subsequent administration.

Dealings at arm's length

In discussions on the management of subsidiaries, the phrase 'arm's length' is frequently used. This phrase refers to the fact that a subsidiary (as opposed to a branch) is a separate company, a legal entity in its own country with its own constitution and articles of association. As a result, there is a requirement that dealings between the parent and subsidiary should be conducted as between independent companies – or as between shareholder and company. This is important to national tax and excise authorities, because tax liabilities and duties will depend on a number of factors like the prices companies charge in moving goods between different units. Since a growing proportion of the foreign trade of the industrialized countries is between units of a company – the highest figure is for the United States, where it is over half – the effect on national taxes can clearly be large. The phrase arm's length is used in other arrangements too and will frequently be found in the literature. Naturally the managerial reality will often be far from arm's length. Direct instructions will pass to subsidiaries which will be treated like any other unit of the company. These instructions often have to be communicated circumspectly because in some cases, where mandatory instructions are seen to be used, tax authorities can declare that the affiliate is effectively a branch and tax its income accordingly.

6.6 A note on disinvestment

Growing international investment is being accompanied by increasing disinvestment – the reduction of a particular holding either by the disposal or loss of assets, in whole or in part. Back in 1973, before the first oil crisis changed the picture, the disinvestment figure for British companies was about £1,800m. in the one year, and there has been a steady increase since then. For a company disinvestment can be anything from an unexpected disaster to a carefully planned change of strategy. The purpose of studying the subject is to have less disaster and more strategy. There are two types of disinvestment.

Compulsory

A government takes steps to reduce or abolish the foreign holding. Where nationalization is official policy, there will be no difference between domestic and foreign companies. The bid to bring more of the country's business into domestic ownership, on the other hand, will affect only the international firm. The change may be carried out by means of a complete take-over by local interests, or by the gradual sale of shares. In some countries, such as Nigeria and India, the proportion of foreign ownership permitted has been reduced – although there are currently indications that it may be increased again. As countries enter more into world trade, policies change. The enforced sale of assets varies from industry to industry. Sectors where foreign capital is considered vital to the economy, notably those in high-technology or those that can build up an export business, are either exempt from the regulations or allowed to retain more of the equity. Disinvestment, then, can be partial as well as total. Under some circumstances the withdrawal may be followed by the negotiation of a management contract. In this case a relationship has continued; there have been other instances where a former subsidiary has become a competitor after disinvestment.

Voluntary

A company takes steps to disinvest a holding, either partly or completely, because:
1 operating in a particular market has ceased to be profitable;
2 there are seen to be commercial or political advantages in selling some of the equity to local citizens;
3 operations elsewhere need extra funding which can most easily be raised by a particular sale;
4 the company is planning for international rationalization either by product, when a particular product is no longer considered to fit with corporate strategies, or

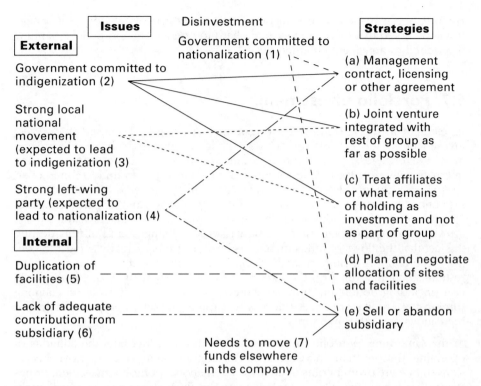

The lines represent the links between issues and strategies

Figure 6.3 Disinvestment

by geography, when some facilities are being closed to concentrate production on others. Sales offices and servicing centres may be similarly rationalized.

Voluntary disinvestment is more common in industrialized countries and in long-
established industries where competition is keen. Studies have shown that a
limited number of companies are responsible for a high proportion of disinvest-
ments, and that in most cases the subsidiary is eliminated completely – although
the information may be biased by lack of data on partial sales.[10]

Conclusion

Disinvestment, then, is sometimes forced upon a company by legislation and
sometimes follows rationalization. In either case it can be incorporated in long-
term plans as part of a restructuring, or it can be a panic measure verging on
disaster. Some of the issues that produce disinvestment, linked with their typical
responses, are shown in Figure 6.3. The figure shows the issues divided into
external (numbered on the left from 1 to 7) and internal (lettered on the right
from a to e). Different linkages are shown by different kinds of line (broken or
unbroken). The external, political risk factors loom large in the eyes of commentators but the internal, corporate rationalization pressures are more influential
in practice. The strategies range from retaining some interest through a joint

venture, or a management contract (and perhaps both), to abandonment or sale. It will be noted that these strategies are hard to operate at short notice; planning is required to anticipate emergencies.

6.7 Portfolio investment

Investment in foreign equity or long-term loans is less discussed than direct investment because it does not include general, as opposed to financial, management. Nevertheless, it probably accounts for as much of the money passing internationally.[11] In 1984, America's mutual funds invested around $13bn in overseas shares, a tenfold increase in five years. In the reverse direction foreign institutions bought £5.2bn of shares in the United States in 1983, an increase of 75 per cent on the previous year. The rapid growth has been aided by the parallel growth of foreign quotations on national stock exchanges, and all this despite the fact that the flows of funds under this heading are particularly subject to controls. The controls include restrictions on investment in specific industry sectors, restraints (often severe) on the export of funds or payment of dividends, taxation (including double taxation, sometimes caused by the difficulty in claiming foreign tax credits), restricted access to capital markets, complex disclosure regulations and other measures.

At the same time, portfolio investors share with direct investors the stimulus of operating in more than one economy. This enables them to smooth over recessions in one area with booms in another. International portfolio investment brings the further advantage of counter-balancing the fluctuations in a national stockmarket which do not necessarily reflect the changes in economic activity. In 1980, for instance, the yield for a Belgian investor of Belgian securities was considerably below that which he would have received from a portfolio of foreign holdings. By early 1983 that position had been reversed.

There are also a number of incentives like the possibility of investing in tax havens or, for personal investors, the chance of placing their money in countries which they may wish to visit or live in, although, in general, longer established, portfolio now tends to follow direct investment. Both move into strong economies even in the face of strong currencies, a paradox which makes an exact charting of the motives of the investor complex. Foreign portfolio investment is particularly attractive to those who are seeking long-term growth rather than income. In Britain, for instance, some growth-oriented unit trusts have all or part of their holdings abroad.

6.8 Conclusion

Investment abroad has been seen to be a major step in a company's development, with the possibility of rapid growth in size and profitability; the chances of disaster are also high. Managing operations in foreign countries, even within an area where there are great similarities, is always a different exercise from domestic management, in kind and not just in degree. Companies that do not understand the differences risk a breakdown or, at the least, a record of missed opportunities. Vigilance over the requirements of foreign investment is needed on a variety of matters which include the following:

1 Understanding foreign accounting systems, financing methods and means of transferring funds.
2 Understanding legal differences and the likely implications for a company of changes of government.
3 Understanding local cultures and especially the varying attitudes to authority, work and incentives.
4 Understanding distribution and logistical difficulties and opportunities.
5 Noting different marketing methods, together with the constraints and opportunities.
6 Understanding the results that can be obtained from foreign investment and exercising vigilance to ensure that these results are being obtained in practice.
7 Achieving the objectives of the foreign operations by attention to the following issues.
   (a) *The speed of development abroad.* The successful company expands step by step and does not attempt to invest in numerous countries at once.
   (b) *An effective means of market protection.* Investment is usually seen in this light, but two questions have to be answered: 'Is investment desirable?' and 'Is the proposed investment the most desirable?'
   (c) *Ownership.* Is 100 per cent ownership possible or desirable for a particular project? What is a general guideline appropriate to this company on the question of ownership?
   (d) *Establishment.* Should a new company be developed from scratch, or should an existing firm be purchased?
   (e) *Organization.* How is the subsidiary to be managed? A vital decision under this heading is whether to adapt the head office system to match the challenge of the overseas operations. The situation will change constantly, so flexibility is needed (see Chapter 11).
   (f) *Legal.* The framework for the subsidiary – type of company and articles of association – has to be determined. Alternatively, there are a limited number of circumstances in which a branch may be preferred. This is more likely for a selling subsidiary than a manufacturing, but can be for either.
   (g) *Control and monitoring.* Adequate provisions have to be made to ensure that head office is kept aware of developments in the subsidiary and whether these are in line with plans. An early warning system is required for possible threats, and to signal successful developments which require action at head office.
   (h) *The need for investment insurance.*
   (i) *Planning.* The exact means by which the subsidiary is integrated into the corporate planning system. This includes rationalization proposals.
   (j) *Staffing.* The recruitment of managers and technical experts for the foreign units.

These issues are discussed in this and the following chapters. Meanwhile, the fundamental options are again brought together in a keyboard analogy diagram. Figure 6.4 shows the type of subsidiary and the ownership possibilities, with both black and white keys which can be played in several combinations.

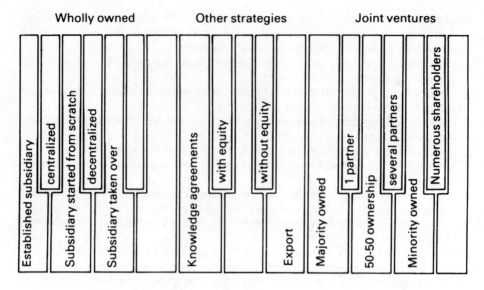

Figure 6.4 The keyboard analogy – investment

6.9 Exercises, questions and further reading

Case examples

Company A: The foreign subsidiary that refused to pay a dividend

Company A (a British company) had a subsidiary in France which failed to pay
a dividend. Each year the directors of the parent company flew over to France,
noted with satisfaction that financial targets had been achieved, and proposed a
dividend. Each year the chief executive of the French subsidiary pointed to a
clause in the articles of association of his company which said that dividends
should only be paid after adequate provision for capital requirements had been
made. Our capital requirements, he claimed, will absorb all the profits. The position of the French chief executive was secure because:

1 he was managing a successful business and the parent company directors were
   unwilling to interfere in a way that might cause damage; no dividend, with the
   prospect of dividends in the future, would be preferable to losing the prospect;
2 he had the support of French commercial law both for his personal job security and the policies being pursued.

A more satisfactory business relationship in the first place would have ensured that:

1 the dividend was not the only way of getting money out of the subsidiary (see
   Chapter 8 on financial management);
2 the dividend was related to the level of profit rather than to the requirements
   of the subsidiary.

The board decided that there was a choice between the following options – all,
in their view, undesirable.

1 Leave things alone in the hope that the situation would change. The advisability of this depended on the amounts at stake. If, for instance, considerable growth was possible in the subsidiary's market, patience might be the best solution. If, on the other hand, there were limits to growth or the income from the French company was urgently needed elsewhere, the costs of leaving things as they were might be enormous. In addition, the effect on other subsidiaries had to be considered.

2 Increase the pressure for a dividend. This was little different from 1.

3 Dismiss the chief executive and risk the consequences, or facilitate his early retirement.

4 Promote the chief executive. If he was as talented as suggested, and as obstinate, his presence might be valuable at head office where he would have to serve the group as a whole.

5 Put in a new finance director briefed to study the figures – evidence of borrowing, rates of return and so on – in the hope that the chief executive could be proved wrong.

6 Threaten to withhold technical and other information required by the subsidiary.

7 Sell the subsidiary, hoping for a capital gain, pull out of France and use the funds elsewhere.

8 Split the subsidiary into two – one company for manufacture and the other for marketing. The existing chief executive could then be left in charge of the one to which his talents seemed most suited and dividends could be taken out of the other. This solution has been tried on a number of occasions for this and similar situations. One danger is that each of the two subsidiaries operates less efficiently than the one replaced.

9 Negotiate afresh with all the above options on the table. The chief executive might decide he has much to lose by continuing resistance.

Company B: the company that failed to support the foreign operations

Lack of support from head office is another common problem that results in disappointment with the performance of the foreign subsidiaries. They are not providing the expected income; they are not developing new markets; they are not feeding in new ideas either commercial or technical. Company B acquired its foreign affiliates in a haphazard manner. Most already existed when company B bought other domestic companies. They became and remained subsidiaries of subsidiaries, and continued to report to their former parents. Other foreign affiliates had been set up by the new parent company and reported direct to a member of the main board. When the chief executive visited the subsidiaries, he came back horrified by the neglect he had uncovered. He considered that they were failing to reach their potential as a result of ineptitude at home. As a result an international division was established to foster and to control the foreign companies.

Vitamore SA: the move abroad

Vitamore SA was a Swiss Pharmaceutical company. Smaller than companies like Hoffman La Roche and Ciba Geigy, but growing rapidly thanks to the discovery of two powerful new antibiotics, Vitamore felt that the time had come to back its success as an exporter with foreign investment. However some major problems caused misgivings and questions were being asked about how wise the policy was, and whether the objectives could be achieved by foreign investment.

Some important considerations are:

1 The company operated in three product groups:
   Antibiotics, sales $350m.
   Analgaesics, sales $450m.
   Veterinary products, sales $200m.

   Roughly 80 per cent of the turnover in each product was export.
2 For the more advanced products in each group, research and production were hard to separate as further developments were taking place.
3 There were numerous strong and usually international competitors in all the product groups. Even the two new antibiotics were only expected to keep ahead of the competition for a limited period.
4 Some of the products were manufactured in stages, which did not necessarily have to be in the same place. Some processes were simpler than others.
5 The more sophisticated products were extremely demanding on skilled manpower, including chemical engineers and bio-chemists.
6 A minimum viable cost in the home country for a complete manufacturing system was $100m; for a plant making the simpler ingredients it could be as little as $20m. In Switzerland there were average sales per worker of $85,000 but this was higher for the more sophisticated processes and lower for the less so.
7 The company considered that it had reached the limit of its expansion alongside powerful competitors also drawing on a limited manpower.

You are asked to draft a project plan for the internationalization of Vitamore, setting out what information you would require to make reliable proposals to the Board.

A joint venture

Go Ahead Plastics plc had a joint venture in Ghana. The parties were a local firm of merchants, who previously imported Go Ahead's products. The joint venture was called Headway Plastics (Accra) Ltd. 40 per cent of the equity belonged to Go Ahead, and the other 60 per cent to a local firm called The Comfortable Enterprises Company. Headway manufactured a number of products for household use like table tops and electrical appliances. These were all Go Ahead products which had previously been imported. Headway had built up the local market and exports to other West African countries. The joint venture, now five years old, had been judged a commercial success; but some troubles were becoming apparent. Go Ahead was considering these troubles, and its point of view was as follows.

1 A much larger company than Comfortable Enterprises, Go Ahead was providing most of the inputs that had made Headway successful. These included both product and market information and techniques. Go Ahead had also helped to raise funds to finance the growth and given guarantees for this purpose.
2 The original agreement prevented Go Ahead from charging for management services. Hence it could only get its money out in dividends, and it only received 40 per cent of these, with the result that it was putting in much work for which it was not being paid.

Comfortable Enterprises argued:
1 that the agreement was being followed to the letter;
2 that its local knowledge and expertise had made a success of the joint venture.

In spite of these arguments, Go Ahead was now determined that some action must be taken; it saw the choices available as:
1 to sell its holding, either to Comfortable or to a third party;
2 to renegotiate the agreement between the parties;
3 to buy out Comfortable and to find another partner;
4 to buy out Comfortable and to make Headway a wholly-owned subsidiary.

Questions

1 'We have no problems in deciding where to invest. When orders from any part of the world exceed a certain level we set up a presence there.' Critically evaluate this approach to international direct investment.

2 Discuss the key variables which should determine the choice between either:
   (a) a joint venture with local interests or a wholly-owned subsidiary in a particular foreign country, or
   (b) a greenfield foreign entry versus the take-over of an indigenous firm.

3 Can any rules be devised to ensure the success of a foreign direct investment? If so, what are these rules? Do they differ between types of firm and types of host country? Do they differ between a first foreign direct investment and later ventures? Give reasons for your answer.

4 Examine the factors that can be expected to determine the choice of joint venture partners.

5 How important do you consider the action of competitors to be in leading to foreign direct investment? Discuss threat and rivalry in direct investment strategies.

6 Analyse the differences between small and large firms in establishing foreign subsidiaries.

7 Evaluate the benefits and dangers of offshore production plants (plants established in low-wage countries to source the firm's home market) in a multinational firm's production network.

8 Discuss the issues raised by foreign direct investment in extractive industries.

9 Examine the reasons for the establishment of a foreign marketing subsidiary.

10 An international retailing company has asked your advice on the possibility of using its know-how and business techniques in other countries of the European Union. Draft a memorandum on this subject as an outside adviser on international business.

11 What are the advantages and disadvantages of 100 per cent ownership of a foreign subsidiary? Discuss your answer in the light of a range of options.

12 Explain how guidelines on the appraisal of large capital projects can be modified to cover multinational operations and their uncertainties.

13 Detail the political considerations that need to be taken into account when selecting between more or less similar, but alternative, capital investments located abroad.

14 A machinery manufacturer with a turnover of £150m is considering the future of its extensive operations abroad. Hitherto subsidiaries have only been established in industrialized countries where 100 per cent ownership is permitted. In the developing countries there are licensing and agency agreements. The company has recently developed some new products considered to have great growth potential, but cash and staff resources are both limited. A number of ideas are being canvassed around the company – joint ventures, management contracts, rationalization schemes and much else. A member of the chairman's staff has been asked to produce a memorandum for the Board advising on policies and the reasons for adopting a particular approach. Write the memorandum for him.

15 An American motor car company has decided to close its factory in France which employs 12,000 people. Assume that the decision to close is irrevocable and that the withdrawal has to be completed in five years. Trace out the steps necessary between the present and the date of closure. Include as many options as possible, but indicate which are to be preferred. The conclusion should be a viable plan for an orderly disinvestment.

Note: question 1 and most of the others depend for an adequate answer on a wider reading.

Further reading

Brooke and Remmers, 1978.
Buckley and Casson, 1976.
Casson, 1983.
Clarke, 1985.
Daniels and Radebaugh, 1995, ch. 8 and 12.
Lall, 1983.
Robinson, 1984, ch. 6 and 8.
Vernon and Wells, 1981, ch. 3.
Wells, 1983.

7 International marketing management

By some definitions of international marketing this whole book is on the subject, especially the preceding chapters (4–6). Chapter 7 concentrates on decisions not covered elsewhere – market research, product strategies, customer identification, pricing, promotion and sales. There is also a section on the growth of barter and countertrade as well as one on external affairs. The subject of cultural differences, including the concept of psychic distance in marketing, is considered in Chapter 14.

A successful international firm is one that has effective international marketing. To many this is a self-evident proposition, but sceptics have cast doubt on it. A good invention can be a substitute for any amount of inefficiency, while luck helps, but a world spread normally comes through effective marketing. It is curious, therefore, to note a tendency that can be compared to pulling up the drawbridge, for an important debate in many companies is about the appropriateness of having an international marketing department at all. Central departments are abolished or slimmed down and their functions delegated to the subsidiaries, while international conferences are held to circulate experiences. Marketing, it is maintained, is a national activity and only a few exceptions, such as pricing, are to be centrally determined. When a company takes this view, there are procedures for answering specific international marketing questions, but it remains that many reorganizations are not so much major restructuring along the lines to be discussed in Chapter 11, but rearrangements of the marketing function – the establishing or abolition of central or regional departments, the reallocation of expertise or other similar changes.

The bias of the reorganizations raises questions about the viability of an international marketing department. Are we not into national marketing in a variety of countries? Those who answer 'yes' point to the heavy overheads incurred by a department which, they consider, contributes little to the well-being of the foreign operations. They also recall a number of notable blunders caused by international marketing policies. Some of these blunders are reported in this book, particularly in the case examples, but many of them have occurred when there was no international marketing department to feed back to other decision-makers intelligence about the foreign markets. The argument from blunder, then, is double-edged. The most powerful support for international marketing is the one suggested in the first paragraph, that the company will need to deploy globally the expertise that has made its expansion abroad possible. This argument underlies much of the discussion, along with three related questions:

1 What are the marketing skills which especially ensure the success of the thrust abroad?
2 Where in the organization are these skills most effectively located?
3 What international standardization is possible or desirable?

The answer to these questions will be related to industry sector and other factors which between them influence corporate policies.

In particular, questions about standardization raise general issues. The applicability of both marketing techniques and product policies world-wide has been much researched over the last 20 years.[1] The issues that have come to light indicate that support for standardization arises from a combination of savings in readily identifiable cost, together with the less tangible savings in mounting a marketing mix world-wide which is already proved in the domestic marketing and of which the company has experience. If a policy starts from such a basis, sound as it appears, it then encounters constraints that cast doubt on the viability of the global scheme. The constraints include the state of the industry and of the accepted selling and distribution channels in the local market, along with cultural factors, population structures and legal problems. An analysis of the costs and benefits of global and local policies is required in each market, and this implies a degree of central decision-making.

7.1 Market research

International market research includes activities that vary from general studies of national markets (considered under corporate planning in Chapter 12) to more detailed investigations that precede a product launch in a new area. Most companies leave the detailed investigations to a local subsidiary or collaborator and, as with domestic research, the investigations are usually contracted out to specialists. Most market research is handled by specialist concerns which match up to their international clients by forming consortium-type arrangements with similar firms in other countries rather than by direct foreign operations. A number of national and international bodies foster these arrangements and endeavour to maintain standards.[2]

Naturally, companies of different sizes relative to the competition will ask different questions. The large company will want to know what market share can reasonably be foreseen within what period of time and at what cost. The answer to these questions may require costly local knowledge. The small company will be looking for a niche, the finding of which will be more critical than detailed knowledge of the market. The amounts at stake are unlikely to justify expensive investigations, but limited research is still vital for success.

The person responsible for market research at head office has a number of options:
1 to leave the decision to the foreign agents or affiliates (hardly feasible when entering a new market, although a regional subsidiary might prove suitable);
2 to act as co-ordinator and adviser to the units abroad;
3 to book research from an international research firm or consortium with a capability in the selected country;
4 to book research with a local company in the market.

For the established international firm, the choice will depend on size and experience. Commonsense would suggest that the services of a consortium, or a market research firm that is international, are most appropriate to an inexperienced operator, but there is no evidence that this is what actually happens. The urgings of advisers, like the British Overseas Trade Board, suggest that many inexperienced operators undertake little serious market research abroad. This could be the reason why product policies, the next subject to be considered, cause so many upheavals.

7.2 Product policies

The usual aim of the exporter is to alter the product as little as possible in order to save costs, to utilize production capacity without expensive changes, and to make the most use of existing expertise. This is where standardization becomes a particularly significant issue. Feedback from the market will, however, frequently suggest changes. In some countries the standard product may be unsaleable; in others hard to sell. In fact, product policies cause a number of difficulties in the process of going international. The following check-list outlines the main issues that will affect the decision.

1 *Product acceptability.* Some products vary little from country to country, although there may well be differences that the consumer does not notice, like changes in electrical equipment to suit local standards. In this connection symbolism is important. A product includes image, packaging, language and presentation as well as the form of the goods or services on offer. In each market the symbolism has to be considered as well as the quality and reliability.

2 *National reputation.* Some products are expected to be international. Alcoholic drinks, for instance, are often judged according to their place of origin. For other products certain countries have established special reputations, like Italy for household appliances. In these cases there is no cause for adaptation but where the reverse applies, national origins are disguised as far as labelling laws allow.

3 *Health and safety regulations.* Each country has its own rules upon items as different as car emission standards (and some car design features, like attachments that might be considered dangerous) and the ingredients of jam or soft drinks. These regulations may force products to change in ways that are not anticipated until the regulations are fully understood.

4 *Consumer protection laws.* These have similar effects, as do other forms of legislation that affect products.

5 *Cultural differences.* Design features and colouring may be unacceptable in some markets.

6 *Other national differences*, like climate, may force changes. A brand of petrol that is designed for temperate areas may not be efficient under conditions of extreme heat or extreme cold.

7 *The product life cycle.* There may well be opportunities to extend a product's life overseas. Goods which have become obsolete in one country (like labour-intensive machinery or soap for hand washing of clothes) may be saleable in another.

Another influence is market segment which will be considered in the next section.

7.3 Customer identification and product image

The positioning of the product in the market will influence the question of standardization, especially in consumer goods. On the whole, up-market products are more universally acceptable than those offered to a wider range of customers to whom national and cultural variations are more important. Some of the issues are illustrated by the contrasting examples of two companies – X and Y.

Company X, in domestic hardware, sold only at the top of the market. Its products were expensive but had a reputation for quality and durability that made the customer consider the price worthwhile. Company Y, on the other hand, pursued a more popular and cheaper segment. Both policies were viable, but the reputation for providing value for money in the chosen segment had taken a long time to build up in each case.

Company X established a chain of subsidiaries around the world. Each enjoyed considerable autonomy so long as it sent home an adequate return on the investment entrusted to it. Two of the subsidiaries decided that more money could be made more easily if they changed their image, and moved down-market. Sales increased in each, but with disastrous consequences elsewhere. The corporate image of quality and reliability was eroded. Sales at the top of the market were reduced without compensating increases elsewhere.

This incident shows how, with international travel and advertising, a carefully established market position in one country can be damaged by actions in another. As a consequence, international management is concerned to ensure that an established segment will be maintained abroad; if there are reasons for a change, a different trademark is required. Company Y suffered an opposite problem when one of its subsidiaries used its autonomy to attempt to move up-market, only to lose trade as customers became confused as to where it stood.

In some countries the appropriate market is harder to identify than in others. The middle class, as known in western industrialized countries, hardly exists in some regions. Greater inequalities of wealth may also produce a different kind of customer at the top of the market from the one the company is accustomed to. Even between industrialized countries there are varying tastes. A degree of ostentation that is appropriate in one country may make an article unsaleable in another. Finally, there is a segment which is itself international. Phrases like 'the jet-set' express a belief in the existence of a group of consumers who have at least as much in common with one another as with their fellow countrymen. Manufacturers of up-market products will be especially concerned with their reputation among this group of big spenders.

7.4 Pricing policies

Market influences on price will vary from country to country and it is the principle rather than the practice which is standard. An important issue is that of the message in the price.[3] This is the statement in money terms of the customer identification. The policy of adjusting prices to the market segment applies universally,

although it will be more familiar in some markets than in others. As a result, international standards are frequently enforced. Local practices, on the other hand,
differ from country to country. The differential, for instance, between an up-market and a more popular product will vary considerably, as will expectations about
the link between price and quality. In a poor country, there may be very wide
margins on goods sold to the wealthy elite, while it may be difficult to recover
costs on goods sold to the poor.

Competition has a double-edged influence on prices, abroad as well as at home.
Low elasticity of demand, found especially in the later stages of a product life cycle,
keeps margins down. On the other hand, the need to provide sufficient incentives
to agents boosts them, especially where exclusive deals are not permitted. Delicate
decisions over agencies are a characteristic of international companies. Place the
margins too high, some companies report of some areas, and they no longer provide an incentive. The agent ceases to make an effort once the income is sufficient
for his needs. Place them too low, and you lose your agent.

Other main influences on pricing include tariffs, price controls, resale price maintenance and sales taxes, as well as less direct influences like other forms of
taxation and consumer protection regulations. Tariffs are, of course, intended to
discriminate against foreign goods but, as they are normally on a percentage
basis, a reduction in the price has a relatively large effect. This reduction may
have to be justified against dumping regulations.

Transfer pricing[4]

One of the most controversial issues for the multinational is that of pricing
between different units. Profits, and therefore tax liabilities, can be moved from
one country to another by raising or lowering the prices at which the goods or
services are transferred, or by lengthening or shortening the period of credit. The
obvious characteristics of such transfers do not help the manager embroiled in
the controversy, and the subject is beset (from his point of view) by emotional
overtones. These can be almost as strong within a company as they are between
a company and outside critics.

The first point to be made is that a decision has to be taken. If the product transferred is of a standard nature, similar to other goods in the same market, it may
be possible to reduce the uncertainties by declaring that the price charged to the
foreign affiliate shall be the standard price that would be charged between two
independent businesses. This is the expectation of the tax and other authorities
as well as of pressure groups who are watching the transfer price. But such a
simple solution is seldom available. Indeed, if the foreign buyer was a separate
company there would be a process of bargaining over the price – a process that
can never be accurately reproduced within a company. Frequently, in any case,
the item transferred will be a component for which there is no market price. In
determining a policy there are a number of options:
1 to fix a price that is as close as possible to an assumed market price;
2 to leave the selling organization to negotiate with the buying – this can be a
   means of arriving at an assumed market price, but the bargaining power is
   unequal if head office is either the seller or the buyer;

3 to determine centrally, either with or without consultation, transfer prices that will assist corporate objectives in the form of saving taxes or postponing their payment.

This last option is to meet the controversies head-on in the belief that the interests of the company require it. An internal problem is that the company's control and appraisal system is sabotaged. The results of a particular unit do not show the true position; they are biased by unearned gains or unmerited losses caused by the transfer prices. Indeed, with so many people watching him, the manager who makes a loss, as a result of instructions from head office, has indeed proved his skill. To overcome the appraisal problem some companies produce elaborate schemes to compensate managers whose accounts show up badly as a result of adverse prices, but the difficulties remain.

At times the problems posed by manipulating prices are ignored. In one example known to the author, instructions to transfer products from one subsidiary to another at a much reduced price were issued by production management at head office. The subsidiary which obeyed these instructions was later reprimanded by another department at head office (the controller's) for the consequential reduction of its profits.

Difficulties with governments are not reduced by the fact that there are always two governments involved (usually with opposing interests). There may also be more than one department within the same administration. A reduction in the transfer price will, for instance, lower the income for the customs and excise at the same time as it increases that for the inland revenue.

Through the controversies, hard evidence is in short supply. A number of dramatic illustrations have been documented of the apparent use of transfer pricing to reduce artificially the profits in particular countries.[5] These have usually been the result of special investigations stimulated by other issues, like monopolies legislation in Britain, although more general allegations have been made as a result of research into the pricing policies of multinationals in developing countries. The piecemeal evidence has, not unnaturally, led to conflicting interpretations. Some commentators affirm that much is being made of a few isolated incidents, others that these same incidents are to be compared with the tip of an iceberg. Different pricing policies – both on the part of companies and their critics – can make a considerable difference (goods can be expected to cost more in a small market, for instance, if allowance is made for the extra expense of small consignments). Even so, the suspicion that companies do have something to hide is nurtured by the secrecy with which pricing policies are surrounded, even in firms otherwise known for their openness. However, against this, companies argue that their unwillingness to reveal prices is due to the difficulties involved, including that of interpretation, rather than the need to conceal practices which might be criticized.

These conflicting statements are accompanied by contradictory perceptions inside companies. The position usually maintained, at least to the outsider, is that juggling with transfer prices brings more problems than benefits. On the other hand, there are some companies where the benefits are strongly maintained. In either case, it is clear that prices have to be determined (goods are unlikely to be transferred free!), that the price is often fixed as a result of tough bargaining – as it would be to an outside customer – and that an ability to reduce the tax bill may well be argued as part of the bargaining process.

The results of bargaining between different units of a company and with outside suppliers and customers (including agents and licensees) will help to determine the costs and benefits of direct investment – what savings (if any) are available by bringing the market inside the company.

7.5 Promotion and sales

A number of issues appear under this heading.

The control of sales areas

That instructions to subsidiaries and other affiliates about which markets they may sell into are a controversial issue has already been recorded. To governments trying to promote national exports it is a scandal that foreign companies impose restrictions; to companies, on the other hand, it is commonsense. It would be difficult to make plans or agreements for local production if it was not possible to calculate the size of the market to be served and this depends on the sales area; and that is not the only problem. Direct competition confuses the customer if salesmen from the same company quote different terms. Some large firms can afford to permit such competition. Most allocate market areas in spite of political hostility.

Advertising

Customs and tastes vary so much from country to country that a message can be reversed when carried across a frontier. Examples of this include cigarette or drink advertisements which appeal in one country, but have the opposite effect in another where the sexual *mores* are different. Most countries have laws or voluntary regulations to control advertising. In Germany, for instance, knocking copy – where one company attacks another in its advertisements – is not allowed, and many other countries have restrictions on comparative advertising as it is called (see *The Economist*, 18–24 May 1991, pages 93 and 96). It is likely that some restrictions will apply throughout the European Union.

The customer who is most suitably reached by one medium (say radio) in one country is not reached that way in another if the target audience is reading magazines. Advertising has itself become an international industry, and there are numerous organizations or consortia to steer a company through the pitfalls. Indeed, advertising is an example of an industry which has become international to service existing customers.

According to a report published in *The Economist*, the proportion of world advertising expenditure handled by international agencies increased from 13 per cent in 1976 to 20 per cent in 1985. The same article refers to the growth of consortia (calling them 'networks') and points to the fact that clients are forcing the pace by reducing the number of agencies they employ.[6]

Selling

The recruitment and training of salesmen is usually left to the subsidiary. A company may organize international conferences to introduce new products or promotional techniques, but selling is a local activity requiring an intimate knowledge of language and customs. Subtle differences in the law also provide traps for those trying to sell in more than one country. There are laws of unfair competition in some parts of Europe of a kind that are almost unknown in others. Restrictions on trading stamps, special offers and other selling devices are introduced to support small shopkeepers in some countries. In spite of these differences, there are occasions when international selling makes especially good sense, like major construction contracts which are usually negotiated by teams from head office. International selling techniques are also practised by franchising companies, when attendance at central training institutions is a condition of the franchise.

Other forms of promotion

The international company provides incentives to its dealers abroad by bringing them to the home country and providing travel facilities for themselves and their families. The transfer of successful trading schemes from one country to another is also possible.

Systems selling

Increasingly, companies are selling systems rather than individual products. In heavy machinery, for instance, the hardware and the software as well as operator training, maintenance and other back-up facilities are required in one package. One implication is the need for co-operation in the sales drive between all the supplying firms. Research has stressed the requirements of interdependence and the extent to which this is a growing feature of technical sales.[7]

7.6 Other elements in the marketing mix

A number of other topics – as diverse as packaging, credit and after-sales back-up – are essential elements of international marketing.

Packaging

Even standardized products may have to be packaged differently when they cross frontiers. Many countries have regulations about the type of container allowed – in some cases a returnable container is compulsory, in others forbidden – and about labelling and other details. In some markets there are no regulations, but local customs and preferences still make adaptation necessary. While packaging that can afterwards be used for another purpose is popular with some consumers, it can breed suspicions of overcharging with others. Many products are suited to a standard international package, but policies on the subject have to be reviewed country by country.

After-sales

The replacement of defective goods is legally enforced in many countries but, whatever the law, exporters will need to match the competition. After-sales service can be regarded as a marketing weapon in its own right. The repair facilities may be the distinctive feature of a product that enables it to achieve its market share. A requirement for these facilities will affect other corporate policies, including the selection of agents and the need for a local subsidiary.

Credit terms

Local conditions may necessitate some ingenuity in formulating credit terms. Statements about interest rates and required deposits vary from country to country, as well as rules about the advertising of credit terms. Inflation rates will also influence the terms offered.

Distribution

This subject will be discussed in Chapter 10.

Trade fairs and exhibitions

Opinions vary about the cost-effectiveness of exhibitions in other countries, but they do allow for making and receiving contacts with likely customers. The costs of these and other special promotions are often defrayed by governments or assisted by Chambers of Commerce, International Trade Centres and similar organizations.

7.7 Countertrade

Boeing and Rolls Royce once agreed to accept between them 35 million barrels of oil in payment for ten 747–300 frames, 40 engines and sets of spares. At the same time, an Australian affiliate of the Netherlands company Van Ommeren International Trade started to supply sheep meat to Iran in exchange for crude oil.[8] The British Government has accepted oil in part payment for military aircraft to Saudi Arabia. These examples illustrate the growth of barter, or countertrade, deals and the dangers they contain – including the risks of taking such large quantities of oil at a time of uncertainty in the market.

Increasingly, the salesman encounters the demand that part payment be made in goods. Countertrade is most common among the wealthier developing countries, including China, but is spreading elsewhere. In the early 1980s a survey undertaken by the General Agreement on Tariffs and Trade found that countertrade accounted for 8 per cent of world trade ($160bn) and 15 per cent of Eastern European trade. A study of the Organisation for Economic Cooperation and Development (OECD), on the other hand, estimated about $80bn for the total, including about 10 per cent of trade between developing nations and 30 per cent of developing-country trade with Eastern Europe.[9] Both the overall figures, different as they are, are smaller than many current estimates which vary up to as much as $720bn.

The OECD study lists 53 developing countries which were reported to be showing an interest in countertrade, in addition to the countries of Eastern Europe. It also reports that western companies favour it as a means of retaining markets where import controls and other restrictions are severe or where competition is fierce. The study was critical of the growth of countertrade on the grounds that it did not effectively conserve scarce currency, while it did add extra costs for both parties and did 'cause additional distortions to the trading system and detract from the efficiency of adjustment mechanisms.'

Some countertrade agreements are highly ingenious. The author's attention has been drawn to the case of a British confectionery manufacturer which has established a factory in India solely to supply the Russian market. The sweets are exchanged (countertraded) for Russian machinery which India imports.

Whatever the force of the arguments against more countertrade, the trend is not likely to change in the short-term because there is no suitable alternative. The international marketer is increasingly likely to find countertrade on the agenda, especially in international construction contracts or in the sale of capital equipment. Once competitors agree to barter, it becomes a necessary part of the business deal. The exporter is then left with two problems: how to value the goods offered, normally a relatively small part of the total payment, and how to sell them. The value is not too difficult to determine, it hinges around a real or assumed market price. The sale, however, presents greater difficulties, especially when the connection between the goods bought and those offered in return is not obvious. For instance, it may seem logical to the buyer to offer products in return for machinery. But machinery manufacturers may have no expertise at all in the sale of the goods produced by the machines. On the contrary, such sales can bring them into competition with their customers.

Larger companies have the option of setting up their own organizations for coping with the products (General Electric, General Motors and McDonnell Douglas have done so) or of setting up specialized subsidiaries in countries where there is already expertise available. Smaller companies will have to use agents or companies that specialize in barter deals. Undoubtedly barter will continue because it carries considerable advantage for countries with payments problems and for those struggling to make an impact on world markets.

7.8 External affairs

A limited number of international companies have developed a new department to co-ordinate their relations with the non-commercial environment – including dealings with governments, pressure groups and other institutions. The following are among the principal activities.

1 Relationships with governments and with intergovernmental institutions.
2 Relationships with pressure groups concerned with conservation, consumer protection, women's rights, the position of minorities, civil liberties and other causes.

3 Relationships with public and private organizations in other countries.
4 Briefing managers on subjects of current controversy.
5 Providing the company with an early warning system about new developments in the business environment which demand some corporate response.
6 Advising the company on issues of social responsibility and about its response to criticisms on this score.
7 Channelling the company's contribution to educational and charitable causes and providing papers, speakers and publications for outside bodies, including the media. This activity includes making known the company's contribution to knowledge in its field of business. It can also include training executives for radio or television appearances.
8 Other activities designed to enhance the reputation of the company and correct criticisms which would come under the remit of a normal public relations department.

Most of the companies that pioneered external affairs departments were large and well-known and with a high profile that made them vulnerable. Usually they have been in the chemical, electronics or petroleum sectors. The department goes under a variety of names, but the organization is similar. The starting-point is pressure on the part of some individual or group concerned about the impact the company is making. The first steps are usually to promote a small specialist unit to monitor the environment. From this beginning other functions will gradually be added, until the department become fully established. The staff will gradually build up relationships with other organizations, including government departments.

For further information, see: Boddewyn, J.J., *Corporate External Affairs* (New York: Business International, 1975).

7.9 Exercises, questions and further reading

Case examples

Car Components AB – export territories

Car Components AB, a middle-sized Swedish company ($500m annual sales) manufacturing a range of automotive parts had begun to build up a network of small manufacturing or servicing subsidiaries in a number of countries. The initial impetus had been to support foreign sales (69 per cent of the business) and especially to provide a more reliable service to international customers. After a few years the company began to encounter problems over sales areas. The growing pace of its aggressive marketing policies led to orders in more countries, and sales teams from head office were encountering those from subsidiaries, while the subsidiaries themselves were competing with one another and sometimes in their home markets. The problem was most acute in the car manufacturing countries in Europe, America (North and South) and the Far East, but others were also included since their products were imported as spares into 34 non-manufacturing countries. The principal subsidiaries or joint ventures were in Brazil, Canada, France, Germany, Japan, Korea, Malaysia, the United Kingdom, the United States and Yugoslavia.

To meet the problem, Car Components AB had begun to formulate some rules which included the following.

1 No member of the group was allowed to export into the home territory of other members.

2 Members of the group were free to compete with one another in other territories *so long as* they used different trademarks. This proved unexpectedly popular with agents who found that they could sell the same products under different names. It was unpopular within the parent company where a loss of international impact against competitors was feared.

Car Components AB was wondering whether the rules needed reframing and if so how this could be done. The company had been warned that if the restrictions on export were leaked in at least one Latin American country, the results could be serious for their business there and cause legal problems for senior executives. In general, the directors were being pressed, often in contradictory terms, between their experts at head office and their affiliates, agents and dealers overseas.

Questions

1 List and discuss some of the ways in which international market research differs from domestic.

2 Assume a company in an industry of your choice with rapidly increasing exports, and outline the reasoning process that might lead to a decision to establish a marketing subsidiary abroad.

3 Consider the advantages and disadvantages of a standard international advertising programme and the circumstances in which it might be used.

4 Examine critically the statement that international marketing is an extension of domestic marketing with no significant differences.

5 International product standardization has been called one of the illusions of the international marketer. Discuss.

6 Transfer pricing is controversial inside a company as well as outside. Identify and analyse the internal conflicts that are likely to arise.

7 Picture a large chemical company suffering from bad publicity in the host country of one of its subsidiaries. What measures, if any, should the parent company take if it suspects that the bad publicity is damaging the business? Explain the reasons for your proposals.

Further reading

Daniels, J.D. and Radebaugh (1995), ch.17.
Håkansson, H., ed., *International Marketing and Purchasing of Industrial Goods*, (Wiley, 1982).
Robinson (1984) ch. 2.
Terpstra, V. (1983).

8 International financial management

This chapter is concerned with management functions often found within the finance department, such as: determining the sources and uses of funds, understanding foreign monetary systems, the management of accounting, control, taxation and insurance, along with two, legal and administration, which are sometimes under finance. Aspects of administration are to be found in Chapters 9 and 11, while corporate planning, which may also come under finance, is the subject of Chapter 12.

The finance department of an international company requires a number of different skills: those of the analyst, the banker, the accountant, the controller, the planner (the 'thruster' who requires different skills from the controller, the 'policeman' with whom the post is usually associated), the administrator and the lawyer are the most obvious. Some activities of the department are listed in Table 8.1 and form the subject of the next seven sections, beginning with the raising of funds.

Table 8.1 Functions of international money management

Sources and uses of funds (including remittance policies and exchange risks)
Project appraisal
Understanding foreign monetary systems
Accounting
Control and planning
Taxation
Insurance
Legal and administrative

8.1 Sources and uses of funds

The main object in raising capital is to ensure that money is available at the right time, in the right place and at the lowest possible cost. Funds can be raised in various parts of the world at different interest rates, but their cost for any particular project also depends on exchange rates and taxes. Sometimes, in countries with high interest rates, inflation is also high. In this case, the cost of capital is less than appears as repayments will be made out of devalued funds, not forgetting that revenues will also be transmitted out of devalued funds – but this devaluation is short-term compared to that of loan repayments.

There may be restrictions on the movement of funds or there may be other constraints which make borrowing in the most favourable market impossible, while the preferred means of raising capital will partly depend on the uses for which the money is intended. The following are some examples:

1 *Export.* Sales abroad will usually be financed by bank borrowings at home, supported by export credit guarantees.[1]
2 *Construction projects* (which also need export credit guarantees) may be funded from a combination of home and foreign sources, perhaps through a consortium of banks, and supported (when appropriate) by international agencies like the World Bank.
3 *Foreign collaborators.* Agents, licensees and other partners are normally financed from their national sources, but may receive funding from abroad, some of it from the parent company.
4 *Foreign investment* is also supported by funds raised both at home and abroad, sometimes from inside and sometimes from outside a company.

In general, deciding how and where to raise capital starts from a review of the resources available within the company. This is followed by a process of ascertaining where outside capital can be obtained at the lowest total cost. A formula is required for determining the costs, which has to allow for taxes, exchange rates and other relevant factors. The next step is to check the effect of any particular source on the risks of the venture and the chances of a reasonable return. Finally, the availability of the funds is rechecked, to be followed by an investigation of returns, likely problems, taxation, rules about transferring funds and other implications of the chosen methods.

Capital structure

There are several types of capital which can provide the funds needed for foreign ventures; the phrase *capital structure* is used of a mixture of sources selected for a particular company or subsidiary. The four main types are: equity (shares), long-term debt (debentures), short-term loans, and retained earnings (depreciation allowances and profits). For the parent company there are conventions, which vary from country to country, on the proportion of equity to debt. There will also be variations between industries, related to risks and opportunities, but the parent company will have similar gearing to that of a domestic firm.

It is a principle of gearing (leverage) that if a high proportion of the capital is in the form of debt, then the shareholders will do well if the company is highly profitable (more money is available for dividends on less shares), but badly if there is a downturn (a higher proportion of the income is required to service the loans). Debt–equity ratios vary from below 30 per cent to above 70 per cent, according to both the country and the industry sector. If a foreign subsidiary possesses local equity capital – shares issued in the host country for the affiliate as opposed to the parent – its capital structure and therefore its gearing is likely to resemble that of any other public company. For a subsidiary that is owned 100 per cent, different considerations apply. The proportion of equity is typically less and the largest part of the capital is from retained earnings. An example of a financial structure for a wholly owned subsidiary is shown in Table 8.2.

This example shows a high proportion of retained earnings. This is normal in foreign subsidiaries, but much higher debt is also not unusual. This is possible because the parent company is consolidating low debt with high debt operations. The loans can come from the parent company, other subsidiaries, local sources or foreign sources outside the company.

Table 8.2 Financial structure of a wholly-owned subsidiary

	%
Retained earnings (profit after payment of dividend + provision for depreciation)	55
Borrowing in the host country (short- and long-term, which may be guaranteed by the parent company)	30
Borrowing from parent or from other subsidiary	7
Other sources	3
Equity from parent	5
TOTAL CAPITAL	100

Criteria for determining the capital structure include:
1 increasing the profits, especially those at the disposal of the parent company,
2 reducing the risks,
3 maintaining maximum flexibility in planning for the future,
4 establishing an appropriate level of gearing (leverage).

Fluctuating exchange rates have persuaded finance managers that, where all other factors are equal, as high a proportion of loan finance as possible should be raised locally. Reinforcing this is the view that bankruptcy costs for individual units are lower than those for domestic firms as well as the need for equity funds elsewhere. However, where political risk is low and restrictions on transferring dividends are light, a low proportion of debt to equity may be preferred.

In either case, there will be equity and possibly loan finance from the parent company. Other sources include funds from government departments and local authorities in the host countries, and from international funding institutions, such as the World Bank and the regional development banks, some of which are described in Chapter 16. The principal sources, classified by whether they arise inside the company or from without, are summarized in Table 8.3.

The availability of finance from the parent company may be restricted by exchange controls (although this restriction is less common than it used to be, the industrialized nations, from which most foreign investment still comes, have been reducing their controls), while other constraints will influence the final structure. A bank guarantee may be required for local loans, and this is not to be regarded as a nominal risk, as has already been demonstrated (see Chapter 3, the example of Wilmot Breeden). This guarantee is important to the outside lender, but the capital structure of the subsidiary is not. The security of the loan rests with the parent company whose own capital arrangements will indicate its stability.

Table 8.3 Sources of funds

Internal to subsidiary:	depreciation
	undistributed profits
Internal to the company:	equity from parent
	loans from parent or another subsidiary
External (in host country):	equity
	long-term debt
	bank loans
External (outside host country):	loans from financial institutions
	international sources

In the changing conditions of international finance, increasing resort to the bond markets is likely.

Remittance policies

A principal objective of the international company is to make the optimum use of its resources; to this end a centralized view of financing is usual. The ability to transfer funds when required is vital and this implies the use of as many different routes as possible, in the hope that the blocking of one route by exchange or other controls will leave another open. In the general tidying up of national finances achieved by the International Monetary Fund (IMF), the blocking of remittances (as opposed to delays caused by controls and conditions) is less common than it used to be, but the memory still influences policies. Some of the options are listed below.

1 *The payment of dividends.* This is usually the most highly taxed route and the one most subject to government restrictions. The money cannot be moved until after the end of the financial year, so the risk is increased by the delay.

2 *The payment of royalties for patents and technical information.* This method usually attracts a lower tax rate, although some countries have now taken to imposing higher levies, alleging that companies are overcharging for the use of their technology. Royalty payments are, as a rule, less restricted than dividends and the money can be remitted when the information is provided.

3 *The payment of fees for management services.* This is often tax-free, with few restrictions, and remitted promptly, although the payment will have to be justified to the tax authorities who may lay charges of fraud if they are not satisfied that the services are being provided.

4 *Payment for goods and services supplied from head office or any other unit of the firm.* Reducing the payments made by the subsidiary will automatically move money into a country and vice versa. However, these payments are likely to be closely scrutinized in both the home and the host countries.

5 *Charges for goods and services provided to other units of the company.* The same considerations will apply as for payments.

6 *Loans between units of the company.* Both the payment of interest and the timing of repayments of the loan are means of moving money.

7 *The timing of any of the payments.* Delaying any of the payments will increase the funds available to the subsidiary, accelerating them will increase the cash available elsewhere in the company.

Numbers 4, 5 and 7 have already been considered under the heading of transfer pricing in Chapter 7. During periods of acute balance-of-payments problems or foreign currency shortages, all remittances may be blocked.

Risk management

Ensuring that as many methods as possible are available for transferring funds across national frontiers, but within the company, reduces the risk. Companies that concentrate on profit (remitted in the form of dividends) may find the money blocked by exchange-control regulations, reduced by taxes or devalued during the delay in payment – or possibly all three. At the same time, other methods have to be justified to the authorities and within the company, and each has its drawbacks. Therefore, a combination of methods is the safest way of ensuring that money is transferred to head office either for paying dividends there or for adding to the pool of capital.

Naturally, a particular subsidiary can be expanded at any time by reversing the procedures for moving money out. One argument for 100 per cent ownership is that the choice of policies for transferring funds is much more restricted when there are local shareholders. They will constitute a pressure group for making, and retaining, profits within the subsidiary. In general, the following risks have to be considered.

Losses through currency fluctuations

There can, of course, also be gains and certain situations need to be scrutinized carefully. For instance, the capital value of a subsidiary may be reduced by devaluation, but its income may be increased when its products become more competitive as a result. There are two kinds of risk to be considered. One is the translation loss which arises if the currency in a subsidiary's country declines in relation to that in the home country. This loss can itself be divided into two. One is the balance sheet loss which may affect the share price marginally, but is otherwise irrelevant unless assets are to be sold; the other is the loss on remittances from the particular subsidiary. The timing of such remittances, to make gains where possible and reduce losses to a minimum, has been described[2] as 'the fundamental challenge' to the finance manager, and this has led to a rapid growth in forecasting services. The other kind of risk is that of *economic* loss which takes account of the relevant conditions to balance the consequences of currency changes.

A subsidiary which is remitting in a devalued currency, for example, is doing this for purchases as well as for profits. Further, the devaluation of the currency may be the result of a boom in spending in the country which has caused a balance of payments crisis. This boom can mean that higher profits are being transferred and that these compensate for adverse exchange rates. These examples oversimplify a complicated sequence of considerations, but the message is that it is the overall gain or loss that matters to the company rather than the effects on one particular transaction. This approach suggests that the most effective way of reducing risks to a minimum is by diversifying sources and increasing income. Nevertheless, companies use a number of devices like loans in different currencies and buying currency forward.

Losses through expropriation or liquidation

A spread of activities is the most effective insurance, a slump in one market hopefully being balanced by success in another, but this option is not available to a small company. Even for a large company a spread undertaken too rapidly, or on too small a scale, can lead to greater risks. A company that is large enough can reduce the risk of loss and, at the same time, increase the possibilities of gain – high profit potential often accompanies high risk – by its spread of investment. The inadequate servicing of a market can also lead to its loss.

One means of reducing risks is to seek a loan that is provided in a number of different currencies at once, like the Special Drawing Rights of the IMF or the

European Currency Units. Such a loan can minimize the impact of exchange fluctuations.

8.2 Project appraisal

The process of deciding where fresh investments are to be placed is considered in the chapter on corporate planning. The role of the finance department is to operate financial techniques designed to indicate the most promising proposals and to eliminate those with little chance of achieving the required return on investment or other criteria. The methods of appraisal are not essentially different from those used for domestic projects with which they are in competition for corporate resources. The main difference is that foreign-exchange and other risks have to be built into the calculation.[3]

8.3 Understanding foreign monetary systems

The discussion so far assumes that corporate finance managers, or their advisers, have acquired some familiarity with foreign money markets, each of which has its own rules and customs as well as its special traps for the unwary. A low-cost loan can turn out to be very expensive indeed if conditions are attached which make unexpected repayments, or interest rate increases, necessary at difficult times. The ideal capital structure may be difficult to achieve in one country because of local traditions about the proportion of debt or equity required, while loans in another may be hard to negotiate because of credit restrictions or a general shortage of capital. In general, however, investors do favour international companies; they are considered highly creditworthy, and therefore eligible for favourable rates of interest.

8.4 Accounting

A finance officer in an international company may have to read the accounts of subsidiaries and collaborators in many different countries, each with their own special conventions. The differences between countries are often puzzling and lead to misinterpretations. To reduce the problems most companies insist that their foreign subsidiaries present their accounts according to the conventions of the home country. Naturally, the insistence can only extend to those affiliates which are actually owned by the parent company – if a finance manager wishes to examine the accounts of collaborators like agents or licensees he must expect to receive them according to local conventions, if at all – but the translation of the financial statements can be a burden to a small affiliate. Some of the differences are comparatively detailed, but can still have a considerable effect on the results. For example, an apparent profit can mask a loss when an item, which at home would be shown as a debit in the revenue account, appears in the capital account of the subsidiary. Depreciation allowances also vary from country to country, both according to accounting conventions and to tax allowances. Other differences concern the underlying philosophy of an accounting system or the main features of corporate performance that are being measured. Four main types have been identified:

1 *The macroeconomic*, in which the firm is seen as a unit of the national economy and the accounts are presented in such a way as to assist government planners. Sweden is an example of this approach.
2 *The microeconomic*, in which the emphasis is on the survival and maintenance, in real terms, of the corporate investment. This method is used in the Netherlands.
3 *The independent discipline*, in which the accounts are held to provide an acceptable valuation of the progress of a company. This is the system that prevails in Britain, Canada and the United States.
4 *The uniform*, in which the accounts are compiled to a simple set of uniform rules which are applied to all circumstances, as in France and Germany.[4]

Note: Within the European Union, accounting standards have now been harmonized. As a result, these differences no longer apply although it has been alleged that the harmonization is 'more apparent than real' (*International Management*, June 1991, page 52; this article illustrates the effects of different accounting systems on profits).

In addition to variations which arise out of different accounting methods, there are varieties of legal system. For instance, the amount of information that a company must disclose varies from country to country in spite of a tendency to greater openness in recent years. Both governments and stock markets have been insisting that more detail be made available, but there are still wide differences. A French company may not be required to publish details of its operations in its own country, but be forced to make public those of a wholly-owned subsidiary elsewhere.[5] Standardized accounting is currently being promoted by the European Union and by the United Nations.

8.5 Control and planning

The finance department will certainly be responsible for the control system and perhaps for corporate planning as well. The control system consists of the operating figures of the subsidiary – financial, marketing and production – submitted at regular intervals. Financial controls vary from a few simple ratios to a demand for full operating figures and variations from budget. Frequently included would be income statements (sometimes broken down by product and by customer), cash balances, export sales, payment details, changes in borrowings and other balance-sheet details – all presented to spotlight differences from plan. The frequency and the detail required are both the subject of controversy. Too seldom can be dangerous as problems go undetected, but intervals of two years are not unknown; too frequent can be an expensive problem for the subsidiary, but weekly reports are also not unknown. Monthly reporting is usually recommended.

The demand for too much detail can also make difficulties for the subsidiary and can divert managerial attention from more pressing matters. Those companies which require reports at monthly or more frequent intervals do, in any case, usually demand greater detail quarterly or annually.

The purposes of a control system are as:

1 a measurement of performance;
2 a means of directing the attention of subsidiary executives to priority objectives (by selecting the items on which reports are required);
3 an early warning of impending trouble;
4 a means of collecting information for salary and promotion decisions;
5 a means of collecting information for accounting, for planning and for answering enquiries;[6]
6 a means of directing attention to the strengths and weaknesses of subsidiary management;
7 an educational process for the executives involved.

There are problems in making the control system convincing as a measure of performance when so many decisions are outside the influence of a particular subsidiary – including its pricing policies and choice of markets if centrally decided. However, a standardized control system does provide a universal language which can absorb an extraordinary amount of information, including comparisons across frontiers. It has behind it a profession and a considerable body of theory. On the other hand, it is considered oppressive and often irrelevant to subsidiary managers who may harbour grievances about information which they consider misleading, especially when obedience to the wishes and policies of head office appears to produce a poor performance. It is also seen as arbitrary, rooted in the past, and not sufficiently sensitive to change.

Corporate planning is related to the control system because much of the data requested is used by the planners. This is considered in Chapter 12, where it is asserted that the control reporting provides the most used information, but that this may not always be in the best interests of a company facing changing circumstances which make previous experience irrelevant.

8.6 Taxation[7]

The development of policies to minimize taxes and negotiations with the tax authorities are among the most complex activities undertaken by the finance department. Domestic taxes, which are themselves sufficiently complex, deal with allowances, depreciation, stocks and the definition of a profit. None of the tug-of-war between different national tax authorities affects the domestic finance manager, whose international counterpart has a number of additional items on his agenda including the following.

I Trading with or within a country

Profits on exports are not taxed in the destination country. Some form of permanent establishment is required to make the profits liable to local taxes; but the affiliate does not have to be incorporated to become eligible for tax, it only has to have a fixed place of business. However, the type of incorporation makes a difference to the taxes paid at home. Typically, branch profits are taxable in the home country, whether or not they are remitted, while branch losses can be off-set against domestic profits. With a subsidiary, on the other hand, only the remitted profits (those sent to head office) are liable to tax in the home country, and losses cannot be offset against profits in any other country. As a result, it is often an advantage for tax reasons to operate through a branch in the early unprofitable years even if, for other reasons, a subsidiary may be preferred – for instance because it offers limited liability which a branch does not. Another advantage of a branch is that most countries do not impose withholding taxes on payments, whereas dividends, interest and royalties are all liable to these taxes. Nevertheless, most companies eventually opt for a subsidiary.

2 The possibility of choosing in which country a profit is shown by manipulating currency transfers within the company

This will be undertaken against the ingenuity of revenue departments who may impute a profit for tax purposes if they suspect that manipulation has taken place. There will also be problems inside the company when the measurement of a sub-sidiary's performance becomes impossible through the action of central finance, resulting in unfair judgements on individual managers and possible demoraliza-tion.

3 The possibility of moving money to countries where corporate taxes are not charged or at least taking advantage of differential taxes

Tax havens (like the Cayman Islands or the Bahamas) are typically small coun-tries or dependencies with some degree of tax autonomy. They promote their facilities for taxpayers as a means of generating business for themselves. The com-pany only requires a small office and the tax concessions are usually enhanced by banking and commercial secrecy, efficient telecommunications and a liberal exchange regime – at least for non-residents. Each tax haven country has its own specialized regulations. There is a view that many countries can be considered as tax havens in certain circumstances – that, in spite of increasing pressure by tax regulators, money can profitably be transferred to save taxes.[8]

The advantages and disadvantages of tax havens are much debated. For the com-pany, the route and timing of the payments will determine whether there is an advantage. There is the immediate benefit that the tax difference between the home and host country is not paid when the money is moved if the tax in the home country is higher than that in the host. Thus tax rates of 45 per cent and 30 per cent respectively mean that the extra 15 per cent is not paid if the money is moved into a tax haven. If it acquires interest while there, or is subsequently moved in the form of a loan rather than a dividend, or is moved to another sub-sidiary in a low tax country, then tax will have been saved.

The growing number of registrations in tax havens suggests that companies do obtain advantages, and many administrations have moved to offset them. In the United States, for instance, an enactment that goes back to 1962 decrees that profits from intermediaries are deemed to have been remitted to the parent company even if they have not. Canada, the German Federal Republic, Japan and many other countries have similar legislation. More generally, tax-haven subsidiaries are excluded from the benefits of bilateral treaties and their transactions are likely to lead to investigations by the authorities.

4 The understanding of widely differing national tax systems

The differences lie partly in the relative proportions of different levies, partly in different methods of assessment and enforcement, and partly in different taxes. The main levies are:

1 Direct taxes on profits. These may be local as well as national, and distributed profits sometimes pay a lower rate than those retained, on the grounds that the recipients will be paying personal income taxes on their dividends.
2 Indirect taxes, usually on sales. In the countries of the European Union, the principal indirect levy is Value Added Tax (VAT). This has the advantage that it can be rebated on exports (a rebate allowed by the regulations of the General Agreement on Tariffs and Trade, see Chapter 16).
3 Withholding taxes on the transfer of funds across frontiers, which usually vary with the type of funds (dividends, royalties and so on) being transferred.
4 Miscellaneous taxes on machinery, on official documents and on other selected targets.
5 Excise duties levied on alcohol, petrol, tobacco and other commodities.

5 The problem of double taxation

This arises when income from a subsidiary is taxed once in the country where it is earned, and again in its home country after being repatriated to form part of the profits of the parent company. A similar problem arises in personal taxation for executives who earn part of their salaries abroad and are typically the subject of complex tax rules as a result. Most countries tax the foreign earnings of domestic companies. There are a few exceptions, mainly in Latin America, where only income generated in a country is taxed, not foreign earnings. If this practice were universal, there would be no problem of double taxation. In any case there are difficulties in identifying taxable profits and deductible expenses between two countries. A number of methods of relieving double taxation occur; otherwise much international business would be impossible. The two most usual methods are: unilateral relief by the home country and bilateral treaties.

1 *Unilateral relief* implies an acceptance that a prior claim lies with the country in which the tax is earned and that, as a result, adjustments have to be made in the home country. These take the form either of exempting foreign source income – as in France and the Netherlands – thereby favouring profits abroad, or of allowing *foreign tax credits*. Most of the larger capital-exporting countries – including the German Federal Republic, Japan, the United Kingdom and the United States – adopt this latter method. There are many variations but, in principle, the home country allows the parent company to credit the taxes paid in the host country against its liabilities at home. The concession, which usually includes withholding taxes, only applies to money actually remitted by the subsidiary. This maintains neutrality of tax burden as between home and

foreign earnings, except where host country taxes are lower and the company does not remit the earnings. In this case, the foreign tax credit system favours investment in a lower tax country.

2 *Bilateral treaties* provide, as a rule, that the home country renounces its claims on foreign taxed income, while the host country lowers or waives the withholding tax. In addition, the treaties usually provide for an exchange of information and for active co-operation between the administrations in the two countries. A network of bilateral treaties exists between member countries of the Organisation for Economic Cooperation and Development which has established guidelines for such treaties. Developing countries are increasingly negotiating similar arrangements.

6 Unitary taxation

This refers to the charging of tax calculated on the profits of a company as a whole and not just on those made within the jurisdiction of a particular authority. The attempt to levy this tax has arisen as a result of suspicions about the manipulation of transfer prices and a general lack of information on the activities of international companies. The subject became especially controversial when a number of individual American states threatened to impose unitary taxation rigorously. The companies argued that such action was contrary to double taxation agreements. The issue was also taken up with the Federal authorities by European governments with investors in the states concerned, and reprisals were threatened.[9] Whatever the conclusion of these particular cases, national authorities will undoubtedly continue to tax companies on the profits they assume they should have earned within the country (the *imputed* profits). This is not, of course, the same as unitary tax; but between imputed taxes and unitary taxes, governments are likely to experiment with various means of achieving the aim of ensuring that companies are prevented from limiting their contributions in countries in which their subsidiaries operate.

7 Tax concessions

These are offered in many countries, especially the developing countries, to attract foreign direct investment. They take a number of forms including:
1 exemption from corporate tax in the initial years (tax holidays),
2 accelerated depreciation or outright investment grants.

Larger companies may use their strength to negotiate concessions but the decisions are usually taken on other grounds. The concessions are negotiated as an addition to the income from a project that has been agreed for different reasons. Smaller companies may be more influenced by the concessions, but to be overinfluenced by tax concessions can lead to trouble. They do not usually repay the costs involved in operating in a difficult area and, in any case, the taxes levied in the early unprofitable years of a project may well be negligible.

To the above seven items should be added:
8 The special taxation of foreign income as well as concessions to avoid double taxation.

9 The general implications for tax purposes of foreign affiliates, their accounting methods and the form and timing of their remittances.

The ability to keep the tax bill to a minimum is undoubtedly an important function of the finance department; it operates through controversial policies like
influencing corporate pricing to more humdrum (albeit time-consuming) decisions about changing the dates for annual accounts in the subsidiaries. The
danger is that tax minimization becomes an aim in its own right, with the result
that long-term objectives are missed for the sake of short-term tax gains. In some
companies a mystique is built up around the importance of tax reduction to corporate income. Unless confiscatory, taxes are a proportion of profits. To sacrifice
profits tomorrow for tax gains today is only helpful in the short-term.

Further reading

Overviews of foreign tax systems can be found in the publications (generally
loose-leaf, for ready updating) of the International Bureau of Fiscal
Documentation, Amsterdam, and in publications by multinational accounting
firms such as Arthur Andersen, Ernst and Young and Price Waterhouse.

Adams, J. and Whalley, J., *The International Taxation of Multinational Enterprises
in Developed Countries*, (Greenwood Press, 1977).

Humpage, O., 'U.S. Taxation of Foreign-Source Corporate Income: A Survey of
Issues', *Federal Reserve Bank of Cleveland, Economic Review*, (Winter
1980/1981).

Kopits, G., *Taxation and Multinational Firm Behaviour: A Critical Survey*, IMF
Staff Papers (November 1976).

Plasschaerts, S., 'The Design of Schedular and Global Systems of Income Taxation
– The International Dimension', *Bulletin for International Fiscal
Documentation*, (August/September 1981).

Sato, M. and Bird, R., *International Aspects of the Taxation of Corporations and
Shareholders*, IMF Staff Papers, (July 1975).

8.7 Insurance

The insurance industry is one which has developed internationally, partly in order
to spread risk and partly to service international customers. Some companies have
established or bought their own insurance subsidiaries to cope with their needs.[10]
A specialized type of insurance is that for export credit which is handled by
government agencies in many countries, although private insurers are on the
increase. Similar arrangements apply to the insurance of investment. Public and
private bodies are represented on an international organization – the Berne Union
– which brings together a wide range of expertise. A problem of export credit
insurance is that it easily becomes a subsidy. To avoid this, the Organisation for
Economic Cooperation and Development has adopted guidelines on the forms
of credit allowed. These have been agreed by all the member countries, but some
of the wording is vague and has produced differing interpretations. The main
clauses provide minimum cash payments (15 per cent of value of contract),

maximum and minimum interest rates (which vary according to the wealth of the country) and repayment terms.[11]

There are many schemes available including:

1 a comprehensive insurance, covering a whole export business,
2 cover for one-off projects,
3 cover for a bank guarantee,
4 underwriting for a particular market.

Selecting the appropriate scheme is itself an important skill, while there are markets which are so risky that no insurance is available. If such markets are important to the company, the risks are usually minimized by committing only a small proportion of the total business. Another necessary use of insurance is for goods in transit. Cover may be required for four different modes of transport, each with its own conventions and characteristic risks, for just one consignment. A particular insurer will not necessarily undertake all the risks of loss or delay, and it may be necessary to employ specialist agents or mutual societies to cover, for instance, strikes or demurrage costs.

8.8 Legal and administrative

The finance department is sometimes responsible for the administration of the company and its legal affairs. The international aspect of administration is described in Chapter 11. The legal affairs sub-department, for its part, is responsible for ensuring that the traps that beset those who operate under different systems of law are avoided as far as possible. Contracts have to be drawn up with local collaborators, and drawn up in such a way as to ensure that the arrangements will be upheld in the other party's country – in particular that the contract can be terminated if necessary. Another duty of the legal department is to negotiate a constitution and articles of association for the foreign subsidiaries. A mistake can have long-term consequences, as in the case quoted of the subsidiary which refused to pay a dividend. Yet another duty is to cope with problems caused by national and, in the case of the European Union, regional competition policies. United States corporations, and foreign subsidiaries in that country, are frequently engaged in litigation over alleged domination of the market or other activities in restraint of trade. Such cases are becoming more common in Europe as well.

Thus contracts, constitutions and competition laws are the most important concerns of the legal department, but there are numerous other issues arising from regulations that vary from country to country. Advice to the marketing department on consumer laws, or to the manufacturing manager on employment and safety regulations, is among them.

8.9 Summary

The finance department is expected to be the largest and most centralized unit of head office in a multinational company. It is designed to maintain close links with the finance departments in the subsidiaries in order to be ready to grasp opportunities and to staunch losses. One reason for close supervision is the possibility of reducing the costs of financing foreign operations by borrowing where interest, taxation and exchange rates are favourable. Another is the fact that decisions made in one subsidiary can affect the taxation of a whole group. The credit, and even the solvency, of the whole can also be affected by the financing methods employed in the parts.

An important aim of the finance department is to raise capital on the most advantageous terms – from any suitable source and for any unit under the corporate umbrella – while continually recognizing that the word 'advantageous' covers complex calculations of short- and long-term advantage. Another objective is to ensure that a fair picture of the financial health of a firm as a whole, and of its component parts, is provided at any time, together with projections into the future. The finance department may also be responsible for providing legal and administrative support. Its expertise is critical for the international cohesion of the corporation.

8.10 Exercises, questions and further reading

Computer simulation

Assume a loan of £20m repayable in ten years. Prepare a table of interest repayments at four different rates of interest (say 5 per cent, 10 per cent, 15 per cent and 20 per cent) and calculate the savings to be made by reducing the interest by 1 per cent at each rate. Then recalculate all the figures providing for eight different changes in exchange rates (from +1 per cent a year to -1 per cent for each year) on the total repayment of loan plus interest. Once the student is familiar with the exercise, the figures can be worked out for a pair of real countries.

Case example (role play)

Mr James Bevan was Financial Controller of the Eatwell Food Co. Ltd, a large international food processing and distributing company. He was under considerable pressure to redesign the control system, but the pressure was coming from opposing sides. The headquarters corporate planning staff were dissatisfied with the information they were receiving. They had been charged to develop plans for new investments in different parts of the world; for this they needed a great deal of information on the progress of each of the company's products in all its markets. Investment appraisal in the food industry requires to be especially sensitive to local conditions.

Bevan himself was finding increasing difficulties in allocating expenses and profits between products as the company expanded. Delays in supplying information, and the fact that some of the subsidiaries had different accounting dates, were among the problems. On the other hand, there was sustained pressure from abroad to relax the control system. There were constant reminders that most of the subsidiaries were small companies in intensely competitive markets. To them the time spent collecting and passing on the information the controller demanded was an expensive and frustrating waste which diverted their attention from their own business. The complaints of the foreign subsidiaries had been strongly emphasized to the Board, and Bevan had either to change the system or to justify current practices. Even stronger justification would be needed if he was to introduce the stricter control system both he and the planners wanted.

What are the criteria which he should be considering? What sort of information would justify each possible choice: keep the status quo, intensify the controls, or relax?

The participants should split into two or three groups, each representing one of the protagonists – head office planners, controller's department and subsidiary management, for instance. Each group should plan its attitude beforehand, and then debate a solution with the others.

A lively group, given adequate preparation time, can produce an interesting debate from this 'case example'. The debate can also provide valuable experience in negotiation.

Case study

Tsurumi, T. International reporting and transfer pricing of multinational corporations CCH 383–018–6.

Questions

1 Outline and discuss the main aspects of the work of the international finance manager.

2 Identify and examine the most important techniques in the management of the currency exchange operations of a multinational firm.

3 Establish a financial structure for a multinational corporation as a whole and for an individual subsidiary in a substantial market.

4 How far should financing the foreign operations of an international company be a central function, and how far should local financing be delegated to the local subsidiary? Give reasons for your answer.

5 What are the connections between inflation rates, interest rates, opportunity costs and cut-off rates? Describe the considerations that must be applied to obtain uniform standards in the appraisal of capital projects at home and abroad.

6 Discuss in depth the opportunities, problems and choices faced by a company in moving funds around the world.

7 Examine the problems of forecasting cash flow in an established subsidiary abroad and in a new project.

Further reading

A review of the work of an international finance manager which is detailed, factual and suitable for the general reader is Eiteman, D.K. and Stonehill, A.I. *Multinational Business Finance*, 3rd ed., Addison-Wesley 1986. A detailed account of the differences between national accounting systems is Choi, F.D.S. and Mueller, G.G. *An Introduction to Multinational Accounting*, Prentice-Hall 1978.

There is a chapter on Control (ch. 4) in Brooke, M.Z. and Remmers, H.L., *The Strategy of Multinational Enterprise*, 2nd ed., Pitman 1978.

See also: Arpan, J.S. and Radebaugh, L.H., *International Accounting and Multinational Enterprises*, Wiley 1985.

Oxelheim, L., *International Financial Market Fluctuations: Corporate Forecasting and Reporting Problems*, Wiley 1985.

Robinson (1984) ch. 7.

9 Personnel and industrial relations

Mr X has been appointed chief executive of multinational company Y. The appointment was widely acclaimed in the business columns. Mr X's ability to turn round derelict companies was so legendary that no one could understand why he was still plain 'Mr'. After a quick review of company Y's position, he increased his reputation greatly by declaring a large reduction in staffing. Most severe was the reduction in research and development staff; 45 per cent of the scientists employed in four countries had to go while around 30 per cent were made redundant in every department. Mr X was given the credit for restoring the company to profitability. He was not blamed for the destruction of the careers of many competent employees; the personnel managers in the various national subsidiaries were pilloried for this. Naturally, the severance terms were generous, exceeding the minimum requirements of each country, but there was still much bitterness.

This chapter is concerned with three groups of issues which normally come under personnel: staffing, industrial relations and other personnel policies. The degree of integration within an international group varies. It is usually said that multi-nationals do not interfere with personnel policies abroad, but there are enough exceptions to make such a statement suspect. Senior appointments in subsidiaries, indeed, are almost always reserved to the centre. Other policies are often prac-tised world-wide and some multinationals have a reputation for transferring labour policies (sometimes this is innovatory). Related issues are considered in Chapter 11 on organization, and Chapter 14 on national differences, while codes of con-duct relevant to personnel and labour relations appear in Chapter 16.

International personnel management is not a recognized specialization in the way that international marketing and international finance are. Indeed, there is a fear that if such a specialization did develop companies might become over-bureau-cratic, wedded to uniformity and inhibited from innovations or agreements in one country by exaggerated fears of the repercussions in another. Subsidiaries could be hamstrung in local bargaining. Nevertheless, a number of developments are occurring – identified in this chapter – which make for greater international co-ordination. These developments are being driven, and have been driven for at least the last 30 years, by a combination of attitudes and technologies. This point, also, will be explored in these pages, beginning with staffing policies and the transfer of personnel across frontiers.

9.1 Staffing policies

Discussions under this heading usually concentrate on managerial appointments, and this section will be no exception, but it should be said that increasing numbers of other employees are being seconded abroad to meet shortages in particular skills or even general shortages of labour, and there is a note on these at the end of this section. In the case of the managerial appointments, it would seem that declarations of policy are less fashionable than they were; companies are becoming more pragmatic.[1] Twenty years ago statements like 'a newly formed subsidiary will always have an expatriate chief executive for at least the first five years of its existence' or 'we now have a policy of promoting local managers to all positions except that of finance manager, which is still staffed by one of our own people because he is expected to bring the money home', were common, even if the relationship of cause and effect in the second statement was always suspect. Now, five stages in the development of international staffing policies can be identified; but it must not be assumed that a particular firm will go through them all, nor that this particular order will be followed.

Stage 1 – the expatriate

This is the policy of employing nationals from the home country in some or all of the senior positions abroad. The traditional method of sending managers out to govern the foreign possessions enabled a regular career structure to be established, normally with a period of overseas service as a condition of a top appointment at home. With this developed a system in which managers knew one another, and knew their companies, so that communications remained relatively informal. The appointment of expatriates to senior positions abroad is still practised by some companies – especially, but by no means exclusively, those that are new to foreign investment. This policy is, not unexpectedly, difficult to sustain indefinitely. It is unpopular in the host country and it is expensive. The cost to the company of an expatriate can be up to three times that of a local national on the same salary. In some countries there is the further difficulty of recruiting expatriates.[2]

Stage 2 – the local national

This concerns the appointment of managers to take charge of subsidiaries in their own countries. It is a policy which appears to be commonsense to many firms, once they feel confident that the subsidiary is established and running well, and is also the only course available in many instances. Local executives will not stay with a company where foreigners block all the avenues of promotion, and many countries will not grant work visas to foreign nationals unless there are no local nationals eligible for appointment. The head office presence will be retained by seats on the local board. Senior appointments in the subsidiary will be controlled from the centre. Hence it is the nationality of the appointee that changes, not that of the appointing authority. This stage sees an increase in formality when older, informal methods of control become hard to sustain. Regular and detailed reporting normally accompanies the emergence of a more impersonal system, although some companies make considerable efforts to retain the informality of the expatriate stage. For instance, local nationals due for promotion are brought to head office, where they are encouraged to familiarize themselves thoroughly with the corporate system and to get to know the staff.

Stage 3 – the third-country national

This is when promotion from any part of the company to any other becomes possible. This stage sometimes begins by chance. An able foreign executive is promoted to head office or to take charge of a new subsidiary. In a joint venture the 'able foreign executive' may be a member of a shareholding family. The appointment is sometimes regarded as an exceptional recognition of special talent, but the exceptions gradually become more common until a new policy has come into existence.

There are companies that formulate international management development programmes. These may not produce results that differ greatly from a more casual change of policy. Eventually a central department is master-minding the global staffing in either case. One constraint on this new-style expatriate system, as with stage 1, is the difficulty of obtaining work permits from the immigration authorities in the host country. However, this is usually easier in stage 3 as the authorities can be assured that there are opportunities for promotion abroad for their nationals if they will grant a permit for a foreign manager to come to their country.

Negotiating salaries is an obvious problem of employing third country nationals. The most common rule is payment according to scales that operate in the host country. But this makes it difficult to persuade executives to go to countries where salaries are lower. There may also be problems over fringe benefits, especially pension entitlements. As a result, special allowances often have to be arranged. Some companies have higher salary scales as a reward for willingness to be transferred anywhere in the world. Others have complicated packages to make up for losses incurred by foreign service.

The third problem with this stage is that some people are not globally disposable, as in the case of a manager whose promotion turned into a personal disaster when war broke out between his native country and that in which he held his new appointment. Political hostility is one of many constraints on transfers, but the third country national system does enable ability to be rewarded, corporate cohesion to be increased and global management development programmes to work. From the subsidiary manager's point of view, promotion across frontiers becomes possible and a centralized system is made tolerable.

Stage 4 – the international grade

This is a modification of the third country national policy designed to cope with the salary problem. An executive is promoted to international grade at a higher salary and this carries with it an obligation to accept transfer to anywhere in the world, sometimes at short notice.

Stage 5 – special secondment

There have always been transfers of managers for specific and limited duties, including the rapid solution of a crisis. But currently secondment for a fixed period, and in a special appointment, is being elevated into a policy. The changing locations of manufacturing facilities are among the reasons for the emergence of shortages of certain skills and types of experience in various parts of the world. For this reason there are increasingly vacancies for specialists on foreign assignments.

Whichever policy is pursued, the numbers involved are likely to be small in proportion to total employment. ICI, for instance, stated in its 1984 Annual Report that 600 out of 115,600 employees were serving outside their own countries (of these about half were third country nationals).

Influencing factors

About 30 factors that help to determine staffing policies have been identified.[3] Some relate to the characteristics of the company, some to the individual and some to the host country. In the following list these are divided according to company, individual and country characteristics.

Company characteristics

1 *Ownership of foreign subsidiaries.* A policy, and indeed a person, suitable for wholly-owned subsidiaries may well be unsuitable for joint ventures. The latter require special skills in diplomacy and understanding. The anticipated time-span is also relevant. An investment which is expected to be short-term can be used either as an opportunity for training an inexperienced manager or as a final posting for one about to retire. The latter policy overcomes personal problems of reintegration when the project comes to an end. Similar considerations may apply where minority holdings are concerned. Longer-term management policies are appropriate when the parent company has majority or total ownership.

2 *Method of establishing a subsidiary.* If this is by take-over, existing local management will continue to be employed, at least at first. If it is by founding from scratch, an initial expatriate period is normal.

3 *Industry group.* Policies will vary at least between manufacturing and service industries. The latter may depend upon intangible knowledge from headquarters (how the company works) and so are likely to continue to employ expatriates, although this does not necessarily apply to banks who employ local nationals for their knowledge of local business conditions.

4 *Technology.* The level of the technology in terms of sophistication, together with the amount of research effort needed to sustain it, will affect the policies of both the technical and the marketing departments. This will apply particularly when the transfer of knowledge also requires the transfer of staff. There is some evidence, too, that companies operating in high-level technologies are more likely to transfer policies as well as personnel.

5 *Market influences.* If the market for the product is purely local and the techniques employed are within the capacity of local management, expatriates or third country nationals are much less likely to have a part to play than where global techniques are applicable in world-wide markets.

6 *Age of investment.* The older foreign subsidiaries are likely to have established staffing systems which are hard to change unless problems arise.

7 *Organization structures* (see Chapter 11). Companies with product group world-wide structures are likely to employ more expatriates; those with matrix organizations are almost certain to require international management

development schemes. This method is highly dependent on calibre of staff and their ability to collaborate internationally.

8 *Commitment to international business.* A company that does not have a substantial part of its business abroad would not consider the more elaborate schemes for international promotion.

9 *Cost factors.* These are debatable and there is no ready formula for working out the costs and benefits of the possible programmes. The costs of expatriates of all types, especially third country nationals, are increasing rapidly, but the benefits can also be great. A manager, especially an international manager, is judged by his performance rather than his cost.

10 *The communication and co-ordination system.* This may affect staffing policies in many ways. One is the use of international transfers, meetings and educational programmes to facilitate the development of more efficient international communications.

11 *Style of management.* Executives will settle for a distinctive style which suits their business or their personalities. This style is likely to be culture bound, however, and may cause difficulties in a foreign subsidiary.

Personal characteristics of executives

These include:

1 life-style, expectations and ambitions,
2 qualifications and experience,
3 record of performance,
4 commitment to international business,
5 suitability for promotion across frontiers, including willingness to adapt and sensitivity to people from other cultures,
6 family commitments and, if accompanied, ability of family to adapt.

Host country characteristics

1 *Level of economic development.* This naturally affects the ability of the company to recruit in a given country either for local or international posts. On the other hand, there will be pressure on the company to assist the development process by establishing educational programmes to facilitate rapid promotion. Applications for permits for foreign residents, wherever they come from, are likely to be scrutinized carefully even in those countries which have most need of foreign management. The industrialized countries place less obstacles to the movement of managers across frontiers, but work permits are normally required except for those moving within the European Union.

2 *Political instability and nationalist sentiments.* Similar considerations apply, but skilled and experienced management may be required to maintain a presence in the face of political instability or to negotiate a withdrawal. Negotiations will also be needed where nationalization or expropriation is involved, possibly leading to a continuing contract for management.

3 *Foreign investment and immigration policies.* Limitations on ownership and the issue of work permits are usually the subject of negotiation, whatever the regulations. If the company has international policies, however flexibly operated, these will aid the negotiations.

4 *Availability of qualified and experienced managers,* and the need to develop and promote local managers and technical staff. These considerations apply in the same way as those already listed.

5 *Socio-cultural setting.* There are clearly problems of adjustment across boundaries of culture, race, language and religion. There are, equally clearly,
boundaries that cannot be crossed, although some obstacles prove imperman-
ent and others mythical. Some of the most difficult cultural boundaries are
crossed successfully and the myths dispelled after brief examination. Selection
and training can frequently minimize the problems to the point where they
become tolerable.

6 *Geographical location.* As with the socio-cultural setting, the location is
obviously an important consideration, but is not usually allowed to impose
impossible difficulties on actions that are otherwise desirable.

Employees other than managers

The transfer of non-managerial employees also features among corporate employment practices, and is of two kinds.

1 *Internal:* the movement of employees from one unit (usually, but not always
head office) to another to fill a gap where some essential skill is not available
locally. The policies for internal transfers will be similar to those already listed
for managers. Most of the employees moved will be on 'special secondment',
and some will regard the move as a first step in promotion.

2 *External:* recruitment in another country to fill vacancies at any level, frequently
of semi-skilled or unskilled workers during periods of labour shortage. During
the 25 years immediately after the last war representatives of manufacturing and
other firms in several European countries recruited labour both elsewhere in
Europe and from further afield. The immigrants, or 'guest workers' as they were
known in some countries, were originally employed on a temporary basis, but
many stayed either because they preferred to do so or because they could not
afford to return home. Switzerland passed a series of laws compelling reductions in the numbers of foreign employees. The recession of the 1970s led many
countries to restrict immigration and virtually to cease foreign recruitment.[4]

Selection and training

Techniques for selection and training (operator as well as management) are
becoming increasingly international, and staff are seconded to the same courses
from different units of a company. Psychological tests and surveys are conducted
uniformly. There is, however, a narrow line between expertise which is transferable and that which is not. Some aptitude tests, for instance, are found to be
culture bound and unsuited to a different environment. At the same time, many
companies are at pains to promote their own corporate culture, and to ensure
that techniques compatible with their specific requirements are introduced world-
wide. The most careful selection and training will not remove all the problems
of transfer for the executive, although there are many compensating advantages.
In the end, some difficulties have to be lived with.[5]

Summary

Staffing policies include an action on the part of a company (a policy and its
implementation), a reaction on the part of the individual, and the influence of

government policies and other external factors. For the international corporation two of the external factors – the availability of suitable persons and the pressures of governments for the promotion of local nationals – sometimes contradict one another. The reaction of the individual is a part of the general problem of international management. The need for a high enough standard of dedication, discipline and willingness to take risks does not fit easily into a culture which inculcates liberty, individualism and the pursuit of leisure. High salaries are supposed to compensate for the trials and perils of international management, but this is not the whole story, as discussions on motivation demonstrate.

9.2 Industrial relations

In most democratic market economy countries, trade unions represent their members' interests in a number of ways. Many, such as legal action and insurance, are routine and attract little publicity although they occupy most of a union's resources in normal times. The two that do attract publicity are:
1 industrial action: bargaining with employers, sometimes supported by sanctions;
2 political action: lobbying the legislature and sometimes supporting a political party.

The emphasis on one course or the other varies according to the country. Where the unions are weak, either for lack of members or because their organizations are fragmented, political action has priority, but normally there is a rough and ready balance, and the bargaining process is little influenced by the political environment.

International industrial relations are a problem for labour interests. Few companies have shown much interest in international bargaining, although there was one notable initiative by Philips which has not been repeated. Most of the other recorded examples have been on the initiative of the unions and have not generally proved of lasting significance. Indeed, one of the major issues that has arisen between the multinationals and the unions is that of companies moving facilities from one country to another. In this case, it is difficult for the unions of two countries to co-operate since the loss of jobs in one is matched by the gain in the other.

There have been repeated forecasts that international labour relations were about to burst upon us,[6] but the forecasts have not been realized. Domestic-style bargaining has not so far gone international although *most* European countries (but *not* including Britain) do have compulsory works councils.

The main problem for the unions is that the balance of power changes when they face international companies. In the home country, agreements may have been bargained for over the years and have produced an equilibrium, even if an uneasy and unstable one. The move abroad, or the take-over of the company by a foreign firm, places the union at a disadvantage. Concessions are less easy to come by and information about the company's trading position more difficult to obtain once there are a number of divisions operating in several countries.

As a result of these and other problems, trade unions have turned their attention to political rather than industrial action. In this they have scored a number of successes both within countries and within international organizations. These latter include the representation of labour interests in the codes of conduct which have been or are being promulgated (see under Organisation for Economic Cooperation and Development and the United Nations in Chapter 16). Successes also include the drive towards worker participation in the European Union. In this instance, a measure of co-determination is proposed with workers' representation at a policy forming level in companies, along lines long since implemented in Germany. Part of the deal is that operating information must be made available to worker delegates. The union contributions to the codes of conduct and the European Union's proposals may have been watered down, but are still strong enough to produce opposition in countries unaccustomed to such regulations.

A consequence of the union decision to act politically has been that much of the strength of international unionism has surfaced in lobby groups, like the European Trades Union Confederation (ETUC) and the Trades Union Advisory Council (TUAC, matching BIAC – the Business and Industry Advisory Council) to the Organisation for Economic Cooperation and Development (OECD). TUAC also has a close relationship with the International Confederation of Free Trade Unions. One of the specific demands of international trade unionism is a modification of the OECD principle of the free movement of capital. The proposal is for conditions to be attached to the movement of capital which will also meet other demands:

1 union recognition,
2 autonomy for the subsidiary with arm's length accounting,
3 compulsory standardized information,
4 wages and conditions to be of the same standards as those of the country into which the investment is moving unless the standards are below those of the International Labour Office Convention.

There is also opposition to investment incentives which encourage competition between countries to the advantage of companies. Some of these proposals are enshrined in codes of conduct for international companies.

9.3 Other personnel policies

The department of the subsidiary that deals with employment practices, conditions of work, industrial relations and related issues is usually held to be the most autonomous. Some firms have only a small central function, providing a limited advisory service. Local laws and local employment customs are difficult for the foreigner to understand. Dismissal procedures, for instance, vary from country to country. Policies that succeed at home can prove inapplicable and a parent company may feel it inadvisable to interfere so long as the results are satisfactory. Inevitably, however, the results are not always satisfactory and there are a number of ways in which head office does effectively set policies for affiliates abroad, the following among them:

1 *Management styles.* The setting of a single management style for a whole group of companies is rare. Usually the local management runs its company in ways

that are familiar in the host country. Participation can be the rule at home, with an autocratic regime abroad. In fact, many combinations occur. Sometimes top executives in the subsidiaries enjoy consultation with their superiors at head office that their own staff do not have with them.

2 *Key issues.* Against declarations that personnel policies are left to each subsidiary to fix in its own way, there are frequently key issues over which head office exerts greater influence. There are two reasons for this:

(a) A particular issue may have implications beyond the internal affairs of the subsidiary. Pension schemes are a common example, and indeed illustrate a number of the problems of international management. On the one hand, such schemes are partly determined by laws which vary from country to country; therefore company-wide policies may not make sense. On the other hand, the affiliate may wish to provide extra benefits to recruit and retain able employees which the parent company, if it guarantees subsidiary borrowing, may end up paying. This latter possibility makes international supervision of pension schemes likely.

(b) A particular issue may have caused difficulties within or for the company outside the unit where it arose.

3 *Intra-company comparisons.* Companies with manufacturing units in different countries produce figures to compare employee performance, among them productivity comparisons. These indicate the condition of the manufacturing process as well as the effectiveness of the employees. The figures may be difficult to interpret as between countries with different labour costs and different standards of mechanization, but personnel policies will certainly be influenced by the results. Subsidiaries with poor productivity figures will be expected to accept new management techniques or productivity deals. International comparisons also influence policies like those on absenteeism, sick leave, injury and disputes. Another influence is that of capital projects when there is competition between subsidiaries. While information about personnel policies may not be important in formulating proposals, labour costs will often be crucial and there will be a premium on policies that help to keep costs down.

4 *Innovation.* The introduction of new techniques of personnel management is another influence on the policies of local affiliates. Productivity bargaining and other techniques have spread from one country to another through international firms.

5 *Education and training.* Management education is becoming increasingly international, and senior staff are often seconded to the same courses from different units of a firm. Within the company, too, courses are mounted which recruit participants from any country in which the firm operates with the aim of improving cohesiveness and communication and developing common policies. Many firms also have specialist courses for financial, marketing and other executives, although less often for personnel staff as such. Methods of operator training are also being disseminated.

There is always a narrow line between experience which is transferable and methods which will work in one culture and not in another. While management is developing its own international culture, there are methods which suit the lifestyles of one region and which are not helpful when transplanted elsewhere. Nevertheless, companies are likely to make efforts to ensure that personnel policies discovered to be most effective in some subsidiaries are used in others.

For two recent articles on 'human resource management' as personnel management is now called, see:

(a) Brewster, Chris, 'Towards a "European" model of Human Resource Management,' *Journal of International Business Studies*, 26.1, first quarter 1995, pages 1–22 and

(b) Bird, Allan and Beechler, Schon, 'Links between business strategy and human resource management strategy in US-based Japanese subsidiaries: an empirical investigation', *Journal of International Business Studies*, 26.1, first quarter 1995, pages 23–46.

9.4 Cases, questions and further reading

Case examples

Gigantic Holdings AB: a staffing problem

Senor Juan Alamos was the chief executive of a Latin American subsidiary of the Swedish international conglomerate Gigantic Holdings AB. The Board had a high opinion of him, and he was often praised as an outstanding manager who had turned in reasonable results in spite of severe difficulties caused by an unreasonable government. His reports persistently complained of interference on the part of the government. Now the Board was hearing some disturbing rumours, and these were confirmed when two members visited the country. It appeared that Senor Alamos was running a private vendetta against the government, that the restrictions against which he was campaigning were quite normal and acceptable, and that he was making many enemies through his unreasonable attitude. He was thought to be using his position in the company to influence local politics, which was totally contrary to group policy.

As soon as the directors realized this they asked him to resign, which he refused to do. They then dismissed him. The next move was his reinstatement by order of a court and a summons against the company for illegal dismissal. It appeared that the law did not allow a foreign company to dismiss local nationals in managerial positions. The directors were caught between an employee who was discrediting the company, the industry group and foreign firms in general, and the fact that the country's law still afforded him protection. Not unnaturally the Board wondered what to do next.

Powerful Engineering plc: staffing an international company

Powerful Engineering plc is a pseudonym for a large international company in heavy engineering. It is London based, and has subsidiaries in the United States, Venezuela, Brazil, France, Germany, Sweden, India, Kenya and Australia. Apart from the appointment of the chief executive in each country, members of the board have not interfered in the staffing or personnel problems of their foreign subsidiaries for many years. Indeed, they are proud of the fact that between 1970 and 1980 they successfully went over to local national control. Apart from general world conditions, this change was stimulated by the loss of able local managers, particularly in two Latin American subsidiaries. Now they have only local national executives overseas, apart from some British staff (mainly engineers) on short-term assignments.

During the process of developing local nationals, the company wanted to retain some elements of the personal control that existed in the days of expatriate managers and to this end it instituted a regular training course. Carefully selected managers in each of the ten countries in which the firm had manufacturing subsidiaries were brought to England for a year. During this time they got to know their way around head office thoroughly, became personal friends of many of the executives with whom they would be corresponding, and carried out limited projects to familiarize themselves further with the way the company worked. After returning to their own countries, the most capable were rapidly promoted to senior posts. Members of the main board were closely involved and had no worries about a scheme which had worked well for ten years. Now they had in front of them a report from the Group Personnel Officer which raised some puzzling questions about the foreign staffing policy. Some points from this report were as follows:

1 Once again the turnover rate among foreign executives was alarming. Indeed, it was worse now than it had been in the mid-1970s when it was taken to signal the need to increase the responsibilities of local managers. But what was being signalled this time?
2 The training scheme was not, in fact, building up the informal network that had been intended. The foreign managers kept in a group to themselves, and formed limited contacts with their British colleagues who often failed to find the time to see them, or were away when needed.
3 Managers in some of the countries were reacting badly to the way the control system was working, and were failing to send in their reports regularly. Other communication problems kept arising, such as a failure in one subsidiary to co-operate in a global marketing promotion.
4 Able personnel in the group, and especially those with much needed skills, always seemed to exist in the countries where their talents could not immediately be used and not where they were required.

The Board was wondering if the situation demanded the development of new policies on staffing.

Case study

Michelin Tires Manufacturing Co. of Canada Ltd. (A and B), Harvard Business School case no. 9–378–668.

Questions

1 How are the diverse units of an international company held together? Sketch out the personal influences involved, and discuss the qualities required of staff with international responsibilities.

2 'The international manager faces rapid change in all the countries in which he operates, but with a bewildering variety of speed and direction in each.' Comment.

3 What external criteria influence the choice of staff in an international business? What practical considerations limit a company's freedom in placing staff in overseas locations? Discuss possible answers to these questions.

4 Comment critically on the statement that: 'The ability, or frequently the inability, of a company to absorb a returned expatriate is a test of an effective international management development scheme.'

5 Discuss the advantages and disadvantages of international personnel policies:
(a) to the company,
(b) to the foreign employees,
(c) to the host country government.

6 Outline the problems which the expansion of multinationals poses for labour organizations.

7 Imagine yourself being asked to advise a union of skilled workers in an industrial country who see their jobs disappearing to less developed countries. Recommend any action you think might be taken, giving reasons for your suggestions.

8 What are the main procedures for international collaboration on the part of labour organizations? List and discuss.

9 Explain how the trade unions are reacting to the multinational company and what further developments are likely.

10 Discuss the view that trade unions are structured in such a way as to make the task of protecting employees in multinational corporations extremely difficult.

11 An American businessman has spoken recently about an 'underlying identity of interest' between governments, companies and trade unions. Do you agree with him? Give reasons for your answer in terms of the cross-frontier operations of companies.

12 Discuss the view that multinational business as a phenomenon highlights the inherent inequality between capital and labour.

Further reading

Bluma, A., ed., *International Handbook of Industrial Relations*, (London: Aldwych Press, 1981).

Flanagan R.J. and Weber, A.R., *Bargaining without Frontiers*, (Chicago: University of Chicago Press, 1974).

Golzen, G., *Working Abroad*, 8th ed., (London: Kogan Page, 1985).

Kochan, T.A. and others, *Industrial Relations Research in the 1970s: Review and Appraisal* (Industrial Relations Research Association, 1982).

Kujawa, D., *International Labor and Multinational Enterprise*, (New York: Praeger, 1975).

Liebhaberg, B., *Industrial Relations and Multinational Companies in Europe* (Aldershot: Gower, 1980).

Robinson (1984) ch. 4 and 5.

Seddon, J.W., 'Issues in practice: the education and development of overseas managers,' *Management Education and Development*, Vol.16, No.1, (1985) pp.5–13.

See also: Sasaki, N., *Management and Industrial Structure in Japan* (Oxford: Pergamon Press, 1981). This book gives a clear and concise account of Japanese personnel policies.

Note: a useful organization is the Management Development Branch of the International Labour Office.

10 Logistics, purchasing, distribution, production and research

This chapter reviews other international departments, mainly in the context of international logistics – the reason for including physical distribution here rather than in Chapter 7.

An international manager has to mastermind a massive exercise in logistics. At the least, this is likely to include ordering supplies from more than one country for manufacture and distribution in several others. At its most extensive, the search for supplies and markets is world-wide and facilities are provided wherever the need to ensure either supplies or markets are the dictating factors. In any of the largest companies, sources, facilities or outlets can be found in about half the world's 200 countries.

Figures 10.1 and 10.2 illustrate the main approaches to corporate logistics. Figure 10.1 illustrates the most usual, head office centred system. In this case, the scheme is put together at the centre where an overview is maintained of all the movements within the system. Naturally this does not mean that all goods and funds must pass through the centre or that no decisions are delegated to the subsidiaries; it does mean that a company is structured and new units are added with an eye on the advantages to head office. The market-centred approach (Figure 10.2) is one in which the system is essentially geared to providing for each market, with head office providing general oversight. In either case, co-ordination is required as the system grows, and each department makes its own distinctive contribution, perhaps drawing on different countries, and having to match the requirements or opportunities of each of the others.

A logistic system is determined by calculations based on a complicated formula made up of size of plant, availability and cost of labour and materials, costs of transport, customs' tariffs, other legal constraints and reliability of supplies. This last consideration dictates that all facilities must normally be duplicated, and that the site of the second or other plants must be in an area unlikely to be affected by a breakdown at the first. Any cause of breakdown that could affect more than one plant, including strikes or transport problems, must be eliminated as far as possible.

In theory a logistical system can be planned according to the maximum advantage of each element. This needs to be worked out in costs and in timing separately, although the two are related. Additional speed is often expensive, but delays at any stage can be even more so. Various techniques have been developed to ensure optimum timing (like critical path analysis) and these can be employed internationally.

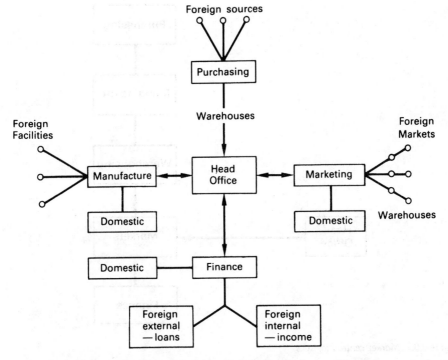

The whole logistic system is master-minded from the centre although many movements of components, goods and finance will by-pass head office, and many logistic decisions be delegated to operating units.

Figure 10.1 Head office centred logistics

Figure 10.3 provides a simplified formula for working out optimum costs. At various of the eight stages in that formula, the costs are related to such items as the siting of facilities, the mode and route of transport, the inventory and the financing. A small reduction in the inventory can tip the balance in favour of one route; but if this is achieved by extra speed (by using air instead of sea, for example) the direct costs of transport may be higher than the savings in inventory. The figures change again when the goods have special characteristics, as when they are perishable.

This chapter is concerned with three components of the logistics equation (others have already been considered) – purchasing, distribution and production. A section on research and development follows that on production.

10.1 Purchasing

The more efficient a firm becomes, the more awareness develops of the difficulties of controlling the costs of supplies. In many multinationals, purchasing has become the main means of further savings, although the buying department

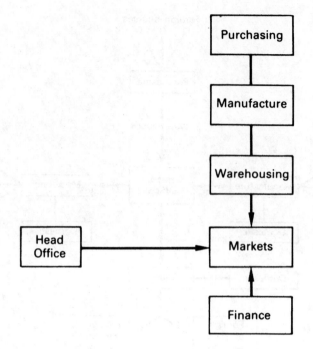

Figure 10.2 Market centred logistics

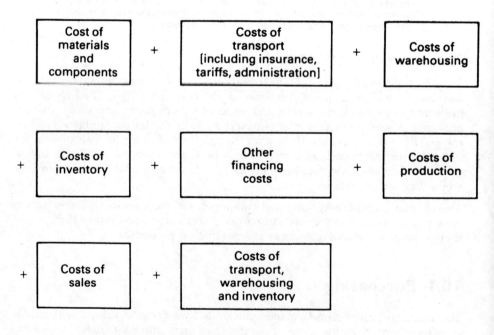

Figure 10.3 Costing of logistic arrangements (from purchase to sale)

is not always accorded the importance that suggests. Policies are determined by two basic decisions, both of which can be interpreted in terms of theories considered in Chapter 2. One is how to identify the most advantageous source of a particular purchase and the other is whether it should be made inside or outside the company. The first decision is not determined on the basis of cost alone. Quality, reliability and acceptability are also important. One research showed that, in the sample covered, reliability was the most important factor in the purchasing of industrial goods. A long-term relationship with the supplier was the norm for the purchasing manager: 'Stability is . . . a clearer, stronger characteristic of industrial markets than is change.'[1]

Most firms do not shop around, but the weights given to different factors depend on the budget available, the quality demanded (itself influenced by the market segment into which the company sells) and the costs of delays. These latter will be higher for machinery manufacturers, but also higher in any industry sector with efficiently organized production.

The other decision, whether to buy internally or from outside, depends on the relative costs of the internal and external markets. In either case, a company may wish to avoid over-dependence on one source. There is the further issue of whether to buy locally or from abroad. Pressures are often brought by governments on subsidiaries to purchase within the host country. The pressures include general measures – import duties, controls, commercial treaties – and particular measures such as conditions attached to investment proposals and to incentives for local production.

Purchasers have to steer a path through the requirements of the government and the commercial practices of the country to ensure that supplies arrive at the right time and in the required condition.[2] They also have to consider the political position within the company. Assertions of freedom to buy inside or out are often made but this freedom is likely to be limited in a corporate system where a purchasing manager in one unit is in a junior position compared with a marketing manager in another. The relationship is likely to be even more unequal when a subsidiary is being asked to buy from the parent company. In the end, it will be argued, the control system will ensure that the purchasing is made in the most favourable market. However, this argument overlooks factors like quality and reliability as well as the influence of corporate politics.

10.2 Distribution

There are three logistical decisions for physical distribution:
1 the choice of channel (export, licensing or investment or one of their variants, see Chapter 3),
2 the choice of mode of transport, and
3 the means of overcoming the various hurdles.

The mode of transport will, of course, be decided after calculating costs and timings, although the timing calculation will often have to take account of the possibility of damage as well as delay. Transhipment can cause considerable delays which sometimes, for instance, reduce the apparent advantage of air transport. An increasing proportion of high-value goods are going by air freight but, in one study, an exporter from Britain discovered that door-to-door air-freight times to other parts of Europe averaged five days, including some destinations that could be reached by road in less than 48 hours.[3] The distribution manager in an industrialized country also has to understand the operation of transport systems in the less industrialized. For instance, Pepsi Cola entered the Mexican market by taking over a firm whose transport facilities consisted of 37 bicycles, a fleet which the new parent company later expanded to over 1000 trucks.[4]

The costs of physical distribution as a proportion of total costs have been estimated to vary according to the product, from around 0.2 per cent for small and expensive pharmaceuticals to 100 per cent for bulky and cheap plastic products. These costs include insurance, interest on working capital for inventories, costs of storage and other requirements at frontiers, duties, taxes and administration, as well as the price of the transport.

The other problem is overcoming obstacles. These include delays at frontiers, either because the authorities are not satisfied that import regulations have been observed or because the documentation is not adequate (a recent British Customs & Excise Department survey found errors in 25 per cent of the documentation of goods being imported into the country). Another hurdle is the need to conform to product and consumer laws in the importing country. To ensure, for instance, that labelling and descriptions match the regulations.

10.3 Production

International production is developed in a number of ways:
1 licensing or other contractual arrangements including contract manufacture, the subletting of the production process;
2 establishing a subsidiary intended primarily to service a local market;
3 establishing a subsidiary to supply international markets. This may sometimes be integrated with other units to make a cross-frontier flow of production.

Among the considerations which determine the siting of facilities are the following:
1 *Strategy.* Where the company predicts its business will occur.
2 *Control of supplies.* Where problems have arisen or are anticipated, companies may decide to bring their suppliers under their own management to ensure a regular flow of components of the required quality. However, other factors must be considered before the results can be guaranteed, especially when planning internationally.
3 *Cost of capital,* together with its availability and transferability. Details of this factor, which can be critical in determining a location strategy, were considered under finance.
4 *Cost and availability of labour.* For many labour-intensive industries – including textiles, footwear and some branches of electronics – lower wages combined with reasonable productivity levels may represent the difference between success and failure. It has been found that even part manufacture

in a country with low labour costs can reduce the costs of production. Some United States' companies fly advanced-technology components to countries like Taiwan for processing and assembly, and return them to the home base for incorporation into finished products.

The wage differentials which produce such strategies may change as countries industrialize – they already have done so in some instances – but the opportunity is likely to remain for the foreseeable future. Wages are also rising in the industrialized countries, as are other labour costs like social security payments and fringe benefits. Workers in the less industrialized nations have improved their standard of living – the factories pay more per hour than the subsistence farms, on which the same workers were previously employed, paid in a day. But the countries that have attracted most foreign industries have more to offer than low wages; they possess a labour force which is quick to acquire the skills as well as the disciplines of industrial life, while productivity rises and breakdowns decline. Nevertheless, there are difficulties, and the removal of a production process to a strange environment requires considerable ingenuity. Even labour-intensive machinery is not all that simple, and is designed to be operated in an industrial environment where the skills and training are readily available and where the operators are educated to read instructions and manuals. In a less developed country it may be difficult to translate the instructions into the local languages, of which there are sometimes several, and some of the workers will be illiterate. The care of the machine and the care of the operator may both prove difficult to instil.

5 *The economies or diseconomies of scale.* These will be related to the labour costs, since labour-intensive machinery will not suggest a large factory unless there are expensive services to provide. With some products, on the other hand – including such dissimilar goods as pharmaceuticals and automobiles – the economies of scale are so important that no factory can serve only one market except in the largest of countries. Competitive advantage is gained by careful site selection. There is also the possibility of multi-stage production, whereby components are manufactured in one country, shipped for processing to another, and perhaps assembled or packaged in yet others. A sophisticated production control and planning department is required, but it is also necessary to ensure that other sources of supply are available in case of breakdowns or other stoppages. A false economy is to depend on one supply factory, where this can be avoided, even if at an otherwise optimum size; the ability to duplicate sources is one advantage of international production. The sources may be small feeder factories or two or three larger units, and may be either owned by the company or by independent suppliers.

6 *Government intervention from the home country.* While government measures are usually designed to increase exports and reduce imports, companies that ship goods abroad for processing and then reimport them may receive favourable treatment, including remission of duties, while the same concessions may apply to the import of raw materials not available locally. This enables companies to plan an integrated production process without undue price increases caused by duties and taxes.

7 *Government intervention from the host country.* Some countries offer incentives to foreign companies as their principal means of promoting employment.

This can mean taking steps to ensure that the foreign investor has reasonable security and relief from constraints. His investment will be safeguarded as long as the regime lasts. The workers will be discouraged from protesting, but will also be provided with better education, while favourable taxes are imposed, funds are made available on reasonable terms and the remittance of profits is guaranteed. In several countries there are *offshore* investments, where factories are built in designated areas to manufacture solely for foreign markets. These allow considerable fiscal and other concessions to firms which bring employment to the country.

8 *Location determined by loan finance.* The availability of funds from a particular source, such as aid funds tied to a particular country in a bilateral agreement or from a supranational bank, may help to determine the location of a particular facility.

9 *Facilities for expatriates.* These include professional support and housing and educational facilities, as well as suitable working conditions. In these days security must also be included.[5]

10 *Internal factors including the allocation of projects between new and existing facilities.* Most companies develop a set of criteria for determining which units are to be offered extra resources. Among the criteria will be the reputation of the unit and the skills of its management.

Most of these considerations also influence how *integrated* production becomes. Arrangements for the flow of components across frontiers have been achieved, notably in the car industry, which have the advantage of meeting demands for part manufacture locally. Such arrangements enable a company to make use of special location advantages and of economies of scale in component manufacture – as well as diseconomies in circumstances where small feeder plants are viable. A means of analysing the advantages and disadvantages of international integration is shown in Table 10.1. It should be remembered that integration is here used in *both* of two possible meanings – the masterminding of production arrangements from head office (or from one centre for each product) as well as for the part manufacture at different sites in different countries which this makes possible. This latter arrangement often has to be modified to reduce over-dependence on one source of supply and to meet situations where final assembly near to the market is required. Naturally, the compatibility of components is important.

10.4 Research and development

The title of the department – research *and* development – suggests that two separate activities are taking place. In fact, there are several, including:
1 thinking out ideas,
2 basic research,
3 applied research,
4 development of a viable product,
5 test manufacture in a pilot plant or experimental unit,
6 final testing before large-scale manufacture.

Table 10.1 The advantages and disadvantages of integrated international production and sources of supply

	Conditions favouring international integration	Conditions discouraging international integration	Conditions disqualifying international integration
Capital	Where cost is low Where availability is high	Where cost is high Where availability is high	Exchange-control regulations in home or host country making movement of funds impossible
Production sources	Where the economies of scale are high Where compatible components can be transported economically	Where there are too many non-standard components	
Labour	Where cost is low Where availability is high Where there are adequate education and training facilities	Where cost is high Where availability is low in required abilities or skills Where there are quality control problems abroad	Where some highly-trained or skilled occupations non-existent
Transport	Where costs are high Where bottle-necks are common (Central control if not integration)	Where transport is no problem and so little is gained by global considerations	
Customers	Where they themselves are international, especially where customers expect international service	Where they are fragmented or local	
Legal	Laws regarding: part manufacture, locally high duties or taxes on finished goods, high taxes on local profits, or withholding tax on transfer of funds	Where legal, customs or tax systems do not impede local decision-making	Prohibitions on specified imports

Some or all of these stages may be performed internationally. Some, like basic research, not by the company at all but in research institutions or universities. When it is said that research is usually concentrated in the home country, this applies to the earlier stages, not the later.

Nevertheless, there is usually less scope for the international operation of research and development than for that of other departments. Most companies accept the logic of a central facility for this purpose, but with a number of qualifications. Some high-technology companies set up research in more than one country to tap local talent and ideas,[6] overcoming the problems of distance by on-line links.

Favouring one central department is the fact that the company will probably have grown internationally on the strength of its research and development success, that it will have a self-perpetuating team of scientists or engineers in a function heavily dependent on personal abilities, and that the dispersal of facilities is expensive. Against this, the most expensive exercise is not research but development, and it may well make sense to move part of this development to a site where the plant will ultimately operate or in which the costs are less. It may also make sense to conduct at least some part of the research in a subsidiary located near to a centre of expertise. Some European companies, for instance, justify the retention of an unprofitable subsidiary in the United States on the grounds that it can be a 'listening post.' This phrase is used to describe the ability of a small research department in the subsidiary to tap into local research. Some companies have spread the location of research and development facilities in different countries but retained the advantages of central direction by means of on-line links.

The ability to tap into local developments in the firm's line of business without the expense of a subsidiary can be provided by a technical liaison office. Some companies organize these offices on a regional basis. Being small and informal, they can easily be closed if they are not justifying their existence.

The following considerations influence the organization required for a research and development department:

1 Basic research will usually be undertaken on a limited scale and in one centre. Where the research is conducted in more than one place, it will almost certainly be under central control.
2 Research aimed at developing new manufacturing processes is likely to be undertaken centrally.
3 Product research is located either at the corporate, divisional or even the subsidiary level. Cost factors often suggest centralized research, but where the product divisions are in unrelated technologies it may be located at divisional level. Highly innovative companies have the most centralized research departments; those less dependent on advanced technologies are more likely to move the research elsewhere.
4 Some products require development to be conducted at the site of manufacture. Close liaison is needed with the production engineers for testing the products and resolving teething troubles as they occur.

Research and development, then, is a function which is usually organized and directed from the centre. Figure 10.4 shows some of the options available. The first – option (a) – is when the central research and development department has facilities in more than one country. Only a relatively small number of companies possess such facilities. Option (b) is where all research and most development is conducted at home, but the foreign subsidiary has its own technical department to cope with problems or to plan modifications. In this case, the foreign development managers report to the chief executive of the subsidiary, but close links are maintained with head office. This is the most usual form of organization. Option (c) is a matrix where the foreign development department is responsible to corporate research and development and to local management at the same time. This is different from the company-wide matrix described earlier and relates to the rest of the organization in a number of ways, the following among them:

1 Where the company as a whole is organized along matrix lines, the research and development function may be separately organized inside the corporate system. Central research may service more than one division and local development more than one subsidiary. The department is likely to be involved in a network of complex relationships.

2 Research and development is sometimes organized into a matrix form when the rest of the company is not. At least the foreign development department is likely to maintain close links with a product division at home if the subsidiary is reporting to an international division.

3 In companies where research and development is treated as a cost centre and little effort is made to price the department's services, the matrix arrangement is one of organization only and is not necessarily reflected in the accounting system.

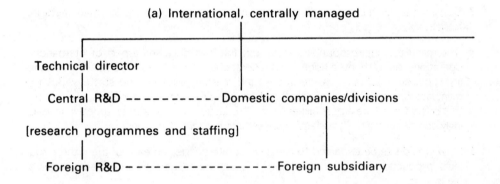

(a) International, centrally managed

Technical director

Central R&D — — — — — — — — — Domestic companies/divisions

[research programmes and staffing]

Foreign R&D — — — — — — — — — — — — — Foreign subsidiary

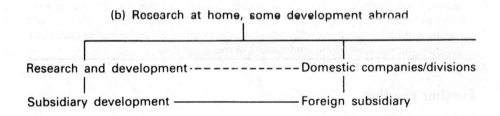

(b) Research at home, some development abroad

Research and development — — — — — — — — — Domestic companies/divisions

Subsidiary development ————————————— Foreign subsidiary

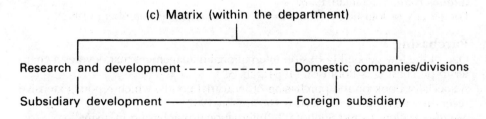

(c) Matrix (within the department)

Research and development — — — — — — — — — — Domestic companies/divisions

Subsidiary development ————————————— Foreign subsidiary

Figure 10.4 Options for research and development departments

10.5 Cases, questions and further reading

Case studies

Best Oil Company – logistics in the oil industry – Rutenberg (1982) ch. 5.
General Foods Ltd (Japan) – distributing processed food products in Japan –
Terpstra (1983) pp.406–8.

Questions

1 Discuss the role of the purchasing or distribution department in an international firm.

2 Discuss the conditions under which an integrated international production system might be recommended.

3 Consider some techniques for determining optimum locations for manufacturing facilities.

4 'The manufacturing responsibility is possibly the least discussed aspect of international operations, often shunted aside in considerations of investment, site selection, financing requirements, tax considerations, and market research and strategy. But the manufacturing sphere is probably the most complex facet of operations and the one that offers the greatest possibilities for cost reductions and customer appeal in increasingly competitive world markets' (Business International). Comment.

5 How would size be expected to affect corporate policies on each of these three subjects: production, location and supply? Discuss the advantages and disadvantages of being large.

6 'The main reason for setting up a research centre outside California was to obtain new technical and scientific thrusts – to avoid what Hammond calls the "bandwagonism" that can follow the grouping of researchers in one location. Hewlett-Packard also wanted a research centre in Europe to reflect the fact that 30 per cent of its sales come from this market.' Discuss the implications of this statement.

Further reading

Logistics
A general book on logistics management is Bowersox, D.J., *Logistical Management*, Macmillan 1978.
For a study of logistic problems in the oil industry, see Rutenberg (1982).

Purchasing
One of the few general books on international management that devotes a chapter to purchasing is Robinson (1984), ch. 3.
A specialist book on the purchasing of industrial goods, which reports extensive recent research on the subject, is Håkansson 1982.
See also: Hallen, L. and Snehota, I, 'International purchasing in a small country', (working paper, Uppsala: Centre for International Business Studies, 1981).

Distribution

Most books on international marketing have a chapter on physical distribution. See, for instance, Terpstra (1983), ch.11.
See also: Brooke and Buckley (1988) ch. 2.7.

Production

Starr, M.K., 'Global production and operations strategy,' *Columbia Journal of World Business* (Winter 1984), pp. 17–22.

Research and development

Robock and Simmonds (1983) ch.19.
See also: Lasserre, P., 'Selecting a foreign partner for technology transfer,' *Long Range Planning*, Vol.17 No.6, (1984) pp. 43–9.
Behrman J.N. and Fisher, W.A., 'Transnational Corporations: Market orientation and R and D abroad,' *Columbia Journal of World Business*, Fall 1980) pp. 55–60.

11 Decision-making and organization

This chapter considers how the various organizational options available to the multinational can be interpreted in terms of the strategies outlined in Chapters 2 and 3. In particular, the consequences of three-dimensional management in causing change are recorded. The organization is also interpreted in terms of the four main purposes which it has to fulfil:
1 to enable decisions to be taken efficiently and at the right time,
2 to provide a channel for the exercise of authority,
3 to provide a system for reporting and other communications,
4 to provide a career structure.

Regional and departmental organizations are also covered; for staffing, see Chapter 9.

The title 'Decision-making and organization', is intended to place organization in its correct context: that of an administrative system required to match the requirements of a decision-making process. In fact, the administrative is just one of the systems that an organization must sustain, but it is the one that usually determines the structure, even if not in the short-term. Other purposes are to provide a means for the exercise of authority, a system of communications and a career structure. An organization will usually emerge from a compromise between these objectives, but if any one of them is ill-served there will be pressure for change. The final form will be determined by an interplay of strong personalities and pressure groups with, perhaps, some guidance from organization specialists.[1]

There are two principal aspects to the subject. One is the structure, the framework represented by diagrams with lines and squares illustrating the various levels in the hierarchy. This provides the *route* for the flow (and interplay) of the decisions and the other purposes of the system. *Where* the decisions are made forms the other aspect, and is usually considered under the heading of centralization and decentralization – the *process* of the decision-making. The *route* and the *process* provide the content of this chapter.

Writing and consultancy on international company organization often seem to start from a description of what exists, unsupported by a theory of how it comes about or of what factors are causing change. There is a descriptive, even aesthetic, base rather than a theory of decision or change. Organizations are charted as if such charts were of interest in their own right, and their merits discussed as if they were decorative rather than commercial activities: resembling pictures for permanent exhibition rather than stills in a scene that is always changing. However, a number of typologies do exist which attempt to interpret the organization options. This chapter uses typologies, both for structure and for centralization, derived from theories of the complex organization mentioned in Chapter 3, especially the conflict theory which reflects the effects of decisions across three dimensions. Meanwhile, the route of the decision-making and the structure of the organization will be considered first both in the company as a whole and in its major departments.

11.1 Organization structure: the route of decision-making

A number of stages can be identified as the corporate system grows more international and the demands of the foreign operations make themselves felt. The diagrams that follow are simplified representations of extremely complicated systems. They show the formal, recognized, aspects of those systems; underlying them, and influencing their development, is a network of informal relationships and pressure groups. These produce lobbies for change along the lines of particular interests – perhaps for specific markets or products. From their action and interaction reorganizations arise; changes are also produced by disturbing experiences or by insights.

In one middle-sized British chemical company, the chairman toured the overseas affiliates and came back horrified at the neglect he had discovered, as well as the openings lost, because the managers abroad could not get decisions from their home-based colleagues fast enough to grasp opportunities. There followed an upheaval at home designed to produce a structure which would serve the subsidiaries better. Such incidents provide the impetus for change. Whatever deeper forces may be at work, changes actually happen when someone unearths a problem or alters a strategy. There is no suggestion that a particular firm goes through all the stages, or that the order is not reversed sometimes. The following are the options between which companies choose their structures, and some of the reasons for these choices.

Stage 1: Exporting and licensing

The priority at this stage is to construct a centre of expertise that will supervise and stimulate the foreign business. Growth is normally haphazard and the foreign operations may well be supervised by executives who have little interest in them. Even when a specialist department is established, its status is frequently pitched too low to match the opportunities, and the appointment is made at a time when problems are already growing out of hand. Many of the mistakes that such a specialist department might avoid have already been mentioned. They include the negotiation of payments on conditions which are not enforceable in a particular country, the appointment of an agent or licensee on conditions which are later held to be invalid, the despatch of goods by an unreliable route or the adoption of a promotion style inappropriate to the market. The list could be lengthy. However, even more important is the ability of an export department to make the company aware of new developments around the world. Naturally, this ability only exists where the department is given sufficient status.

Policies for the expansion of foreign trade start from decisions about the priorities of the business and the relevant routes abroad. The possibilities were outlined in Chapter 3 and include, as a first step, the choice between the sale of goods and the sale of knowledge. Figure 11.1 shows two options for the export department. In (a) it is a sub-department of marketing, while in (b) it is an independent department. The internal organization of the department itself has been outlined in an earlier chapter (see Figure 4.3).

Licensing is more difficult to place. Ideally the staff would be recruited from research and development and employed by marketing or export. Some positions are shown in square brackets in Figure 11.1. In practice, licensing often remains part of research and development although integral to the marketing strategy. A liaison arrangement is needed to ensure a satisfactory relationship between the needs of the foreign market and of new product development.

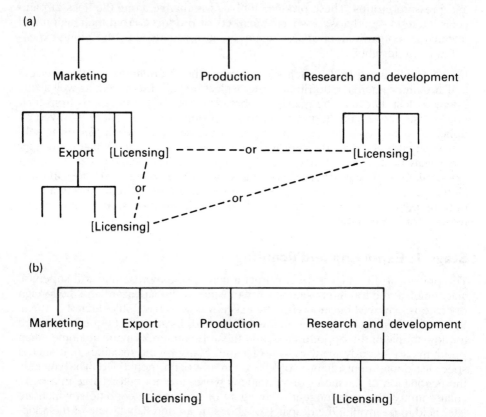

The usual choice for export is shown at (a), a sub-unit of the marketing department, but sometimes the department has a higher status and that is demonstrated at (b).

Figure 11.1 The emergence of an international organization: two options

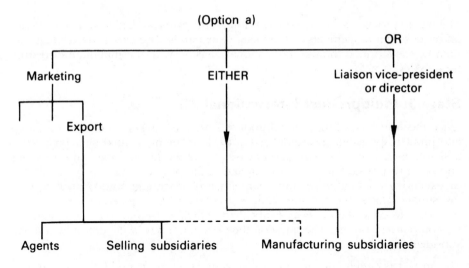

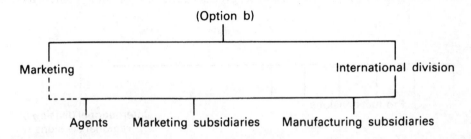

Figure 11.2 The beginnings of international investment

Stage 2: Simple international

As foreign business grows and a network of foreign collaborators and subsidiaries develops, there are two main options for the organization and these are shown in Figure 11.2. One option, (a), is for a manufacturing subsidiary to report either to the chief executive or to one of his colleagues, sometimes named a liaison director. This is an *overall* system, whereby the oversight of the foreign operations is in the hands of executives with overall, company-wide, responsibilities.[2] The export department acts in an advisory capacity for the manufacturing subsidiaries as well as continuing to manage the marketing affiliates and the agents.

The other option, (b), is to form an *international division* (not necessarily using that title) either from scratch or, more usually, by upgrading the export department. The coming of the international division causes two problems. One is that managers in the subsidiaries consider themselves demoted; there is now a level between them and the top of the company. The other is that the division will have a difficult relationship with the marketing department. Marketing often retains control of sales offices abroad during a transitional period.

The whole process is facilitated when long-term plans are laid to upgrade agency and licensing arrangements as the business expands. The export department can then be transformed into an international division with the minimum of disruption.

Stage 3: Multiproduct international

Once the firm has a formal multiproduct structure – when operating decisions and profit responsibilities are delegated to departments named after products – a simple international organization ceases to be workable. Operating decisions and profit responsibilities are concentrated in the product divisions, with a board or executive committee retaining supervision of strategy and control of new investment. Under these circumstances it ceases to be logical for a member of the board to control an overseas subsidiary which is itself one of the contenders for corporate resources. The question then becomes: who will control the foreign subsidiaries?

The answer is either a geographical arrangement (an upgraded international division or a series of regional divisions),[3] product divisions, or some combination

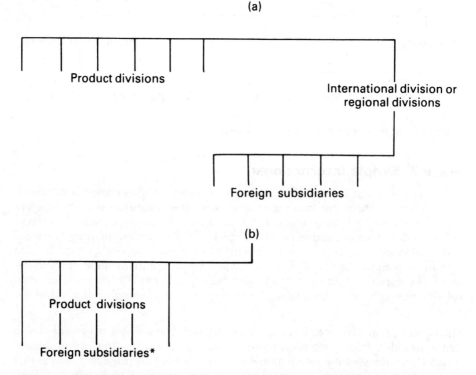

(a)

Product divisions

International division or regional divisions

Foreign subsidiaries

(b)

Product divisions

Foreign subsidiaries*

* In some countries one product division may act as an agent for another

Figure 11.3 Multiproduct, multinational companies, standard organizations: two options

of the two. Figure 11.3(a) shows the international division solution. This division is managing a complex structure and providing a channel for a steady flow of information between the centre and the foreign affiliates. Expertise in all aspects of international trade is concentrated in the division; knowledge of the technical and marketing aspects of a many-sided business is also required. Decisions have to be taken about which products are to be developed and where, and the international division will be caught in a crossfire between the foreign subsidiaries and the product group managers. Nevertheless, the specialist division has proved a vital tool for masterminding foreign policy, and the tensions have often turned out to be constructive. Some companies have moved into regional divisions instead, with the world divided into two or up to five regions.

The other option, shown in Figure 11.3(b), is to give each product group responsibility for its operations world-wide. This is most likely to be effective when the product groups are large. In such cases, each division can carry its own staff expert on international trade. Where the units are small, this system may not incorporate adequate skill in foreign business. There may also be duplication when each division sets up its own global organization. Naturally, however, the divisions themselves favour this arrangement and press hard for it. The advantages are greatest when the products are unrelated. It is difficult for an international division to handle a number of products which have little technical or marketing relationship to one another.

In addition to the standard options, there are experimental options of two main types. One is the matrix. This elaborate organization follows closely the principle that the organization should match the decision-making process. As a result the international (or regional) division and the product divisions exercise joint authority. The lines of multiple authority and of reporting are intended to ensure that as many elements of the decision-making as possible are brought into the structure. Figure 11.4 represents a simplified version of an arrangement that can be extremely complex. Since the word became fashionable, many companies have declared that they possess a matrix organization, but the true matrix only exists where there is more than one line of authority and where the accounts are made up each way. The chief executive of the subsidiary illustrated in Figure 11.4(a) reports to each of the product groups and to the international division. Usually the relationship with staff officers at headquarters is advisory, but there may be a line of direct reporting to central finance. The international division consolidates the accounts for operations outside the home country, while each product group makes up the books for its division at home and abroad. The subsidiary manager may find himself caught in a conflict of interest when the international division agrees to increase his investment but the relevant product group disagrees. Such clashes are sometimes resolved by allocating priority to one or other of the divisions or they may be left to a debate between the parties – to be settled, if necessary, by the board or executive committee.

This type of organization brings into the management system conflicts of interest that exist anyway, and by bringing them into the open helps to resolve them. It is an organization-type based on the conflict theory. Each issue that has priority in the decision-making has its executive champion to ensure that it is not

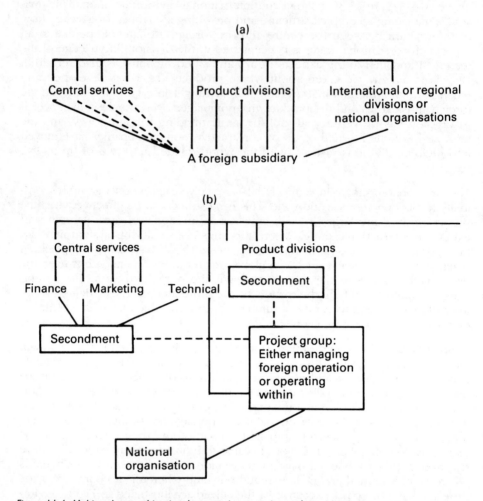

Figure 11.4 Multiproduct, multinational companies, experimental organizations: two options

neglected. Thus managers with functional, geographical and product group responsibilities have similar status to those in the foreign subsidiaries. This gives rise to the danger of expensive overheads, if the number of posts grows out of proportion to the size of the business. The matrix company needs an internal consultancy which will watch that growth and ensure that a post only survives if it remains necessary.

After a rapid growth in the early 1970s, this type of organization has not spread as fast as was then expected. Some early hopes have not been realized. Indeed, some research has suggested a decline.[4] In the main the matrix type has been espoused by large companies, principally in the chemical industry and in capital intensive firms which require a large number of specialist managers. It is also found in smaller service companies, including consultancies. One reason for its decline is the difficulty of operating the system – it proves too demanding. Another is the rise of an even more flexible organization, the project-type. Illustrated in Figure 11.4(b), this type has emerged from aircraft manufacture, where an *ad hoc* organization is set up for each new design, sometimes internationally. Many project organizations operate within consortium arrangements. As consortia spread through other high-technology or large-scale fabrication or extraction industries, it is likely that an increasing proportion of managers will find themselves spending more time in project-type organizations in which the chain of command changes to suit changing circumstances.

The five main types of international structure can be summarized as:
Type A – overall (Figure 11.2(a))
Type B – geographical (Figure 11.2(b) and 11.3(a))
Type C – product group (Figure 11.3(b))
Type D – matrix (Figure 11.4(a))
Type E – project (Figure 11.4(b)).

Other authors use different classifications for the same phenomena, frequently distinguishing between the international division and the regional types.[5] Since the same factors produce the two and similar results follow in terms of the conflict theory of organization change, these are treated here as different aspects of one type.

Not every international company fits neatly into one of the categories. Due to compromises, partial reorganizations and other causes, many are mixed. For purposes of analysis these can be regarded as in transition. There are pressures towards a particular type in some industry sectors. For instance, the geographical type is common where product divisions are small, where geographical spread is large, where the company is mainly in consumer products or where governments are large customers. The product group is found more commonly with industrial products or where the company is widely diversified and where the divisions are large. Some companies have merged divisions to increase their size when they have gone over to the product group world-wide system, while others are so large that each division is itself a separate type of organization. Exxon, for example, is a type C organization with each of its petroleum and chemical divisions being type Bs, having regional divisions in their own right.

Modern trends

This framework for analysing multinational company organization is rapidly being out-dated by two tendencies that have already been noted.

Rapidly increasing involvement in joint ventures
Most of the listed structures were devised in the days before joint ventures were common. The structures were not devised to organize these joint ventures and now, arguably, means of handling them dominate the requirements placed on the organization. These may be handled by a product division or they may be handled by a co-ordination unit (a new version, whatever the title, of the international division), or it may be handled more informally by a main board director from each of the collaborating companies.

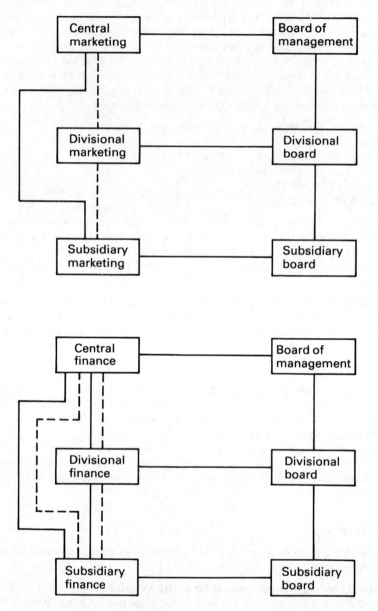

The broken lines represent advisory and communications links only; authority is exercised along the unbroken lines.

Figure 11.5 International departments: marketing and finance

Rapidly increasing informality

This informality makes it difficult to analyse modern organization structures as convincingly as was previously thought, but the structure must still meet the fundamental demands outlined in the first paragraph of this chapter. The management of departments has also altered.

Organizing the departments

A major issue is whether individual departments manage the affairs of their opposite numbers abroad. Is there, for example, to be one marketing department throughout the company or will marketing report to general management in each division or subsidiary? The answer varies from function to function as well as from company to company, while adopting a divisional structure will produce different arrangements from those that were appropriate to the simpler organization. Some options for particular departments are set out below.

The central marketing department sets policies for the company as a whole, promotes market planning, and perhaps develops techniques that are new to the company for improving the total marketing performance. In a divisionalized company the department will be smaller, perhaps even non-existent; where there are no divisions, central marketing will be larger and with more powers. Direct line management from marketing at head office to the subsidiary rarely, if ever, exists. The links, indeed, are usually tenuous except in a matrix organization where they may be very complicated. Information links between headquarters' marketing and sub-units of the foreign subsidiary are not unknown but the only situation in which the marketing department manages units abroad is where there are sales offices or selling subsidiaries.

Central finance is usually more involved in overseas operations than marketing, as both financing and control imply direct instructions from the centre. Submissions and reports must be entered on the correct forms and submitted by the required dates. Nevertheless, subsidiary finance managers will usually report to local chief executives. In matrix organizations direct reporting lines, from one finance department to another, do exist but only occasionally. There may also be some foreign finance subsidiaries that are used either for funding or for tax purposes. These come under the direct control of head office. Figure 11.5 illustrates the principles.

Production is similarly organized to finance, although part manufacture in different countries makes closer links necessary. Personnel, on the other hand, is more like marketing, but the links between the personnel departments in head office and in the subsidiary can be even more tenuous. Complete integration internationally is rare (found very occasionally in finance or production); almost invariably the departments in each subsidiary report to the chief executive of that subsidiary and not to a departmental chief.

Organizing the subsidiaries

The company that invests abroad needs to develop a suitable organization for its subsidiaries. Each unit has to be sufficiently integrated into the management system of the whole corporation to contribute its part to the general well-being, and to match the legal and commercial environment in its own country. At the same time, the managerial structure may not coincide with that prescribed by law. For legal purposes, a subsidiary is usually incorporated in the host country. It is therefore under an obligation to fulfil the requirements of a local company in, for instance, providing the information stipulated by company law. There is also an assumption of independence which is maintained, at least in form. As a rule, a subsidiary will be organized in a way that is normal in the host country and thus familiar to managers recruited there. If the subsidiary has been acquired as a result of the purchase of an existing concern, this is almost certain to be the case, but three circumstances modify the set-up.

1 *A mirror effect.* The affiliate is sometimes led to restructure itself to reflect more closely the pattern of organization that obtains in head office rather than that usual in its own country. This effect can be produced on instructions or voluntarily, as a result of reproducing the structure of head office. The change frequently comes about, gradually and almost imperceptibly, to meet the demands of the control system. Subsidiary executives find that they need appropriate skills and areas of responsibility to match up to the issues on which they are expected to report. This need gradually distorts the organization.

2 *A reorganization masterminded by head office.* Even where there is no mirror effect, the organization may be changed as a result of instructions or advice from the centre.

3 *A liaison department.* The complexities of international decision-making, particularly inter-subsidiary relationships, produce liaison departments which are not needed in domestic firms. These departments are designed to ensure the dissemination of policies and of information. Sometimes they are also centres of authority, as in a case outlined in the next section – that of a subsidiary with regional responsibilities.

Organizing the regions[6]

Some companies are developing an organization to control or co-ordinate their operations in groups of countries. Four types of regional organization have been identified:

1 *A national subsidiary which is given authority outside its own country* to prepare a market plan for nearby territories and to mastermind sales and servicing facilities for the area. This is the only type of regional centre that is appropriate to the small company. It is particularly relevant when increasing competition makes a corporate presence necessary, but where there is not enough business to support such a presence in any one country. This can occur in machinery manufacture as well as in some branches of the construction industry. Rapid response is possible to a potential customer, while spare parts and accessories can be held by the centre.

Examples of national subsidiaries that have become regional centres, outgrowing the parent company in the process, have been identified in research into Swedish foreign investment.

2 *A subsidiary which administers a region,* with line authority, and with responsibility for profits and for consolidating the accounts of companies under its

jurisdiction, and is separate from a national subsidiary in its own country. Some companies (mainly in the United States and in sectors like chemicals and food-processing), operate closely integrated regional policies with this type of organization. Like other centres this type is criticized for burgeoning bureaucracy, but extra staff are not necessary when the centre is drawn partly from head office and partly from the subsidiaries. Corporate logistics can be controlled from such a centre in addition to manufacture. This type is common in companies that have a matrix organization.

3 *A regional centre that has staff responsibilities only* exists in some large companies where high-level expertise can be made more readily available in this way. It proves, however, difficult to identify the relevant expertise which would be under-utilized if allocated to subsidiaries and not sufficiently available if retained in head office. Nevertheless, the conviction that some services fit with a regional approach ensures that advisory centres often come into existence, but are frequently short-lived. Subsidiaries put pressure on head office to set up such a centre, but when it is brought into existence they come to consider it an expensive irrelevance which they bypass.

4 *A regional centre which provides advisory services to successful subsidiaries in its area, and takes over line responsibilities for those in trouble*, exists in a few companies in sectors as diverse as electronics and food processing.

Regional centres often have difficulty in becoming accepted by subsidiaries; diplomacy is a necessity. This can be a problem in units which have a floating population of expatriates from head office who consider themselves in temporary exile, and successful managers from the subsidiaries who are being groomed for a corporate appointment. Neither the expatriates nor the successful managers are selected because they are natural diplomats.

In spite of the criticisms, the regional centre does provide expertise and co-ordination to make national subsidiaries more competitive. Also provided are: the ability to negotiate with supranational treaty organizations like the European Union, as well as the ability to develop marketing programmes with customers who are also organized by region. In the planning process, the geographical can be an important unit. The centre can collect and interpret the information required by head office planners. The centre can also be a training ground, useful for regional management development programmes. Companies sometimes assert that their growth has only been made possible by the development of a regional centre.

The rise of joint ventures is expected to produce a new form of regional organization when a joint venture is used to mastermind a specific market.

Communications

Much of this book is about communications and one of the tests of a satisfactory organization is the extent to which it facilitates and does not hinder the flow of messages. The 'problem of communication' is a hard-worked phrase, sometimes, one suspects, representing a shallow diagnosis of problems that have other causes. The conflicts of interest and opinion which are unavoidable in managing an international company will not go away because communications are improved. On the contrary, improvement may make the problems more obvious

and cause more serious disputes. As a subsidiary manager remarked: 'Our problem of communication is to avoid telling head office things it is best for them not
to know.' No doubt such a statement can be dissected, interpreted and criticized
in a myriad of ways.

Communication is always selective and the selectivity has been made more difficult by the introduction of technology that can carry almost unlimited quantities
of information; communications are biased by the interests of the sender and the
receiver. In an international system there are tensions which distort the sending
and receiving of messages, however technically efficient the system.

The position of foreign managers, even of expatriates, is complicated by a different set of loyalties and priorities from those of the head office staff with whom
they are corresponding. Issues like the interests of the host country and its economy will influence the views of local management. Different commercial and
national interests are bound to affect the interpretation of messages as well as
the response to them. The interests of the whole are not necessarily the sum of
the interests of the parts. Head office executives are often quick to point this out,
but slow to realize that many of the communications difficulties that puzzle them
are a consequence. Personal interests will normally supplement and emphasize
commercial and national. Career prospects, time horizons and personal aspirations will affect communications at each point in a network

Sometimes there are pressures that operate against the commercial and national
interests. Such pressures are felt by a manager who believes that corporate
policies are in conflict with his personal ambitions. Indeed, the consequences for
other company policies are an important consideration in developing international career opportunities. Communications, it has often been pointed out, are
culture-bound and this particularly applies to managerial aspirations and interpretations.

Another personal influence is the ability to ignore messages. Upward messages
are lost because recipients are too busy or have lost the art of listening. Subsidiary
managers, who think they spend a disproportionate amount of their time on
reports, are often disillusioned to find how ill-informed are visitors from head
office. On the other hand, foreign managers are known to complain that they
have been kept in ignorance on subjects about which information has in fact
been sent to them. One in-company investigation showed that nearly 90 per cent
of complaints about lack of information were unfounded.

Problems in communications may reflect commercial, national, cultural or linguistic differences. Organizational arrangements may also cause difficulties. The
geographical type is often associated with communications problems in head
office, whereas in product divisions, problems are found in the links between
head office and the foreign subsidiary. The required organization is selected on
other grounds and the need to live with the problems has to be accepted. The
mistake, so often made, is to change the organization in order to solve communications problems. There is little evidence that this works.

A pattern emerges made up of a number of specific points at which communications difficulties can be anticipated, overshadowed by major issues lurking in the
background. To match this pattern there are some remedies, along with a general

need to anticipate problems and thus understand the implications of those that arise. Where there is an excess of messages being transmitted, and they are being ignored, indirect information can be more effective than direct. Thus the circulation of productivity figures (for both sales and production activities) has been found more effective in persuading subsidiaries to introduce new methods than notices advocating these methods. The control system can also be used to transmit the need for more advanced management techniques. Investigations often show confusion about what is being put into the system as well as about what is coming out. Regular checks which isolate what is happening can make a considerable improvement, but the informal links need to be emphasized. These are links which do not follow the lines laid down by regulations and organization charts.

Some companies disapprove of any short-circuiting of official arrangements, and make efforts to stop them. Not only are these efforts themselves expensive, but the informal links may be more efficient even if they do cause inconvenience. Some companies, on the other hand, assist the emergence of unofficial arrangements by management development programmes and regular international meetings of managers.[7]

11.2 Centralization and decentralization: the process of decision-making[8]

Delegation sums up an age-old worry. Is the organization best served by keeping the authority at the centre or by decentralizing as much as possible to subordinate units? The issue becomes even more acute when these units are in different countries and when quick decisions have to be taken. The situation is complicated by legal, commercial and personal influences which pull in different directions.

The amount of autonomy possessed by a particular subsidiary will be influenced by the country, the industry sector, the size, the age and many other factors. Some of these can work both ways. A large subsidiary, for instance, may be more independent because of its size, maturity and general ability to manage its own affairs without interference from head office; or it may be tightly controlled, on the grounds that any setback will be serious for the whole company. The position can be summarized by listing the pressures which induce either greater control from the centre or more autonomy for the local unit.

Pressures within head office towards greater centralization

These include:
1 the need to take a global view of resources, particularly the financial but also the personal like scarce skills;
2 the need to ensure sufficient information at the centre for resource allocation through budgets, investment appraisal and corporate planning;
3 other issues where the interests of the whole corporation may well differ from those of an individual subsidiary, including rationalization and disinvestment;

4 where the level of expertise at the centre makes delegation inexpedient or wasteful – this argument can be double-edged: sometimes head office carries expertise which the subsidiaries could profitably use to decide in which unit the necessary specializations are most usefully employed is a fine judgement;

5 sometimes the status of the senior staff at headquarters makes them more able to deal with representatives of government and other pressure groups even in the host country; where there are tensions, there may well be fears that local managers could not cope with sensitive issues.

Pressures within head office towards greater autonomy for a subsidiary

These include:

1 expensive overheads, centralization means extra staff to process proposals and decisions;

2 the opinion that the recruitment of able managers and their motivation are both made difficult when discretion is limited;

3 a belief that decentralization is an appropriate policy;

4 the problems of communication caused by over-centralization.

Pressures within a subsidiary towards greater autonomy

These include:

1 the desire for independence, and the opinion that the subsidiary can be more efficiently managed without interference from the centre;

2 the need for rapid decision-making on occasions; the actions of competitors may require responses which are too rapid to allow the mandatory consultation with head office;

3 pressures within the host country against foreign decision-making on matters vital for the local economy.

Pressures within a subsidiary towards greater centralization

These include:

1 a sense of dependence on head office;

2 a career structure leading to head office (where this occurs);

3 attempts by technical and other experts in a subsidiary to maintain direct links with their opposite numbers at the headquarters, even where the decision-making has been delegated.

This last pressure leads to a phenomenon that has been called *inverted centralization*, which arises when a subsidiary is expected to be self-sufficient and a centre of authority for its staff.[9] This does not suit local specialists who find no relevant expertise among their own managers, through whom they are nevertheless obliged to communicate with head office. As a result, efforts are made to bypass local management. Once direct links with head office are established, these reduce the level of independence of the subsidiary. The specialists, be they engineers or marketing experts, are more interested in their professional links than in those of nationality.

The conflicting pressures reviewed under the above four headings produce different effects under each of the following sets of conditions.

Features inherent in the business

Standardized products, integrated manufacturing operations and large-scale or politically sensitive contracts are conditions which make for greater centralization. A subsidiary is likely to gain greater autonomy when there is little business with head office, when the products are consumer goods and when local decisions have to be taken rapidly to sustain the business. Among the other issues that come under this heading are the size and age of the affiliate together with the method of its funding. A long-established company that has been purchased is likely to be more independent than one that has been started from scratch.

Experience

If a company has sustained a loss through ineptitude in a subsidiary or become involved in a controversy for a similar reason, the pressures towards centralization will increase. Frustration through delays caused by head office decision-making or the loss of executives in the subsidiaries pushes the relationship in the opposite direction. The 'direction' is illustrated in Figure 11.6 where a company can select, or drift into, any position between that of high decentralization (at 1 on the figure) to high centralization (at 8 on the figure).

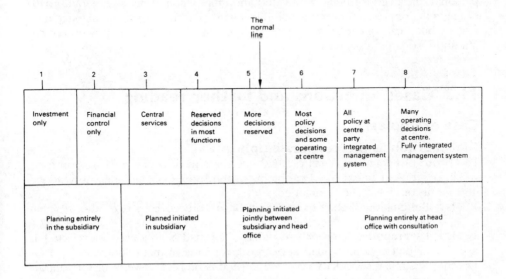

Figure 11.6 A scale of decentralization: centralization

Attitude

There is a general view among senior businessmen, but not among specialist managers who often hold the opposite opinion, that decentralization is a correct policy. 'Appoint the chief executive of the subsidiary and then leave him to manage' is a common expression. The opinion, however, frequently differs from the reality. Statements about decentralization can mask a reality of centralization.

The whole process of centralizing and decentralizing the relationship between head office and the subsidiary can be seen to resemble a pointer moving along a scale from maximum autonomy at one end to close oversight and central decision making at the other. Figure 11.6 also includes the concept of the normal line, a position on the centralized side of the middle of the scale to which rival pressures move the typical company – a kind of organizational equilibrium. Some firms will settle at other points, but for many the counter-pressures that come into play maintain the relationship near to the position indicated. Also illustrated, in the lower part of the figure, is how a planning system can match the degree of centralization.

Summary

The conflicting pulls and pushes which determine the allocation of authority in the international company have been outlined in this section. Where other factors are equal, there is a bias towards centralization because the expertise at head office, and the fear of problems in the subsidiary, emphasize the pressures in that direction. On the other hand, too little discretion leads to unsatisfactory management in the subsidiary, and the consequences of this stimulate a move back to greater autonomy. Among the conflicting influences, the commercial (such as the need for a global oversight of resources) pushes towards centralization, while the personal (the need for better motivated and more inspired management abroad) suggests the opposite. Decentralization is regarded as improving the management system, but it can also lead to disaster when the subsidiary has the power to commit and lose large resources.

11.3 Cases, questions and further reading

Case examples

Global Products plc: corporate upheavals

The Board of Global Products plc had been in almost continuous session for a week. A series of unexpected problems in the foreign subsidiaries now added up to a major crisis. These included:

16 May   Resignation of chief executive in Brazil (preceded by two other resignations earlier in the year).

29 May   Loss reported in French subsidiary. This had been totally unexpected as market conditions had appeared favourable in that country.

12 June   Australian subsidiary involved in serious problems over a major contract – numerous delays and customers complaints.

24 June   Advance warnings of losses in two other subsidiaries precipitated the present series of Board meetings.

It had indeed been a long, hard summer.

Twenty years ago the first foreign subsidiary had been founded in Canada. The market there for one of the company's most successful products, an electrical component, had grown to the point where local manufacture would increase profitability and provide a defence against aggressive local competitors. As a result of the success of the first foreign ventures, a policy had been developed whereby the company put as much new capital each year into operations abroad as at home. For some years this policy had appeared to pay off handsomely. The foreign subsidiaries had been profitable and had cushioned the firm against the ups and downs of the domestic economy.

During the growth of the international side of the business, two major reorganizations had taken place. The first had happened seven years earlier with the formation of an international holding company, and the wholesale decentralization of the subsidiaries by country. Up to that time, most policy and many operating decisions were reserved to head office. The foreign management reported to a liaison director on the main board, and his personal staff were the principal means of communication and decision-making. The subsidiaries had been set up with finance from the United Kingdom and were owned 100 per cent by the parent company. They were manufacturing products to head office specifications and patents. No deviations were allowed, and changes needed the sanction of the liaison director. He and his staff kept up a steady stream of instructions that had to be followed.

When the international holding company was formed, the intention was that a considerable measure of decentralization would take place. On principle, operating decisions were to be taken by the subsidiary; conformity to central policies was only required on major issues like the raising of long-term capital, entry into a new market and changes in a product line. Board-level appointments were also reserved to head office. Members of the staff of the international holding company were to provide a close link with the subsidiaries. They were to ensure that reports came in regularly and were analysed. The reports were to be kept to a minimum and to consist of key monthly financial indicators, together with a few other figures like market share. The policy decided by the Board was for a minimum of formal control together with a maximum of contact. The international staff were expected to visit the foreign companies regularly to discuss problems and opportunities on the spot. Mandatory orders, however disguised, were not to be used.

The transition to the new system was not altogether smooth. There were some resignations in the subsidiaries, but these were considered a natural reaction to change. Some problems did arise within head office, and the position of the international holding company was always a difficult one. This was generally assumed to be a result of the personality of the man in charge. Mr Green was abrasive, rubbing his colleagues up the wrong way; and they did not agree that the performance of the group or of the subsidiaries had improved as a result of his efforts. Eventually, some four years later, a further reorganization was decided on. The international holding company was to be abolished, and the product group divisions were to take responsibility for their foreign operations. In some countries this meant splitting the local subsidiary, in others it meant that one product group acted as agent for others. Once the reorganization was completed the foreign companies were to be guaranteed the same degree of autonomy as before.

By the time of the Board meetings with which this report started, it had become clear that the autonomy of the foreign firms was much less than anticipated. Although the new system had now had plenty of time to settle down, decisions were being taken at head office which had been delegated to the subsidiaries. Further, an ever-increasing amount of information was being demanded from the local managers. These latter were complaining that they were being tied to their desks by the pressure of a well-staffed headquarters which was making impossible demands on smaller organizations.

Questioned about the allegations, head office executives were able to give convincing replies. The progress of the business depended on achieving at least the same level of sophistication as their competitors, so they needed to ensure that new products and new techniques were quickly adopted throughout the group. They also needed to ensure that there was adequate reporting for the planning system to function efficiently. Some of the questions raised at the meetings were:

1 Where, if anywhere, have we gone wrong?
2 Is it just a coincidence that these problems have arisen all at once?
3 Are our controls too loose or too tight?
4 Do local managers operate best when left to their own devices?
5 Why, above all, did some of the problems take them by surprise in spite of complaints that the reporting was already burdensome?

Exhibit 1 shows the organization as it had been when the international division existed and Exhibit 2 the announcement of the reorganization.

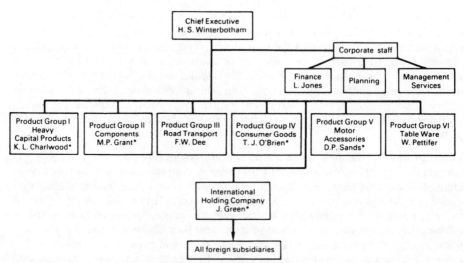

*A member of the main board, together with four part-time directors: one banker, one customer of the heavy engineering group, one car manufacturer and one lawyer.

Exhibit I Global Products plc: corporate structure after the formation of the international division

---

CONFIDENTIAL   6 September

Circulation to:
All Directors,
Executives and Managers.

GROUP REORGANISATION

I have decided in the interests of group operating efficiency to make some changes in our organisation.

As from the first of next month, the International Holding Company will cease to exist and its functions will be reallocated between the product divisions. Mr J. Green, who has served the company well for over 30 years, will be retiring. I am glad to say that we shall continue to have the benefit of his assistance as a consultant. Other staff will be offered alternative employment, if available, in the next two weeks.

There may be some disturbance at first but I am confident that the whole group will be feeling the benefits of these changes within the next few months.

H. SEDLEY WINTERBOTTOM,
Chairman and Managing Director

Exhibit 2 Letter announcing reorganization

A German food-processing company: corporate expansion

A German food-processing company with sales of DM4000m possessed manufacturing subsidiaries in eight countries and agencies and marketing subsidiaries elsewhere. In the eight countries there were 30 factories which manufactured five main products all closely related. Each country had a national subsidiary reporting direct to a senior executive on the Committee of Management. At home, product group divisions had just been introduced. A consultant was asked to advise on what, if any, changes should be made to the international organization. The first reaction of the corporate management had been to tell the subsidiaries that nothing would change as far as they were concerned. Effectively the chief executives of the foreign subsidiaries were to have the same status as the newly-appointed divisional heads. The consultant advised against this, but the committee of management said that any other arrangement would be unthinkable.

Case studies

Albion International Petroleum Co. (Davis 1979, pp. 255–272).
Bancil Corporation (Robock and Simmonds, 1983, pp. 733–747).
Eaton Corporation (Davis 1979, pp. 105–141).
YKK (Yoshida Kogyo KK) Davis 1979, pp. 434–464).

Questions

1 Comment critically on the classification of company organization contained in this chapter. In particular discuss the possibility of other ways of interpreting the trends in international company organization.

2 What is the likely future for regional organizations? Give reasons for your answer.

3 The chief executive of an international food preparation and canning company is worried about the slowness of communications which appears to be damaging the competitive position of the subsidiaries. He has commissioned a report by his personal assistant which concentrates on problems in the decision-making process. Write the report. Do not hesitate to introduce assumptions about the company.

4 Explain where a product-group organization would be preferred and the steps necessary to overcome likely problems.

5 Under what circumstances would you expect decentralization to be dangerous? Give reasons for your answer.

6 One of the realities which complicates the work of an international manager is what has been called 'three-dimensional decision-making' – decision-making grouped around functional, product and geographical issues. In the light of this complication, discuss some possible plans for the management structure of an international company and the conditions under which particular plans might be preferred.

7 Meanwell Plastics Ltd is having trouble with its international division. This division controls plants in four European countries and five less developed countries in Africa and Asia; it also masterminds the company's marketing efforts in most other parts of the world. Growth has been fast, but profits are flagging. The main worry is about increasing friction at head office between international and the other divisions. This has produced a dearth of technical information abroad.
Write a memo to the Managing Director advising on some measures that will improve the situation. Do not hesitate to tell him what further information you will need to make more confident recommendations in your role as outside adviser.

8 Do you regard the degree of autonomy as a significant element in the development of a foreign subsidiary? Give reasons for your answer.

9 Discuss the matrix organization in an international company. Include in your answer an outline of a probable future, if any, for this type of organization.

Further reading

Brooke (1984).
Brooke and Remmers (1978) ch. 2–5.
Davis (1979),
Hulbert, J.M. and Brandt, W.K., *Managing the Multinational Subsidiary*, (New York: Holt, Rinehart and Winston, 1980).
Robinson (1984) ch. 9.
Robock and Simmonds (1983) ch. 16.

Samiee, S., 'Transnational data flow constraints: a new challenge for multinational corporations', *Journal of International Business Studies*, (Spring–Summer 1984), pp. 141–50.
Vernon and Wells (1981) ch. 2.

12 International corporate planning

This chapter brings together various implications of the thrust abroad in outlining the work of a department responsible for co-ordinating corporate development. A philosophy of planning is the starting-point, with the reasons for moving from an informal to a formal system and the methods of doing so. The various stages are then examined, from strategy formation to implementation, and the chapter ends with information processing and organization. Much of the content of the planning, including diversification policies, has already been discussed in Chapter 3.

The corporate planning process unlocks doors, answers problems and makes extensive logistical arrangements possible. Product and indeed industry changes can be foreseen and potential disasters averted. These statements can be supported, but they are by no means incontrovertible or truisms. Company planning has had a chequered career. Once deplored as an expensive way of putting the firm into a straitjacket, planning became the faith of the 1960s. At an international conference of top executives back in 1970, the overwhelming majority replied 'planning' when asked on which subject they most sought further help. Then came 1973 and planning was back in the doghouse, since most planners had not anticipated the oil crisis and companies had written stable, long-term energy prices into their projections. From this shock the reputation of planning was gradually rebuilt, but rebuilt with a new philosophy – one that was already held by the more sophisticated planners – that emphasized the word 'contingency' – the ability to plan for a range of possibilities rather than for a set course. Throughout this chapter such an approach will be assumed.

The phrase 'international corporate planning' is used in many contexts, usually to identify basic strategies and their implications. The present purpose is to take a wider view, looking at the whole range of company planning from vague speculation about the future to details of implementation. Each section of this chapter deals with a major activity but the tools available to the planner are not considered (apart from a brief section on the collecting and processing of information) because they are not specifically international.

Figure 12.1 illustrates the approaches to planning discussed in the following pages. In the figure, the line across the top represents a range of planning arrangements from all planning in the subsidiary to all planning at head office with varying degrees of sharing in between.

The next line shows another range of options, from formal planning (at home and abroad) only for capital budgets to a complete corporate system. The inverted triangle shows the gradual expansion of planning horizons from domestic, at the bottom, to completely international at the top. Various combinations are possible between local, participative and head office planning, on the one

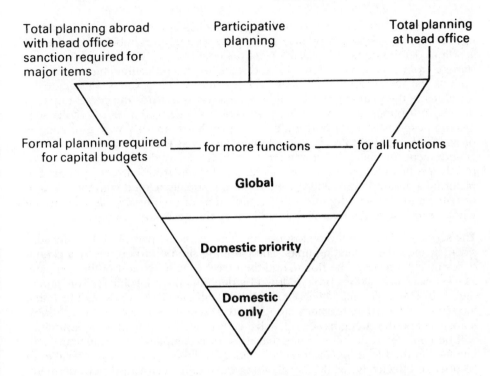

Total planning abroad with head office sanction required for major items

Participative planning

Total planning at head office

Formal planning required for capital budgets ____ for more functions ____ for all functions

Global

Domestic priority

Domestic only

Figure 12.1 A philosophy of international corporate planning

hand, and planning in different departments on the other. With this background, the underlying approaches to planning will be examined.

12.1 A philosophy for international planning

Planning is not to be regarded as an out-of-the-way activity for a few specialists with little relevance to normal business: to some degree everyone plans – if only with a gleam in the eye, a calculation in the head or a note on the back of an envelope. Formal plans vary from a general review of a company's intentions to detailed proposals with dates and financial projections. Once the natural activity, which goes on anyway, is systematized into a set of professional activities, a number of approaches are seen to be possible. For instance, planning could imply that the direction in which a company is going can be laid down, with answers to questions likely to be encountered along the way. For a number of reasons this approach is largely discredited. It is not flexible enough to be effective in a fast-changing environment and the mathematical models used in the past were often unable to cope with many relevant variables. At the other extreme is the view that planning should provide a few general indications about the future of the business. This approach is apt to produce proposals that are of little interest to anyone except the planners.

More firms are now going over to the *contingency* approach which is adopted in this text. A company works systematically through a number of courses of action to determine how its basic objectives could be met in the years to come, starting from a general review of the distant future and examining the various options for achieving its objectives. The amount of detail varies, but gradually increases as the planning horizon moves backwards towards the present time. A number of options are worked out from which are derived a set of criteria suggesting responses to opportunities and problems. In this way guidance is provided about how to react to *contingent* factors as they arise. In an uncertain environment this method is preferred to a more clearly defined route. The proposals are flexible and start from scenarios derived from current options, but picturing a distant future. These scenarios are gradually refined with the addition of dates and financial figures so that each unit of a company, as well as the whole, can readily discover its role and make the necessary arrangements.

The second element in the philosophy of planning is the part played by the subsidiaries and other operating units. The planning can be carried out by a central department, agreed by the Board, and then passed on to the rest of the company as a series of instructions broken down by department or subsidiary. This procedure is usually called *top down* planning, although the phrase does not mean that the views of the operating units are ignored. Discussions will be held with local managers and the strengths of each subsidiary as well as its market opportunities will be considered. It still remains that most of a company's managers are little involved in the planning, and may not understand the results or even be able to co-operate effectively, while the planning documents can cause bewilderment. As against these difficulties, the advantage of planning from the top is that a truly global, rather than a sectional, standpoint is being taken over corporate resources.

The reverse approach is *bottom up*. In this case the central administration brings together, co-ordinates, amends and finally sanctions the plans presented by each operating unit. Normally, although not always, the proposals are organized by a timetable. Outline plans are required on one date, five-year projections on another, one-year budgets on a third, and so on. Although much effort goes into persuading the subsidiaries to adhere to the deadlines, an advantage of this method is that plans are being worked out by those who are going to implement them. The consequent understanding of the proposals is considered by some companies to be critical.

The difficulty about the fashionable *bottom up* approach, popular as it naturally is with the subsidiaries, is that the advantage of the group may be different from the well-being of its component parts. A particular subsidiary may benefit from using all its earnings to expand its own business, whereas the company as a whole would be better-off if the money was transferred to another unit in which a higher rate of return was possible. Even when considering financial priorities alone, as in the case of a conglomerate, marketing and other aspects of the business have to be taken into account. A capital decision cannot be taken in isolation from all other issues. However, the expertise may not exist, in the head office of a company pursuing *bottom up* policies, to determine realistic priorities.

In sum, two related problems arise:

1 the inefficient use of the world-wide resources of the firm where each unit is plotting its own course;

2 the lack of staff at head office to judge adequately between the proposals being made, or indeed to react quickly enough when sanction is required.

Naturally, the second problem can be overcome by increasing central staff but, beyond a certain point, any increase will become inconsistent with the *bottom up* philosophy. The first problem is less easily resolved. To make the best use of global resources, the plans still have to be finalized at the centre in the light of criteria developed there for the future of the company as a whole, but with the full involvement of the local managers. Given this approach, and if the company is large enough to warrant a central planning department, central staff are likely to concentrate on:

1 educating and stimulating the planners in the subordinate units to work out their own proposals in the light of overall company policies and sound planning principles;

2 developing clear criteria for judging, amending and integrating the proposals that come from below.

Between the top down and the bottom up approaches is a third philosophy of international planning which upholds the global view but promotes a participative relationship between head office and the subsidiaries. This approach takes on board many of the issues discussed in this book, enables the company to make the imaginative leap across frontiers, and attempts to ensure that business expectations are not frustrated by a misunderstanding of local cultures or legal systems. International planning has to cope with an organization fraught with divided loyalties. Local units and local managers are likely to push their national interests and resist the transfer of funds.

One *contingent factor* which grows in importance is international competition. In the face of threats from firms based in many other countries, planning has to provide for the moves of competitors and to ensure that a company retains a strong strategic position.

Conclusion

This section has considered the outlook that the corporate planner requires to underpin his activity. The argument revolves around three words.

1 *Contingency.* The planner is providing a sense of direction and a choice of route. Both can readily be changed if conditions change. They provide the company with guidelines for any circumstances that can be foreseen and, hopefully, for the unexpected as well. Contingency planning aims to prevent the company being cornered in an emergency.

2 *Participation.* The relationship between planners in the various units of the company is a subtle one. Local opinion has to be modified in the interests of the company world-wide, as seen through the eyes of head office, to ensure that neither the national nor the international considerations are overlooked.

3 *International.* The planning in which we interest ourselves here has an international content, and the various stages of international planning are examined next.

12.2 The role of international planning

The planning process brings together all the activities of a company and tries to produce order out of a tangle of policies, sometimes inconsistent, that emerges. The subject as a whole can be viewed in terms of time and space.

Time

There is a sequence of events which stretches from the occasion when a project appears on an agenda to the day when a new product is launched in the market-place. The following gives some notable dates along the time-line; the first three stages cover the formation of strategies, a subject already outlined in Chapter 3.

Stage 1: the idea
A senior decision-maker gives the go-ahead in some such terms as: 'This idea is worth considering.' After this the briefing can take many forms, such as:
'If we are to continue to sell product X at our present level of profitability, it seems that we need to expand into the United States and eventually to begin to manufacture there;'
'At what time and under what conditions can we introduce our new product line in France?'
'Consider the options for product Z in Nigeria and identify the three that appear most viable.'
'Examine the economic and political conditions in Malaysia and advise on the facilities required to expand in that country.'

A long-term planning exercise may start from a briefing even less precise than any of those – a review of the future of the company as a whole. More detail will be provided for a short-term project.

Stage 2: the decision preparation
This is the stage in which the planners review the information required and the options available for developing proposals. Outline schemes will be prepared stretching years ahead and supported by market information, capital requirements and possible returns and projections for manufacture and staffing. The options considered may include entering a new geographical or product area, expanding an existing one, holding production stable while deriving more income from greater efficiency, and many others. The exercise may be far-reaching, with questions about where the company will find itself in 30 years' time and what steps are needed to arrive at the destination or, as is more likely, the project may be to consider the routes out of whatever crisis is currently exercising the management.

Stage 3: the decision to proceed to the next stage
'Option X seems to be the most viable and further planning will proceed along the lines suggested.' Such a statement sparks off stage 4. On the other hand, all the proposals may be rejected, in which case stage 2 is repeated.

Stage 4: translation
The all-embracing decision has now to be reformulated in greater detail. Guidelines will demonstrate how the decision can be carried out and how

hazards are to be avoided. The foreseeable contingencies have to be provided for. Sometimes the process will be a long one. For instance, investigations may show that the only profitable way to enter a market is to buy an existing company. Lengthy research may follow before a suitable company is found. During the waiting period the planners will be monitoring numerous sources of information about the country; they will also be rejecting incompatible opportunities. Funds and other resources will be kept available for a quick response when the opportunity occurs. The search process can be useful to the implementation of the plans when the acquisition is made, if it is conducted in such a way as to build up a body of knowledge relevant to business in the country. This stage will include the drafting of a list of dates when developments are expected to occur. At the translation stage the strategies are developed and the tactics worked out.

Stage 5: decisions on further action
This stage will include a series of decisions, among them: fixing a budget, confirming personnel requirements, launching a sales drive, and agreeing to the implications for each department.

Stage 6: detailed plans for implementation
Capital and revenue budgets are prepared and formulae used to forecast how much cash is required and when each infusion of fresh capital will be needed. Techniques are employed to decide the lead-times (deadline dates) for each project and to ensure that supplies and personnel will be available.[1]

Stage 7: operating the project
By now everything is ready to start, and the decision-making is delegated to the unit managers. The role of planning at this stage is to monitor progress and to make recommendations for altering the arrangements as necessary. In particular, the planners have to watch the co-ordination of the departments and subsidiaries which are contributing to the project.

Space

The planner's other major contribution, besides working out the various stages over time, is to ensure that, at any given moment, the implications of the project decisions are being recognized and that the consequential actions happen. This aspect of the planner's role can be described under three headings.

1 Objectivity
The planner needs a reputation for objectivity, to stand outside the corporate politics and the power struggles to keep the implications of the agreed plans in focus. This is a hard assignment, made harder still if the planner has other duties. There will be a number of biasing factors, the planner's own career expectations among them. The need for objectivity may sometimes lead to the use of an outside consultant, but the honest insider is likely to be more effective.

2 Linking
The planner provides links between the different functions – marketing, production, finance, staffing, research and the rest – to ensure that each fits with the time schedules of the others.

3 Bridging

This is the other activity of the planner, to ensure that production keeps pace with sales, that financial resources match the needs, and that all the other requirements are in balance. The need for the matching works both ways. Materials and funds, not to mention customers, must not be late, otherwise expensive delays will occur. Equally, if they are too early there will be unnecessary charges on a line of credit borrowed before it is needed, or on stocks bought too soon. Under certain circumstances the balancing process may involve rationalization across frontiers. This is a delicate exercise which can be made less traumatic by local participation. The much-discussed *just-in-time* approach is intended to overcome, this problem – but the difficulties are naturally, much more acute internationally.

Conclusion

Figure 12.2 brings together the dimensions of time and space, and shows how they fit within an international framework. The subjects listed are those discussed in this section, and the diagram is intended to show them in a suitable context. This outline provides an introduction to the next section where the reasons for international planning are discussed.

It should be noted that phrases like *long-term* or *short-term* are not accurately defined here for the reason that the definition varies from industry to industry and from country to country. A mining company may know that 20 to 25 years will elapse after the decision to go ahead is made and before the income begins to flow. Ten years would be medium-term planning for a company in that industry, while such a period would be long-term for a clothing firm or one in consumer electronics. Similarly, the time horizons for a stable country might be different from those for an unsettled one.

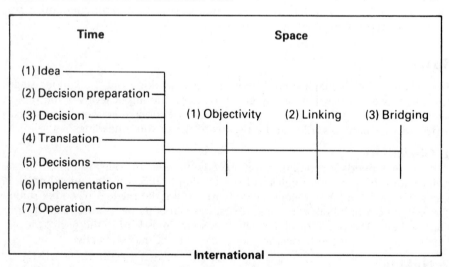

The numbers correspond to those in the text

Figure 12.2 The dimensions of international planning

The exercise of planning, then, is along the lines of time and space, in addition to its domestic and international dimensions. In the succession of stages, each is concerned with a shorter time horizon than the one before. The first is a broad, general declaration of interest in an idea and the last brings the project into operation; the process continues with the monitoring of the route taken and the identifying of factors that are impeding progress or forcing a change of course. Spatial considerations – objectivity, linking and bridging – provide a reminder of the various contributions to the well-being of the company that are required of the planner at any one time.

12.3 The purposes of international planning

The distinction between formal and informal planning has already been hinted at. Informal planning – ideas and suggestions – goes on anyway, is continuous and is cost effective. A few minutes of inspiration, when available, may well be worth many hours of perspiration. But there is also a place for formal planning which:

1 provides a broader view – informal planning is restricted by the knowledge, experience and prejudices of the planner;
2 can establish priorities closely related to the objectives of the company;
3 can fulfil all the other purposes listed in Figure 12.2.

These reasons apply to all planning, but can equally be applied to the distinction between the domestic and the international. Where no-one is committed, even part-time, to international planning, the opportunities abroad will not be effectively reviewed and are not likely to be assigned the priority needed to exploit them. Indeed, the reasons for formal international corporate planning are more powerful than those for domestic. The increasing complexity of global operations, the bewildering variety of factors that can affect the results, and the complicated logistics that have to be provided for, all point to the need to ensure that deadlines are set and criteria determined for coping with change.

Formal international planning, using systems and techniques to map out the corporate developments, also serves other objectives including the following.

To ensure that the operations abroad are not treated just as an extension of those at home

A subsidiary in Nigeria, Malaysia, the United States or wherever, has a life of its own. It is a part of a national economy. Its government can make life difficult by, for instance, blocking remittances to head office if the subsidiary is considered to be acting against the national interest. Skilled planning is needed to ensure a proper autonomy while also ensuring conformity to corporate policies.

To make certain that the foreign operations are sufficiently integrated into the company's global strategies

For most firms, too little integration is a greater danger than too much. Strategies are painstakingly developed and then individual exceptions are permitted which conflict with those strategies and may, in the end, make them unworkable. Another pitfall under this heading is neglect. The foreign subsidiaries may not be able to make the expected contribution as a result of being left out of the scheme of things.

To make delegation possible

This becomes necessary as the organization becomes more complex, and to ensure that individual managers operating in various parts of the world take part in the decision-making system. Specialist skills can be drawn on wherever they exist and, conversely, career possibilities become better known.

To broaden the horizons of head office

In particular to bring together into comprehensible patterns the information and insights which flow from overseas.

To watch the movements of competitors and to guess their strategies

This is hard enough in the case of a domestic firm; it becomes much more difficult with foreign operations, especially when a competitor makes apparently inconsistent moves. The decision-making process seldom allows for total adherence to a chosen strategy.

In sum, valuable information and profitable opportunities will be misused or wasted if a continuous international planning process is not operating, and some formality is required to ensure that it is.

12.4 Collecting and processing information

Strategic and planning decisions are based on a mixture of fact and judgement. A fashionable phrase – *the management of uncertainty* – sums up the judgement. The search for certainty is fruitless; the need is to discriminate between options and to make sure that the judgement is as well-informed as possible. There are planning techniques designed to reduce uncertainty. Naturally, the techniques will be appraised according to their efficiency at carrying out this purpose, but they will not be expected to provide one sure way to a goal or be condemned if anything goes wrong. A tool is chosen according to its ability to deliver reliable guidance at a reasonable cost. As with all data collecting or processing aids, the expenses have to be weighed against the advantages to be gained. Are the costs of ignorance higher than the costs of knowledge? The viable costs of research and planning will be related to the possible rewards of success and the penalties for failure.[2]

The information required by the planners is of a number of types, including:
1 information about the company – its progress and opportunities, its problems, its strengths and its weaknesses;

2 information about companies with an existing or possible business relationship – customers, suppliers, advisers;
3 information about competitors;
4 information about social, economic and other trends that are likely to affect the market;
5 information about relevant legal and political factors.

The information can be collected within the corporate system, both through regular reporting and as a result of special enquiries. There is evidence that this internal information is the most used, although the use of data banks is increasing. External sources may provide a more objective review of the environment, but it is with the company and its current position as well as the views of its managers that the planners are mostly concerned.[3] Dangers which have to be safeguarded against are not only that the information provided internally may lack objectivity but also that it is too rooted in the past. The plans that emerge are liable to be a simple continuation of existing business and lack an element of innovation, including entry into new foreign markets.

Among the external information needed, the review of potential markets and new centres of manufacture or supply is specifically international. Many techniques for country appraisal are available, usually designed to assess political risk.[4] A comprehensive scheme can be designed for the purpose, or taken from among those on offer. The hallmarks of one that is viable are that it covers all aspects of the national life relevant to the business and that it can be used at various levels of complexity – from a simple back of the envelope type calculation to an elaborate statistical analysis.

There should be a scoring system, to establish the state of each item in the particular country, and a weighting which corresponds with the company's priorities. For instance, one scheme (referenced in note 4) divides 78 items under eight main headings. Main heading number 1 is 'The national economy', sub-heading 1.4 is 'energy consumption per head'. This particular variable will be rated from 1 (well below average, consumption is low) to 5 (average) to 10 (consumption is very high). The score will then be multiplied by the weighting, which will be high if the company supplies energy equipment or low if this item is irrelevant to the company's business. The main heading will also be given a weighting. The final calculation will give some such messages as: below 30 per cent (not worth pursuing); above 70 per cent (almost a certainty); between 30 per cent and 70 per cent, worth more detailed examination. This method can be used, with different variables and weightings, for different purposes, including whether to enter a market in the first place and, if so, by what route (exporting, licensing or investment).

Market surveys are required at each stage of the planning process – the decision-preparation, the translation and the implementation – but in varying levels of detail. Other techniques for assembling and for appraising data are used at different stages. These techniques are no different from those employed in domestic corporate planning, although the uncertainties are greater when they are used internationally.[5]

In general, the decision-preparation stage requires broad-brush methods based on qualitative judgements rather than accurate calculations. Long-term forecasts of the market and of social, political, economic and technological change are accompanied by scenarios describing where the company might be going during the next ten, 20 or 30 years. Relevant techniques are those that present most clearly the probabilities and possibilities within the company and can develop the options that match the environment. At the translation stage, moré quantitative methods are required, and at the implementation stage exact figures are essential to lead to the formulation of budgets.

Plans, both long-term qualitative and short-term quantitative, need to provide options for the various contingencies that are anticipated in achieving strategic objectives. The ideal is a continuously updated model, which any authorized executive can review at any time, showing the expected position of the company and the opportunities open to it in the short- and medium-term, with a number of options, giving their advantages and hazards into the distant future. From this model can be derived sets of criteria for judging opportunities as they arise. Planning is normally as much concerned with responding to offers and threats from would-be collaborators or competitors as it is with stimulating fresh initiatives within the company. A major advantage of systematic planning is the ability to avoid short-term responses which sabotage long-term aims.

12.5 The organization of a planning department

The three major options for international planning are shown in Figure 12.3, where (a) and (b) are described as 'integrated', because the respective planning departments are closely interrelated. In option (a), the divisional, regional and national departments report to general management, but long-term and tactical planning activities are only carried out at the corporate and divisional head offices. Other levels are responsible for implementation planning. In option (b), central planning manages the divisional and regional departments, but not the national subsidiary. In option (c), each unit, including the national subsidiary, is responsible for its own strategies and tactics. Fully competent planning departments are required at each level, and their links to one another are more restricted.

In each of the options shown in Figure 12.3 executives in the most senior level of planning are servicing top management for decision-preparation and their colleagues in other head office departments for both decision-preparation and translation. The divisional planning department is involved in decision-preparation in only one of the options, (c).

12.6 Conclusion

Planning is about taking the extra care that can turn a difficult route into a successful one. Each channel for foreign business has its problems. Exports can be blocked, licensees can turn into competitors, investment can be ill-placed. The selected channel is chosen in the knowledge that problems will occur since no choice is trouble-free. Foreseeing the problems in order to resolve them is one of the purposes of planning. This chapter began by discussing the philosophy.

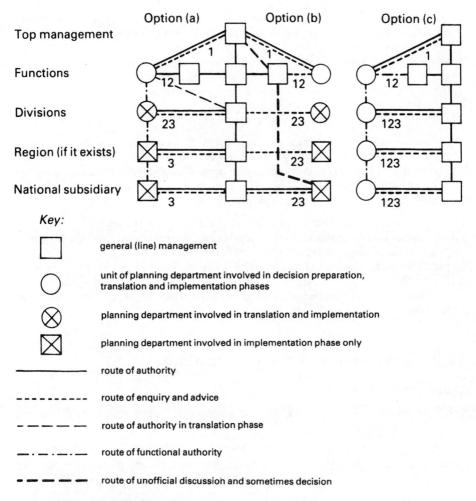

Key:

☐ general (line) management

◯ unit of planning department involved in decision preparation, translation and implementation phases

⊗ planning department involved in translation and implementation

⊠ planning department involved in implementation phase only

───── route of authority

- - - - - - - - route of enquiry and advice

─ ─ ─ ─ ─ route of authority in translation phase

—·—·—·— route of functional authority

▬ ▬ ▬ ▬ ▬ route of unofficial discussion and sometimes decision

1 = Decision preparation (strategic planning)
2 = Translation (tactical planning)
3 = Implementation (operational planning). These terms are explained in the next chapter.

Figure 12.3 The organization of corporate planning – three options

It was argued that there were three important considerations:
1 to allow for contingencies and to be flexible enough for plans not to be invalidated by change in the environment or within the company;
2 to be participative, guided by head office in the interests of the company as a whole but with subsidiary managers involved;
3 to be international, fully accepting and using the international dimension.

These considerations were accompanied by those of time and space. Figure 12.2 listed the stages that a project has to go through over time, and is the outline for a planning cycle. Alongside are the requirements for the planners to produce an objective, linking and balancing service within the company at any one time.

It has been pointed out that planning will be happening informally even when it is not recognized as such. But formal planning can achieve a number of extra goals including:

1 ensuring appropriate treatment for the foreign operations,
2 ensuring the co-ordination of global and of local policies,
3 making delegation possible within a recognized framework,
4 broadening the horizons of head office,
5 monitoring the strategies of competitors.

Once a diversification programme is authorized, it can take one of two forms. The international route, with its various approaches, is one, and product diversification the other. The two routes, geographical and product, can go together when a company buys another which is already international or when the most profitable means of launching a new product is abroad.

Finally, there are numerous techniques available. Long-term, mainly non-quantitative, methods for systematically analysing the material for the strategic decision-making; and quantitative methods designed to reduce the uncertainties in the short-term. International corporate planning is at one and the same time a means of steering the company along a chosen route, and of signalling the opportunities and the problems that are likely to arise. Measures can be taken to reduce the uncertainties, but these will never disappear.

12.7 Questions and further reading

Questions

1 List the main activities associated with international corporate planning, and discuss one of them in some depth.

2 It is asserted in this chapter that forecasting for foreign markets is a particularly difficult activity. State whether you agree or disagree with this and give reasons for your answer.

3 Write a briefing for an executive who has recently been appointed to introduce international planning into a company. Select for yourself the size (by net assets) and industry group of the firm.

4 What do you understand as a synergistic use of resources? Explain how difficulties arise in developing synergy.

5 What are the main problems associated with planning across frontiers? Explain some solutions.

6 Discuss some consequences of size and industry sector in international corporate planning.

Further reading

A thorough review of the subject, which amplifies the brief statement here, can be found in: Brooke and van Beusekom (1979).

See also: Channon and Jalland (1978).

Kuno, T., 'Comparative study of strategy, structure and long-range planning in Japan and U.S.,' *Management Japan*, 13.1, (Spring 1980), pp. 20–34.

For a review of the subject, *see*:

Dymsza, W.A., 'Global strategic planning: a model and recent developments', *Journal of International Business Studies*, (Fall 1984), pp. 169–83.

There are textbooks which cover most of the relevant techniques, although not usually from an international point of view. See, for example: Butler, W.F. and others, *Methods and Techniques of Business Forecasting*, Prentice-Hall 1974.

Appendix to Chapter 12
Internal consultancies in multinational companies

This Appendix is by Michael Hurford and is reproduced with his permission

Even after the cutbacks of recent years, many companies still carry central service staff which provide consultancies to the domestic and foreign subsidiaries.

Consultants provide to their host organization something otherwise missing from it, such as:
- special knowledge or skill
- intensive professional help
- arguments, with evidence, that justify action by the host organization.

These things are, usually, seen by the host organization as worth acquiring to address a problem, manage a change, or to improve the current way of doing things.

All consultants operate within the following operational conditions:
- they do not have any hierarchical or structural authority or power in the host organization except that given to them temporarily by the client: all they have is sapiential authority;
- responsibility for taking action lies with the host organization; thus the role of the consultant is advisory or catalytic;
- consultancy is not a means of performing miracles. It is a burdensome, time consuming, and often untidy process in which the ideal has always to be balanced against the attainable.

I will now take two examples common to many multinationals and indicate some of the difficulties of putting their initial precepts into practice.

Centres of expertise

1 Most multinationals have, in their head offices, groups of experts in the company's major functions. The higher the technology of the company, the greater the pressure to establish these groups.
2 They are responsible for:
   (a) transmitting to operating units advice about the best practices in their disciplines;

(b) formulating policy, standards and procedures which, when approved by the company's management, will be mandatory on operating units;

(c) doing research in order to do (a) and (b) properly.

3 It is necessary for these units to be staffed by well qualified people to avoid reinforcing mediocrity. However, they should also be trained in the subtleties of their role. The heavy hand must be replaced with the sensitivity of the consultant.

4 The most difficult aspect of their role is to distinguish between being advisors and inspectors. It is very difficult, too, for the subsidiary to grasp whether it is receiving genuine advice or whether that advice is, in fact, mandatory.

5 Many multinational companies have introduced forms of profit centres whereby headquarters' services are only used if subsidiaries request them and then, usually, a charging out system is used. I have doubts about profit centres anyway, but there is a risk, in the theory's application to centres of expertise, that group expertise is diminished.

6 My final comment on centres of expertise is that they are a strong centralising influence.

Internal management consultancies

All multinational companies have debated the pros and cons of these against external consultancies.

1 Apart from cost, the advantages of internal management consultancies are:

External

Overt independence

Freedom from hierarchy

Prima facie competence

Freedom from conditioning

Internal

Provided overt (senior) client support, then independence and freedom from hierarchy can be overcome.

Knowledge of the vocabulary, ethos and behaviour patterns – this is a great advantage.

Knowledge of what is possible.

2 Relationship with the client. Most consultants would subscribe to the dictum, 'Begin where the client is, not where you are'. This implies that their role is selected to fit the expectations of the client, the circumstances of their agreed contract and the nature of the assignment. However, consultants will possess a variety of skills and attributes which are at the disposal of their clients. As a consequence, the roles which consultants perform may well vary throughout any assignment. Clients are presumed to be more familiar with the substantive functioning of their own organization than consultants. However, analysis and diagnosis of organizational process and design represent areas in which consultants would probably claim greater expertise than their clients. This differentiation of expertise represents the interdependence between consultant and client. Sensitivity to each other's expertise and knowledge is thus the foundation upon which an effective client–consultant role relationship is based.

The essential characteristic of the client is that he is, at the same time, authority, problem owner and en route advisor.

3 There are problems that are specific to multinational companies:
   (a) a lack of trust of someone from head office.
   (b) a language barrier
   (c) an often unanswered question: 'Is the solution mandatory?'
   (d) a need for mixed teams from centre and subsidiary.
4 It should be noted that centre of expertise operations require a client just as much as consultancies.

Holism against reductionism

'Since we are assured that the all-wise Creator has observed the most exact proportions of number, weight and measure, in the make of all things, the most likely way, therefore, to get any insight into the nature of those parts of the creation, which come within our observation, must in all reason, be to number, weigh and measure.' (Stephen Hales, 1677–1761)

There is a book called *God and the New Physics* which, at first sight, would seem to have nothing to do with the study of organizations. However, when I read it, it struck me how good an illustration to one of the perils of finding out the truth about organizations was the chapter that dealt with the problem of life force.

The author makes the point that a study of the constituents – the atoms – will not reveal the secret of life; it is to be found in their pattern of association. Atoms do not need to be animated to yield life, they simply have to be arranged in the appropriate way.

The main thrust of western scientific thinking during the last three centuries has been reductionist. The use of the word analysis illustrates the scientists' almost unquestioning habit of taking the problem apart in order to solve it. But some problems, like jigsaws, can only be solved by putting them together. An illustration could be a flashing electric sign. If you asked an electrical engineer to explain this, he could give an accurate description in terms of electric circuit theory, but to claim that the display is nothing but electrical impulses in a complex circuit is absurd. Obviously his explanation is accurate at its particular level of description, but it omits any mention of the message. This concept is outside the engineer's terms of reference. Thus, one could say that the message is on a higher level of structure than circuits and lamps. It is an holistic feature.

The characteristic of such an holistic feature is described as *emergent*, that is, it emerges when the whole is seen rather than just the constituents. There are many illustrations, though one of the best is an ant colony. Ants possess an elaborate and highly organised social structure based on division of labour and collective responsibility. Although each ant has a limited repertoire of behaviour, the colony itself displays a remarkable level of purpose and intelligence. Clearly, each ant does not carry a mental picture of the final design as each is programmed to execute a single task but, if one considers the colony as a whole, the emergent picture is complex. Thus, any structure must be looked at both at a reductionist and an holistic level.

The idea that an organization has a personality separate from the personalities of its members is not new. All the Companies Acts state that this is so. There was an interesting American book called *Corporate Deviance* which tried to explain why some companies were crooked and others were not.

You should aim, therefore, to be able to describe an emergent view of your organization, one that transcends and yet embodies the strengths and weaknesses of its members.

Trawl through the following check-list

There are many methodologies, but an effective one is to structure interviews by asking questions under the following headings:
- Tasks
- Performance assessment/accountability
- Authority/decisions
- Workload
- Organization
- Hindrances to effective work
- Information volunteered by the interview.

PART THREE THE ENVIRONMENT AND THE FUTURE

This part rounds off the book by examining the business environment in which the international manager operates. The subject is divided among four chapters – economic, cultural, governmental and inter-governmental. Finally, Chapter 17 summarizes the book and looks into the future.

13 The economic environment

'The gross national product does not allow for the health of our children, the quality of their education or the joy of their play. It does not include the beauty of our poetry or the strength of our marriages, the intelligence of our public debate or the integrity of our public officials. It measures neither our wit nor our courage, neither our wisdom nor our learning, neither our compassion nor our devotion to our country. It measures everything, in short, except that which makes life worthwhile.' (Robert Kennedy quoted in *The Guardian*, London, 3 June 1995.)

This chapter covers issues which make up the economic environment of the international firm. Naturally it, along with Chapter 15, rests heavily on economic statistics and readers should bear the above quotation in mind. Other aspects of the environment, like the cultural and political, are considered in the following chapters; inevitably there is some overlap. The underlying theories proposed in Chapter 2 are assumed as background to this chapter.

The economic and technical factors which influence international business policies are legion. The following is a selective list of some of the key components of the economic environment: trade flows, commodity trading, investment flows, trade between East and West, trade between South and North, capital markets, financial instruments, balance of payments, exchange rates, inflation, banking, insurance and technology. Most of these are considered here; other factors, like technology transfer, government and inter-government interventions, are examined in other chapters.

13.1 Trade flows

The steady increase in world trade has already been noted (Table 1.1), and this has been accompanied by changes in composition and direction. The most outstanding change has been the increasing proportion of trade that is intra-company. For the United States, income from foreign assets has long since reached 25 per cent of all foreign income, and the figure is rising in most of the industrialized countries. While companies claim that their subsidiaries are free to deal with outsiders as well as suppliers within the company, the high level of internal trade imposes restrictions on new entrants and is itself a motive towards vertical integration.

The flows of trade have retained some remarkable similarities during the last quarter of a century in spite of dramatic changes in the influencing factors.[1] For instance, the list of the top ten exporters has contained much the same names (although Saudi Arabia came in and Benelux dropped out) as it did in 1970. The

215

directions of trade have also changed slowly. The most dramatic change in the 1970s was the rise of the oil-rich countries; there has also been a move towards greater trade within regions.

In the European Union, where intra-regional commerce has increased from a third to a half of all trade, this can be accounted for by the removal of tariff barriers. However, this explanation does not fit the Pacific basin countries where trade within the region has increased from a little over half to about two-thirds of their total in a quarter of a century. Here the trade between members of a regional group (the Association of South East Asian Nations, ASEAN) has increased more slowly than that for the region as a whole. This is partly accounted for by a reorientation of the exports of Australia and New Zealand – now 50 per cent to other Pacific countries, a proportion that has doubled in the period. In the Americas most trade is regional; 30 per cent of South American exports go to the United States.

Table 13.1 gives the global directions of trade in the mid-1980s. It shows that, in spite of the rise of the oil-rich nations, over half of all world trade is still between industrial countries – a proportion that has only declined slightly in recent years.

Table 13.1   Directions of trade in 1993 (exports in US$m)

| TO | FROM | |
	Industrial countries	Developing countries
Industrial countries	1,776.9	663.5
Developing countries	728,121	461,414

Source: *Direction of Trade Statistics Yearbook 1994* (1995) Washington DC: International Monetary Fund

All observations on the directions of trade must be seen against the background of a general increase. The exports of Eastern European countries to the West, for instance, have increased rapidly (by about 700 per cent) over the last 15 years but have remained static as a proportion of world exports (roughly 10 per cent). One consequence of the growth of world trade is the parallel growth of dependence on trade for sustaining national economies.

Table 13.2 shows the dependence on trade of some of the industrial nations. It also shows the differences between the relatively low dependence of the United States and Japan, which are nevertheless high exporters, and the high dependence of some European countries. The following three propositions stem from the growth of world exports, together with the growth in the proportion of exports to gross domestic product:

1 That export trade aids economic growth more than import substitution; the fastest growing economies in the 1970s and early 1980s, mainly in the Far East, were export-oriented. Naturally, however, other factors are involved and this relationship may be coincidental.

2 That as the part played by exports in a nation's wealth increases, its ability to control its economic decision-making is reduced; it also becomes more vulnerable to currency revaluations which raise exporters' prices. The nightmare for

many a government is the reaction on the part of the nation's customers to economic policies which influence imports, protection, inflation, labour relations, support for exporters or other measures that appear to influence international competitiveness or increase the difficulty of entry to national markets.

3 A consequence of the contradiction between 1 and 2 is an inconsistency in policies which support long-term measures for the liberalization of trade while, on particular issues and in the short-term, adopting protectionist regulations. Countries, like companies, concentrate on domestic policies in times of financial crisis often at the expense of their foreign trade interests. The struggle between free trade and constraint remains a feature of the economic environment which companies have to take into account.

Table 13.2 Dependence on trade (exports as % of gross domestic product, 1992)

	(1) Gross domestic product ($m)	(2) Exports ($m)	(3) (2) as a % of (1)
France (1992)	142,869	231,452	1.7
Germany (1992)	184,508	429,754	0.03
Japan (1992)	203,736	339,492	11.6
United Kingdom (1992)	106,502	190,481	22.4
United States (1992)	1,011,563	420,812	0.8

Source: *World Development Report 1994*, The World Bank, Washington DC.

Further reading

Daniels and Radebaugh (1995), ch. 5.
Williams, A.O., *International Trade and Investment: A Managerial Approach*, (Wiley, 1982).

13.2 Commodity trading

Many of the industrial countries grew rich as a result of the exploitation of their own resources, together sometimes with those of dependent territories as well, and by turning those resources into manufactured products. Market entry was relatively easy and yet monopolistic advantages could be acquired in rising industries. Entry into world trade is more costly today. Some developing countries are dependent on a limited range of agricultural or mineral products, and are affected by frequent fluctuations in price. Companies can be made or broken by changes in world prices for the commodities they buy or sell. The futures markets are designed to even out price changes for the manufacturer while various systems, including the holding of buffer stocks and the control of prices, are designed to make life easier for the supplier.

The commodity which has most influence on world trade is, of course, oil. So dominant has this been in recent years, that it is hard to remember the impact that prices of other commodities, like wheat and rubber, once made. Present evidence is that the dominance of oil in an increasingly energy-hungry world is not

likely to decline. In 1973, oil provided over half (54.6 per cent) of energy requirements in market economy countries. After 13 years of intensive search for other
sources, that figure had only dropped to 45.0 per cent in 1986. This decline is
unlikely to go much further for a number of reasons. One is that the comparative glut of oil in the last few years has brought an end to some of the efforts to
develop other sources (like the processing of shale in North America). Another
is that one increasing source, hydro-electric power, seems to be reaching the
limits of its expansion, while nuclear energy and coal are encountering environmental problems.

For the next 20 years, oil is likely to retain its dominance and, after a decline
in the short-term, the overall increase in energy demand will boost prices however much other sources are developed.[2] Oil production (market economy
countries) in 1987 averaged 43.7 million barrels per day. Estimates for 2000 vary
between 23 and 58 million barrels per day. The most likely estimates are well
above the 1987 figure, showing an increase in production of about 15 per cent
in each decade. No-one is yet certain when falling supplies will begin to cut
production.

While the oil producers succeeded in maintaining prices to a certain extent,
attempts were made to support commodities like copper and sugar – two products whose price fluctuations radically affect several national economies (from
Guyana to Zambia). Attempts to introduce some order into world markets may
have benefited consumers who can purchase futures, but they have not helped
producers as much as had been hoped. The message to them has been to process commodities inside the country where possible. This statement does not,
perhaps, do justice to the skills employed in the markets but, from the point of
view of the producer, the large buyer has great power. Some attempts to offset
this have been made where suppliers are particularly fragmented. These include
co-operative farm buying organizations and, among sugar producers, the development of nucleus estates. In this arrangement, a factory is established to process
the products of a large group of small farms. The farmers remained independent
but received assistance, advice and an assured market from the firm which ran
the factory. This firm had access to world markets.

Table 13.3 gives an insight into the fluctuations of commodity prices. Attempts at
control have been carried out by means of buffer stocks, production quotas and
export quotas. When the first edition of this book went to press efforts were still
being made to stabilize the price of tin, albeit at a much lower figure than that
at which it began to collapse. Several years later the saga continues.[3]

Table 13.3 Fluctuations in price of selected commodities (US$000)

	1990	1992	1995
Iron	70.8	31.60	25.5
Petroleum	22.05	18.72	16.5
Copper	120.72	103.64	136.23

Source: *Yearbook of International Financial Statistics 1994* (1995), Washington DC, International Monetary Fund 1995
See also: ICCH Commodities Yearbook 1990 (Macmillan 1990)

Further reading

Daniels and Radebaugh (1995), ch. 7.
Robock and Simmonds (1983), ch. 2.

13.3 Investment flows

Investment flows, we have already noted, have increased to the extent that some industry sectors are dominated by firms which operate world-wide. Some indications are provided in Table 13.4, where the percentage increases and the absolute figures both demonstrate that substantial sums are flowing across frontiers. The patterns sometimes defy expectations and are full of paradoxes. For instance, one motive for direct investment is the opportunity to buy companies cheaply when a currency is strong. This would explain Japanese moves abroad based on a strong yen, but would not explain European investments in the United States which have even gained impetus at times when the dollar was strong. This suggests that to diversify into an economy, whose growing strength is demonstrated by a rising exchange rate, is also a motive. Yet another motive for direct investment is to retain markets where tariff barriers impede exports. However, the .experience of the European Union shows that investment also increases when tariff barriers come down, although non-tariff barriers may remain.

Different ground-rules come into play when capital can be transferred more easily.

The bulk of investment, like most trade, is between industrialized countries, but the developing countries are making their presence felt as the following paragraphs will demonstrate.

Table 13.4 Increases (decreases) in flows of investment in recent years: growth (decline), 1986 to 1990

INTO THE UNITED STATES (US$BN)	
(1986)	18.56
(1988)	41.82
(1990)	12.45

OUT OF THE UNITED STATES (US$MN)	
(1985)	78.27
(1987)	98.76
(1989)	57.65

Source: *World Tables 1994* (The World Bank) Washington DC, 1994

Further reading

Daniels and Radebaugh (1995), ch. 8.
Hood and Young (1979), ch. 4.
Robock and Simmonds (1983), ch. 2.
Stopford and Turner (1985).

Vernon and Wells (1981), ch. 7–10.
Williams, A.O., *International Trade and Investment: A Managerial Approach*, Wiley (1982).

13.4 Trade and investment: East and West

Before the political changes in Eastern Europe, it was already possible to say: 'Trade between the socialist countries of Eastern Europe and the rest of the world increased rapidly during the 1970s, albeit from a very small base.'[4] Apart from the word 'socialist,' which is currently unfashionable, that statement could be made of the 1980s and early 1990s. Further, the progress is taking similar forms – slowly developing trade backed by limited investment in the form of joint ventures of which 1991 has seen a succession. One was a major investment by Gillette to manufacture razors in the then Soviet Union (reported in the *Financial Times* for 5 March 1991). Also reported in the *Financial Times* (27 April 1991) was an increase in joint ventures under the headline: 'Joint ventures gleam amid economic gloom'. The report showed a nearly five-fold increase in joint ventures between 1989 and 1990 and a quadrupling of the production of these ventures (with foreign partners owning 38 per cent). The average size of the ventures was small and together they added up to a tiny, but rapidly growing, niche in a large economy.

From the point of view of western companies, the most noticeable change has been in the reliability of payments. In the days when they dealt with government departments, they were subject to hard bargaining and many frustrations, but once a contract was signed payment was prompt and reliable. Now that individual enterprises have to stand on their own feet, it has proved very difficult to ensure timely payment. Another difficulty for the western businessman is that the abolition of central planning – however desirable on other grounds – removes the advantage of knowing where demand will lie five years ahead.

Table 13.5 gives recent figures for trade between Eastern Europe and the industrialized world. Much of the export total is in raw materials, especially energy sources from the former Soviet Union, although the smaller countries export a higher proportion of manufactured goods. Imports are mainly manufactures.

Table 13.5 Exports from Eastern Europe to the industrialized countries (US$m)

	1990	1991	1992	1993
All industrial countries	2,453.7	2,503.3	2,650.1	2,561.1
France	194	1163.8	1408.9	1509.5
Germany	3027.8	3447.6	3254.5	4971.4
Japan	297.7	199.4	473.1	489.5
United Kingdom	833.3	637.8	989	945.1
United States	1001	1681.1	1846.4	1485.6

Source: *Directions of Trade Statistics Yearbook 1990*, Washington: International Monetary Fund

Currency problems (compounded by large debts, especially in the case of Poland) are going to constrain trade for many years to come. One solution for the shortage of currency has been an increase in countertrade. This has steadily grown during the 1970s and 1980s and probably stands at about a third of all East–West trade now.

Technical assistance agreements are another component of trade that is likely to grow, matching the general increase in sales of knowledge recorded in Chapter 5. The western exporter obtains royalties from the licensing of technology, and sometimes management fees and component sales as well. This trade is not all one way. The former Soviet Union was, for a long time, a source of foreign licensing agreements and a company was registered in Switzerland in the late 1970s to promote the licensing of eastern technology in the West.

13.5 Trade and investment: North and South

The economic divisions in the world are growing even as the political divisions seem to be easing. The Brandt Commission[5] estimated that in 1980, 800 million people (nearly 19 per cent of the world's population of about 4.3 billion) were on the verge of extreme poverty and starvation. Since then, the number has certainly increased. It has also been dramatized by natural and manmade disasters in Bangladesh, Iraq and several parts of Africa. The fact that in total the developing countries' share of world trade is also increasing (see Table 13.6 and note that this generalization excepts African developing countries) demonstrates that there are large and growing differences between countries classified by the World Bank as 'developing'; the average growth is made up of some large increases and some declines. Chapter 15 proposes a classification which includes oil-rich, richer developing and poorer developing nations. These three categories together with the poorer (non-European) socialist nations make up 147 out of 173 countries classified and the differences between rich and poor among them are of recent origin. Thirty-five years ago Japan was still classified as a developing country, while other South East Asian countries are now regarded as 'newly industrialized'. Singapore, for instance, has achieved a gross domestic product per head above those of some poorer industrialized nations. There are also Caribbean countries like Trinidad and Barbados reaching into the wealthier classifications.

Table 13.6 Trade of different regions – changes in share over ten years

	Share of world trade (%) (US$bn)		Change (%)
Exports from	1980	1990	1980–90
Developed market economies	1,258.9	2,445.2	+48.5
Developing countries	586.9	774.8	+24.3
Africa	94.9	66.7	−42.3
Economies in transition	155.1	171.9	+9.8

Source: *World Economic and Social Survey 1994* (1994) New York, United Nations

Poverty

The word 'South' is taken to mean poverty although some countries so classified have become very rich indeed. The 'South' includes also the poorest with a standard of living well below the international average. In 1995, the British press contained accounts of growing relative poverty in some developing countries.[6] These showed small gains in revenue in very poor countries more than offset by a rapid increase in population. Also shown was a decline in investment in these countries. 'Charity groups' were said to be advocating a cancellation of developing countries' debts.

A characteristic of the developing nations, especially but not exclusively the poorest, is dependence for trade on a limited number of raw materials. The Niger, for instance, is one of the ten poorest countries. A United Nations report of the early 1980s showed that one third of the income of its government came from uranium whose price was depressed by a global surplus.[7] Other minerals and the products of tropical agriculture form the main source of wealth of another 60 countries. This situation makes up a poverty trap whereby a country does not earn the foreign currency to buy the equipment and know-how to diversify.

One result has been that the wealth of some countries has actually declined in recent years in spite of international concern about the poverty trap. These countries have been hardest hit by the oil price rises and by the recession in the West which kept commodity prices low. For instance, in 1983 world gross domestic product increased by 1.9 per cent from the previous year, but the average of non-oil producing developing countries in Africa was down by 0.7 per cent, and this was an average measured against some striking increases (like +16.1 per cent for Botswana). Central and South American non-oil exporting countries declined (−2.1 per cent), while those in Asia increased by 5.5 per cent.[8] In spite of the problems, however, trade has increased. The value of exports from non-oil exporting developing countries increased between 1973 and 1983 from $68bn to $265bn (390 per cent); but market share, at 23.5 per cent, is still very low in proportion to the size of the developing world.

The main proposals of the Brandt Commission were as follows.
 1 The establishment of an action programme for the poorest countries to cover water and soil management, health care, afforestation, solar energy, mineral and petroleum exploration, support for industry, development of transport and other infrastructure needs.
 2 Remedies for high birth rates and protection for the rights of migrants and refugees are proposed. Pressures on the environment, caused by expanding populations in the industrialized countries, which produce irreversible ecological damage, were identified.
 3 Disarmament has to be treated as an urgent need if poverty is to be fought.
 4 The task of the South is to be seen in terms of social and economic reforms which include the redistribution of wealth, improved social services, more spending on rural areas, more small-scale enterprises and improved tax administration, together with greater co-operation between countries.
 5 The countries of origin need to play a greater part in the marketing and processing of commodities. Prices need to be stabilized, while new financial arrangements and facilities are required. Tariffs should be modified in

industrialized countries to allow the entry of processed minerals. Behind this proposal lies a bias in the tariff systems of the wealthy nations which has been discouraging industrialization among the poor producers of raw materials. They are unable to enrich themselves by establishing their own processing industries because of the difficulty of selling the products.

6   The transition to new sources of energy should be speeded up and the United Nations should establish a global energy centre.

7   Tariffs are likely to be liberalized, but fair standards of employment will be expected in return. New patterns of world industrial production are needed under the surveillance of some international organization, perhaps incorporating the General Agreement on Tariffs and Trade (GATT, now WTO) and the UN Conference on Trade and Development (UNCTAD). There should be free trade in food.

8   Laws and codes for transnational corporations are required to ensure that:
    (a) reciprocal obligations are agreed between the home and host countries to control foreign investment, the transfer of technology and the repatriation of profits, royalties and dividends;
    (b) ethical behaviour is enforced, information is not withheld, restrictive practices are outlawed and labour standards maintained;
    (c) national tax policies are upheld and transfer prices monitored;
    (d) national incentives for foreign investors are harmonized.
    In addition, steps should be taken to improve the bargaining power of less developed countries and their access to international finance. Countries should insist on control over their own natural resources, but pay adequate compensation where this involves expropriating a foreign firm. Appropriate technology should be transferred at reasonable prices.

9   A world monetary order should be established with an improved exchange system, the creation of a new currency and reform of the International Monetary Fund.

10 Development finance: a complete reorganization of the system is called for. This would mean a new organization; the World Development Fund is the suggested title.

11 The strengthening of the United Nations and the establishment, under its auspices, of a high-level body to oversee international negotiations.

The Brandt Commission was an attempt to ensure that the subject of rich and poor comes to the top of the agenda for statesmen against the current resistance and apathy. The position outlined in the Commission's report suggests the possibility of massive famine and disease. Expectations have been raised but not fulfilled; despair can produce disaster. If the gap between North and South widens, there will be a North–South conflict to replace the dialogue.

Further reading

Aw, B.Y. and Roberts, M.J.,'The role of imports from newly industrialized countries in US production'. *The Review of Economics and Statistics*, Vol.67, No.1, February 1985.

Balassa, B. and Michalopoulos, C., 'Liberalizing trade between developed and developing countries', *Journal of World Trade Law*, Winter 1986, pp. 3–28.

Lall, S. and Streeten, P., *Foreign Investment, Transnationals and Developing Countries*, Macmillan, 1975.

North-South, A Programme for Survival, Report of the Independent Commission on International Development Issues under the Chairmanship of Willy Brandt, Pan Books and M.I.T. Press, 1980.

13.6 Capital markets and financial instruments

Three trends have been noted in the capital markets in the last few years: a steady increase in the growth indexes of all of them, a shift of emphasis to South East Asia and further developments in international currencies. The increases have been dramatic in many cases, with new high levels being recorded. In 1985 all the 18 principal stock markets, except Singapore, showed increases ranging from 123.9 per cent for Italy (second and third places were taken by Austria and Germany) to 13.3 per cent for Japan (−23.7 per cent for Singapore). For Italy this was the second year running at the top of the table. Although not among the front runners, the South East Asia markets have gained considerably in significance. Japan has the greatest volume of business after the United States (Britain is currently in third place); Hong Kong suffered a setback in 1982 (a fall of 44.2 per cent) but has come back strongly since then; Singapore had other falls in the 1980s as well as 1985, but has grown rapidly from small beginnings and established itself as an important money market.[9]

The third trend was the growth of international currency and bond issues. Although this growth has still not matched the optimistic forecasts of the early 1970s, new records are continually being achieved. For instance, the total of Eurobonds on issue reached US$81.5bn in 1984, a 63 per cent increase on the previous year.[10] Eighty per cent of the bonds were denominated in US dollars, but the rest were in the currencies of ten different countries (four from the Pacific rim and the others from Europe). Of the borrowers, only 8 per cent were in non-industrialized countries, while among the issues were a small proportion, less than 4 per cent, which were themselves denominated in an international currency – the European Currency Unit (ECU).[11]

These modest statistics mask considerable changes on the international financial scene in the last ten to 15 years. The changes are now taken for granted by those who operate on the markets and by the finance managers of a limited number of large firms, but are relatively unknown or misunderstood outside a small circle. The occasional brief report that another company has obtained a loan in European Currency Units does not adequately reflect the new horizons that are opening up for developing international business. On these horizons are to be found the development of instruments for other purposes besides raising loans for international operations. There are increasing facilities for buying currencies as well as commodities forward. Financial futures were first introduced in the United States in 1972, and the London International Financial Futures Exchange opened ten years later. This development has been followed by a series of instruments for hedging against exchange risk.[12]

A question alongside all these developments is the extent to which they are designed to facilitate trade, or whether a maze is being created which will make life harder for the trader. One answer is that the maze already exists; the movement of money across frontiers is a complex operation involving a mass of national regulations (some of which appear to conflict with one another) as well as of hazards, some obvious and some hidden. The argument would further maintain that fluctuating exchange rates have not inhibited trade and investment because of the availability of skilled financial services. Turnover in the principal foreign-exchange centres doubled between 1979 and 1984. The skills appear to be available to a limited range of companies and efforts may well be needed to make the services more widely available. Some such efforts are under way and a report of the World Bank[13] listed what it called 'three innovative financial instruments':

1 flexible maturity loans where interest rates are held constant but maturity dates are negotiable and can be tied to export receipts;
2 graduated payment loans, where interest rates begin low and increase in later years;
3 shared equity loans, where the lender takes a part of the equity.

These are examples of arrangements within which repayments can be made easier without the trouble of a major renegotiation. Inasmuch as they increase the lender's risk, they also make the risk more identifiable and therefore easier .to offset by insuring or hedging.

Further reading

Dufey, G. and Giddy, I.H., 'Innovation in the international capital markets', *Journal of International Business Studies* Vol.xii, No.2, Fall 1981, pp. 37–51.

13.7 Other landmarks in the economic environment

The international scene contains a number of other economic activities which directly affect the business decision-maker. These include the threat of national bankruptcy; although no one knows what this would involve exactly, the consequences of a series of near-misses are all too well-known. In late 1994 and early 1995 an acute crisis in Mexico caused a panic in international financial circles. As long ago as 1935, four Latin American countries did fail to pay interest on any part of their foreign debts, while others failed in part. Today debt rescheduling, balance-of-payments crises, domestic retrenchment, exchange-rate fluctuations and government intervention are part of a continuing national and international debate – often couched in language which seems to change from the grimly apocalyptic to short-sighted over-optimism and back at every small swing of an economic indicator. A review of the current position will begin with the question of indebtedness.

Balance of payments and national indebtedness

National debts were one of the talking points of the 1980s. In fact, the problem reached a dangerous peak in 1981 when two countries (Brazil and Chile) reported between them a current account deficit (incoming funds minus out-going) of about $25bn, and four other countries (Argentina, Chile, Korea and Nigeria) each had deficits between $4bn and $6bn. With rescheduling, international loans and domestic retrenchment measures, the immediate problems passed and conditions improved rapidly. Mexico was in surplus two years later, in 1983. But the measures to overcome the immediate prospect of a major international crisis also caused lasting damage. Retrenchment measures, including severe cuts in imports, slowed down growth and the introduction of new equipment as well as having a destabilizing effect, socially and politically. All these have made further crises in the future more probable.

The 1981 emergency produced some political oddities – such as the United States Government providing assistance to banks which were helping in the rescheduling of debts, including those of countries against which the same government was taking political measures at the time (including Poland and Nicaragua) while also running up a huge indebtedness at home.[14]

Balance of payments crises will continue to be endemic in much of the world while a limited number of countries are in surplus at any given time. A particular national balance can be affected by the economies of its trading partners. Each market has to be watched for the possibility of measures to reduce imports, to cut consumer spending or to restore the balance of payments in other ways. The price of oil is a major factor. When it goes down, some of the oil producing countries have severe problems; when it goes up, oil-consuming countries are likely to be in trouble.

Exchange rates and inflation

The fact that floating exchange rates have not destroyed world trade has already been noted; it has been put down to a mixture of skill and determination on the part of traders, together with the ability of the financial services sector to produce new instruments for countering ill-effects. The problem is compounded by the fact that any move has contradictory results. A decline in a national currency will be good news for exporters but bad for importers whose prices will ultimately affect exports. It will be good news, too, for investors wanting to bring their foreign income home, but bad when those same investors want to strengthen their foreign bases. An assumption has usually been made that currencies would change in value to reflect changes in the economic life of countries, thus smoothing out price fluctuations. In practice, the reverse often happens and appeals for fixed exchange rates stem from this. The short-term movements of currency undermine trading plans and expectations. While some maintain that these cancel out in the long-term, others think that the price in damage to trade is too high.[15]

Graphs in the current issue of the International Monetary Fund's Annual Report show the extent, and limitation, of exchange-rate changes over the last four years for the major industrial countries. For the United States, for instance, the nominal effective exchange rate varied between 111 and 92 (index figures, 1980 = 100); on the same scale, Japanese figures varied between 201 and 152 and Britain 82 and 72. In each country, the figure for the middle of 1991 was approaching that for the beginning of 1988. These figures put the problem into perspective, but the choice of date makes a substantial difference, as does adjustment for inflation. The fact that the changes are so much smaller after the adjustment (shown in figures entitled 'real effective exchange rates' – in some cases positive and minus results are reversed) supports the view that exchange rates compensate to a certain extent for inflation. It can also be said to support the view that other people's problems are imported through currency speculators.

Fear of inflation has, further, been one of the factors which have brought intervention by central banks. A depreciating currency is a cause of the inflation which has plagued most countries since 1972. This has always hit the developing countries harder than the industrialized, while the changes have in the past moved roughly in parallel for both. Inflation peaked in 1973–74, declined thereafter for about three years, and then reached a fresh peak in 1980. Since that date the figures have drifted apart with inflation remaining in double figures for the developing countries, in treble for some, but declining steeply to around the 1972 level of 5 per cent for the industrialized nations.

Another reason for central bank intervention is to prevent a currency rising too much. Like so many features of the economic environment, this reflects a contradiction. If a declining currency can lead to inflation, an increasing one loses exports and produces unemployment. There is a further nightmare for the richest countries, that of the currency becoming an international one and prone to speculation. This is still a problem for the United States dollar, in spite of official efforts to the contrary; other currencies are used by international dealers as well, but the proportion of non-dollar funds floating outside their own countries is small – in 1983 it was 17.5 per cent. Attempts to reduce inflation while not damaging employment lie behind many of the interventions on the part of governments and intergovernmental organizations. These are considered in Chapters 15 and 16.

Further reading

Eiteman and Stonehill, 1989, ch. 2.4.
Vernon, R. and Wells, L.T., *Economic Environment of International Business*, Prentice-Hall, 1976.

13.8 Exercises, cases and questions

In this chapter the further reading has been put at the end of each section.

Computer simulation

Take a country and compile on a spreadsheet programme the facts required for Table 13.7. These can be found in the current (monthly) issue of *International Financial Statistics* (Washington, DC: International Monetary Fund). Use the spreadsheet's facilities to calculate average annual changes and project these into the future. Calculate also the average influence of different factors like import prices, energy prices and others. Then repeat the calculations for different assumptions about likely changes over the next five years. Calculate a best possible circumstance, a worst possible one, and an expected outcome in five years' time for the balance of payments, debt and any other factors considered significant.

Table 13.7 Exchange rate changes, selected countries

	1989	1990	1991
Australia	1.26	1.28	1.28
France	6.40	5.45	5.64
Germany	1.90	1.62	1.66
Italy	1,372.10	1,198.10	1,240.60
Norway	6.90	6.26	6.48
Sweden	6.40	5.92	6.05
United Kingdom	0.60	0.56	0.57
United States	1.00	1.00	1.00
National currency units against US$			

Source: *The World Economic Factbook 1993*, Euromonitor Plc 1993, Great Britain

Case studies

Engineering company entering an LDC, M.H. Harper, CCH: 382–007–1.
Massey-Ferguson-Agromont-Motoimport (Poland), R.W. Hill and S.J. Paliwoda, CCH: 580–004–1.
Nestlé in LDCs, J.A. Murray, CCH: 383–089–1.

Questions

1 Name the main subjects evoked when mention is made of the 'economic environment' of international business. Discuss one of the subjects in some depth.

2 What is a reserve currency? How can such a function embarrass a national economy? Explain the difficulties that can arise.

3 'Trade theory has been groping its way to new sets of explanations' (Helleiner). Comment.

4 Discuss the development of financial institutions internationally and their part in the development of new patterns of business.

5 Examine the trends of international portfolio investment.

6 Outline the main sources of government funding for foreign companies.

14 National differences

This chapter considers the vexed subject of cultural differences – the tightrope that has to be walked between an exaggerated respect, which can appear insulting, to differences which sometimes turn out to be ephemeral and a crass insensitivity which is even more damaging. The topic is examined in the light of research going back to 1970. The study of culture is less time-bound than other aspects of international business and the sub-headings represent some of the issues under which the differences can be observed – work (money, leisure), authority (power, social stratification) and the role of the family.

14.1 The elusive differences

'The need for comparative, cross-cultural research has long been emphasized. Equally, the difficulties of conducting such work on a meaningful basis have become apparent. Though the potential for such projects seems unlimited, the reality has been disappointing and much of the difficulty has arisen from either (a) the lack of adequate conceptual frameworks or (b) the severe logistical difficulties of conducting such work.'[1]

Understanding the different cultural systems in which business is carried on is often considered the most important skill for the international manager but the search for a key to this understanding, as the quotation suggests, is often frustrating and elusive. Everyone is aware of national differences, but this awareness is compounded of many half-truths and stereotypes. It is hard to be precise even about the meaning of the word 'culture'.

In this chapter, culture is being used in the broad sense of a bundle of attitudes, perceptions, memories, prejudices, and other guides to action which can be identified as characteristics of a particular group and which condition the direction of change in that group. The most obvious characteristic of culture is that it is always changing and this fact alone increases the elusiveness. For the purposes of studying international business, attention is concentrated on differences between the culture in particular countries. But how are these differences identified? There is a strong suspicion that some generalizations which are alleged to represent national differences actually reflect company size or type of ownership, or some variable which has become inextricably mixed with others, while the particular combination of influencing factors is itself part of the culture being studied. Further, there are differences within a country (regional, occupational, class) which may be more noteworthy than the differences between countries. The English miner and the German miner, for instance, may have more cultural resemblances through their occupation than they have differences as a result of nationality. The same can be seen in other occupations. The professional manager is becoming increasingly internationalized and a force for cultural change himself as his professionalism increases. To say this is not to deny that overlooking cultural differences can be a special problem for the new breed of international manager.

The difficulties of identifying these differences are only exceeded by the problems caused by ignoring them. This has considerable implications for the development of international management skills and there are other reasons for interest. The international firm itself provides a focus of study for cultural change – a framework for controlled observation. While social anthropologists could well study the international company, management experts could certainly make more use of the work of social anthropologists. It might help if the evidence painstakingly collected by students of management, could be interpreted in a more convincing framework of anthropological theory.[2] Meanwhile, this chapter will try to trace a path through cultural differences and offer some guidance relevant to the international manager. If some of the guidance is still by 'rule of thumb,' this stems from the present state of the art.

An early writing[3] which surveys the management literature on this subject detects three schools of thought. One is called *universality*, where the view is taken that cultural differences are unimportant. The activity of management is the same throughout the world and so are the conditioning factors. Local variations are determined by differences of style or situation rather than culture. The second school is called *cultural cluster* and takes the opposite view. Managers bring their beliefs and values to their activity and conduct it accordingly. The third school is labelled *economic cluster* and claims that the level of industrial and economic development in a country is the main influence on managerial behaviour. Each school of thought emphasizes points to be considered in constructing a general theory. The stage of economic development of the country and of the professional development of its management cadre are influencing factors, and the significance of some of the 'cultural clusters' is being reduced as managers in one country learn from those in another.

The study in question shows a preference, nevertheless, for the latter approach. In the following pages little support is found for extreme universalist assumptions which are apt to produce more problems than are solved, as superficial resemblances are pressed into support for minimizing the cultural differences. Undoubtedly, there is much to be learnt by one culture from another in tackling the problems of industrialization, but the universalist view suggests that the learning is all one way. Who is to say, on currently available evidence, whether the American emphasis on individual responsibility is more effective than the Japanese on group decision-making in either or both countries? Or vice versa? It may be that one method or the other will eventually be found to be more suitable for all mankind, but the more reasonable assumption in the present state of knowledge is that each is effective in its own cultural setting, and each can learn from the other.

There do appear, however, to be a number of questions that are related to the stage of development of an industrial society. If group responsibility is a culture-bound characteristic, the transition from family management and appointment by inheritance to professional management and appointment by qualifications, does seem to be universal. Although there may be evidence that in some advanced industrial societies the divorce between ownership and management has not gone as far as is sometimes assumed, the trend is surely unmistakable. Indeed, as was shown in the discussion on management contracts in Chapter 5, the divorce between ownership and management is moving a stage further still – and this trend is certainly universal in that it is found in all kinds of country, albeit to a limited extent.

The concern with cultural differences, apart from the interest they possess in their own right, is related to both the problems of general management and those of marketing, although conceptually these are distinct. For general management, cultural differences mean those issues that need to be recognized for the way they affect the motivation and control of subordinates in other countries. Styles and techniques are both involved inasmuch as they impinge upon value systems. The marketing aspect is not just concerned with relations with subordinates abroad, even in the marketing function, but with a bundle of changing demands and expectations on the part of the consumer which again vary from country to country.[4] The implications of the demands and expectations may be difficult to assess and are sometimes contradictory.

For some products local prejudices are important, for others a foreign label may be preferred. Food and drink is an industry which comes on both sides of that distinction, and success is related to the ability to identify cultural attitudes. The obtaining of government contracts, too, involves perceptiveness as to what is important to the legislators and voters in a country. Most of the issues discussed below have both marketing and management implications. They have been chosen because they are relevant and frequently mentioned – motivation including attitudes to work and money, authority and stratification, family and sex, and a whole range of social beliefs and practices.

An interesting article[5] emphasized the importance of culture in considering the consequences of formalization for performance.

Work

Attitudes to work and money affect both management and marketing policies. They are also the subject of stereotypes, beliefs and prejudices that sometimes have little substance. Companies which have developed international productivity comparisons with some degree of sophistication have discovered that deeply ingrained views about attitudes to work in different countries are untrue. But this does not mean that more effective management can change the approach to work at will in a situation where leisure is highly valued. Managers themselves appear to say 'enough is enough' at different levels of salary and work-load in different countries. Attitudes to leisure vary from country to country; higher incomes may produce more work or more spare time. The work ethic means, in effect, that preoccupation with work is considered a virtue in some parts of the world and a vice in others. As a result different types of appeal, reward and penalty, are effective in different cultures. But even beside this cautious and general statement there must be placed some reservations. One is that studies of morale in different countries[6] show this to be a complex variable: motivation depends on numerous factors, some of which may be only slightly influenced by national cultural traditions. Another observation about attitudes to work and money is that the national situation must be considered. The willingness to work and the acceptability of certain products will be different in times of war from times of peace, and may be affected by other national crises as well. Further, the labour situation will affect the demand for labour-saving equipment both in factory machinery and in domestic goods.

Most managers are inclined to regard themselves as pragmatic in outlook. This seems to be a generalization that a wide assortment of writers allow themselves, but even so an alleged pragmatic approach can lead to a number of different results. Three studies of Indian and United States managers showed, for instance, that the former opted for strategies which led to optimum results but with high risk; the American managers preferred lower risk and lower expected pay-off.[7] Other studies[8] have shown that managers rate their subordinates in contrasting ways in different countries. In particular the differences within an occupation are greater in western countries than in some developing countries, although differences between occupations may be greater in the developing countries.

Some customs may not be part of the culture but may nevertheless be deeply felt as IBM discovered when an attempt to introduce Sunday working at the German plant provoked outrage on the part of the Roman Catholic church and a section of the ruling conservative (Christian Social Union) party as well as the trade union (IG Metall).

Social class, education and the family

The factors which determine a person's role and expectations in society vary considerably between cultures, but again the stage of industrialization may be as important as the cultural traditions. At least the two influence one another in determining factors like social class. *Stratification* is a word that is used as loosely as culture. It may refer to the prestige in a society of various groups selected because of their hereditary or religious standing or because of their wealth, occupation or education; many combinations of these factors exist. In considering the environment of international management, information is required on the usual means of recruiting for different occupations within a particular country, the provision of education, the availability of suitable people for conducting the business, and the life-styles adopted by different classes. To this should be added the nature of the class distinctions, how rigid they are or how socially mobile is the population.

It has been pointed out that, in a traditional industrialized society, the labour demand is roughly triangular.[9] There is a narrow peak of top management broadening rapidly with a wide base of semi-skilled and unskilled workers. During the process of the industrial revolution, the societies concerned developed a supply of labour which roughly corresponded to the demand. At the peak, the supply may have been narrower than the demand and there may have been some indentations lower down, especially among the skilled occupations; but the labour required was usually available, albeit the reverse was not always true. In times of economic depression supply was ahead of demand especially at the bottom. The sizes of the triangles may have been different, but the shape was normally the same.

The traditional non-industrialized society had a labour requirement which could be compared to an inverted T, with a narrow band of leaders and middle classes and a large number of peasants and workers at the bottom. The process of industrialization, as a country develops, produces a labour demand in a triangular shape similar to that of the traditional industrialized countries, but some societies have much more difficulty than others in producing a labour supply that matches the new requirement. Some countries in the Far East seem to have found this transition easier than those in other parts of the world. There is a tendency in many cultures to produce bulges in the original upright of the T rather than a triangle. Thus there may develop a surplus of people with advanced qualifications and a lack of skilled workers or of people capable of filling lower managerial positions.

Interestingly, the labour supply in some of the industrialized countries, notably in the United States but also to a certain extent in Europe, is beginning to acquire a similar shape. The triangular demand is also becoming distorted but in a different way. The requirement exceeds the supply at the top, but a little lower down the supply is exceeding the demand at least in certain professions. Below that again, among skilled workers and certain semi-professions, the demand runs ahead even in times of unemployment, while expansion is increasingly constrained by severe shortages of electronic engineers, mechanics, plumbers, computer operators and others. Among the unskilled, unemployment remains endemic in spite of forecasts to the contrary going back to the first days of compulsory education. The base of the demand triangle is narrowing all the time. Companies which have invested with inadequate knowledge of the type of labour available have encountered trouble.

Much has been written about relative costs as an incentive to companies to move to low wage countries, although the availability of labour capable of exercising the levels of responsibility and skill required by a particular firm may be more critical. If the home country can no longer supply the junior supervisors and skilled workers required, there may be few countries that can. Hence the search is limited.

The class structure of society and the factors by which it is shaped influence the respective status of different professions and with it the shape of the customer's market as well as the allocation of jobs. A society without too many constraints on social mobility may accord prestige to the teaching profession and a larger part of the national income will be spent on educational equipment than in a society which is more rigidly stratified. Educational institutions are sometimes resented in countries where children are regarded as a source of income, and social mobility (one incentive for education) is limited. Other countries, by no means always the same ones, will be opposed to welfare support for adults. The subject of education also brings up methods of managerial training. Some methods of sensitivity training, for instance, have been strongly criticized in Africa where they have been regarded as aimed at non-existent inhibitions. This kind of training is regarded as culture-bound.

There has been a tendency in some countries towards a more participative management system which is also centralized. In countries where the military class has high prestige, a disciplined but decentralized system may prevail.

Military regimes incline to a paternalistic attitude and do not favour the hire-and-fire outlooks they find in foreign firms, eager as they often are to co-operate with foreign businessmen.

A study quoted earlier also sheds light on the exercise of authority by managers in different countries.[10] It shows that out of 90 comparative investigations of managerial styles carried out internationally before 1970, the overwhelming majority emphasized the differences rather than the resemblances. Some writers warned against the dangers of reading too much into the occasional success of a company which sets out to ignore the national differences or pretends that they do not exist.[11] One common characteristic is that managers express a preference for a less authoritarian system than the one they actually have, but there the resemblance ends. Questions about whether managers think their subordinates wish for more responsibility or not are answered differently in different countries, as are questions about the reliability and trustworthiness of subordinates. Deference is a virtue in some countries, while phrases like 'to stand on your own feet' express preferred attitudes in others.

Management styles are affected by such differences. More recent studies have stressed that the individualist management style typical of the United States has not been adopted in the collectivist society of Japan, although many American techniques have been adapted by that society.[12]

Attitudes to the conduct of family life, and to the roles of family members, vary considerably. Local customs are often supported by powerful religious beliefs but education and industrialization bring change, while observers have noted the survival of older relationships even in the most industrialized of cultures. In few cases do cultural conditions remain static. The changes which especially affect business can be listed as a series of transitions.

From the extended to the nuclear family[13]
The nuclear family consists of two generations and becomes the norm in most industrialized countries. The term 'extended family' is used where three or four generations live together, including aunts and uncles as well as parents and children, and support one another. Each member has a role to play, designated by tradition and the extended family is often called the traditional family.

From the family to the firm or the state as the provider of social security
The extended family provides the support required at different stages of a person's life – eliminating, for instance, the need for pensions and housing for the elderly – and a childcare arrangement while the parents work. With different services provided for one another by the different members, the extended family carries within itself a miniature welfare state which works so long as the resources are adequate. Elements of the extended family do, of course, survive as a part of the social structure even in cultures where it has otherwise disappeared – if only when the grandmother is the baby-minder.

From the family business to the joint stock company
Business organization is also influenced by the extended family which may provide the total management structure of a small business. Indeed, it is impossible to understand how companies work in many parts of the world without

understanding the local patterns of family life. In some circumstances relatives will be almost the only source of recruitment considered eligible for management positions in a firm. The eventual emergence of the joint stock company occurs when the business grows beyond the resources of a family unit.

From male domination in earning and spending to a degree of equality
Although the female influence may be greater at this stage (or even in the previous stage) than the outsider realizes.

From a position where the child is an earner, and an economic asset, to that where children are seen as spenders and economic liabilities
In cultures where children are regarded as money-earners, there is naturally resistance to the spread of full-time education.

Changing attitudes to family life, and in particular to the role of children, may yet reduce expected population increases. From the point of view of the market for baby equipment and toys, less children can, however, mean greater demand because of increasing wealth.

Other cultures, besides those where the extended family is strong, may have prejudices against labour-saving devices in the home and the spending power of the women and the young people will be limited. Strongly held social and religious beliefs resist changes which industrialization might otherwise be expected to bring. Different ways of allocating jobs – by qualifications or by social class, religion, sex, region, race or tribe – and the pace and direction of change are significant elements in the business environment. There are also unspoken signals which identify cultural differences, from politenesses and taboos to less significant but noticeable practices like the time taken to answer a letter.

In some cultures an important issue is dealt with immediately; in others promptness is taken as a sign that the matter is regarded as unimportant, the time taken corresponding with the gravity of the issue. Another aspect is the volume of communication that takes place between managers. It has been shown, for instance, that there are considerable differences in the rate of interaction between managers in different countries.[14]

Authority

The class structure of society usually provides the basis of authority. At least it provides a normal recruiting ground for authorities and a source of their legitimation, although some cultures make it easier to break through barriers to promotion than others. The exercise of authority varies according to the management style, but different styles are likely in different cultures.

One research relevant to this has also produced a measure of the cultural differences – *the power distance* measure.[15] This is defined as 'a measure of inter-personal power or influence' between a boss and a subordinate 'as perceived by the least powerful of the two,' while the distance is seen as the extent to which either participant can influence the behaviour of the other. It is suggested that the distance is 'to a considerable extent determined by their national culture'. The evidence for this statement has been provided by research in 39 countries in which questions were asked on such subjects as the fear subordinates have of expressing disagreement with bosses (answers expressed by 'I am afraid very frequently' through to 'I am afraid seldom'). The answers have been assembled in a series of tables showing Power Distance Index values varying from 94 (very often afraid) for the Philippines to 11 (very seldom afraid) for Austria. As often with similar studies, the national differences are greater when examined by nationality alone than by occupational sub-headings. But these results do not entirely support the opinion that the differences go by occupation – for the technical experts, clerks and service technicians indeed, the differences are greater than they are when averaged across all occupations. Only for unskilled plant workers are the differences considerably less.

This is an abbreviated account of a detailed study in which international comparisons have been comprehensively documented and sources of error controlled. Even so, the problems of comparability are great and no doubt there is scope for refinement. The Power Distance Index has proved of value in research – both academic and commercial – and has provided a means of assisting managers to grasp the complexities of cross-cultural management. The index is linked to a number of variables like income inequalities, educational systems, political systems and historical factors.

Three other factors measured in the same study were uncertainty avoidance, individualism and the masculine–feminine relationship. These have been considered already – the first as a fundamental element in a theory of the complex organization, and the latter two as parts of the transition seen in many countries from the personal to the joint stock company and from male domination to greater equality between the sexes.

Another classification of cultural differences

Hutton[16] classifies the cultural differences by means of a list of the key issues of which culture is said to be composed. Although apparently arbitrary this list (which should be consulted) provides, with its sub-headings, an illuminating review of the subject. The main headings are: language; religion; values and attitudes; law; education; politics; technology; social organization. Among the many issues mentioned is that of the technology in American homes which many non-Americans find confusing.

Other characteristics cited include the frustration period which is a normal part of the cycle for the expatriates and which can be expected to be followed by a period of 'coping'.

Conclusion

The discussion can be summed up by saying that there are differences in the cultural environment between one country and another which are hard to identify and are in a state of continuing change. Nevertheless, the skilled international manager understands and respects them. With all the prejudices and travellers' tales which bedevil the understanding, some key issues do need attention when framing an international management system or developing a market. The differences are as easily exaggerated as they are underestimated, and the reactions of companies vary from serious attempts to acquire the colour of their surroundings to brash efforts to be conspicuous. As with national frontiers, the boundaries of culture have a way of reasserting themselves even when they are expected to disappear.

The following is a list of the subjects (not all of them discussed in this chapter) on which cultural differences can be expected.

1 *Work*: the attitude to work, the relative importance of work and leisure.
2 *Individualism* or *collectivism*: the relationship between individuals in a society.
3 *Money*: either the desire to accumulate more money or the view that 'enough is enough'.
4 *Class structure*: the availability and source of recruitment of labour at all levels.
5 *Education*: the development through the educational systems of relevant outlooks and skills.
6 *Family*: the comprehensiveness of the family and attitudes to women.
7 *Social security*: the respective roles of the family, the employer and the state.
8 *Authority*: the sources of authority and its legitimation.
9 *Social, moral, religious, and political outlooks*.
10 *Cultural resources*: the physical and mental heritage which makes the country distinctive.
11 *Professional status*: some professions are more powerful in certain countries than in others.
12 *Advertising and other methods of promotion*: the relationship to the general outlooks, educational standards and laws of the country.

14.2 Questions and further reading

Questions

1 'Comparative management stands between theory and practice as:
  (a) it borrows from and contributes to our systematic knowledge of management and organization theory ... and
  (b) is relevant for the training and effectiveness of managers.' (Jean Boddewyn).
  Discuss this view of the value of studying management in different cultural settings.

2 Outline the main features that should be noted about the local culture by a company going into a foreign country of your choice. Both management and marketing issues should be considered.

3 'And, at the same time, comparative management studies add to fundamental knowledge in the behavioural sciences by allowing for more diversity and variation in how problems are handled, decisions made and controls affected by managers from differing cultures.' Discuss.

4 Discuss the development of international management, and the extent, if any, to which you think there is going to be a disappearance of cultural differences in the profession.

5 Outline the provision for management education and the main differences between countries (select three specific countries for discussion).

6 'The multinational firm no longer has to pay any serious attention to the so-called *cultural differences.*' Discuss.

7 Compare and contrast some of the evidence available on styles and patterns of management in different countries.

8 Identify and illustrate some of the main features that the marketing manager of a consumer goods company has to look out for when commencing operations in a new market.

Further reading

Barsoux J.-L. and Lawrence, P., *Management in France*, Cassell 1990.
Daniels and Radebaugh (1995), ch. 4.
Hofstede, 1984.
Hutton, J., *The World of the International Manager*, Philip Allan 1988.
Joynt, P. and Warner, M., *Managing in Different Cultures*, Oslo, Universitetsfordaget, 1985.
Weinshall, T.D., (ed.) *Culture and Management*, Penguin, 1977.

15 The company and the nation state

'In Western Europe some 25 major companies belong to the exclusive 'multi-nationals club.' The only controls over the big multinationals are national boundaries but they leap these virtually without hindrance. So one of the most important requirements of national and international social democracy is the creation of a 'multinational' – or, better, an international – forum of public opinion which could work as a corrective to this particular power development.'

These words of a former Chancellor of Austria (Bruno Kreisky) illustrate one view of the multinational firm – the moderate opposition, it might be called – which comes in the middle of a range of opinions running from extreme opposition to whole-hearted support. Kreisky's fears are supported in a recent statement by the chairman of Ford of Europe.[1]

If we find we have major assembly facilities regardless of the country involved, which for one reason or another – perhaps uneducated government action (giving longer holidays, or a shorter working week) or union intransigence – cannot be competitive, we would not shy away from a decision to close them.

Multinational companies emphasize the contribution they make to material well-being, technical progress and management standards. In spite of these arguments, the climate of opinion has become increasingly hostile in recent years. The hostility is no doubt partly due to a growing dislike of the large organization as well as a response to the much publicized activities of a limited number of companies, but that is not the whole story. The interaction of national and corporate decisions, whether in conflict or in co-operation, leads to a series of problems, many of them unavoidable.

Government decision-making is often more complex than that of companies. The justification for this statement, which will be treated with incredulity by some corporate executives, lies with the problem of simplifying and limiting objectives. Corporate aims – such as an x per cent return on shareholders' funds or a y per cent growth in net investment – and their implications, may be difficult to achieve but they can be identified, simplified and accorded priorities. Projects can be axed when they are not contributing to immediate objectives, or when corporate survival is under threat. A government, on the other hand, cannot close down a country's education system and invest instead in the health service, or vice versa. The balancing act is more precarious and leads to short-term measures designed to support a number of interests which cannot be ignored. Projects have to proceed side by side, and there is an election date to be considered as well.

Short-term measures frequently bedevil relations with companies who are constrained by different time-scales – the short period between annual reports and the much longer period between a decision to invest and the earning of an income from the investment. A company, with its greater single-mindedness, becomes impatient at the labyrinthine decision processes of government, especially when that government is operating in a different cultural setting. This is not to say that the company's task is simple. The complex issues that can face a firm intending to invest abroad were illustrated many years ago by the example of BASF and the State of South Carolina.[2]

The German company BASF (Badische Anilin und Soda-Fabriken) undertook a prolonged evaluation of a number of possible sites in the United States. The main requirements were deep sea docking facilities, with good communications inland, and plentiful supplies of fresh water. The site eventually chosen was on the coast of South Carolina (on the eastern seaboard) where deep sea and fresh water facilities were excellent while local unemployment was high. Inland communications were more of a problem, but the state government undertook to build a new highway and railroad system to service the plant. Docking facilities, river dredging and a five-year tax holiday were also promised. The governor of South Carolina travelled to Germany to mark the importance of the deal by signing the agreement himself, but by that time a storm of controversy was already brewing. One issue was racial. The right-wing government of South Carolina was criticized by its own supporters for spending so much taxpayers' money on finding jobs for the mainly black unemployed who were expected to work in the plant, but more serious trouble was not far behind.

A few miles from the site was Hilton Head Island, at that time claiming to be the most expensive holiday resort in the world. The resort developers maintained that the chemical plant would seriously damage their business by polluting the air and the water. They were joined in their protests by a group of inshore fishermen who feared the consequences of the dredging of the channel. The company denied the charges and announced steps to ensure against pollution but the environmental issue had already turned a local argument into a national controversy. The Hilton Head developers found powerful, if improbable, allies in the conservation lobby, notably Friends of the Earth. A scientific department of the Federal Government also became interested, questioning the company's calculations on water pollution. In this connection, BASF's record on the Rhine was held against it. But the company was not without supporters, and an equally unlikely alliance emerged on its side which included the state government of South Carolina and the National Association for the Advancement of Coloured Peoples (NAACP). At the height of the controversy, the Hilton Head developers announced plans for an expansion which would employ the same number of people as the chemical plant if that project was cancelled. To this the NAACP retorted that the quality of work was not comparable. BASF offered skilled industrial employment, whereas the holiday resort would only provide routine jobs in hotels, golf clubs and car parks. But the scheme was already doomed. After incurring high costs, in time and money, during the protracted controversy, the company decided to abandon it and adopt a less controversial site in Louisiana. Later the Hilton Head developers cancelled their expansion too.

This case illustrates a number of issues that face the international company, even in places where it is officially welcome. Environment, employment and race add up to powerful influences, no less powerful when they are on opposing sides, leaving the company in the eye of a storm. Also illustrated is the danger to a company of government incentives. Even when these do not lead to a major controversy, they are by no means guaranteed to match the costs that a project may incur.

A recent (June 1995) much-publicised case when an oil company decided not to proceed with plans to dispose of a redundant oil-platform by sinking it in the North Sea has proved another example of the large multinational being influenced by public opinion, in this case public opinion in many countries although in this case too, there were supporters as well as opponents of the company's intentions.

Other issues – especially finance, taxation and trading areas – will be considered later in this chapter, but first a means of classifying countries when analysing their problems is discussed.

15.1 The types of country

The case of BASF was that of a company based in a rich, industrialized country wishing to invest in another wealthy country. The controversies vary with the type of country but classifying countries is not an easy exercise. Even the number of countries is in some doubt. The United Nations has 159 members, but some are not at present regarded as independent, while there are a number of sovereign states (including Switzerland and Taiwan) which are not members. Every country has its distinctive characteristics and even the distinction between rich and poor can be deceptive. There are many grades of wealth and poverty, and a poor country in a warm climate may be better off than one that appears to be statistically its equal in a region where fuel costs are heavy. However, it is generally assumed that some valid generalizations can be made according to wealth and political system, and Table 15.1 follows a widely accepted classification modified from United Nations usage, in distinguishing between market and planned economies, and between industrialized and developing nations.[3]

Table 15.1 lists 182 countries which are usually (although not all universally) regarded as independent. While there is some overlapping in terms of relative

Table 15.1 Country classification

[The figures in brackets show the estimated gross domestic product (or net material product) per head in $US, see note at foot of table. The first figure refers to 1987, the second to 1989. A comparison can however be misleading: a steep rise or a steep decline may only reflect changing parities with the dollar.]

1. Richer industrial market economies (GDP per head over $10,000 in 1987)

Australia (13083) (17039)	Austria (15457) (16727)
Belgium (14187) (15537)	*Canada (16258) (20462)
Denmark (19951) (20402)	Finland (18023) (23211)
*France (15954) (17071)	*Germany (18243) (19202)
Iceland (21769) (20611)	*Italy (13223) (15166)
*Japan (19467) (23046)	Luxembourg (16748) (18866)
Netherlands (14673) (15208)	Norway (20063) (21651)
Sweden (19303) (22703)	Switzerland (25986) (27497)
*United Kingdom (12172) (14752)	*United States (18292) (20749)

Table 15.1 continued

2. Other industrial market economies

Cyprus (5232) (6393)
Ireland (7915) (9273)
Malta (5307) (6365)
New Zealand (10528) (11915)
San Marino (NA)
Turkey (1293) (1461)
Yugoslavia (former) (3033) (3456)

Greece (4603) (5401)
Liechtenstein (NA)
Monaco (NA)
Portugal (3591) (4413)
Spain (7443) (9601)
Vatican City (NA)

All the above (except Liechtenstein, Monaco and the Vatican City) are members of the Organisation for Economic Cooperation and Development (OECD). The countries marked * belong to the Group of Seven (G7) major industrial countries.

3. The oil exporting countries

Algeria (2786) (2027)
Ecuador (1072) (1005)
Indonesia (436) (520)
Iraq (3499) (3652)
Libya (5691) (5081)
Oman (5875) (5872)
Saudi Arabia (5831) (5606)
Venezuela (2716) (2352)

Bahrain (6420) (6549)
Gabon (3252) (2978)
Iran (5868) (8537)
Kuwait (11088) (11430)
Nigeria (216) (157)
Qatar (16841) (19068)
United Arab Emirates (16239) (17497)

All in this category are members of the Organization of Petroleum Exporting Countries (OPEC), except Bahrain and Oman.

4. Former socialist countries of Eastern Europe

Bulgaria (3201) (2566)
Hungary (2460) (2731)
Romania (2524) (2312)

Czechoslovakia (2697) (2572)
Poland (1400) (1909)
Russia (3337) (3751)

5. Developing countries with command economies

+Afghanistan (306) (485)
China (235) (313)
Kampuchea (NA)
+Laos (174) (343)
Vietnam (105) (109)

Albania   (791) (820)
Cuba (1520) (1562)
Korea North (830) (897)
Mongolia (805) (804)
+Yemen Peoples Republic (513) (551)

6. Richer developing countries (exporters of manufactured goods)

Brazil (2146) (3270)
Korea, South (3190) (5029)
Singapore (7735) (10277)

Hong Kong (8423) (10877)
Mexico (1693) (2396)

Many of these are known as newly industrializing countries (NICs.)

7. Other developing countries

Andorra (NA)
Angola ((637) (717)
Antigua (3000) (3805)
Bahamas (9643) (10788)
Barbados (5736) (6694)
+Benin (380) (355)
+Bhutan (195) (196)
+Botswana (1333) (1983)
Brunei (9851) (9101)
Cambodia (81) (106)
Chile (1511) (1958)
+Cape Verde (710) (813)
+Central African Republic (385) (374)
Chile (1511) (1958)
+Comoros (413) (417)
Congo (1112) (1031)

Anguilla (3250) (4250)
Argentina (2647) (1894)
+Bangladesh (189) (217)
Belize (1446) (1701)
Bermuda (24509) (27103)
Bolivia (601) (609)
British Virgin Islands (9000) (11231)
+Burkina Faso (215) (216)
+Burundi   (232) (207)
Cameroon (1244) (975)
Cayman Islands (NA)
+Chad (140) (165)
Colombia (1169) (1219)
Cook Islands (2056) (3167)
Costa Rica (1622) (1807)
Dominica (1537) (1878)

Table 15.1 continued

Djibouti (1261) (1236)
Dominican Republic (765) (959)
El Salvador (939) (1255)
+Ethiopia (118) (124)
French Guiana (2674) (2800)
Ghana (354) (353)
Guatemala (840) (954)
+Guinea (389) (480)
Guyana (435) (239)
Honduras (868) (980)
Ivory Coast (992) (849)
Jamaica (1226) (1612)
Kenya (380) (368)
Lebanon (701) (467)
Liberia (464) (497)
Malawi (157) (192)
+Maldives (408) (617)
Martinique (7348) (7705)
Mauritius (1749) (1933)
Morocco (812) (915)
Myanmar (262) (401)
Namibia (1042) (1100)
Netherlands Antilles (6467) (7198)
Nicaragua (7503) (240)
Pakistan (354) (361)
Papua New Guinea (869) (886)
Paraguay (1155) (1049)
Polynesia (14112) (13805)
Reunion (5986) (5674)
St. Kitts-Nevis (1769) (2000)
St. Vincent (1179) (1391)
+Samoa (612) (637)
Senegal (679) (690)
Sierra Leone (164) (200)
+Somalia (236) (173)
Sri Lanka (388) (406)
Suriname (2749) (3362)
Syria (2917) (1502)
Thailand (915) (1269)
Tonga (990) (1295)
Tunisia (1304) (1319)
Turks and Caicos Islands (600) (700)
Uganda (252) (257)
Vanuatu (828) (786)
Yemen Arab Republic (515) (761)
Zambia (294) (416)

Egypt (1396) (1403)
Equatorial Guinea (401) (391)
Fiji (1487) (1549)
+Gambia (305) (357)
Grenada (1724) (2186)
Guadeloupe (5801) (6013)
+Guinea-Bissau (182) (179)
+Haiti (324) (439)
India (319) (326)
Israel (8722) (10256)
Jordan (1426) (1098)
Kiribati (375) (530)
Lesotho (223) (245)
Madagascar (167) (140)
Malaysia (1925) (2156)
Mali (225) (236)
Mauritania (437) (454)
Montserrat (3231) (4077)
Mozambique (101) (84)
Nauru (NA)
+Nepal (153) (152)
New Caledonia (9377) (15353)
+Niger (307) (266)
Panama (2334) (1919)
Peru (2171) (2046)
Philippines (593) (729)
Puerto Rico (7874) (8799)
+Rwanda (329) (310)
St. Lucia (1378) (1480)
Sao Tome et Principe (487) (381)
San Marino (NA)
Seychelles (3687) (4232)
Solomon Isles (505) (608)
South Africa (2492) (2592)
+Sudan (322) (320)
Swaziland (852) (845)
+Tanzania (141) (107)
Togo (385) (381)
Trinidad and Tobago (3957) (3172)
Tur (NA)
Tuvalu (NA)
Uruguay (2541) (2736)
Virgin Islands(US) (10423) (11670)
Zaire (118) (102)
Zimbabwe (618) (630)

+   classified by the United Nations as 'least developed' and eligible for special aid
The figures are intended to give some indication of relative wealth, and should be treated with caution. No countries have frequent censuses, and four have never had one. Hence a degree of estimation is involved and whether exaggeration or understatement is likely depends on a number of factors – some social and some related to the tax system (the introduction of compulsory education in one country, where understatement had been suspected, demonstrated the opposite – there were more children than anticipated). Figures for gross domestic product are also difficult to determine accurately, and will be influenced at any given time by the relative strength of the dollar. Nevertheless, the figures provide useful indications and comparisons. Even when deciding whether a market is rich enough to sustain a product, care has to be taken since average figures can hide great inequalities. India, for instance, rates among the poorer countries but 5% of the population is very affluent, and a much larger proportion is industrialized. 5% of the population of India is 34 million people, many more than the total populations of Denmark, Finland, Norway and Sweden added together.

Source: UN National Accounts Statistics 1988–89 New York: United Nations and UNCTAD annual reports

wealth, measured by gross domestic product per head (see the note at the foot of table), the following are the distinctive characteristics of each type:

1 *Rich industrial market economies.* These countries are members of the Organisation for Economic Cooperation and Development (OECD), and each has a gross domestic product per head of more than $8000. They also have elected governments that are subject to change, some more frequently than others. Most have low inflation rates. They have all experienced ups and downs in unemployment and industrial production, but have sufficiently strong economies to keep their problems under control, while providing rich but highly competitive markets.

2 *Poorer industrial market economies.* These include other members of the OECD plus five small states. They vary more among themselves than the previous category, and overlap in wealth with some of the richer developing countries. Nevertheless, they remain rich by the standards of most of the world. Many of them suffer from chronic problems of balance of payments, unemployment or inflation – sometimes all three.

3 *Oil exporting.* The 15 countries in this class include all the members of the Organization for Petroleum Exporting Countries (OPEC) plus two other Middle East oil producers. Some are net debtors (Algeria, Ecuador, Gabon and Nigeria) in spite of their oil resources. A priority for all of them is rapid industrialization before their oil supplies run out. They form most of the leaders in a trend towards the reallocation of industrial sites around the world.

4 *Former socialist countries.* The seven countries of Eastern Europe.

5 *Developing countries with command economies.* Eleven developing countries including China.

6 *Richer developing.* The six developing countries which export manufactured goods, including the newly industrialized. Many of these countries are industrializing fast and are already richer than, for instance, OECD members such as Turkey or Portugal. The gross domestic product of all of them is over $1000 per head and many have substantial urban populations, sometimes combined with a considerable gap between rich and poor. Increasing wealth is enabling these countries to bargain more strongly in dealing with foreign companies and in negotiating trade treaties.

7 *Other developing.* These countries fall outside the other classsifications. Some report a gross domestic product per head similar to the 'richer developing'; others are struggling with a poverty that is sometimes extreme, and have difficulty in taking part in trade on any but the most disadvantageous terms. Since the first oil crisis, many of them have found their wealth per head declining in real terms, while others are now engaged in infrastructure projects and looking forward to growth.

The relations between companies and governments are influenced by the bargaining powers available to each side. The powers of industrialized nations are high on account of their rich markets, but reduced by the difficulty of imposing sanctions when a country is both home and host to foreign investors. For developing countries, the bargaining power is low against a company that brings technology and other much-needed assets, but increases as the know-how becomes more familiar. A Canadian study has provided a formula to enable relative bargaining powers to be assessed:

Bargaining power = (technology $\times$ W_1) + (management $\times$ W_2) + (inputs $\times$ W_3) + (exports $\times$ W_4) + (market $\times$ W_5) where W stands for weightings to be determined for each factor.[4]

15.2 Authority and the nation state

The causes of conflict between companies and governments can be seen as a series of controversies. The former planned economies still have restrictions in practice while even countries with regimes most dedicated to private enterprise have laws restricting business activity and sectors forbidden to the foreigner.[5] The controversies arise from allegations that companies are acting against national interests and that restrictions are needed as a result and are often conducted in an atmosphere of mutual incomprehension. The corporate executive who is accused of political interference may in fact be all too aware of the reverse – that their careers will be at risk if they tangle with the local government. However ill-equipped they are to play the diplomat, their company is likely to repudiate them if they put a foot wrong. They may also be refused entry permits to places where they need to operate. The principle is not altered by the fact that there have been a few much publicized cases, mainly in South America, where foreign companies do appear to have tried to change a political regime. Usually companies are circumspect about political intervention and, where this does happen, they claim that a subsidiary is behaving like a local company.[6] Complaints about direct interference with a nation's internal affairs are regarded as absurd by corporate staff.

Representatives of governments see the matter differently, as do concerned citizens. They regard the known examples of intervention as the tip of an iceberg; they are worried by subtle pressures and especially the consequences of the meetings that are understood to take place between the leaders of international firms.[7] They are also conscious that size means power, however responsibly it may be used. The small or poor country, in particular, feels itself compelled to appease the large foreign company on which it has come to depend for employment and wealth creation. This is true of a dominant national company also, but the problems of controlling a large foreign firm are perceived to be more acute. The political problem of rival centres of power within a country is as old as government itself, and has frequently been complicated by international affiliations whether religious, political or commercial. The complexity should not be underestimated. For instance, a company can make itself unpopular with shareholders who consider the income derived from some of its foreign markets to be in no way commensurate with the risks. The investment, they consider, could more profitably be placed elsewhere but management stays because it does not want to acquire a reputation for being footloose and deserting a nation where it is a substantial employer, especially if the market is likely to grow. At the same time, public opinion in the country is condemning the firm for its dominance although an even greater outcry would follow if it were to leave.

The issue is one of authority not, as is sometimes thought, of sovereignty. The government is always the sovereign power in a country and can expropriate a company by the passage of a law, but this does not alter the genuine worry about who is in charge in a situation where a close-knit group of managers have the ability to exercise considerable influence. The situation is further complicated for a company that finds it difficult to be neutral – where, for instance, government policies are influencing company plans and performance. Even a simple enquiry to discover government intentions on subjects like tax reform or import controls may be seen as an attempt to influence those intentions. Lobbying can be regarded as a normal commercial practice by a company and as unwarranted political interference by a government, while the balance of advantage and disadvantage can be equally hard to determine.

It is optimistic to suppose that a company, legally obliged to consider the interests of its foreign shareholders and often adopting centralized policies, will always act in accordance with the interests of the host country. The nightmare for a government, however, is not the recognition that conflict is likely but the difficulty of asserting national authority without turning companies away and depriving the country of the benefits they bring. A solution is not made easier when it is recognized that the benefits are more readily quantifiable – in terms of taxes, development aid, jobs generated and technology transferred – than the disadvantages. These are headed 'problems' in Table 15.2, where a selected list of issues between companies and governments demonstrates that the same issues carry problems and benefits.

Table 15.2 also shows in which chapters the issues are considered further. Clearly their consequences vary from business to business and from country to country. There is no formula which provides an over-riding means of determining where the balance of costs and benefits lies. International companies do provide a massive reallocation of the world's resources, and many people are enriched as a result; but this does not necessarily make these companies the most efficient or discriminating allocators of those resources. Nor, on the other hand, would more people necessarily benefit if the companies did not exist. What can be said is that the freedom and the constraints will vary with the national priorities at any given time, although even this statement requires some qualification.

Neither companies nor governments (however dictatorial) are to be regarded as monolithic. They are more realistically understood as coalitions of interests in which various groups will strive to win support for their views; the policies emerge through the strivings. In a company, for instance, there may well be a lobby trying to promote greater sensitivity to local interests, and a government official may work with its members.[8] The lobby is unlikely to defy the dictates of commercial viability, but where the choices are finely balanced or viability depends on time-scale (short-term losses can be absorbed to produce long-term profits) the changing balance of power can change the policy. Among the exercises at the end of the chapter can be found an example of such a conflict (see 'Speizeprov AG – influencing subsidiary policy'). This is a relatively straightforward example of an opposition group in head office finding itself in a changed position when its expertise became valuable to the chief executive after a crisis in a subsidiary. More subtle examples of the interplay of groups also occur. This understanding of conflicts between companies and countries is illustrated in the following section.

Table 15.2 Issues affecting the relationship between companies and governments

Issue	Benefits to country	Problems for country	Where considered
Authority (influence, power, sovereignty)	–	Exertion for undue influence on political and economic policies	This chapter
Competition (consumer interests)	Provision of greater choice through international trading	Restriction of competition	This chapter Chapter 7
Education	Support for local research	Damage through centralized research	This chapter
Employment (labour, manpower staffing)	Provision of jobs, often of high quality	Movement of some jobs to head office, expatriates in senior positions	This chapter Chapter 9
Environment (physical)	World use of beneficial technologies	Ability to move to areas of lax pollution legislation	
Finance	Ability to enrich country	Damage to money market and to national economic policies	This chapter and Chapters 8 and 13
Information (accountability	Development of new techniques	Ability to conceal financial position in host countries	Chapter 12
Management	Development of new techniques and raising standards	Too little consideration of local culture and aspirations	Chapter 14
Regional development	Responsiveness to national regional policies	Limited commitment to location	This chapter
Resources (use of experience, funds, knowledge, materials, people, techniques and other resources)	Efficiency improves their use	Channels to own interest	Chapter 12
Taxation (transfer pricing)	The wealth generated makes the companies large tax payers	International movement of funds facilitates tax avoidance	This chapter and Chapters 7 and 8
Technology	Ability to bring useful knowledge to country	Centralization of research and development	This chapter and Chapters 10 and 11
Time horizons		Difficulty of reconciling time horizons of governments and companies	Chapter 12
Trade	Increase in trade	Controls over exports from subsidiary, also dumping and unfair practices	This chapter and Chapter 3

15.3 Some major issues

The issues around which the conflicts occur are varied and far-reaching. In the following list they are arranged in alphabetical order, but their significance for governments and for companies varies considerably.

Competition policies and consumer interests

The best-known national competition policy is that enshrined in anti-trust and related legislation in the United States. The confusing enforcement of this legislation also indicates the uncertainties with which companies have to cope. In one famous case, where a number of electrical components manufacturers were prosecuted for price-fixing, the defence claimed that the alternative was a price war. This would have led to bankruptcies and the survivors would then have been accused under the same legislation of acquiring monopoly powers.[9] In the past some European companies have benefited from anti-trust suits, like BAT which came into existence after one. Many others have been frustrated by uncertainties and delays while the courts decided whether their American take-over bids came within the terms of the legislation.

The United States' law, which is over 100 years old, was given a considerable impetus in the 1940s. One reason for this was the discovery that international agreements between chemical companies resulted in Germany being able to produce a synthetic rubber before the allies in World War II because a vital part in the research effort had been allocated to a German firm in a pre-war cartel. Elsewhere, legislation is more recent and has been gradually implemented. It has also been accompanied by uncertainties and lengthy hearings. One example was a case that the European Commission brought against IBM. The issue was the refusal of the company to make information available about its mainframe (370 series) computers so that other manufacturers could produce compatible equipment. The compromise agreement (signed in August 1984) illustrated the tortuous logic and uncertainties of such cases. IBM undertook to make information available on new equipment and software within 120 days of announcing that they were coming on the market, and in Europe no later than elsewhere. The agreement was to be renegotiated after a few years.[10]

Another uncertainty is the chance of civil action where a criminal case has demonstrated the possibility of success. The various suits which followed the withdrawal of criminal proceedings brought as a result of charges laid by Laker airlines against other trans-Atlantic operators illustrated this. A more recent series of cases has been between Virgin Atlantic Airways and British Airways.

Competition legislation now exists in most industrial countries as well as in regional organizations like the European Union. Various forms of regulation aim to prevent control of the market either by agreements between companies or by the exercise of monopoly power by one or two large concerns. European countries have been wary of operating legislation on monopolies because a company can be large in its own domestic market but still small in the face of world competition. This accounts for their willingness to leave enforcement to the European Union. There is also a fear that action against national firms is positively helpful to the foreigner attempting to start business in a country. The purpose of the legislation is to protect the consumer by enforcing competition and to keep down the costs of market entry for newcomers. Companies, for their part, argue that they lower prices and raise customer choice through their international operations – they can obtain supplies in the cheapest markets and launch new products even where returns will only be long-term. They also point to the number of lengthy and expensive cases against them which end up unproven. In spite of these claims governments are impressed with the need for counterbalancing measures against threats of monopoly.

Education, research and technology

The claims of multinational companies to be disseminators of innovating technologies and techniques have been investigated and generally upheld.[11] A worry for governments is over the centralization of that research. In Canada, for example, the 'branch economy' is a phrase used to convey the finding that a high proportion of foreign investment (over 60 per cent of the total in manufacturing industry) means the removal of research posts to foreign countries, especially the United States. Modern technology makes the centralization of research in the home country less necessary than before, as has been demonstrated by one multinational (Alcan), itself of Canadian origin, which has located research facilities in three different countries connected by on-line links. In spite of this example, most research facilities remain concentrated, and the spread of multinationals is increasing the concentration. One consequence is damage to higher education, when incentives to study advanced technologies as well as research grants for further study, disappear. The link between business innovation and higher education is not straightforward, but fears exist both of a lack of support and an increasing brain drain to centres of high-level research.

The solution urged in Canada, and existing elsewhere (in Italy, for instance), is to press for product mandate status – the assignment to the national subsidiary of one complete division. The subsidiary then exercises all the head office functions, including research and new product development, for this division. In this way the company retains the advantages of centralization, but the country acquires a wider range of outlets. Although only applicable to diversified firms, more is likely to be heard about world product mandates which have already been tried in firms as different as Philips, Black and Decker and Litton.[12] However, government intervention is not likely to promote them to any significant degree. Any problems caused by companies centralizing research are more likely to be countered by support for national research in advanced technology.

Employment (including regional development)

Because multinationals bring jobs, often jobs of high quality, governments are wary about imposing restrictions on them. However, research into job creation has tended to modify that accepted view because when a local company is taken over there are also job losses. Even when a subsidiary is started from scratch it may require scarce skills and, as a result, local employers find themselves faced with stiff competition for a limited pool of labour. If local employers go out of business as a result, the job creation turns out to be an illusion. At the same time research posts may disappear along with management and planning positions if services are moved to head office. But, on the assumption that job gains do exceed job losses, some governments have developed a battery of incentives and controls to direct foreign investors into starting new businesses. And the interventions seem little related to the political complexion of the government; similar negotiations with foreign investors are undertaken by right-wing as well as left-wing governments.

Several American states have permanent representatives in Europe seeking foreign investors, while countries like Switzerland have controls on foreign business. Ireland is a country that has aimed, with considerable success, to cure an age-old problem of inadequate opportunities at home leading to high levels of emigration, by encouraging foreign companies. The facilities include the provision of off-shore zones where companies can service foreign markets free of customs and other regulations. A number of countries, both industrialized and developing, now provide such facilities which appear to have made a substantial contribution to the Irish economy.

Incentives and constraints can be divided into direct and indirect measures. Most countries exercise some control over take-overs and, where controls exist, government consent is required for any foreign investment above a minimum sum. Since most countries are anxious to encourage the inflow of funds, these controls are used to control rather than to stop foreign investors, and to steer them towards greenfield ventures and away from take-overs that are considered harmful to national interests. Difficulties for companies are sometimes caused by their willingness to respond to these measures and invest in regions which the locals shun, as two examples earlier in this book have already demonstrated – one where communications with a region were much worse than the foreigner thought possible, and the other where an area of high unemployment did not contain relevant skills and production was delayed for two years because this elementary fact had been overlooked.

Most firms decide in the light of other commercial considerations and treat government concessions as providing some assistance after the decision has been taken. Nevertheless, there are areas of unemployment in most European countries, as well as in the southern United States, that would be almost completely derelict without foreign investment. There are also snags to this over-dependence on the foreign firm, such as its ability to pull out when depression or technical development produces rationalization. Nevertheless the existence of foreign concentrations shows the contribution the international firm can make.[13]

Government measures are more usually indirect than direct and include grants, loans at zero or low rates of interest, tax holidays and the provision of facilities in the form of offices and factories, new roads or rail sidings. The facilities are provided especially to encourage the greenfield development, which may still be subject to planning controls as well as the hostile lobbies demonstrated by the BASF example with which this chapter opened. Since the number of would-be investors is limited, there is competition between governments. This has led to an escalation in incentives which, in its turn, has produced a demand for international agreements restricting them. Some implications of this demand have been incorporated in the codes of conduct discussed in the next chapter. It has to be said that the same companies which are exacting a price for entering countries that offer a relatively free market anyway, are also negotiating to enter socialist countries where they are bargaining to reduce constraints rather than to be granted assistance. It is the market that counts, however strong the pressure for grants.

The employment policies of governments, and the provision of work and residence permits, vary considerably. One constraint is on the employment of expatriates – a restriction that is almost universal except where treaties exist to guarantee free movement of personnel – and sometimes in spite of such treaties. In addition to immigration rules there may be laws safeguarding established professions. In France, for instance, the chief executive of a pharmaceutical company must be a pharmacist.

The question of employment, then, illustrates the love-hate relationship between a government and the foreign companies that operate within its jurisdiction. It also illustrates the complex variety of objectives which the government has to consider and which produces the apparently contradictory policies so bewildering to the corporate negotiator. Immigration laws are examples of measures designed to protect local nationals, which may yet reduce job opportunities by discouraging the foreign investor. Such laws exist almost everywhere from a rich country with high employment like Switzerland (where immigration laws, first introduced after a referendum based on social issues, were partly justified on the grounds of reducing economic pressures) to poor countries with problems of national identity.

Finance and taxation

Finance is always a delicate issue. In Chapter 8 the capital structure of the foreign subsidiary was discussed and its typically high proportion of loan capital demonstrated. Since the loan capital is usually raised locally, this fact has given rise to the claim: 'they are buying us with our own money'. The phrase, which has been used in the French press among others, illustrates the point of view of the local businessman, especially at a time when funds are scarce and expensive (although it has to be added that some businessmen are only too pleased to sell their enterprises to the foreigner who can afford to offer a high price). The money market is further weakened when foreign companies remove shares in attractive sectors of the economy by buying high technology companies. The resulting pressure is one of the reasons for controls exercised by some governments. These take two principal forms to meet the two main objections:

1 an insistence that a minimum foreign equity is imported before a project is sanctioned;
2 an insistence that part of the equity in the local subsidiary is sold locally.

The contradiction in these measures is to be traced to the problems that produce them. While few industrialized countries yet insist on local equity (at least formally, there are unofficial pressures), the less developed find themselves compelled to give priority to fostering an infant money market and opportunities for their own investors. Greater opportunities for the local entrepreneur as a prime mover in industrial development, and a more secure mover than the foreigner who can withdraw, are a topical issue in most developing nations. In Nigeria, for instance, frustration has been expressed at the way foreign companies control a high proportion of the national economy and at the same time mop up an even higher proportion of scarce funds. This frustration led to indigenization decrees which have become increasingly strict over the years. Their provisions restrict foreign ownership in different industry sectors, with 60 per cent the highest allowed in those industries where foreign know-how is most in demand. Nigeria does at least possess oil revenue – and it is no coincidence that the pace of indigenization has varied with the price of oil as did the enforcement of measures like consents to the repatriation of funds – but other countries have to build a financial future without such assistance and that requires skill in encouraging foreign capital on terms that will also assist the local money market. Malaysia, for instance, has relaxed laws on foreign investment in order to give industrial development priority over the local money market (during the 1970s foreign investment had to be below 50 per cent). In spite of this the money market is booming in that country – the New Straits Times Industrials Index reached 5666 in June 1995.

The dilemma for a government official is clear enough; what is not always recognized is the problem for the private sector. The local executive of an international bank can find himself in the position of having to approve funds to a foreign customer of his bank, although he considers the project harmful to his country, and having to reject other applications he would much like to foster. In a poor country it is harder than in a rich one to accept that market forces can determine investment decisions. Foreign investment is welcomed when it brings fresh funds into a country, but the terms on which the funds are introduced are increasingly questioned. In particular, the consequences for the local money market, for local entrepreneurs and for the long-term well-being of the country. Measures to counter the problems can lead to contradictory solutions – when, for instance, a higher proportion of equity over loan capital is demanded and, at the same time, a lower proportion of total equity. The circumstances of the country will determine the bias in a particular case, but companies have to expect countries to regard financial arrangements in the light of their effects on general economic development.

Transfer pricing

One subject of interest to companies and to countries is that of taxation. While claiming the right to minimize their taxes by legitimate means – and hiring for this purpose experts capable of using reliefs and concessions to the utmost – companies also claim to boost government incomes as a result of high profits generated by efficient operations. Some companies, like the uranium concessionaires in The Niger, provide virtually the whole of a poor nation's tax income. The counter-claim is that the multinationals are manipulating their affairs internationally so as to avoid tax or to pay it in low-tax countries. An official of the United States Treasury once said that multinational companies could run rings round his staff. If this can be said of a sophisticated administration, how much more can it be said elsewhere. The basis of the accusation is the charge that prices between units of a company are being manipulated; since a proportion of the foreign trade of industrialized countries is intra-company, there is plenty of scope for manipulation, even though the opportunity is normally limited to occasions when the product is unique (a component used in an assembly in another country, for instance). If a product has a market value, the tax authorities should be able to identify overpricing.

The managerial issue has already been discussed under pricing in Chapter 7, but there are political issues both within a company and within a government as well as between the two. The political issues illustrate the point that neither companies nor governments are to be regarded as monoliths in which a single corporate view can be identified: an insight often overlooked by those who seek to influence policies. Much has been written on transfer pricing with little hard evidence to support the generalizations.[14] This lack of hard evidence is due to the strict confidentiality which is maintained by both executives and administrators, although the veil is lifted occasionally as in the Monopolies Commission investigation of the pricing of Hoffman Laroche's pharmaceutical products in Britain. In this case evidence was made available as a result of legal sanctions and appeared to show overpricing which had the effect of moving profits to a low tax country. In other instances the evidence is hearsay, but still adds up to a strong case.

The author has himself spoken with numerous executives (to date in upwards of 60 companies) who have had experience of transfer pricing. Many have expressed a duty to keep down the company's tax burden by all legal means; a majority have been opposed to manipulating prices, while making clear the problem of negotiating a price for a unique product (the question of internal markets always gives rise to problems, see Chapter 7). One reason for their opposition to using transfer pricing as a technique is related to company politics; if a subsidiary is being appraised on its profitability (to which executive bonuses are frequently attached), there is little guarantee that losses due to unfavourable transfer prices are taken fully into account. One subsidiary provided evidence to the contrary; in spite of assurances from one department in head office, it was severely criticized by another for the losses. The chances that playing games with prices will damage the management information system should not be underestimated; nor should a company be tempted to show losses in order to justify closures decided on other grounds or to counter the power of organized labour.

The main pressures within a company towards use of transfer pricing come from the finance department seeking to minimize taxes and to move funds. The latter purpose may be more important than the minimizing of taxes, although the two go together when different methods of moving money (like dividends and royalty payments) are taxed differently. In countries where remittances are blocked, pricing may be the only means of moving money out. Even in a company where each unit has a relative autonomy, there may be pressure from the centre to resolve problems between the buyer and the seller when both are inside the company.

This political balance within a firm has a parallel within government; if the products are liable to pay duty, the customs administration will be as interested in ensuring that the prices are not too low (when duty is payable on value, as is usual) just as the tax authorities are in seeing that they are not so high as to reduce profits. One department's gain is another's loss, within governments as within companies. The general conclusion from the limited evidence available is that manipulating transfer pricing is not as common as is sometimes alleged, but that some centralized companies are using it to considerable effect even at the expense of problems within the company. Sometimes the difficulty of fixing prices may produce distortions; at other times the difficulty of moving funds may be a conclusive argument for adjusting prices. Skills at identifying over- (and under-) pricing will always be required by agencies enforcing competition law as well as those assessing taxes.

Trade

The most controversial issue of all is that of restrictions on trade. This topic has already been mentioned more than once in earlier chapters, but the size of the dilemma needs to be re-emphasized in this context. Most companies take it for granted that subsidiaries and licensees will be restricted in their sales areas. From a company's point of view this is commonsense and few allow unrestricted competition between subsidiaries. There are numerous examples of the problems that can arise from such competition. A carefully fostered corporate image can soon be destroyed when one national subsidiary aims at a different market segment from the rest. Salesmen from different subsidiaries offering contradictory prices and terms do not help either. In many cases, too, a subsidiary or a licensee will have been established to service a particular market, and heavy investment elsewhere may be threatened if unrestricted exports are permitted. None of these arguments appear convincing to a country whose export effort is hampered because national companies (foreign subsidiaries are by definition locally registered and hence national companies) are taking orders from outside.

The situation is made worse when a local company has been taken over and directed to concentrate on its home market, and worse still when the instructions are forced upon head office by its own government. An example of this occurred in the early 1980s when the United States Government instructed American companies to prevent both their subsidiaries and licensees abroad from selling materials to the Soviet Union for the construction of a gas pipeline, during the period of sanctions arising from the Russian involvement in Afghanistan and Poland.

In spite of these problems, it has been shown that multinationals can still be larger exporters than local companies even when they impose restrictions.[15] They have the contacts and facilities to make the most of the opportunities in markets where exports are permitted. For this reason governments are wary about driving away good exporters for the sake of penalizing the bad. At the least it should be possible, where investment controls exist, to stipulate that export outlets are not abandoned and to make this a condition for permitting a take-over. Increasingly, countries are allowing concessions to companies undertaking to export a minimum proportion of their output. The problem of a foreign company controlling a subsidiary's exports is not entirely straightforward.

Conclusion

To match the benefits and problems listed in Table 15.2, governments adopt a number of measures. These can be subdivided into those that apply to all companies, domestic as well as foreign, and those that apply only to the foreign:

1 Government measures that foreign firms need to take account of but which apply to domestic firms as well include:
   (a) regional incentives,
   (b) labour laws,
   (c) health and safety regulations,
   (d) accounting rules,
   (e) competition laws,
   (f) commercial legal codes,
   (g) company law (including supervisory boards as in Germany),
   (h) measures against dumping or unfair practices.
2 Government measures that only apply to foreign firms include:
   (a) special incentives,
   (b) measures to ensure compliance with national trading policies,
   (c) government procurement guidelines,
   (d) insistence on local equity or joint ventures,
   (e) insistence on employment of local nationals,
   (f) insistence on part local manufacture,
   (g) tariffs and other barriers to trade,
   (h) taxation (especially withholding tax),
   (i) restrictions on repatriation of funds.[16]

Incentives are not as effective as is often hoped because companies are looking at markets. The general state of a national economy and its prospects are more important than specific concessions, which are likely to influence the decision only when there is a fine balance between investment sites. This is one example of the need to understand one another's motives which is critical to any negotiations between companies and governments. Another example is that of time-scale. Changes in government policy cause confusion to business (for instance, in Britain the statutory grants and allowances for manufacturing industry changed 15 times in one period of 21 years). The disincentives produced by frequent, short-term measures are likely to be more obvious to companies than concessions which, in any case, may not match the costs they are paid to offset.

15.4 A rent for your place in our society

A disservice is done to policy-makers in both camps by claiming that there is no inevitable conflict between companies and governments. A company pursuing benefits for its shareholders (as it is legally bound to do) cannot always be acting in the best interests of each of the countries in which it happens to be operating at any one time. There is unlikely to be an identity of interest on every issue between a company and its own government, let alone a foreign one. The major concern of government is to identify the conflicts that can arise, along with the issues on which an identity of interest exists, and to try to cope with both as effectively as possible.

Naturally, the bargaining powers of governments will be influenced by the nature of the market, as well as by the facilities that their countries can provide. Some are able to exercise more influence than others. The next chapter discusses the codes of conduct that are being promoted to provide a framework for negotiations, but a consensus seems to be emerging on a relationship that appeals to most administrations. The following paragraph attempts to express this consensus.

You (the foreign firm) must find something attractive in this country to invest here. You would not be here if you didn't. We (the local government) accept that you pay your taxes like other corporate citizens, but we expect a more substantial contribution from you: a rent for your place in our society. This will compensate us for building up the market as well as the infrastructure and cultural resources which you are able to tap relatively cheaply. It will also compensate us and our national firms for any unfair advantages you may possess as a result of your international status. The expected contribution may include any or all of:
  an undertaking to bring in an agreed minimum amount of foreign capital,
  an undertaking to export an agreed percentage of the products manufactured,
  an agreement to provide education and training facilities for your employees beyond what the law prescribes and to facilitate promotion to all positions for local nationals,
  an agreement to keep imports to a minimum and to sell components to the local subsidiary at a fair market price,
  an agreement to operate where feasible in areas of unemployment in this country and to make a contribution to the well-being of those areas that goes beyond the payment of local taxes.

This statement provides a set of criteria for judging the state of the relationship in both non-interventionist and interventionist countries. It takes thinking on the subject beyond the love-hate relationship which confuses so much policy-making.

15.5 Cases, questions and further reading

Case examples

Speizeprov AG: influencing subsidiary policy

Herman Braun was an established and able member of the international division of Speizeprov AG, a multinational with investments in over 50 countries. The company's stated policy was to allow autonomy to its foreign subsidiaries subject to the regular payment of a dividend representing at least 50 per cent of the net profit, or 8 per cent on their net investment after allowing for all taxes. This arm's length policy was modified in practice by frequent visits from head office executives who would offer advice, derived from company experience elsewhere, which the local managers usually took. Braun was known as a critic of this policy, alleging that decisions were being taken that did not represent the best interests of the company. He took the view that there was both too much independence and too much interference at the same time. Local managers were free to take decisions whose consequences could be disastrous internationally for a company which maintained a high profile. At the same time they were prevented from carrying out schemes which were sound by freakish interference on the part of visiting executives. 'We're getting the worst of both worlds,' was Braun's familiar plea. The international division was split into rival factions between those who supported Braun, and those who argued that a profitable mix between central and local interests had been achieved.

Eventually Braun was moved sideways into a liaison post between the international division and the research and development department. As a result his supporters lost interest and criticism was effectively stilled. Some time later a major controversy erupted in one of the countries in which Speizeprov operated. This concerned a marketing programme in which, it was alleged, improper pressures had been brought to bear on consumers. The debate was enlivened by statements that some members of the government favoured the company's products, despite allegations that they were being promoted in ways damaging to health. Questions were asked about how members of the government had been persuaded to favour the products. In trying to cope with the damaging publicity, which included threats of a boycott in other markets, the chief executive of Speizeprov heard worrying rumours within the company. These alleged that the marketing programme had been launched after one of his colleagues (Karl Weiss) had exerted extreme pressure on the subsidiary concerned to produce a rapid increase in market share. Although the actual form of the programme had been left to the local subsidiary, Weiss had limited its options by turning down those that were long-term. Casting around for any source of advice within the company, the chief executive remembered Braun's name and sent for him. The outcast had suddenly come into the limelight and found his views treated with a new respect throughout the company.

This case example provides an opportunity for a role-playing exercise with a number of groups pitted against one another – the chief executive and his staff, the dominant faction in the international division, the Braun faction, the supporters of the controversial programme in the local subsidiary, and their opponents.

Questions

1 'In all business operations, the enterprise has common interests and potential areas of conflict with governments and must recognize governmental policies and actions as constraints in business decision-making' (Robock and Simmons). Comment.

2 Describe conflicts that might arise between a company's objectives and the public interest when the 'company' is an Italian subsidiary of an American firm. Discuss, with examples, ways in which such conflicts can be resolved.

3 Discuss the view that a country should curtail incoming investment, what restrictions can be used and why.

4 Consider the criteria which in your view should be adopted in developing countries for determining the amount and nature of multinational company activity in those countries.

5 Critically examine the statement that direct investment has more to offer a developing country than the equivalent amount of aid.

6 In what ways are governments sensitive about the political and economic power of multinational companies? List the issues that you consider most important and discuss one in depth.

7 Identify some of the criticisms that are likely to be made against a large chemical company operating in Latin America. Write a memorandum to the chief executive from a confidential adviser giving an appraisal of these criticisms and the extent to which they should be expected to influence corporate policy.

8 Evidence indicates that host country controls on foreign companies are increasing. Give reasons for this development and consider the kinds of problem likely to develop from it, if any, for the country.

Further reading

Barnet, R.J. and Muller, R.E., *Global Reach: The Power of the Multinationals*, Simon and Schuster, 1974. This book contains a confrontation view of company–government relations.

Behrman, J.N. and others, *International Business–Government Communications*, Lexington Books, 1975. This presents a more optimistic view.

Bursk, E.C. and Bradley, G.E. (eds.), *Interdependence and the International Corporation*, International Management and Development Institute, 1977, provides trenchant support for the multinationals (it is one of a series of similar booklets on the subject).

Cronje, S. and others *Lonrho: Portrait of a Multinational*, Penguin, 1976. This is a critique of a controversial firm.

George, S., *How the Other Half Dies*, Pelican, 1976. This provides a devastating account of multinational agribusiness.

Goldberg, W.H. (ed.), *Governments and Multinationals*, Oelgeschlager, Gunn and Hain, 1983.

Gladwin, T.N. and Walter, I., *Multinationals under Fire*, Wiley, 1980. This is a scholarly and well-documented review of both sides of the argument.

Lim, L., 'States vs. Market in the rapidly growing economies of East and South-East Asia', *South East Asia Business*, Summer 1985, pp. 4–10.

Lloyd, Bruce 'The identification and assessment of political risks,' *Moorgate and Wall St Journal*, Spring 1975. An old article but one which sets out an interesting scheme for assessing political risks.

Neghandi, A.R. and Prasad, S.B., *The Frightening Angels*, Kent State University Press, 1975. This describes the multinationals and their contribution to the Third World together with some problems that arise.

Pines, S. Melvin and Bogdanowicz, Christine A., The Supranationals, Euromoney.

Poynter, T., *Multinational Enterprises and Government Intervention*, Croom Helm, 1985.

Vernon and Wells 1981, ch. 10.

16 International organizations

This chapter reviews the organizations which have grown up as a result of international treaties or other agreements to regulate commerce. They are of four types:

1 those whose membership is, in principle, unrestricted;
2 those whose membership is regional;
3 those whose membership is limited by a common interest;
4 those negotiated between pairs or groups of countries.

The commercial implications of these organizations are discussed in this chapter, especially their consequences for the restricting, or derestricting, of trade and investment. In spite of a general policy of avoiding abbreviations in this book, the lengthy titles of some of these organizations are abbreviated when they appear more than once.

Attempts to regulate the world by means of treaty organizations have always existed. They achieved a new dimension in the founding of the League of Nations after the 1914–18 War: a treaty organization designed to become comprehensive. Since the war of 1939–45, organizations have proliferated with global, regional or other (more restricted) access. Some are mainly political or military – even these have commercial implications since they provide markets for armaments – most are concerned with trade and investment to some degree. This chapter looks at some of these organizations and their characteristics and follows with sections on the main issues on which international organizations influence commercial policies directly, including international finance, free trade and direct investment.

16.1 World organizations: the United Nations and its derivatives

The United Nations has 184 members. All its activities are relevant to the international manager, but those that directly affect the decision-making are carried out by affiliates like the World Bank, the International Monetary Fund, the General Agreement on Tariffs and Trade (since January 1995, the World Trade Organization), the Food and Agricultural Organization, the United Nations Conference on Trade and Development (UNCTAD), the International Labour Office, the World Health Organization and the Centre on Transnational Companies (now part of UNCTAD). These will be considered under later subject headings.

16.2 Regional organizations

The accelerating growth of regional organizations has been a feature of the world scene since their tentative beginnings in the 1940s and 1950s. Ten years ago there were 27 organizations of neighbouring states designed to promote economic, political and other forms of co-operation; now this number is increasing. They have grown slowly, but some exert a considerable influence on world trade. The most developed is the European Union but other regional groupings, such as the Andean Group, the Association of South East Asian Nations and the Economic Community of West African States, are gaining ground. The success of the European Union in the eyes of the rest of the world has stimulated the growth of similar organizations, ironically since its progress is treated with more scepticism in Europe itself. Among the reasons for this scepticism are two problems which are common to most regional organizations:

1 the apparent slowness of the decision-making, a slowness exacerbated by the fact that each member upholds policies on which it is adamant but which do not claim such high priority among the others;

2 the fact that the benefits of the organization are usually more evident to the richer than to the poorer members.

The force of this objection, it must be said, depends partly on the political complexion of the government. Left-wing governments in poorer countries (such as Greece, Portugal and Spain in the European Union – at least in the past) are inclined to see the higher standard of living in other members as a means of raising the standard of their citizens. This is probably true of the new Latin American organization, Mercosur (see below).

Ironically, two other problems follow as a result of the pioneering of the European Union. First is that embryo organizations elsewhere have often felt inspired to follow the example of the European Union in determining their objectives even when those objectives do not fit their own regional requirements. The other problem is that many of the members of these embryo organizations trade more with the European Union (one reason for its attractiveness) and with other industrial countries than with one another – a fact which gives their regional affairs a lower priority.

This problem was one of the causes of the break-up of two associations – the Latin American Free Trade Area (LAFTA) (the Latin American Integration Area (ALADI) largely replaced it and most members are now with Mercosur), and the East African Community. Most of the associations, however, have funds through which the development of the poorer members is assisted.

Regional organizations are of three kinds:

1 those that aim to be economic communities;

2 those that aim to be free trade areas;

3 those with more modest aims, including a promotion of common interests.

The following selective list provides some idea of the range that already exists. Although not all fit readily into the above categories, and some have aims that are very modest indeed, the growth of others has demonstrated that the trend to regionalism has become and will remain an important feature on the world trade map.

Africa

There has been a considerable development of regional organizations on the African continent with two aspiring communities, five emerging free trade areas and a number of other associations designed to promote specific aspects of economic development. To local observers progress has been very slow and the problem of differences of interest between richer and poorer members has caused difficulties, as in the break-up of the East African Community. Political differences also contributed to this break-up, and these have been exacerbated, here as elsewhere, by the difficulties that unstable regimes have in committing themselves to opening frontiers and entering far-reaching agreements. A problem that is more specifically African is that regionalization cuts across the current drive to nationalism. The fact that frontiers, largely inherited from colonial times, cut across traditional boundaries and tribal loyalties has prompted governments to make a drive towards greater national consciousness – a drive similar to that found in the United States, although for different reasons – and it is hard to promote nationalism and a supranational regional consciousness at the same time. This difficulty has partly accounted for slow progress in most of the organizations; nevertheless some frameworks are coming into place.

There are two organizations which aspire to both comprehensive membership and to becoming economic communities: the Economic Community of West African States (ECOWAS) and the Organization of African Unity (OAU).

The **Economic Community of West African States** has progressed furthest and fixed some deadlines for the future, although progress towards these deadlines is still slow. Its 16 member states, mostly along the West African coast or (like Mali) land-locked but on the West, did tie themselves to a customs union by 1992; this might eventually include duty-free trade. An agreement on the free movement of people was signed as long ago as 1979, but the implementation has been delayed by fears of mass migration. Indeed the wealthiest member, Nigeria, has since then expelled numbers of immigrants who had come from other member states, but in 1985 a limited agreement on the movement of people was signed.

Progress within ECOWAS has been slow hampered partly by a conflict of interest between the member states but especially by political uncertainty within the largest member, Nigeria. Nevertheless, a summit of heads of government held in Nigeria in 1993 added some fresh objectives to the Economic Community including the establishment of a regional parliament along with an economic and social council and a court of justice. Also included was the keeping of peace within the region. As a result of this, there are (at the time of writing, early 1995) ECOWAS troops in Liberia to keep the peace there.

The Community also has a co-operation fund to develop priority projects and a secretariat working on agricultural and infrastructure development, industrial co-operation and other programmes. The membership of ECOWAS, which looks eventually to a continent-wide common market, partly overlaps with the Organization for African Unity. This latter body is mainly known for its political activities, including conflict resolution among its members which include most independent African countries. It has economic and commercial aims, including a declaration of intent that foresees a customs union, but these are still under

investigation except for a continental news agency which has come into existence. An information commission was established in 1990.

In addition to information, work has been progressing slowly on communications and infrastructure, development, defence, energy, agriculture and a social
programme.

The **Organization of African Unity** has tried to follow a similar route on a larger
scale and at an even slower pace. An economic community covering most of the
continent is planned and may yet spring into existence.

There are a number of associations among the francophone African countries
(including the franc zone which is a common interest organization). Of these the
most active is the **Communauté Economique de l'Afrique de l'Ouest** (CEAO).
All six members of this community are also members of ECOWAS, but the CEAO
has progressed more rapidly. Agreements include the abolition or reduction of
duties between the member states, a development fund and co-operation programmes for water supply and transportation. Less ambitious aims are a feature
of other regional treaties which also overlap in membership with those mentioned.
These include: the **Conseil de l'Entente**, the **Organisation Commune Africaine
et Mauricienne** (OCAM) and **l'Union Douanière et Economique de l'Afrique
Centrale** (UDEAC). All have development funds to promote inter-state projects,
as does the African Development Bank of which 48 states are members.

The Middle East

Founded on 25 May 1981 – during the early months of the Iraq–Iran war – the
Gulf Cooperation Council (Saudi Arabia, Kuwait, United Arab Emirates, Oman,
Qatar and Bahrain) was primarily seen as a defence alliance. This did not deter
the invasion of one of its members, Kuwait, in 1990. The members are mostly
very small countries; in area, Saudi Arabia is six times the size of the other members added together. A main aim now is to establish a common market and this
is officially scheduled for 1997 although progress is still slow.

America

The American continents provide several examples of organizations which are of
increasing importance to traders in the area. Although they have suffered as much
as any by the common difficulties of reconciling conflicting interests, and progress
has been slow, these organizations are strengthening their positions rapidly. They
bear witness to one of the advantages of regional associations – that they can
influence the terms of trade in ways which member countries find difficult when
acting alone. The common strength, of course, partly depends on the strength of
the economies of the member countries. This is where the weaker economies
gain, a fact which they sometimes fail to recognize. The attractiveness of the association to the outsider is heightened by the purchasing power of the richer
members. But bargaining power and market entry remain a problem and, in an
attempt to strengthen their bargaining powers, member countries of the organizations discussed below have set up joint ventures among themselves to operate
abroad and to collaborate with incoming investors. These ventures are designed

to overcome the financial and marketing barriers experienced by local firms entering into competition with foreign multinationals. They suffer, however, from disadvantages, especially when attempting ambitious projects or through over-dependence on political power.[1] The following are the characteristics of the main American associations.

The North American Free Trade Area (NAFTA)

This at present includes Canada, the United States and Mexico. An ambition is that this will eventually stretch to most of the American continent. This Free Trade Area is an example of the reverse of the usual problem whereby the poorer nations perceive that the richer members take most of the advantages. In this case, the greatest doubts have come from those belonging to the two very rich members (Canada and the United States) taking the view that Free Trade has removed their jobs to the benefit of the low paid Mexicans. In fact labour interests in the United States were already accustomed to this happening but Canadians reacted strongly when the threat was noticed. The hope of the promoters of the agreement is that the enrichment of Mexico will provide a large market for their neighbours to the North.

The Free Trade Area has a secretariat committed to promoting free trade between the member countries and working out the implications in social and economic guidelines. These are simple in a free trade agreement, dedicated to removing barriers to trade as opposed to a common market which requires more complex regulations enabling the members to share common economic policies. North America has one main free trade treaty; Central and South America, on the other hand possessed or have possessed numerous ones. The position is changing rapidly with the emergence of APEC (see below).

Mercosur

On the first day of 1995, a new regional organization came into existence. Mercosur (an abbreviation of Mercado Comun del Sur, meaning southern common market) is a common market of the four countries which cover most of the land area of South America: Argentina, Brazil, Paraguay and Uruguay. Efforts are being made to integrate the four economies, previously divided by protectionism and hostility between them. According to the *Financial Times* (25 January 1995), the opening of the economies of Brazil and Argentina followed the coming of democracy in the 1980s. This has also led to an escalation of trade between the two countries and with the other two members of Mercosur. By the time of the launch of the organization almost all trade between the four countries had been freed, but the common external tariff only applied to 80 per cent of products. Work continues on the remaining issues while communications in the region are being rapidly developed. Mercosur is swiftly replacing the other main organizations in South America of which the most important is the Grupo Andino.

The Grupo Andino

Composed of Bolivia, Colombia, Ecuador, Peru and Venezuela, the Andean Common Market (ANCOM) has long been the most advanced in common regulations and a common external tariff. It is now likely to be absorbed into Mercosur.

The Latin American Integration Area (ALADI)

ALADI included Argentina, Bolivia, Brazil, Chile, Colombia, Ecuador, Mexico, Paraguay, Peru, Uruguay and Venezuela. This was founded some years ago after the break up of an earlier regional grouping, and is also likely to be absorbed into other organizations. Its achievements at regional organization were never more than modest.

The Caribbean Community and Common Market (CARICOM)

This association consists of 12 islands in the Caribbean plus Belize and Guyana and aims to become an economic community. It grew out of an earlier free trade area, but economic problems in some of the member countries have delayed progress. Conflicts of interest occur between members who show even greater inequalities than most similar organizations. Some – notably the Bahamas, Barbados and Trinidad – are among the wealthier of the developing countries; others, such as St Lucia and St Vincent, rank among the poorer. Gross domestic product per head varies from about $500 to over $3000. Another problem is the small size of each individual market and of the whole. As a consequence, the area has problems in promoting any trade. The products are limited in range and many of the countries are dependent on commodities which are depressed on international markets. Communications are also difficult, given the geography of the region but common efforts are being made to improve the infrastructure and significant achievements have already been recorded. CARICOM has taxation arrangements designed to increase the flow of funds to the poorer members; a common external tariff was gradually being brought into effect during 1991 (see *Financial Times*, 16.2.91).

Other organizations in the area include:
1 the Central American Common Market which has not progressed far, due partly to political difficulties, and whose future is chronically in doubt;
2 the Democratic Community of Central America, whose objects are mainly political and military;
3 the Organization of Eastern Caribbean States, all of whose members also belong to CARICOM;
4 the Organization of American States (OAS), a comprehensive organization based in the United States which is primarily concerned with political and social issues; and
5 the Organization of Central American States and URUPABOL (Uraguay, Paraguay and Bolivia), neither of which have commercial aspirations apart from limited co-operation agreements.

Asia and the Pacific Rim

The huge continent of Asia, stretching from the boundaries of Europe to the borders of the Pacific and includes two-thirds of Russia. The current regional organizations (apart from the Commonwealth of Independent States covering former Soviet territories in both Europe and Asia) are concentrated in the South East. One, ASEAN, is long-established but comparatively inactive; the others are new or in process of formation.

The Association of South East Asian Nations (ASEAN)

Originally founded as a military alliance, the Association acquired economic objectives as the threat of war within and between the member countries receded. The members now are: Brunei, Indonesia, Malaysia, The Philippines, Singapore and Thailand. Laos and Vietnam have observer status for which Cambodia has now applied. All the members are fast-developing newly industrializing countries (NICs) but are outstripped by one member, Singapore, which rates a higher gross domestic product per head than most so-called industrialized countries.

The economic measures have developed slowly and mainly through joint projects in the chemical industry. One reason for the slow growth has been the limited intra-regional trade. The member countries look beyond one another for their trading partners and are now looking, albeit with some misgivings, to wider organizations such as the **East Asian Economic Caucus (EAEC)** – with few definite rules at the moment but a general aspiration to foster Asian 'togetherness' (Mahathir, Prime Minister of Malaysia) – and the **Asia-Pacific Economic Cooperation Forum (APEC)** which looks outward to the other countries bordering the Pacific.

The Asia-Pacific Economic Forum (APEC)
This is an organization of which more will be heard, although progress is at present slow as a result of suspicions between the member countries which are competitors as well as partners. The 18 members include some from Asia (Brunei, China, Hong Kong, Indonesia, Japan, Korea, Malaysia, The Philippines, Singapore, Taiwan and Thailand), Australasia (Australia, New Zealand and Papua New Guinea) and from America (Canada, Chile, Mexico and the United States). Although APEC overlaps with other organizations on both sides of the Pacific it has begun to develop trade promoting institutions. These include: the Trade and Promotion Working Group, Trade and Investment Data Review Working Group, Investment and Industrial Science and Technology Working Group, Human Resources Development Working Group, Regional Energy Cooperation Working Group, Marine Resource Conservation Working Group, Telecommunications Working Group, Transportation Working Group, Tourism Working Group and the Fisheries Working Group.

The Malaysian Prime Minister (Dr Mahathir) considered the deadlines fixed for creating these institutions too tight and argued for their relaxation (see *The New Straits Times*, 19 November 1994).

Europe

Three organizations have dominated the European scene: the European Union, the European Free Trade Area and the Commonwealth of Independent States (CIS). Other organizations include:
1 **Benelux**, the customs union between Belgium, Holland and Luxembourg;
2 the **Nordic Council**, consisting of the four Scandinavian countries plus Iceland;
3 the **North Atlantic Treaty Organization** (NATO), which still operates some restrictions on the export to the Eastern bloc of high-technology equipment with military uses.

Some older agreements (like the **Council for Mutual Economic Assistance**, CMEA also known as COMECON in the former socialist countries) have become obsolete. NATO has been searching for a new purpose, while new agreements like the Schengen Accord between France, Italy, Germany and Benelux are coming into being, as well as the CSCE (the Conference on Security and Cooperation in Europe) which is of military rather than commercial significance).

The European Union (EU)

Member countries (as of the end of 1995) are: Austria, Belgium, Britain, Denmark, Finland, France, Germany, Greece, Ireland, Italy, Luxembourg, Netherlands, Portugal, Spain, Sweden. In addition, special arrangements have been made for trade with neighbouring countries and with former dependent territories.

The change of name (from the European Community to the European Union) since the last edition of this book represents a further development in the integration of European countries – a development that is controversial in all of them but especially in Britain. It would appear that the process of integration is now unstoppable. It is also bound to be controversial and extremely slow with each country watching over its supposed national interests before agreeing to further progress. The 1996 summit will be the scene of further difficult negotiations and is unlikely to produce any sensational results.

The decisions of the EU affect business so directly that many firms and trade associations retain representatives in Brussels to keep a watching brief, to lobby and to ensure that their views are adequately represented. Hence an understanding of the decision-making process is required as well as knowledge about its results. A minor industry has indeed grown up in helping interested parties to find their way around the Union's procedures in the three main centres of Brussels, Luxembourg and Strasbourg.

A *Council* of Ministers makes the final decisions, as with most regional organizations, and it is to the Council's secretariat that much attention is directed, but there are three other units in the structure. The proposals for legislation are framed by the *Commissioners* who hold full-time appointments – unlike the Ministers who belong to member-country governments – and have considerable powers in their own right. Unless politically sensitive, the Ministers accept most of the proposals presented to them by the Commissioners. The third unit is the *European Parliament* which considers the Commissioners' proposals before passing them to the Council. (It remains a consultative body only.) The fourth unit is that of the *judiciary* which interprets the EU legislation and can issue directions to national courts on commercial as well as other issues that come under the legislation.

A major step forward in the development of the EU was the Single European Act (1987). This altered the constitution by allowing majority voting on most issues in the Council of Ministers. It also gave more authority to the European Parliament, although still keeping its consultative role.

This Act and other measures towards greater European integration have been stimulated by the observation that the EU, the largest trading unit in the world (which exports 45.7 per cent of world total exports in 1992, far higher than the United States, at 16.4 per cent, and Japan, at 12.4 per cent), was losing out in competitiveness to other countries. Various measures have been taken to increase competitiveness by reducing obstacles to Europe-wide activities by local companies.

The EU has, as its aim, the creation of a unified internal market, in which all the factors of production (money, materials, people, know-how and so on) and of consumption can move freely, and of a common trading policy with the rest of the world. The internal market is still incomplete, but companies that assume that it will not progress further or faster, should be wary. Some issues were agreed early on; others, where national interests are in greater conflict, are taking longer, but blockages have a way of disappearing.

A much publicized aspect of EU business is the Common Agricultural Policy. It is easy to whip up emotion around evocative phrases like the cost of producing unwanted products, but few countries can be satisfied with their agricultural sectors. The United States also has surpluses, while countries as diverse as the Soviet Union and Zambia have chronic shortages. It was famine in Europe that produced the Common Agricultural Policy in the first place. This may be an additional reason for considering the policy outdated and irrelevant to present-day conditions. Nevertheless, the difficulties of tampering with the agricultural sector and devising means of keeping the countryside healthy without under- or over-production are notorious. At the heart of the policy is a system of levies and payments designed to introduce some stability into prices which, from the producers' point of view, over-react to the balance of supply and demand, and to enable the farmers to think ahead without imposing detailed plans upon them in ways that have proved counterproductive. No doubt reforms will eventually be agreed, but they are unlikely to come without some extension of countryside management to ease the transition.

More immediately relevant to the majority of the population, who are in non-agricultural occupations, are the attempts at an industrial policy. The progress in this field can be seen as a case study of how an intergovernmental body develops. After what must have seemed to the negotiators imperceptible progress, common standards have been achieved, and are being achieved, in a growing range of products, despite the technical complexities and the vested interests. The standards so far agreed, or under discussion, include a long list of parts for cars, weighing and measuring instruments, electrical equipment, dangerous substances like pesticides and corrosives, lifts and lifting apparatus and many others. There are also some specialized agencies like the European Committee for Standardization and an organization for the electricity industry called CENELEC. As this edition is being prepared, the Commission is discussing a regulation to abolish withholding taxes for payments between units of a company in different countries in the EU. It is hoped that this measure will encourage European companies to plan their facilities on a Europe-wide basis.

The industrial policy is designed to remove some of the so-called non-tariff barriers, which still restrict the internal trade of the EU. Tariffs themselves have been largely abolished except for new members during transitional periods but there are non-tariff barriers, including the fact that frontier inspections continue. The reduction of other restrictions on trade still seems a long way off since it depends on the harmonization of taxes and of a variety of health and safety rules. Value Added Tax has always been accepted as a condition of membership but, since the rates are different for each country, the tax acts as a form of import duty levied on goods moving between EU countries. In this way the benefits of a common market are partly cancelled out – only partly because the tax is applied impartially to foreign and domestic products – but it still provides a hindrance to trade which would be avoided if member countries harmonized their tax rates. Efforts in this direction are currently under negotiation.

Company law is another issue on which progress has been slow. A common form of company registration has been on the horizon since 1972, and was accepted by a vote of the European Parliament in 1982. This provides a voluntary two-tier system, based on the German model now adopted in several of the member states. A first tier – a supervisory board representative of workers and share-holders – has general powers over policy issues. The running of the company is normally left to a second tier, the board of management. A more radical scheme for compulsory information for, and consultation with, employees in larger companies has been discussed.[2]

The proposal has been supported by European trade unions but opposed by employers. It stipulates that multinational companies operating in the EU, both locally based and foreign, must provide regular information to their employees on production plans, management changes, employment trends and other issues that concern them. This scheme still is a long way from acceptance and is likely to undergo continuing debate.

The increasing pace of integration has unearthed some problems and provided some opposition mainly on nationalistic grounds. Nevertheless, a poll among citizens of the member states in late 1993 showed overall support of nearly three-quarters (73 per cent) with much higher figures for Greece (85 per cent) and Italy (84 per cent) as well as higher figures for Spain, the Netherlands, Ireland and Portugal. Only Britain and Denmark among the then member countries showed more than 20 per cent against.

An issue that has proved most difficult, as it has with other regional organizations, has been to implement the principle of the free movement of people. The EU has tackled the problem from two directions: the removal of restrictions and the encouragement of the transfer of people. The latter measure has been mainly confined to students in the encouragement of students from one country to study in another. The elaborate Erasmus programme was designed to enable students and professors to move between institutions.

The removal of restrictions on movement has proved a more complicated and long-drawn out exercise. The original Treaty of Rome was clear on this point. Article 48 (clause 1) specified that 'Freedom of movement for workers shall be secured within the Community not later than by the end of the transitional period.' This clause, along with the implications for professional qualifications, as well as pension and health rights, has been reaffirmed several times since and the rights of immigrants and refugees added. Restrictions on the movement of people have been further removed by the so-called *Schengen Agreements* between member states.

The Schengen Agreements
France, Germany, Luxembourg and Belgium signed an agreement for the removal of all frontier controls on people travelling between those countries. This was signed at the Luxembourg town of Schengen which stands on frontiers with

Germany and France. Other member countries of the EU have either joined or signified their intention of doing so apart from Denmark (which has applied for observer status), Ireland and Britain. The Agreement includes measures for efficient policing and control of foreign (non-EU) nationals. It is administered in Brussels although the Agreement is not yet part of the EU constitution.

The Economic Interest Grouping

Another kind of measure of the Union is the **Economic Interest Grouping**. This is a facility designed to ease partnership arrangements between companies from which they can benefit without contravening competition law. The grouping, following a practice well-established in France, allows companies to merge part of their activities while remaining independent – allowing considerable flexibility in co-operation agreements. To protect shareholders and suppliers from abuses that might result from this flexibility, extensive publicity is required and the partners in the Grouping have unlimited liability. This arrangement could be invaluable to large projects, especially in major transport ventures, but it is hoped that it will be of even more value to small companies who will be able to enter into such agreements without losing their identity or compromising their existing businesses.

The Economic Interest Grouping measure has been more readily accepted than others because it is voluntary and does not appear to conflict with the interests of governments or pressure groups. However, all the measures are designed to harmonize, throughout the EU, legislation that already exists in at least one member state. A related issue, that of the harmonization of banking laws, demonstrates the reasons for and the difficulties in such a process.[3] This measure is an essential part of the free movement of capital which was supposed to have become a reality in 1973 but has been hindered by widely varying laws in the member countries – for instance, conditions attached to mortgages and safeguards for lenders, the non-tariff barriers.

A first attempt to harmonize the banking regulations in the early 1970s was along the lines of the EU-wide legislation intended to come into operation everywhere at the same time. This encountered opposition on the grounds that it set up over-strict supervision and was replaced by a step-by-step approach – with co-ordination in supervision between states as a first step, followed by proposals for standardized accounting and for the liberalization of mortgage loans. Working parties have been considering other measures which cover various financial activities and are designed to free the movement of capital along with other banking services.

More progress has been made on competition law where there is less conflict of interest and a strong motive for common action. The struggle to limit monopoly powers and enforce competition proves a problem for a country even when it is the size of the United States. In a smaller country, a company can have a dominant position at home, but still not be in an over-powerful position in relation to its international competitors.

EU policy was formulated in articles 85 and 86 of the Treaty of Rome and has been interpreted in a series of judgments by the European Court. Article 85 outlawed agreements between undertakings which fixed prices, limited production, shared markets or supply sources, applied dissimilar conditions to similar trans-actions and entered into contracts subject to conditions not related to the main purpose of the contract. However, the courts were given discretion to permit agreements that would otherwise be outlawed, if considered to be beneficial to consumers. Article 86 expanded on the issue of abuse of dominant position in the market. The judgments that have resulted have attacked monopoly and restrictive practices at a number of levels, from exclusive arrangements with agents to dominance in a particular industry sector. One criterion is to prevent arrangements which make for a monopoly position or other abuse of economic power. However, the legislation allows for discretion where an agreement appears to improve quality of service and exempts small businesses and sub-contracts so as not to prevent useful collaboration. In spite of the competition policy, the largest companies in the EU have continued to grow and efforts are being made to ban mergers which lead to a high level of market dominance.[4]

Since the mid-1980s another issue has come to the fore – the European Monetary Union and the possibility of a European central bank. The European currency unit[5] was first devised in the 1970s as a basket of European currencies, but its use has only gradually developed with the issue of some Eurobonds in ECUs during the 1980s. The significance of the ECU was much enhanced in May 1991 when a then non-EU country (Sweden) announced that the Swedish krone would in future be tied to the ECU. A few weeks later, the Finnish government made a similar announcement. Final plans for the European Monetary Union have now been postponed until 1999.

Another aim of the EU has been assistance to poorer nations. Some members, former colonial powers, supported a number of client states for which provision was needed. The Convention with African, Caribbean and Pacific Countries (ACP) – its official title, it is usually called the Lomé Convention after the capital of Togo where it was signed – provides for special assistance to 66 developing countries backed by the European Development Fund which derived from the Convention. The Fund finances construction projects, agricultural improvements, supply contracts and consultancy. In addition, the EU operates a Generalised Scheme of Preferences (GSP) which covers 148 countries including the 66 members of the Lomé Convention. The amounts of aid available include 8500m ECU voted over five years (an average of £1000m a year) for the Lomé Convention and Mediterranean countries, while other developing countries are receiving about £185m a year.

A distinctive feature of the Lomé scheme is known as STABEX. This recognizes that aid tends to be less effective in countries suffering from instability in their export earnings, and compensates member countries for loss of earnings from 48 agricultural products.[6] A related facility is SYSMIN which recognizes the problems caused by high dependence on a limited range of minerals and compensates for adverse market conditions. SYSMIN was introduced in 1980 and is restricted to avoid the benefits going to multinational companies.

16.3 Other treaty organizations

There are three other kinds of treaty organizations.

Treaties with military, political or social objectives

The North Atlantic Treaty Organization, the Conference on Security and Cooperation in Europe (CSCE) and the League of Arab States are all examples of this kind of treaty. The Commonwealth of Independent States (CIS, Russia) also has its defence department replacing the defunct Warsaw Pact. These are of interest for international marketing since they provide customers for relevant goods or services, but will not be considered here.[7]

Bilateral or multilateral treaties

Most countries, and some regional organizations, have signed treaties to promote trade usually freeing specific goods or offering general preferences. Some countries, including Japan and Canada, have bilateral treaties with the European Union, along with membership of newly developing regional organizations in the Pacific and (in the case of Canada) in America.

Special interest organizations

A number of arrangements which do not come under any of the other headings include the Organisation for Economic Cooperation and Development as well as the Organization of Petroleum Exporting Countries and the other international commodity agreements (see Chapter 13).

The Organisation for Economic Cooperation and Development (OECD)

The OECD was set up in 1961 and its 24 members include, on principle, the most industrialized countries. The OECD operates through over 200 committees to promote and co-ordinate trade between member countries and with the Third World. It also has a role in facilitating currency exchange and in liberalizing trade generally.[7] A recent report criticized the growth of protection against imports, producing evidence that it only has a limited influence on employment in the protected sectors even in the short-term and that this is balanced by job losses in other sectors as well as higher prices and other disadvantages. The OECD code of conduct for multinationals is considered later.

The Organization of Petroleum Exporting Countries (OPEC)

OPEC was founded in 1960 to co-ordinate the petroleum policies of member countries, and became a household name in the 1970s when it raised the price of oil steeply. Its policy of sustaining high prices and of regulating production has brought great wealth to some of its members. Qatar, for instance, is the world's richest country measured by gross domestic product per head. The economies of some members have suffered from subsequent fluctuations in oil prices which have also placed strains on the organization. The fluctuations and the strains are much publicized, but countries like Nigeria are still richer than neighbours without oil and the strains are no greater than those in other international organizations. The Organization's annual report for 1984 speaks of a 'determination to defend the price structure,' but in the following months this proved increasingly difficult.

Among the purposes of OPEC is to channel a proportion of oil revenues into development aid, and a list of 50 of the poorest countries receive loans and aid – mainly for long-term projects, but also for emergencies – from the OPEC fund.[8]

Intellectual property

A subject that has become increasingly on the agenda of the international organizations is that of copyright and intellectual property protection. An affiliate of the United Nations dedicated to this protection – **the World Intellectual Property Organization (WIPO)** – has achieved a much higher profile during the 1990s than in all the previous years since it was founded in 1967. Some companies claim large losses through the pirating of copyrights and patents mainly in South East Asian countries, but the governments of those countries (most of whom now belong to WIPO) have been cracking down on the piracy. A seminar on copyright and the new technology was held in Malaysia recently.

16.4 International financing

The world trading system is increasingly dependent on international funding agencies, without which large projects outside the industrialized nations could not go ahead at all. Some of these, like the European Development Fund, have already been mentioned. The dominant figure is the *World Bank* (officially known as IBRD[9] – the International Bank for Reconstruction and Development). An offshoot of the United Nations, the World Bank has disbursed over $300bn in loans since it was funded. These loans are at or near to commercial rates and are granted to both the public and the private sectors, but increasingly to the latter. The Bank has two affiliates – the International Finance Corporation (IFC) and the International Development Authority (IDA) – which also fund projects in less developed countries. The IDA provides interest-free credits to governments of very poor nations while the International Finance Corporation provides loans to private sector initiatives. In recent years, more private capital has become available to the developing nations, but the World Bank reports that 40 per cent of all capital funds for these countries still comes from official sources including the World Bank itself, the regional banks, the European Union, the United Nations and the Organization of Petroleum Exporting Countries (OPEC).

The regional banks provide a specialist resource: in Asia (the Asian Development Bank), Africa (the African Development Bank) and the Americas (Inter-American Development Bank).[10] These attempt to fulfil three functions: that of financial institution, of development promoter and of regional agency. They provide consultancy services and attempt to ensure that their projects are brought to successful fruition. The World Bank has declared that there are three criteria by which its activities are to be judged:
1 *flexibility*, the ability to adapt to changing conditions in the economic and financial environment;
2 *stability*, the maintenance of a stable flow of financing, without interruptions or wasteful accelerations, as far as conditions permit;

3 *balance*, the provision of a variety of instruments and facilities to suit the varying conditions among borrowers.[11]

The other major international funding body is the **International Monetary Fund (IMF)**, also an offshoot of the United Nations. It has 146 members (13 less than the parent body) and is designed to promote stability in currency exchange. In particular, it provides assistance to countries with acute balance-of-payments problems. Assistance is available to members in a series of tranches according to their contributions. As one tranche (based on a percentage of that country's quota) is used, more stringent conditions are attached before another tranche can be drawn on. In 1974 special facilities were set up for those countries in difficulties over the price of oil. Originally a temporary measure, these facilities have been increased since. There is also an Extended Fund Facility which allows support of adjustment programmes for three years.

Since 1978 the International Monetary Fund has been given increased powers of overseeing the exchange-rate policies of member countries and any other policies that influence those rates.

The near insolvency of Mexico has led the International Monetary Fund to rethink its role, in particular to consider how it can influence the rapid outflow of capital from a country in a future panic. It has been suggested that the Fund should take on a role more like that of a receiver in a national bankruptcy (see *The Economist*, 22 April 1995, p. 111) – so far this is only an extreme proposal.

The World Bank and the International Monetary Fund act as financiers and as advisers. They stand between wealthy donor countries and client governments who need help but resent interference in their economic policies, especially from powerful outsiders whose biases many of them suspect. Most of the donor governments are opposed to government intervention in commerce but are, at the same time, fearful of a breakdown in the international trading system. The political repercussions of pressing nations too far when they face financial problems have been considered incalculable but, as already explained, are now being calculated.

16.5 The international regulation of trade

A number of treaties and treaty organizations have been designed to stimulate or regulate trade, currency exchange, commodities and investment. In the past the accent was on negotiating freer movements of goods and funds across frontiers where barriers were growing. There is now also a demand to reverse the liberalization of investment flows and use international bodies to strengthen the resolve of governments to attach conditions to the movement of capital, and to ensure that companies cannot play one country off against another. This section deals with the four elements in the international framework: trade, currency exchange, investment and commodity agreements.

The General Agreement on Tariffs and Trade (GATT)

Now known as **The World Trade Organization (WTO)** this is an organization designed to promote freer trade.[12] The organization grew out of a treaty signed in 1947. Legally the General Agreement, usually known as GATT, was a set of principles regulating trade. However, it became, in practice, an organization to formulate ways of maintaining the principles. The name was changed at the beginning of 1995 to the **World Trade Organization**. The original agreement covered four subjects.

1 The most-favoured nation principle

This is the principle whereby any favour that one member showed to another should be extended to all. Exceptions to this included customs unions and free trade areas. Impartiality in trade is a key principle of GATT.

2 The reduction of tariff barriers

This is done on a basis of general agreement. Countries can raise them again so long as they make some reciprocal concessions. The reductions are known as 'rounds', of which there have been seven since the agreement was first signed. The one before last was the Tokyo Round whose conclusion was long delayed because of disagreements on a number of issues including terms for agricultural goods, safeguards against excessive imports, and the question of whether there should be differential reductions of duty on manufactured goods. The latest was the Uruguay Round which failed to resolve many outstanding problems but which did establish: some reductions in tariffs, an agreed dispute-settlement mechanism, an agreement on intellectual property rights creating a framework to assist technology transfer and foreign investment, and a phasing out of the Multifibre Agreement. The Uruguay Round also established a new institution – the World Trade Organization – with broader objectives and a simplified decision-making process.

In the event the new Organization came into existence on a wave of optimism. The results of the Uruguay Round were inherited and the new disputes procedures swung into action to resolve two disputes over duties on oil between member countries: one between Singapore and Malaysia and the other between Venezuela and the United States.

It was assumed that all 128 members of GATT would join and others were applying. Nevertheless, there were some problems and internal disputes which were more difficult to resolve. One was the appointment of a director-general for the new World Trade Organization. Eventually the head of GATT was persuaded to stay on for an extra three months and a successor (Renato Ruggiero) was found during that period. Different interpretations of the various agreements will undoubtedly take longer to sort out, especially the Multifibre Agreement.

At the time of writing there is still a possibility of a dispute with the European Union over the adjustment of the tariffs of countries joining the Union. GATT had already permitted the European Union to retain certain duties on imports and it has been assumed that new members would take on these duties, although this would mean an increase on some products while lowering others. The round ended indecisively, bogged down with the problems of agricultural production. This round also tackled trade in services, another topic which produced stalemate. As with other GATT initiatives, liberalizing trade in services was held to favour the industrialized countries with long-established financial, legal and accounting institutions against developing countries where these institutions were embryonic.

3 Non-tariff barriers

These are to be abolished as soon as possible.

4 Arrangements for membership and resignation

These arrangements and how to deal with infringements were also covered by the agreement.

GATT developments

GATT handed over to the World Trade Organization 128 members (Slovenia was the most recent), although some non-members apply its rules, and is currently undergoing strains, like other international organizations during a period of economic depression. The developing nations have for long criticized an organization which they regard as biased towards the industrialized countries, while some of the richer members are negotiating bilateral trade treaties which appear not to uphold the principle of impartial trading. In the United States, for instance, speakers have advocated the bilateral treaty route rather than that of GATT. At the other extreme is Switzerland which has no bilateral treaties or trade quotas, but feels the effect of other countries' agreements when exports are diverted as a result.[13] There have been powerful warnings of the dangers of protectionism, including the OECD report which pointed out that import restrictions do not save many jobs and that protected industries do not take advantage of the opportunity to achieve restructuring. The work of GATT is partly supplemented and partly opposed by another affiliate of the United Nations, UNCTAD.

The United Nations Conference on Trade and Development (UNCTAD)

This was established in 1964. It operates through four committees: commodities, manufactured goods, invisible trade and finance, and shipping. Major decisions are taken at conferences; one was UNCTAD VI in 1983. Results were limited as a result of continuing confrontation between the industrialized countries and the Third World. There were few agreements, apart from one on commodity price stabilization. This was ratified by 108 countries, but the position of most commodities and the countries dependent upon them has grown bleaker since. A report once referred to a 'persistent, even growing, excess supply in the world markets.'[14] There were general resolutions against protectionism and in favour of aid while special provisions were agreed for the transfer of technology and for extra support to land-locked and island territories.

16.6 Codes of Conduct

In January 1977, all 250 employees of the Belgian subsidiary of the Badger Corporation, an engineering consultancy company and itself a subsidiary of Raytheon, were dismissed.[15] The dismissal was without notice or payment of redundancy on the grounds that the company was bankrupt. Ironically Belgium has, from the company point of view, lenient redundancy laws but even so the employees – who were mostly professional engineers – should have received between them BF125m. After the unions had failed in their efforts to gain compensation, the Belgian Government took up the matter with the company but still compensation was refused. Then the government approached the Organisation for Economic Cooperation and Development.

Another irony of the Badger case is that a few months earlier – and after many years of discussion – the OECD had promulgated a code of conduct for multinational companies. This 'code' was a voluntary agreement, without any procedures for enforcement. It excluded action against individual companies and was produced by a treaty organization whose decisions were not binding on member governments. However, the code had been agreed by representatives of employers and trade unions as well as member governments. It stated that companies were responsible for the social obligations of their affiliates. The Badger company argued in response that its affiliate was a registered Belgian company with limited liability in Belgium and its liquidation had been through the normal process of the courts. Badger's legal position was unassailable. Finally, as a result of pressure after the OECD debate, the company did in the end pay.

The Badger case is a pioneer demonstration (there have been others since) that a code of conduct regulating the international behaviour of companies can have practical results. The employees of Badger Belgium received their money and almost certainly would not have done so if the code had not existed. Besides the emphasis on observing the social regulations and customs of host countries, the code called upon companies to mitigate any ill-effects their international policies might have on a particular unit. Companies were also asked to be more open and informative about their activities. In return, countries undertook not to discriminate against foreign enterprises; competition between countries in offering incentives to promote incoming investment was outlawed. The tenor of the document is to strengthen governments in the face of companies, but the implementation remains voluntary.

The subject of freeing cross-frontier investment is now covered by the rules of the World Trade Organization.

The limited principles of the OECD code have been expanded into a more ambitious document being implemented by the United Nations.[16] This code is also voluntary and is intended to provide a universal guide to correct dealings between governments and international companies. It echoes the complaints made against companies, even if its provisions are milder than many critics would have wished, and it also has provisions for safeguarding companies against unfair or discriminatory action on the part of governments. There are six main stipulations.

Control

The code is designed to assist in the policing of international firms and ensuring that their activities contribute to international development.

Scope

The scope of the code includes business activities of whatever nationality or type of ownership – in which an enterprise in one country has substantial authority over an affiliate in another.

Political interference

Companies must respect the sovereignty, laws and policies of the countries in which they operate, and the right of those countries to regulate their activities. Respect for socio-cultural values and traditions is demanded, as is active opposition to policies of apartheid.

This section proscribes political interference and corrupt practices, while a series of clauses cover ownership and control. The subsidiary is to be structured in a way that will allow it to play a full part in local development and economic plans. Personnel and training policies are to give priority to the benefit of local nationals. Exports from the subsidiary are to be promoted. Financial policies must conform with the laws of the country and not conflict with its economic policies. In particular, the repatriation of capital, the transfer of profits and other cash transactions are to be timed to minimise the damage to the balance of payments. The subsidiary is also expected to avoid practices that may harm the local capital markets, to consult with the government when engaged in share issues or long-term borrowing and to co-operate in efforts to establish local equity participation.

Transfer prices should be based on an arm's length principle – dealings as between independent companies, albeit with a common shareholding. Restrictive practices, the transfer of technology, consumer protection and the physical environment are all considered in detail. Companies are called upon to disclose full information about their total business, and about their operations in each country, each region and each product under the following headings:
(a) balance sheet,
(b) income statement,
(c) allocation of net profits,
(d) sources and uses of funds,
(e) new long-term investments,
(f) research and development expenditures,
(g) the structure of the enterprise (parent and subsidiary),
(h) ownership distribution,
(i) operations,
(j) employment,
(k) accounting practices,
(l) transfer pricing.

The provision of information is subject to some safeguards where confidentiality is important, otherwise representatives of labour are to be kept fully informed of developments and plans likely to affect the future of the employees.

Relationships between companies and governments

There are paragraphs on the role of foreign companies in host countries, the rights of countries to prohibit their entry into certain sectors, their treatment by governments, including their acceptance on an equal footing with domestic companies, the safeguarding of the confidentiality of the information that they do supply, and their rights in the case of nationalization, compensation and jurisdiction.

Bilateral and multilateral agreements

Such agreements between states on issues arising out of the code are provided for, and governments agree not to use companies to further their policies in other countries but, on the contrary, to try to prevent companies interfering in the internal affairs of host nations.

Promotion

The code is to be publicised by member countries and to be administered by the United Nations Commission on Transnationals. The final clauses provide for annual consideration and a complete revision in at least six years.

There are other codes promoted by international bodies to match their more specialized interests. The World Health Organization for instance, has produced a code on the sale of formula milk by multinational companies in developing countries. This code has been accepted by the manufacturers after prolonged debate. The International Labour Office has produced a code on the social policies of multinationals, as has UNCTAD on the transfer of technology and on restrictive practices. There are also conventions like that on intellectual property, and these do have legal support. Increasingly, companies will need to be informed on these codes. Those that are voluntary can still be enforced and the codes will increasingly provide minimum acceptable standards for international behaviour. But even the most conscientious adherent will find one dilemma hard to overcome. There is an assumption that dealings with subsidiaries should be on an arm's length basis, but many of the complaints against which the codes are directed – like improper marketing procedures in the case of formula milk – have occurred in subsidiaries.

Thus to ensure that the codes are carried out, companies will have to police subsidiaries more effectively as the formula milk companies discovered. Adequate supervision of subsidiaries can hardly be carried out on an 'arm's length basis.'

Formula milk is still a controversial issue but the other questions considered in these codes are currently not considered to be important as most member countries of the United Nations are more concerned to promote foreign investment rather than to control it. This is a state of affairs that may well change again before the year 2000.

16.7 Questions and further reading

Questions

1 Outline the main thrust of company law in the European Union and discuss some of its implications.

2 It has been said that: 'More than any other body the IMF can claim to have been the guardian of international probity since the Second World War.' Do you agree? Give reasons for your answer.

3 Comment critically on the statement that: 'Codes of conduct are window-dressing; they have no effect on corporate policies.'

4 Sketch out a progress report on *one* of the regional organizations.

5 It has been asserted that regional organizations strengthen the bargaining powers of governments against countries. Discuss this assertion.

6 Examine the significance for patterns of trade and investment of *either* the Organisation for Economic Cooperation and Development *or* the Organization of Petroleum Exporting Countries.

7 Outline measures taken to regulate, or liberate, trade and comment on how far they have succeeded.

Further reading

All member countries have European Union publications offices as well as libraries in which relevant documents are deposited. Many non-member countries also have representative offices. Publications of the United Nations and the other international organizations listed in this chapter can to be found in many libraries.

The other organizations listed in this chapter also publish reports about themselves.

For codes of conduct see:

Blanpain, R. *The OECD Guidelines for Multinationals*, Kluwer, 1979.

Value and Limitations of Codes of Conduct as regulating instruments for Multinational Corporations, European Centre for Study and Information on Multinational Corporations, 1979.

17 International management: the future

This chapter offers a fresh look at issues raised earlier to provide a conclusion which looks into the future. The order of subjects has been reversed. We begin with anticipated changes in the business environment in a chapter that is dominated by new routes of trade and investment (the New International Economic Order (NIEO)) and new technology, as well as changes in strategy formation and organization within companies. Issues already raised and discussed are recalled and summarized, while likely trends are suggested for discussion and speculation.

Business is conducted in the future, not in the past. This simple fact is easily overlooked as firms allow past experiences, and trends that turn out to be temporary, to determine their policies. Phrases like 'rapid change' have become clichés in management writing, but a glance back to the pre-computer, pre-database world in which many companies still live is a sufficient reminder of its truth. All the changes are not technical; the thrust towards national identity and independence, for instance, brings new demands on corporate planning. The emphasis in these pages has been on decision-making, and the material has been arranged around strategic and tactical issues. Information on practices has also been included and most of the knowledge normally required for the international side of a business is here – apart from detailed description of the paper work – even if only in brief, with references to sources of further information.

The story began with elements of a theory of international business and then plunged into the first moves abroad – the planning and undertaking of an export drive – followed by a discussion on the sale of knowledge. Exporting and licensing do not require a major commitment of funds outside the home country as does investment, the subject of the following chapters which culminated in corporate planning. Time spent on planning can save problems and money particularly in anticipating difficulties to be encountered abroad, contingencies that are likely to arise and the means of overcoming them. A writer in the *Financial Times* once described how a British company faced with a construction contract to be completed in 14 months spent six of those months deciding and planning and eight building. A Japanese firm with the same deadline spent 12 months deciding and planning and two building, completing the project at much lower cost.

After considering the business environment, this final chapter summarizes much of what has already been said and in the context of the future. Accounts of the emerging economic order, the problems between rich and poor nations and the increasing interventions of governments and intergovernmental bodies are followed by discussion of the impact these changes are making on corporate strategies and organizations. This reverses the order followed earlier in the book, a reversal appropriate to a conclusion.

17.1 The New International Economic Order (NIEO)

The old simplicities of world trade no longer apply, and the distinction between the industrialized and the non-industrialized is becoming blurred. The less developed countries are seeking industrial expansion – and some are achieving it rapidly – while the more advanced are still trying to protect the remains of their agricultural sector, as well as some of their traditional manufactures. The emergence of new centres of production and of financial services, together with the decline of established centres, marks a process that has been described as the rise of a new economic order. Wealth has been shifting to the extractors of oil and the general balance between primary and other stages of production has been changing. The rise of countries without natural resources is also a feature of the time, reversing the earlier position when wealth came to countries with resources. Nowadays, wealth comes with value-added or service industries.

New centres of commercial activity

The **New International Economic Order (NIEO)** is a phrase that is currently used in two senses: to describe the actual changes that have been overtaking the patterns of world trade and to summarize the *potential* changes towards which proposals are being directed. Under both meanings, a new international division of labour is seen as reducing the gap between primary producers and countries in which the products are processed. In the short-term new centres of manufacture and of service industries are emerging, among them:

1 extensive petrochemical, steel and oil-processing plants in the oil rich countries along with processing plants in countries with mineral resources to replace the export of raw materials;
2 the further development of Singapore as a financial centre and increasing competition between countries like Korea, Taiwan and Thailand for world markets in manufactured goods;
3 a financial centre can also be expected to emerge in West Africa, perhaps in the Ivory Coast or Nigeria and there may be developments in Central African countries like Zimbabwe;
4 some Latin American countries, notably Brazil, will be competing in steel and heavy machinery;
5 an enhanced role for South Africa in world trade on the further side of political change in that country;
6 an increase in direct investment based on the less developed nations.

However, discrepancies between rich and poor countries will continue, and become increasingly dangerous to the world order, while industrialization will be accompanied by problems, such as over-demand for some resources and pollution by wastes.

In recent years, South East Asia has replaced Latin America as the most rapidly developing area. Singapore has already achieved an income per head higher than that of some members of the European Union, while South Korea is the home base of about 400 multinational companies. One reason for the success of these and other countries in the same region seems to be that they have achieved rapid growth without inflation and by export oriented rather than import substituting economies.

New routes of trade

For most developing countries the changes have seemed impossibly slow and have led to demands for less protection in industrial markets in order to encourage their exports. Various sessions of UNCTAD (see Chapter 16) have been devoted to attempts to reach agreement on this. The overall figures show changes which demonstrate both improvement and deterioration. The success of some countries is represented by the fact that the developing countries are becoming less dependent on primary products. Between 1987 and 1993, the imports of industrial products from developing countries increased from $689.00 to $1168.30 (*IMF Direction of Trade Statistics Yearbook 1994*). Most of the increase was accounted for by manufactured goods while primary products declined. On the other hand, the average gross domestic product has not improved since the first oil crisis. Any temporary downturn in the price of oil may give a respite to hard-pressed economies, but will not be helpful in the longer term if it leads to a slowing down in research on other sources of energy. Indeed, cheap energy from renewable sources could change the balance of advantage towards at least some of the less developed nations more rapidly than any resolutions in the councils of UNCTAD.[1] Photovoltaic cells, enabling sunshine to be converted into electricity, are coming down in price and are particularly suitable for such uses as pumping water in hot, dry countries and in providing air conditioning.

The rise of alternative centres of production has left the industrialized countries with problems of adjustment, and these are likely to continue into the foreseeable future. As has often been pointed out, the swing to service industries has not occurred to the same degree in exports. In Britain, for instance, manufacture forms only 25 per cent of national output but earns 40 per cent of foreign exchange.[2] National economies, especially in Europe, have become more dependent on exports of goods at the same time as patterns of trade are changing. This gives them a long-term interest in increasing wealth among the poorer nations to gain new customers for their more advanced products. At present they are seen as competitors for traditional manufactures. At the same time, once developing countries do become customers, their bargaining power in world trade talks increases.

The ultimate aim of UNCTAD and the movement for a New International Economic Order is to assist in smoothing over the transitional difficulties for both the developing and the industrialized countries. If a forum can be achieved in which agreements are reached without being frustrated by confrontation, a peaceful reorientation of world trade will become possible. Reports of recent meetings make this appear a long way off, but major industries (in construction, for instance) are already dependent for large projects on the development banks and other similar means of funding.

Further reading

Mirza, H. 'The new international economic order' ch. 1.6 in Brooke and Buckley (1988).

UNCTAD, *Report on the United Nations Conference on Trade and Development in its Sixth Session*, document no.TD/325 UNCTAD, 1983.

17.2 Some transitions in the business environment

A number of changes can be detected in the business environment in addition to those already described, the following among them.

The emergence of the communicative society

Yesterday's transition for the industrialized countries was from the manufacturing society – production was the basis of the national economy and the main source of employment – to the service society. The richer developing countries are in the middle of this transition now. Service became the basis of the national economy and the main source of employment. An illuminating theory holds that the current transition (which may leap over the earlier transition) is to a *communicative* society in which information is the basis of the national economy and a main source of employment.[3] Of course there are rough edges and overlaps in this as in all transitions. Most countries have not yet reached the service society stage, and those that have still depend on manufactures to earn a high proportion of their foreign currency.

One feature of the communicative society is that information-handling becomes a typical occupation. Its operators service a large and growing number of pieces of electronic equipment – telephones, fax machines, computers, televisions, satellites and many others. They also operate travel, tourism, publishing, broadcasting and other facilities. As national economies expand, the communications infrastructure grows at an increasing speed. As the same time it becomes more difficult to control the flow of information from the centre. The opportunity, often the necessity, of greater openness is reinforced by the attitudes of employees who believe that their skills should make information more available to the public, not less. There is a kind of self-reinforcing process in the information society as a result of which phrases like 'the right to know' have become fashionable. It is no coincidence that leaks of state and corporate secrets have become a feature of democratic as well as dictatorship countries. The whistle-blower has become a hero, which has not prevented him being a martyr as well on occasions.

A different style of management is also required for the information operative. An earlier hierarchical style is one in which information flows are from the top to the bottom. Sideways communication is discouraged and employees are exhorted to loyalty while being kept in the dark. The communications society requires effective interactions between experts while high-level information people form databanks and other stores of knowledge. Flows of information tend to be sideways, the organization is likely to be more egalitarian and leadership styles vary with the need to solve different problems and to perform varying tasks. Information has become a more important factor of production than land, labour, capital, materials or energy. This makes communications' operators the typical and increasingly dominant employees of today. These operators can be divided into a number of classes: the organizers (managers), the transmitters (secretaries, telephone operators, postmen and others), the storers and retrievers (librarians, indexers, clerical assistants and computer programmers), the creators (scientists, artists, statisticians, designers and authors) and the receivers (students).

More companies in a more competitive environment

Competition policies in industrial countries and the growth of new centres will combine to ensure that more companies compete in international trade. The costs of market entry will be reduced by national and regional legislation. With these developments, more companies in a more competitive environment are a likely scenario. Subject to the laws of competition, however, more self-regulation within industry sectors is also likely, aimed at keeping further legislation at bay without lowering the costs of entry.

Policies of growth and of the limits to growth

Two contradictory norms apply to economic as well as to physical improvement. One is the fatalistic view that accepts the status quo and regards poverty and bad conditions as unalterable; the other sees all progress, defined as technical and material change, as good or at least unavoidable even in the face of damaging side effects. Between these two extremes, a double transition can be glimpsed. One is taking countries away from low expectations to rapidly increasing demands for a higher standard of living. The other, mainly in countries that are already relatively rich, emphasizes the limits to growth and the need to forego some benefits while side effects are investigated. One form of growth that is a certainty, and has long been a worry, is that of population. United Nations' projections suggest an average population increase of 1.6 per cent per year for the rest of the century, leaving over 6000 million people alive in the year 2000 compared with 5000 million in 1991. The increase will be almost entirely due to improved health measures and higher standards of living, and despite smaller families and efforts to promote birth control. The implications for agriculture and the food industry are enormous.

National and international policies of stimulus and control

Governments are likely to take stronger measures to promote the thrust abroad of businesses in their countries, and more governments will be in a position to do this. International competition will be further increased as a result of the growing presence of government owned or supported companies. This presence may well increase the influence of non-commercial policies, and the appraisal of business success in the light of its contribution to the national welfare. The appraisal will be along such lines as the hypothetical contract described in Chapter 15. As a result of its experience and outlook, a particular government may use such a framework as a reason for ignoring, accommodating or restricting foreign companies. More subtle means of steering business towards fulfilling non-commercial national priorities (including regional development and indigenization) can be expected, but companies are always likely to be wary of incentives which do not compensate fully for the costs of observing the policies. Intergovernmental restrictions are also likely to follow as the effects of those already in existence become more evident. In particular, the current impetus to regional organizations is likely to be stimulated. Governments will seize the opportunity to pool their resources and thus overcome frustrations caused by an individual weakness in the face of foreign companies.

Technological change

The growth of some industries and the decline of others will accelerate as new technologies come on stream especially in electronics, bio-engineering, transportation, energy and the development of new materials. The problem for the business planner, to whom timing is all-important, will be to calculate the rate of change. The need for advance warning of new technologies is acute and will influence the structure of the corporate technical and information services. The period of gestation is usually long but once the innovation becomes public, the time taken to reach commercial sales is short. Technological forecasting will be a much sought after business asset, but this will not make it any easier. Who now recalls the conversations in the 1960s that prophesied the demise of newspapers by the early 1980s? Perhaps they would have died without the warning given by those conversations. One problem of technology forecasting is to take sufficient account of the reactions of those likely to be affected. Product improvements and customer resistance combine to thwart prophecies. Technology forecasting has been too much concerned with technology and too little with its acceptance. Nevertheless some inventions, like the microcomputer, have beaten expectations and demonstrated – in a foreshortened form – the traditional product life cycle with added hazards for companies that depend on international sales almost from the beginning of their existence.

The growth in the number of people working at home, both as a result of office automation and to feed that automation (systems analysts and programmers), is an example of a potential change – and one that rests on social acceptability rather than further technical inventions – that could dynamite two growth areas of international business: the sale of transport equipment and the construction of office blocks. Although telecommuting, as it has come to be called, has not yet taken off, the technology is in place. When it does become common the international implications are enormous. Distance is no object to the transfer of data, as opposed even to the transfer of voice, let alone of people. A packet of data can be sent anywhere in the world at the speed of light and at a minimal cost of maintaining the system. The telecommuter will be able to live in any country and work in any other, or in several simultaneously, with links that will cost much less than his journey to work does now.[4] Change will obviously come slowly, and will be resisted both for commercial and for social reasons, but is presumably no harder to make than was the change to commuting in the first place.

The rapid increase in sales of modems and familiarity with e-mail must surely mean that the changes will come sooner rather than later. One of the implications is sure to be an international competition for residences for footloose telecommuters. Tax concessions will feature in this competition which may be a reason for the greater harmonization forecast in a later paragraph.

Business travel could also be reduced for the same reason and as a result of growing acceptance of video-conferencing. Already an initial face-to-face meeting with business associates followed by regular meetings through a video link is considered adequate in some cases where a physical presence would have been considered essential in the past. Only the difficulty of personal adjustment stands in the way of change, although another development – the space-plane which can cover 3000 miles in 12 minutes[5] – may restore some advantages to business travel. But this is much further into the future and, by the time it comes into existence, video-conferencing is likely to be well-entrenched and considerably cheaper than it is now.

A different kind of prospect is raised by deep sea mining, another advancing technology. This development could have the effect of finally capsizing national economies already in difficulties because of over-dependence on a limited number of raw materials. A likely scenario, on present evidence, is that the rich will grow richer and the poor poorer once the raid on the seabed begins and world markets are saturated by cheap minerals. A less likely possibility is the emergence of a new internationalism. Just as the Organization of Oil Exporting Countries (OPEC) has set aside a proportion of its income for the support of the poorest victims of the oil price rises, so an international agreement on sharing the benefits of the new regime of cheaper minerals could help the poorer nations.

One feature of much modern technology is the requirement for large amounts of long-term finance to fund lengthening research periods with little certainty of success at the end. The private financing of new generations of aircraft, for instance, has now become impossible in most countries and is only practicable in the United States as a result of military orders. The erosion of opportunities for the private investor may well have political consequences.

Greater strength of international pressure groups

Consumer groups, conservationists and labour organizations are among those forming more international links to match up to the problems that international companies pose to their interests. Greater responsiveness to these pressures is a virtual certainty. This will come about in two ways. One is that diplomacy, the ability to look beyond the immediate commercial implications of a policy, will form an increasing part of the equipment of their managers and will play a larger part in his training. The other is that departments dedicated to dealing with the non-commercial environment are likely to become more common.

Harmonization of tax systems[6]

A more mundane possibility is that governments will respond to greater internationalism by some effort to harmonize tax systems. The logic of the growth of international investment is that tax administrations will be called upon to co-operate more to prevent both duplication and leakage in international transactions. Efforts are already being made in the European Union[7] for instance, but there are many problems – like allocation of head office expenses (including research and development) to subsidiaries. Tax harmonization may also extend to other issues, like the wider use of Value Added Tax.

17.3 Corporate strategies

Greater attention to mixed objectives is among the changes in corporate strategy likely to be noted in the next 20 years. Steering between restrictive regulations and increasingly sophisticated moves by competitors will require more than public relations exercises. At the same time the expansion of departments concerned with external affairs will strengthen lobbies inside companies that advocate greater sensitivity to the non-commercial environment. In recent years companies have been criticized, often in trenchant terms, for:

1 adopting policies harmful to national economic interests, damaging local money markets,
2 causing ill-health by over-selling goods with harmful side effects,
3 dismissing staff on unfair terms,
4 hostility to trade unions and accepted means of collective bargaining,
5 political interference,
6 undue restraint of competition,
and much else.

At the same time, multinationals are strongly supported as a result of the benefits they bring. Hence they are not likely to find themselves under irresistible attack. Currently (1995), large international companies are indeed finding themselves courted since they have the resources and the know-how to meet the investment needs of the former communist countries. This courting season may turn out to be a brief one. Some governments which expelled foreign investors are encouraging their return, even if under strict conditions, and countries previously closed are providing openings. Yet some voluntary and compulsory restrictions are likely to become universal.

Among probable responses by the corporations to the changing environment are the following:

1 Closer checking of each project and policy for its implications for the reputation of the company.
2 Improvement and upgrading of departments which have to cope with the non-commercial environment but, at the same time, a desire to lower the visibility of a company where the nature of the business makes this possible. One implication is that companies may prefer to promote brand names rather than corporate images internationally. The food industry is a notable example of the choice between high and low visibility. Some of the largest companies, like CPC (the Corn Products Corporation) and Unilever, are little known to the general public while their products are household names. Others, like Kellogg and Nestlé, publicize their products by their company name.
3 A reversal of the trend to larger units, with small firms operating in close collaboration. These will be less vulnerable to changes in the economic or political climate.

The trend to smaller companies is likely to develop for other reasons as well. These include the operation of competition laws, the increasing number of countries of origin of multinational companies, the growth of small firms in high technology and of service companies, the internal problems of control and motivation, and external pressures from political and other interest groups. The climate of opinion against large companies is also likely to grow worse and will influence decision-making in a number of ways. But the trend will emerge slowly. Some probable changes in corporate strategies are listed below.

More intra-company trade

An increasingly important motive for international investment is likely to be the assurance of supplies or markets, and goods will be moving between different units of the same company. The intra-company flows are already more than a quarter of all world trade and the proportion is likely to be over 35 per cent by the year 2000.

More knowledge agreements

The development of more specialized technologies in a number of industry sectors – electrical, engineering, chemical, pharmaceutical – is likely to produce more licensing agreements, as is the increasing ability to fit these agreements into company planning and to make money from them. Management contracts are almost certain to increase in popularity as conventional licensing agreements become less viable. The provision of a package of business knowledge will replace the straight permission to use patents.

Service industries will grow internationally

The biggest factor in the growth of the international service industry has been expansion in the wake of customers who have gone international. This trend is likely to grow partly because it will feed on itself. Once a bank, a consultancy company or an accounting firm is established in a foreign country to serve existing customers, it soon finds itself in a position to extend its activities – in countries where this is permitted. Banks, for instance, find a niche in promoting trade with their home country. Other service industries are developing saleable techniques and related know-how. These are especially relevant in rapidly growing urban areas in businesses like retailing and property development. The emergence of new large cities in the Third World will accelerate the demand for such services, as will the problems of inner city areas in established centres of population.

A wider choice of strategies

Major changes are likely to come about as a result of greater emphasis on the strategic approach to business abroad – the ability to see a range of proposals rather than drift into a casual decision. Questions will increasingly be asked about the relevance of options which have previously been considered, if at all, only after other possibilities have been ruled out. The need to raise income in a form that can be repatriated is a contributing factor to the need for strategic thinking. The decision involves an understanding of how the different elements in the business system – the financial, the marketing and the rest – interact.

The questions to be asked include:

1 Where are the profits made?
2 How can we add to the profits by export?
3 Which is the optimum route to the foreign market?

The answers to this last question will replace the incremental approach to foreign operations that is usual at present. All the keys on the strategy keyboard confront the international executive all the time (see Figure 4.4).

The growth of databases will enable small companies as well as large ones to assemble information on the risks and rewards to be incurred in any particular project or in the use of a particular strategy. Business abroad will require more of the skills that this book sets out to provide.

17.4 Patterns of organization and management

Changes in management systems can be expected in the next ten years, with more informal styles combining with tighter controls. Some of the expected changes already exist and are likely to spread. Others take us further into the future.

More flexible organizations

In addition to the product group world-wide and the geographical structures described earlier, organizations will come into existence that are more fluid and can be altered quickly. These will be designed to set up a subsidiary or partnership abroad, or to manage a new organization once established. After a predetermined time the structure is changed. Effectively, there will be management teams especially equipped to cope with different stages in a product cycle. The need for change and the need for continuity will both be built into the organization.

Integration and local autonomy

A line which runs from centralization through to decentralization, with various shades in between, has already been described. So has the lure to centralization. Greater consciousness of the available options and understanding of the decision-making process are likely to result in firms aiming for more varied policies nearer to either extreme of tight integration or broad autonomy.

It is probable, for instance, that loose federations of organizations will become more common – often between companies with mutual shareholdings and close business arrangements: there may not even be a shareholding. The result will resemble that of existing joint ventures and management contracts, but there will be a common strategy and sometimes a common image, as with franchising arrangements. One difficulty will be the need for global planning for so many small and semi-independent units, but it will be worth overcoming a number of problems to achieve the results. Highly decentralized organizations will aim to gain the advantages of size and global spread without the problems associated with the large multinationals. The advantages of international investment, like a global use of resources, will be acquired without drawbacks such as slow decision-making.

At the other extreme, some companies will operate in a more integrated manner. This will be easier to organize managerially but more difficult politically. Nevertheless, it is a logical development for process industries in which production control and after-sales servicing are required in more than one country at the same time for the same operation. The legal and other difficulties surrounding a highly integrated international thrust can be overcome by countries granting special concessions where the need for such an organization is established. These concessions would be similar in nature to the tax and other incentives used to encourage foreign investment now. Between these two extremes of the global and the federal companies, other new approaches will no doubt come into existence. The federal approach has some resemblance to the Japanese system, where a range of services including a bank are included under the general umbrella of a trading company. There are numerous difficulties in applying this in a western industrial system but in some countries a closer liaison between the banks and their corporate clients is likely to develop. In any case, competition will speed changes to a system which is already partly in place in Italy and Germany.

Staffing

Both the more integrated and the more decentralized arrangements will require an increase in the movement of staff between countries. The integrated will demand this because promotion across frontiers will compensate for the lack of autonomy in a particular subsidiary, while the decentralized systems will be most effective if there is exchange of personnel. A common understanding and sense of purpose can then develop. Mobility of staff should meet other difficulties that are not likely to grow less. One is the personal difficulty that limited numbers of executives seek international careers, and those with the most relevant experience tend to get senior jobs in their own country and so have even less reason to move. International career structures, once the only route to the top in many companies, have gone out of fashion. They are likely to be restored in a way that is relevant to modern conditions. This would be in keeping with the requirement to encourage executives to work abroad. Nevertheless, the demand for foreign service is likely to continue to fluctuate and to be strongest in specialized services.

Industrial relations

Sometime in the next boom the trade union response to the multinational is sure to become stronger and more organized. The form that this reaction will take is likely to be influenced by the growing power of the white collar unions who have more identity of interest across frontiers than manual workers. At the least, companies will be faced with better informed negotiators working to more common policies. The great unknown is how the unions will respond to telecommuting, or its effects on staff selection and promotion policies. American unions are already campaigning against a development that, they argue, will lead to exploitation. The home worker pays his own overheads and means of devising collective protection hardly exist. The unions could find a new international role in protecting the home worker who is operating across frontiers.

Ownership and management

A new relationship between owners and managers already exists in international management contracts and looks set to become more common. Just as the historical change has been from the owner-manager to the professional manager, so the professional owner is a new feature – the individual or firm which is not just a sleeping partner and with whose role the professional manager has to come to terms. There is a resemblance to the relationship between the politician and the civil servant, except that in the present case the parties belong to different countries. Where management companies and proprietors enter joint ventures a voluntary (but legally enforceable) relationship comes into existence. This is usually discussed in terms of problems, rather than as the emergence of a new style of partnership in which the two roles are going to change considerably before stability is achieved.

17.5 Peace and war

The tensions in the world contribute to the problems of international business, they also stimulate its growth. Long-term plans are made hazardous by the threat of disruption. Moving staff abroad can be dangerous for the people concerned, especially if they find themselves interned as enemy aliens. This has been demonstrated many times over the years, but was illustrated even more dramatically during the Gulf crisis of 1990–91. There is also a positive side to the problems caused by international disputes as follows:

1 The significance of the arms trade in stimulating inventiveness and progress in the relevant industries is widely recognized however much the trade may be regretted.
2 The effect of a period of post-war reconstruction on a wide range of industries is less frequently noticed. Companies tend to shy away from areas of conflict, naturally enough, but the period immediately after a cease-fire is a major trading opportunity and a chance to establish a permanent market.
3 Further, a military peace can be replaced by an economic war in which new trading routes and centres of production are established.

None of the above statements apply to global conflict or are intended to overlook the horrors of war, but simply to suggest that the effects of local (and perhaps more widespread) conflagrations are less harmful to business than is often assumed. Instead of being put off by instability in an area, companies could be more prepared to play a part in the reconstruction. International competition for contracts in Kuwait is a recent example of business in a post-war situation. The ultimate possibility of world catastrophe lies beyond the scope of this book but armaments do form a substantial part of international business. In spite of their destructive nature, part of their development can be constructive – thrusting beyond accepted technical boundaries and into new organizational frameworks as well, with joint ventures stretching between the public and private sectors of several nations at once. In many countries (possibly most), officer training is also producing expertise in administration and international logistical management, an expertise which is valuable in commerce as well.

Ironically, the commercial value of the military rests on the continuation of a precarious peace in the world. Remove the precariousness and the military will no longer command the resources to make its contribution; remove the peace and the commerce is likely to disappear. No doubt the present super-powers can maintain the status quo for many generations, but they may not be given the chance. The rise of a new power in a different part of the world (a Hitler of Africa, for instance) could render current political divisions obsolete. No doubt many ambitious leaders will have learnt lessons from the Gulf war.

The international manager will have limited influence on developments which may change the rules of his profession but he has produced a world in which rising expectations are taken for granted and have to be fed. The logic of this is surely that the new technology, as well as the managerial and marketing skills that go with it, will produce disaster if they do not produce greater equality – a redistribution of wealth which can only come about if nationalism, along with concepts like sovereignty, is modified in the interests of a common worldliness.

17.6 Conclusion and summary

The scene has changed in one lifetime from trade as the activity of the few, and investment of the fewer still, to a massive influx into both routes to world commerce. At the same time, ironically, the management of international trade and investment has become more specialized, requiring greater expertise, meeting stiffer competition and incurring more government intervention. Table 17.1 traces out some of the issues which are likely to be on the agenda in the coming years.

Table 17.1 International management – some landmarks of the future

	Certainties	Probabilities	Possibilities	Further details	
				Chapter 17	Other chapters
In the business environment					
The New International Economic Order	New centres of commerce and finance			17.1	15, 16
The communicative society	Dominance of communications workers as the typical workers in the future	Systems of government (democratic) suitable to these workers		17.2	
Competition	More companies in a more competitive environment	More regional legislation restricting economic power	A reversal of these trends towards greater concentration	17.2	15
Growth and the limits to growth	Rising expectations and demands producing instability in many areas, but also growing markets	Reaction against growth for its own sake		17.2	

Table 17.1 continued

	Certainties	Probabilities	Possibilities	Further details Chapter 17	Other chapters
National policies of stimulus and control	Encouragement to national enterprises	More world product mandates	Return of laisser-faire A world forum for international trade and investment	17.2	15
Technological change		Increase in telecommuting	Decline of the - city centre office block Decline of business travel Threats to peace from new directions	17.2	13
Greater strength of international pressure	More attention to managerial skills in coping with the non-commercial environment			17.2	15
Harmonization of tax systems		Closer harmonization		17.2	
Within the company					
Corporate strategies	Closer scrutiny of policies, for social and other implications	Search for lower corporate visibility	Trend to smaller units	17.3	3
	More intra-company trade, stimulating even more companies to become international investors	A higher proportion of trade being transacted in knowledge agreements			
	International growth to service industries	More joint ventures and consortium arrangements			
	Changing patterns of organization and management	More flexible organizations – matrix and project-type	More integration and large organizations; more local autonomy ceasing to be viable		
		More pressure for international labour bargaining	More international career structures establishing a framework for international industrial relations		

A table cannot adequately bring out the flavour of the upheaval which is taking place. Another 20 years may well see the global market-place come much closer to a reality. If that is to happen, however, corporate policies will have to change as well as government regulations. If companies fail to make more acceptable arrangements for their foreign operations, the regulations will grow tighter and the more acceptable arrangements will include a willingness to maintain fair practices in international competition, and satisfactory conditions for both capital and labour in host territories. Some reappraisal of the concepts and rights of ownership and of management will be required to lessen the conflicts of interest which currently bedevil attempts at accommodation between international companies and national aspirations. This conflict looks, on current form, set to intensify before any accommodation is worked out.

17.7 Exercises, questions and further reading

Exercise

(This can be elaborated into a series of computer simulations.)

Consider *one* of the following situations or issues and construct an appropriate scenario:

1 A future with accelerating inflation rates in most countries (nowhere less than 8 per cent and an average of 15 per cent in the main trading nations) and rising·interest rates, increasing protectionism between trading blocs, and increasing foreign manufacture by companies and trade between subsidiaries. The effects on the environment, especially government reactions, and the effects on the corporate management system should be considered. The probable effect if any one of the above factors does not increase or accelerate could also be examined.

2 A future with intense competition between trading blocs (for example, the European Union, the CMEA, North America, Latin America, East Africa, West Africa, the Middle East, South East Asia) should be considered. Assume that each bloc will be offering constraints and incentives for trade and investment both outwards and inwards designed to further the commercial and personal interests of citizens of member countries.

3 Assume that the relative positions of different countries remain the same and that the international framework would not alter greatly, and assess likely changes in company and government policies in a situation of limited change. Estimate the conditions which could make the limited change situation untenable. Then make assumptions of radical change in individual countries and see how these are likely to alter the scenario.

Questions

1 Identify one issue which, in your opinion, can reasonably be considered a 'landmark of the future' in international business. Present a general review of the selected issue.

2 Take a company of your choice and write a scenario describing the anticipated state of the business in ten years' time. Research the company to the best of your ability first; then make some assumptions about how probable changes in the commercial environment would be likely to affect it. Finally, prepare a statement of the best state of affairs conceivable from the company's point of view, the worst state and the one you consider most probable.

3 Define the phrase 'New International Economic Order' and discuss the hopes and problems that underlie the idea.

4 What changes do you foresee in the directions of trade over the next ten to 15 years? Give reasons for your answer.

5 Comment critically on the phrase 'more companies in a more competitive environment' as an account of international commercial activity in the future.

6 Discuss probable changes in government strategies in relation to companies.

7 Examine the changes in international management methods which are likely to accompany expected changes in technology.

Further reading

Hewlett, N. 'New Technology & Banking Employment in the EEC,' *Futures*, February 1985, pp. 34–44.

Macrae, N. *The 2024 Report: A Concise History of the Future*, Sedgwick and Jackson, 1985.

Robock and Simmonds, 1983, ch. 24.

Stonier, T. *The Wealth of Information: A Profile of the Post-Industrial Economy*, Methuen/Thames, 1983.

A review article that is very relevant to the future of the multinational is:

Streeten, Paul, 'Interdependence and integration of the world economy: the role of states and firms,' *Transnational Corporations* 1.3, December 1992.

See also 'A Survey of Multinationals,' *The Economist* 24 June 1995.

Notes

Chapter 1 International management

1 The World Council of Churches' report, originally published in German, was produced in English in 1976. For a right-wing reaction to the multinationals, see Tugendhat, C., *The Multinationals*, Eyre and Spottiswoode, 1971. For a general discussion of ethics and the multinational, see Gladwin, T. and Walter, I., *Multinationals under Fire*, Wiley, 1980; 'questionable payments' is the subject of Chapter 9 in that book. See also *North-South: A Programme for Survival*, Pan Books and MIT Press, 1980 to be discussed in Chapter 13. A graphic discussion of the ethical problems of international business is: S. George, *How the Other Half Dies*, Penguin, 1976. For a more recent appraisal see Turner and Hodges (1992).

2 This thought is expanded in Farmer, R.N. and Richman, B.M., *International Business*, 2nd edn., Cedarwood Press, 1974.

3 On principle, only books published since 1980 are recommended as international management is a rapidly developing subject. In practice, classic works from before 1980 are included mainly in Chapters 1, 2, 3 and 14.

4 This section is compiled from interviews with a number of career and manpower consultants. The author is grateful for their assistance.

5 Female readers may be interested to know that the results of a survey on women as international executives, conducted in the United States, and published in the journal *Business Horizons* in December 1979, found that a large majority of those questioned believed that: (1) foreign service was necessary for promotion for both men and women and (2) the opportunities for foreign service for women were limited; some notable exceptions were quoted, such as one woman who led a team of negotiators in the Middle East on behalf of an American oil company. The position is, of course, changing!

Chapter 2 Trade and investment

1 See Le Play, F., *Voyage dans la Russie Méridionale*, Ernest Bourdin 1847.

2 The full figures (apart from military earnings) are:

	1972	1982
	%	%
Exports of goods	67.0	60.5
Exports of services	4.5	24.5
Income from foreign assets	28.5	15.0
TOTAL:	100	100
Actual earnings	$299,937	$726,948

Source: Calculated from *Statistical Abstract of the United States 1984*, (US Department of Commerce, Bureau of the Census).

Note: income from foreign assets includes payment for services provided as well as dividends.

A later edition of the *Statistical Abstracts* (1987) gives the following figures: Export of goods ($214,424m), export of services ($45,082m), income from foreign assets

($89,991m of which $34,330 is from direct investment and $5,491m from 'other private receipts'). All figures exclude military income.

3 There are many studies of Japanese trading companies. See, for example, Sasaki, N., *Management and Industrial Structure in Japan*, Pergamon Press, 1981, ch. 5.

4 See, for instance, Corden, W.M.,'The theory of international trade,' ch. 7 in Dunning (1974). For a general review of economic theory, see Gray, H.P., 'Macroeconomic theories of foreign direct investment: an assessment,' (University of Reading, Department of Economics, research paper no.54, 1981).

5 This is known as the Heckscher-Ohlin theorem after its authors. For a statement of the theorem see Ohlin, B., *Interregional and International Trade*, Harvard University Press 1933.

6 The Leontief paradox, as it has been called, is detailed in a number of papers. See, for example, Leontief, W.W., 'Factor proportions and the structure of American Trade: further theoretical and empirical analysis', *Review of Economics and Statistics*, Vol.38 (November 1956). This article shows that United States exports and imports as well as investment did not necessarily follow the predictions of Heckscher-Ohlin. For a critique of both the Heckscher-Ohlin and the Leontief contributions see Caves (1983).

7 For a detailed statement of the product cycle theory, see Vernon and Wells (1981) ch.1 and 5. See also Mullor-Sebastian, A., 'The product life cycle theory: empirical evidence.' *Journal of International Business Studies*, Winter 1983.

8 The theory flourished in the late 1960s and early 1970s although based on earlier models. For an exposition see Prachowny, M.J.,'Direct Investment and the Balance of Payments of the United States: A Portfolio Approach' in Machlup, F. and others, *The International Mobility and Movement of Capital*, New York: National Bureau of Economic Research, 1972.

9 See Borts, G.H., 'Long-run capital movements', ch.8 in Dunning, J.H.(ed.), *Economic Analysis and the Multinational Enterprise*, Allen and Unwin, 1974.

10 For a discussion of this theory see Buckley and Casson (1985), ch. 1 and 2. See also Rugman, A.M., 'Internalization as a general theory of direct investment: a re-appraisal of the literature,' *Weltwirtschaftliches Archiv*, 116. 2, (1980).

11 See Dunning (1981) ch. 2 and 4, especially table 4.2, pp. 80–1. The reference to 'psychic distance' can be found on p.81. See also Dunning, J.H.,'Towards an eclectic theory of international production,' *Journal of International Business Studies*, Spring/Summer, 1980, pp.9–31.

12 The classic statement of these concepts is Cyert, R.M. and March, J.G., *A Behavioural Theory of the Firm*, Prentice-Hall 1963. For an illuminating study of authority, see Etzioni, A.I., *A Comparative Analysis of Complex Organizations*, 2nd edn., The Free Press, 1975.

13 This theory has been developed by the present author and explained in a number of writings; see, for instance, Brooke (1984) ch. 17.

14 An illustration of the ability to operate successfully in apparent defiance of economic advantage is provided by the British sweet manufacturer Bassett. This company transports bulky and cheap materials twice round the world (from a source in China to a factory in Britain and then to a market in Australia) at a profit. The case study based on the company is recommended at the end of Chapter 3. This case provides a review of corporate strategy, although it does not mention this particular achievement.

Chapter 3 Strategies and policies

1 Some press reports on the uproar caused in Britain when the company ceased to pay dividends can be found in Brooke and Remmers (1978) pp.218–20. A case study written about the development of strategies in Crown Cork is: 'Crown Cork and Seal' (Harvard case studies no.9–378–024, 1977). The Wilmot Breeden example (see following page) has also been the subject of a case study; see: Bishop, J.R.A. and others 'Wilmot Breeden (Holdings) Ltd.,' (INSEAD case F-3135, ICH no.9–210–117, 1964).

2 The conflict of attitudes has already been sketched (see Figure 2.1) and the importance of attitudes, at least in the early moves abroad, is a theme of the literature on pre-export noted in the next chapter.

3 Some years ago Business International conducted a survey which demonstrated that horizontal diversification was considered (both by short-term returns and by the perceptions of the managers concerned) the most successful expansion, with conglomerate diversification the least. For a more detailed discussion of diversification strategies see Brooke and van Beusekom (1978) ch.5 and 6. In particular pp.108–20 summarize the conditions under which each method is likely to be used and list the problems encountered.

4 This is relevant to the licensing decision (ch.5). The transfer of technology is discussed in ch.10.4 as well as later in this chapter (3.5).

5 For a discussion of non-dominant companies, see B.Mascarenhas, 'International strategies of non-dominant firms,' *Journal of International Business Studies*, Spring 1986, pp.1–25. Table 4 in that paper outlines the characteristics of the four niche strategies mentioned here.

6 For an account of the incrementalization theory see, for example, Johanson, J. and Vahlne, J.-E., 'The Internationalization process of the firm,' *Journal of International Business Studies*, Spring/Summer 1977, pp.23–32. For a study of companies in a small and open market which also illustrates the incremental process, see: Luostarinen, R., 'Towards the dynamics and behavioural theory of the internationalization of the firms in small and open economies,' paper presented at the 9th annual conference of the European International Business Association (Oslo, Dec. 18–20). This paper uses the behavioural theory of Cyert and March mentioned in the last chapter (see note 12, Chapter 2). See also: Sullivan, Daniel 'Measuring the degree of internationalization of a firm,' *Journal of International Business Studies*, 25.2, second quarter 1994.

7 See G. Leroy, *Multinational Product Strategies*, Praeger 1976.

8 See above, note 6. Some of this research is mentioned also in Chapter 4 in the context of preparation for export (see notes 1–3 in that chapter).

9 This technique is discussed in more detail in Brooke and van Beusekom (1979) pp. 149–50.

10 There is a considerable body of literature on this subject. See, for instance: Behrman, J., *Transfer of Manufacturing Technology within Multinational Enterprises*, Ballinger, 1976; Contractor, F.J. and Sagafi-Najan, J., 'International Technology Transfer: major issues and policy responses', *Journal of International Business Studies*, 12.2 (1981), pp.113–35; United Nations *Draft international code of conduct on technology transfer*, United Nations, 1979; UNCTAD has also published a series of reports. For marketing know-how see: Terpstra, V., and Aydin, N., 'Marketing knowhow transfers by MNC's,' *Journal of International Business Studies*,12.3 (1981), pp. 35–49. For management know-how see: Desatnik, R.L., and Bennett, M.L., 'Transferring managerial expertise' in *Human Resource Management in the Multinational*, Gower 1977.

Chapter 4 Trade in goods and services

1 Some of this evidence is contained in the literature on the internationalization of the firm. See, for instance: Wiedersheim-Paul, F., and others, 'Pre-export activity: the first step in internationalization,' *Journal of International Business Studies*, 9.1 (1978).

2 See Welch, L.S. and Wiedersheim-Paul, F., 'Domestic Expansion: Internationalization at Home', *South Carolina Essays in International Business*, no. 2(1980).

3 See Bilkey, W.J. and Tesar, G., 'The export behaviour of smaller-sized Wisconsin manufacturing firms', *Journal of International Business Studies*, 8.1 (1977), pp. 93–8. Other references to articles which report a similar outcome from research can be found in Welch, L.S. and Wiedersheim-Paul, F., 'Initial Exports – A marketing failure', *Journal of Management Studies*, 17.3, October 1980, pp. 333–4, reprinted in the Reprint Series of the Centre of International Business Studies, Uppsala University (1981/1).

4 See Attiyeh, R.S. and Wenner, D.L., 'Critical Mass: Key to export profits,' *Business Horizons*, December 1979, pp. 28–38. This article has been reprinted frequently.

5 See *Concentration on Key Markets*, London: BETRO Trust for the Royal Society of Arts, 1975. The step by step approach is usually recommended by export advisers although there are exceptions.

6 This is a common observation. For a detailed study of personal interaction in the sale of industrial goods see Håkanson (1982) pp. 304–16.

7 The International Chamber of Commerce in Paris is an example of an institution that provides arbitration services.

8 For European Union competition law and its application, see *European Competition Policy*, European File no.6/85 (Luxembourg: Office for Official Publications of the European Community, 1985). See also *The ABC of Community Law* 3rd edn. (Office for Official Publications of the European Community, 1991).

9 Examples of such publications are *Sweden Now*, *British Business* and *Business America*. A review of the problems of selecting agents was published in *International Management*, August 1976, pp. 18–22.

10 A readable passage on the relationship between the principal and the agent can be found in Czinkota and others (1995) pp. 74–7. The whole chapter is valuable (ch.4 'Taking your first steps'). A check-list on selection can be found in Spencer (1994) p. 110.

11 For evidence of this statement, see: Davies, G.J., and Gray, R., 'The export shipping manager in the UK,' *International Journal of Physical Distribution and Materials Management*, vol.10 no.1 (1979) pp. 51–67.

12 For notes on export organization see Sherlock (1994) pp. 36–42.

13 Quoted from a personal conversation. For a case for closer supervision of export documentation see Brooke and Buckley (1988) ch. 2.2. For an example of the losses caused by incompetence see: *Letter of Credit Management and Control*, a report published by the Simplification of International Trade Procedures Board (SITPRO) (1985). The report claims that British exporters lose £60m a year because of errors in paperwork. It is thought that similar figures apply in other countries.

14 These abbreviations are explained and their implications costed in Sherlock (1994) pp. 49–63. Further details can be obtained from the International Chamber of Commerce or your local Chamber of Commerce.

Chapter 5 Trade in knowledge and expertise

1 Know-how and knowledge. These words are used in a normal business sense; this may differ from their usual legal definitions.

2 A discussion on this subject couched in terms of internal and external markets of international companies can be found in Casson (1979), see especially ch. 3.2.

3 Transfers of funds and relevant taxes are considered in Chapter 8.

4 Most, but by no means all, academic research into knowledge agreements concerns this issue – the conditions under which knowledge agreements are to be preferred. See, for instance, the reference in note 1 and Buckley, P.J. and Davies, H., 'Foreign Licensing in Overseas Operations,' *Research in International Business and Finance*, vol. 2, (JAI Press, 1981) pp. 75–89. This article showed that during the 1970s know-how sales were increasing rapidly (by 323 per cent between 1968 and 1977) but more slowly than manufactured exports (413 per cent between 1968 and 1977). See also E.T. Penrose, 'International Patenting and the Less Developed Countries,' *Economic Journal*, September 1973.

5 'Jam on the bread' is the phrase often used. This passage is based on the author's observations.

6 Source: *Statistical Abstract of the United States, 1992* 104th edition (Washington, D.C., Bureau of the Census, 1994).

7 See Telesio, Piero, 'Foreign Licensing in Multinational Enterprises,' ch. 9 in Stobaugh, Robert and Wells, Louis T. (eds) *Technology Crossing Borders*, Harvard Business School 1984. This is a stimulating and well-researched chapter covering many issues of international licensing.

8 The author is indebted to Mr John M. Skilbeck for advice on this list and on other issues discussed in this chapter.

Chapter 6 Foreign investment

1 All three reports are from the *Financial Times* and for the following dates: 8 November 1985, 13 December 1984 and 15 November 1985.

2 Organizations that lag behind changing business circumstances have frequently been commented on – originally, although not in quite the same form, in E.T. Penrose, *The Theory of the Growth of the Firm*, Blackwell 1959.

3 The rise of the multinational based on the less developed country is mentioned again in Chapter 13. With regard to size, it is notable that many studies are based on samples drawn from the world's largest companies which may well be unrepresentative in the 1990s. As an exception, see Newbould, J.D. and others, *Going International – The Experience of Smaller Companies Overseas*, Associated Business Press, 1978.

4 For a pioneer research on the foreign selling subsidiary, see Ruff, H.J., 'Ground rules for the establishment of foreign selling subsidiaries,' *Indian Administrative and Management Review*, July/September 1974.

5 This classification is elaborated in Buckley, P.J., The Motives,' ch. 4.1 in Brooke and Buckley (1988). The reference in the following sentence is to: Buckley, P.J., 'The entry strategy of recent European direct investors in the USA,' *Journal of Comparative Law and Securities Regulation*, vol.3, (1981) pp. 169–91. See also: Hornell, E., and Vahlne, J.-E. 'The changing structure of Swedish multinational companies' (Working paper, University of Uppsala, Department of Business Administration, 1982).

6   For the 'drive for unambiguous control' see Stopford, J.M. and Wells, L.T., *Managing the Multinational Enterprise*, Basic Books 1972, ch. 8. In the years since that book was written, more companies have become willing to compromise but the 'drive' still exists. Recent writings on joint ventures include: Walmsley, J., *A Handbook of Joint Ventures*, Graham and Trotman 1982; Harrigan, K.R., 'Joint ventures and global strategies,' *Columbia Journal of World Business*, 19.2, Summer 1984, pp. 7–16. This article contained a detailed bibliography on the subject; it was one of a series in the same issue of the Columbia Journal.

7   Policy standardization in marketing is mentioned in Chapter 7 (see note 1 to that chapter).

8   See 'Survey: Finance and Investment in the US' *Financial Times*, 6 May 1980.

9   The author is indebted to Professor P.J. Buckley for suggestions for this diagram and for other contributions to this chapter.

10   See Bulcke, D. van den, 'Disinvestment,' ch. 4.7 in Brooke and Buckley (1988); for a theory of disinvestment see Boddewyn, J.J., 'Foreign divestment theory: is it the reverse of FDI theory?' *Weltwirtschafliches Archiv*, 119.2 (1983).

11   'Probably' because world figures can only be calculated approximately. In 1992 the United States income from *unincorporated* affiliates was 76.7 per cent of that from direct investment, although the figure changes to 62.3 per cent when retained earnings are taken into account (percentages calculated from: *Statistical Abstract of the United States 1992*, Washington DC: US Bureau of the Census, 1994). Since United States' companies are large direct investors, the statement in the text assumes that other countries will have a higher proportion of their funds in portfolio investment. The figures in the following sentence in the text are quoted or calculated from an article in the *Guardian*, 1 July 1985, p. 9.

Chapter 7 International marketing management

1   The issue of the international standardization of marketing was the subject of a seminal article which has been frequently reprinted and commented on since. See Buzzell, R.D., 'Can you standardize multinational marketing?' *Harvard Business Review*, November–December 1968, pp. 102–13. For a more recent review of the issues see Terpstra (1983) pp. 230–7. For a research report on the subject, see: Kacker, M., *Marketing Adaptation of US firms in India*, Sterling Publishers 1974.

2   In Europe, for example, there is ESOMAR: the European Society for Market Research. For reviews of international market research, see: Barnard, P.D., 'Conducting and co-ordinating multi-country quantitative studies across Europe,' *Journal of the Market Research Society*, 24.1, January 1982 and Barnard, P.D., 'Marketing research in non-Western economies,' *Journal of the Market Research Society*, 24.2, April 1982.

3   See Baker, M.J., *Marketing*, 3rd edn., Macmillan, 1979, pp. 240–3, where this is called 'skimming the market' or 'prestige pricing;' there is also a reference to 'dual pricing strategy.' For an article on pricing policy, see: Baker, J.C. and Ryans, J.K., 'International pricing policies and practices of industrial product manufacturers,' *International Marketing: Management and Direction*, 1.3 (1982), pp. 127–133.

4   This section does not claim to say all there is to be said about transfer pricing, which it examines solely from the point of view of a marketing manager. An example will be found at the end of the chapter; the political issue is considered again in Chapter 15. For a review of the subject see: Plasschaert, S.R.F., *Transfer Pricing and Multinationals: An Overview of Concepts, Mechanisms and Regulations*, Saxon House,

1979. See also Remmers, H.L. and La Torre, J de, 'Towards acceptable transfer prices in multinational enterprises,' unpublished paper (Fontainebleau, Institut Européen d'Administration des Affaires,1980).

5 An example from long ago is contained in *Chlordiazepoxide and Diazepan*, a report of the Monopolies Commission, Her Majesty's Stationery Office 1973. For a fuller discussion of the subject see Helleiner, G.K., *Intrafirm Trade and the Developing Countries*, Macmillan 1981.

6 See 'Business Brief,' *The Economist*, 16 March 1985, pp. 72–3.

7 See Mattson, L.G., 'Cooperation between firms in International systems selling' (Uppsala University, Department of Business Administration, Reprint series 1980).

8 The first two items were reported in the *Middle East Economic Digest*, 3 August 1985, p. 25. The Saudi Arabian oil deal was widely reported in the British press at the end of September 1985.

9 Quoted from Yoffie, D.B., 'Barter: looking beyond the short-term payoffs and long-term threat', *International Management*, August 1984, pp. 36–7. This article makes the point that all the details of a countertrade contract are negotiable; the first proposal may be unnecessarily disadvantageous to the seller. For an article on the OECD study see: Miramon, de J., 'Countertrade: an illusory solution,' *OECD Observer*, May 1985, pp. 24–9.

Chapter 8 International financial management

1 Export credit guarantees are provided by different institutions in different countries, mostly state-owned. The now privatized British Export Credit Guarantee Department is owned by the Dutch insurance company, DSM. A comprehensive and regularly updated review of the subject, which also lists the facilities available in most trading nations, can be found in Clarke, Brian W. (ed), *International Trade Finance*, Chiltern (updated twice a year), ch. 6. Forfaiting is a system of non-resource finance for exporters and an alternative to credit guarantees.

2 By Dufey, G. For an example of research on reducing exchange risks see: Dufey, G. and Giddy, I.H., 'Forecasting exchange rates in a floating world,' *Euromoney*, November 1975, p. 28. See also: Yang, J.G.S., 'Managing multinational exchange risks,' *Management Accounting* February 1986, pp. 45–52.

3 Readers unfamiliar with investment appraisal techniques should refer to any standard description of net present value. See, for example, Merrrett, A.J. and Sykes, A., *The Finance and Analysis of Capital Projects*, 2nd edn., Longman 1973. Dufey (see note 2) has queried whether the net present value is the most appropriate calculation for international project appraisal, preferring the terminal rate of return on the grounds that less dividends (or none at all) will be remitted in the early years.

4 For a study of comparative accounting, see Choi and Mueller (1978). New Belgian legislation on the subject was summarized in *Kredietbank Weekly Bulletin*, 1 June 1984.

5 This is the kind of statement which soon dates and readers should check for any countries in which they are interested; laws about disclosure are apt to change when a country revises company law. International and regional moves towards standardized accounting (like the 7th directive of the European Community) are considered in Chapter 16.

6 The items listed are not exhaustive and might be considered biased in that they emphasize the disciplinary aspects of control. Control in international companies is considered in detail in another book by the same author, see Brooke (1984), ch. 14.

7 The author acknowledges the help given by Professor Dr. Sylvain Plasschaerts, of Antwerp University, who provided much material for this section.

8 See Finney, Malcolm J., 'Tax havens in international tax planning,' ch. 6.3 in Brooke, M.Z. (ed), *International Financial Management Handbook*, Macmillan, 1990. This chapter lists 32 tax haven countries but also provides a broad definition which includes many others.

9 The position on the unitary taxation argument is changing all the time. A summary of the origins of the present controversy can be found in *ICC Business World*, January–March 1984, pp. 14–16; see also Krijgsman, P., 'Unitary taxation', *Multinational Info*, no. 4, February 1984, pp. 5–8. This subject was much in the news and highly controversial in the 1980s when earlier editions of this book were published. It has since been largely defused. In 1993 California scrapped its world-wide unitary tax.

10 See Duffy, K.J., 'Deciding on insurance programmes: the role of captive insurance companies', ch. 4.5 in Brooke (1990); the same publication has two chapters on insuring credit risks (3.4 and 3.5). A list of export credit insurers for major countries includes Cie Belge d'Assurance-crédit, Compagnie française d'Assurance, Hermes Kreditversicherungs (German Federal Republic), Export Insurance Section of the Ministry of International Trade and Industry (Japan), Nederlandsche Kredietverzekering, Exportkreditnamnden (Sweden), Export Credits Guarantee Department (United Kingdom), Export-Import Bank of the United States.

11 For a detailed survey see: *Les systèmes de financement des crédits à l'exportation dans les pays membres de l'OCDE*, 1982, OECD.

Chapter 9 Personnel and industrial relations

1 The evidence for this statement comes from conversations with executive employment agencies in Britain. The policies outlined in the rest of this section may be still more firmly held in other European countries and South East Asia, but the point made later that policies are dictated by opportunity as well as intention should be noted.

2 Attitudes of American executives to service overseas have been extensively studied in the University of Michigan. See, for example, Miller, E.L., 'Managerial qualifications of personnel occupying overseas management positions as perceived by American expatriate managers,' *Journal of International Business Studies* Spring–Summer 1977, pp. 57–69.

3 Some of the information in this section is based on unpublished research carried out by Michael Ng at the University of Manchester Institute of Science and Technology.

4 See Ertkin, E. and Walbank, M., 'The economic benefits of migrant work programmes,' unpublished paper, Department of Management Sciences, University of Manchester Institute of Science and Technology, 1979. See also 'Migrants in the European Community', *European File*, August–September 1979.

5 For two articles on the personal side of executive transfer see: 'Executive stress goes global', *International Management*, May 1984, pp. 42–8; and 'Coping with the ordeal of executive relocation', *International Management*, December 1984, pp. 66–79.

6 For an example of such a forecast from 20 years ago, see D.H. Blake, 'The internationalization of industrial relations', *Journal of International Business Studies*,3.2, (Fall 1972), pp. 17–32.

Chapter 10 Logistics, purchasing, distribution, production and research

1 Håkannson (1982) p. 2. The following pages consider this 'stability' in more detail. The interaction between purchaser and supplier is a main theme of the book.

2 For a summary of pressures for and against international integration, see 'production' (10.4). Two other valuable checklists are:
(1) A list of the specialized skills required by a purchasing department, see: Robinson (1984) p. 66.
(2) A list of the main items for which the importer has to watch, see: Brooke and Buckley (1988), ch. 2.9.

3 See 'Physical distribution,' ch. 2.7 in Brooke and Buckley (1988).

4 See Terpstra (1983) p. 395. On the following page, the author gives another example – that of goods being imported into Zaire which have to be transhipped five times (between ship and train twice and finally onto a truck) before reaching some inland destinations.

5 On the growth of terrorist attacks against companies, see 'Terrorism: why business is now a prime target,' *International Management* (August 1985), pp. 20–6.

6 An example is Hewlett Packard who have a research department in Europe; see: 'Keeping close to reality,' *Financial Times*, 6 November 1985.

Chapter 11 Decision-making and organization

1 Amid all the research effort expended on the multinational firm in recent years a high proportion has gone into various aspects of organization, but little into the extent to which the organizations in current use subserve their purposes or which of these purposes actually influence the structure – apart from the studies which concentrated on the relationship between structure and a rather limited view of strategy in the 1960s and 1970s, stemming from the work of Chandler. See Chandler, A.D., *Strategy and Structure*, MIT Press, 1962.

2 In other writings by the present author this is called 'A type,' with 'B type' the geographical, 'C type' the product division world-wide, 'D type' the matrix and 'E type' the project (see Brooke and Remmers (1978) ch. 2 and Brooke (1984) ch. 15).

3 The use of international divisions is more common than that of regional divisions and is treated as a separate category in some classifications (see Table 11.1); the two are placed together here because the same pressures apply to each. Two suggestions of increases in the geographical dimension were recorded in a 'Business Brief' in *The Economist*, 9 March 1985, pp. 72–3, where it was suggested that international advertising agencies are moving from product to regional organizations. The same publication claimed (in the issue for 24 June 1995) that regional organizations were increasing. For such organizations in a different context, see *Unilever's Management and Organization* (Rotterdam: Unilever, 1983). See also 'Apple moves counter slump,' *Apple User*, August 1985, where the Apple Computer company is described as having abolished its product divisions and strengthened its international division.

4 See Pitts, R.A. and Daniels, J.D. 'Aftermath of the Matrix Mania,' *Columbia Journal of World Business*, 19.2, Summer 1984, pp.48–54. For another view which discusses the problems, but expects them to be overcome, see Davis, S.M. and Lawrence, P.R., 'Problems of Matrix Organizations,' *Harvard Business Review* May–June 1978, pp. 131–42.

5 See: Robock and Simmonds (1983) ch. 16 and Davis (1979) pp. 193–248.

6 Among the limited number of writings specifically on regional organizations, see Daniels, J.D., 'Approaches to European regional management by large US multinational firms', paper read at the Academy of International Business Annual Conference, New York, 1985. The Swedish research mentioned in the following paragraph is reported in Ghauri, Pervez N., 'The management of headquarter-subsidiary relationships in Swedish multinationals,' paper presented to the UK Chapter of the Academy of International Business, Strathclyde, 1990.

7 For a study of data flows within multinational corporations and the constraints upon them, see: Samiee, S., 'Transnational data flow constraints: a new challenge for multinational corporations', *Journal of International Business Studies*, Spring–Summer 1984, pp. 141–50.

8 For a detailed study of centralization see the present author's book on the subject – Brooke (1984) – which studies the concept in its various applications together with several chapters about the multinational firm. Another work devoted to this subject is Otterbeck (1981). A recent article is: Negandhi, A.R., 'Management strategies and policies of American, German and Japanese multinational corporations,' *Management Japan*, 18.1, Spring 1985, pp. 12–20; an earlier case study of a French company is: 'Decentralization and Control at Thomson-Brandt' *International Management,* April 1977, pp. 10–13. See also Ghauri, Pervez N, 'The management of headquarters–subsidiary relationships in Swedish multinationals,' paper presented to the UK Academy of International Business, Strathclyde, April 1990.

9 'Inverted centralization' – the concept is explained in Brooke 1984 pp. 218–20.

Chapter 12 International corporate planning

1 A stimulating article which stresses the need for a close relationship between planning and other departments and especially for ensuring that implementation planning is the key to the whole process is: Hill, R., 'Corporate planning gets a reappraisal', *International Management*, December 1983, pp. 24–30.

2 For a discussion of the value of information see Lehmann, D.R., *Market Research and Analysis*, Irwin 1979. An earlier study on the economics of information can be found in Coyle, R.G., *Decision Analysis*, Nelson 1972.

3 For a pioneer study of information sources for international companies, see: Keegan, W.J., 'Multinational scanning: a study of the information sources utilized by headquarters executives in multinational companies,' *Administrative Science Quarterly*, September 1974.

4 See Brooke and Buckley (1988) ch. 5.1 for the system described below. A discussion of political risk can be found in: Kobrin, S.J., *Managing Political Risk Assessment*, University of California Press 1982. See also Eiteman and Stonehill (1989) ch. 4 and 6, which cover exchange as well as political risk and assess some of the techniques for appraising and minimizing them. Another publication is: Hofer, C.W. and Haller, T.P., 'GLOBESCAN; A way to better international risk assessment', *Journal of Business Strategy*, Fall 1980.

5 Since many, especially of the longer-term techniques, are both controversial and requiring detailed appraisal they are not discussed here. A resume of planning techniques can be found in McNamee, P.B., *Tools and Techniques for Strategic Management*, Pergamon 1985. The relevance of techniques for international planning is discussed in Brooke and van Beusekom (1979) ch. 8.

Chapter 13 The economic environment

1 The figures used in this section have been collected from a variety of sources, primarily the publications of the International Monetary Fund, the United Nations, the General Agreement on Tariffs and Trade and the Organisation for Economic Cooperation and Development. For a model presentation of the different facets of international trade, the reader should consult *Barclay's Review*, various issues had centre spreads covering aspects of world trade (e.g. May 1984 and August 1985).

2 The likelihood of a brief 'hiccup' when oil prices will be low is mentioned later in the chapter. Some of the figures used here are from Telesio, P., 'Energy: is the crisis past?' ch. 6.1 in Brooke and Buckley (1988). For a thorough review of oil and other energy sources see: Stobaugh, R. and Yergin, D., (eds.) *Energy Future*, 3rd edn., Random House, 1983.

3 See, for instance, 'Tin men in search of a wizard,' *The Economist*, 9 November 1985, pp.85–6, and 'Death rattle of an old tin market,' *The Economist*, 2 November 1985, pp.85–6. In March 1986 newspaper reports were still expressing hopes for restoring order to the tin market although a rescue package had by then collapsed.

4 See: Paliwoda, S., 'The Richer Socialist Countries,' ch. 5.8 in Brooke and Buckley (1988).

5 See: *North–South: A programme for survival*, Pan Books and MIT Press, 1980, p. 267. This publication is normally called the Brandt Report after the chairman of the commission which produced it. After the long passage of time, it is still relevant.

6 See, for example, 'Poorest nations getting poorer says UNCTAD' *Financial Times* (reviewing a United Nations report entitled *The Least Developed Countries 1995 report*). See also 'Capital flow to Third World slows to 16pc of 1993 rise' *The Guardian* (23 January 1995).

7 See: *Transnational Corporations and Contractual Relations in the World Uranium Industry: A Technical Paper*, United Nations Centre on Transnational Corporations, 1983, UN sales no. E.83 II.A.l7.

8 See: *International Financial Statistics Yearbook 1984*, International Monetary Fund.

9 The growth of Singapore as an international financial centre was recorded in *International Management*, October 1984, p.7. In the same issue it was stated that there were already 10,000 people working in the Asian dollar market. In 1993 Singapore held S$76,196 million in foreign assets and US$48,361 million of international reserves.

10 See 'The international capital markets in 1984,' *Weekly Bulletin*, vol.40 no.7 (Brussels: Kredietbank, 15 February 1985).

11 The European Currency Unit is made up of a basket of currencies subscribed by member countries of the European Union. The value of the unit is fixed by the value of the underlying currencies multiplied by weightings that approximate to the importance of each. Further details are given in Chapter 16, note 5.

12 In Chapter 8 it was pointed out that companies can take two kinds of measure against exchange risks: (1) by obtaining loans in the currency in which the cash is needed and (2) by the use of the instruments mentioned here. For an account of financial futures see Brooke and others (1990) ch. 5.6.

13 *World Development Report 1994*, Oxford University Press 1985.

14 The story is well documented in: Khoury, S.J., *Sovereign Debt: A Critical Look at the Problems and the Nature of the Problem*, South Carolina Essays in International Business no. 5. Columbia, South Carolina: College of Business Administration, 1985.

15 Thus the French President was quoted as demanding that world trade talks must be accompanied by discussions designed to stabilize currencies on the grounds that 'trade liberalisation is undermined when currency movements can make producers uncompetitive within weeks in foreign markets' (*The Guardian*, 4 May 1985).

Chapter 14 Cultural differences

1 Quoted from a notice issued by the European Institute for Advanced Studies in Management about a meeting on organization and industrial cultures, 26 May 1976.

2 One example of the possibility of doing this was briefly indicated in Brooke, M.Z. and Remmers, H.L., *The Strategy of Multinational Enteprise*, first edn., Longman 1970, ch. 5, where the theory of the *intercalary* position is used to interpret some puzzling evidence about role problems among senior executives in the foreign subsidiary of an international company. The *intercalary* position is that of the local national official who represents a foreign power to his subordinates and a foreign response to that power to his superiors. See Gluckman, M., *Custom and Conflict in Africa*, Blackwell, 1959. See also: Rogers, Rolph E., 'The application of anthropological systems analysis to international management and organizations,' paper read to the Academy of International Business annual conference in London, 1986.

3 See Barrett, G.V. and Bass, B.M., 'Comparative Surveys of Managerial Attitudes and Behaviour' in Boddewyn, J.J. (ed.), *Comparative Management*, (New York University 1970), ch.8. This book has a detailed discussion of the subject. The following is one example from each school of thought. Universality: Likert, R., *The Human Organization*, McGraw-Hill, 1967; cultural cluster: Haire, M. and others, *Managerial Thinking: An International Study*, Wiley, 1966; economic cluster: Kerr, C. and others, *Industrialism and Industrial Man*, 2nd edn., Oxford University Press, 1964. Barrett and Bass prefer the cultural cluster approach.

4 A bank advertisement once hinged on knowledge about the significance of colour in clothing in Nigeria. Another example, as several firms have discovered to their cost, is that of brand names which sell well in one country but turn out to have hidden meanings in another.

5 Sangeev, Argawal, 'Influence of formalization of role stress, organizational commitment, and work alienation of salespersons: a cross-national comparative study,' *Journal of International Business Studies*, 24.4, fourth quarter, 1994.

6 There have been numerous studies of industrial morale. A pioneer example was Crozier, M., *La Phénomène bureaucratique,* Seuil, 1964; English edn., Tavistock.

7 At the least, their 'pragmatism' leads them in different directions. The facts referred to are quoted in Boddewyn, see above note 3, from: Thiagarajan, K.M. and Bass, B.M., 'Differential preferences for long versus short-term payoffs in India and the United States', *Proceedings, xvith International Congress of Applied Psychology*, Swets and Zeitlinger, 1969, pp.440–6. See also: Negandhi, A.R., and Prasad, S.B., *Comparative Management,* Appleton Century Crofts, 1971.

8 Also quoted in Boddewyn (1970). See above note 3, p. 201.

9 In Farmer, R.N. and Richman, B.M., *International Business*, Cedarwood Press, 1974.

10 See above, note 3.

11 See Granick, D., *The European Executive*, Doubleday, 1962.

12 See Hofstede, G., 'The cultural relativity of organizational practices and theories,' *Journal of International Business Studies*, Fall 1983.

13 The extended family is a phrase used to describe a society in which a high degree of interdependence between the members is normal, and where members in several degrees of relationship live together. The head of an extended family may take responsibility for several generations as well as numerous cousins within a generation. This contrasts with the nuclear family, consisting of a husband and wife and their children, which is considered normal in most Western societies. The strength of the extended family can vary considerably from the situation where the head of the family has quasi-judicial powers to that where only a shadow of the institution still exists.

14 Several studies have made this point. For an example see Weinshall, T.D., (ed.), *Culture and Management*, Penguin, 1977.

15 See Hofstede (1984) This book contains a detailed bibliography on the subject of cultural differences. Hofstede himself refers back to the work of Mulder (see Mulder, M., *The Daily Power Game*, Martinus Nijhof, 1977). An academic study using this technique is to be found in Hajimirzatayeb, M., *Cultural Determinants of Organizational Behaviour and Responses to Environmental Demands*, (Unpublished thesis, Oxford University, 1979). For a report on a commercial use of the technique see Seddon, J.W., 'The development and indigenisation of Third World business: African values in the workplace', ch. 7 in Hammond, V., (ed.) *Current Research in Management*, Frances Pinter 1985.

16 See Hutton, J., *The World of the International Manager*, Philip Allan (Oxford and New Jersey) 1988, ch. 6.

Chapter 15 The company and the nation state

1 Quoted in the *Guardian*, 5 February 1986. The Kreisky interview was reported in the *New Statesman*.

2 The full story is told in Wood, O.G. and others, *The BASF Controversy*, Essays in Economics no. 25 (Columbia, SC: University of South Carolina, 1971).

3 This classification is used in Brooke and Buckley (1988), ch. 5.1.

4 The formula is quoted from Poynter (1985) p. 86 with permission of the author. The whole book is an illuminating study of company-government relations. For an attempt to measure company resources in bargaining with Latin American governments see: Fagre, N. and Wells, L.T., Bargaining power of multinationals with host governments', *Journal of International Business Studies*, Fall 1982, pp. 9–23.

5 A review of restrictions, incentives and taxation of foreign companies can be found in: *National Legislation and Regulations Relating to Transnational Corporations*, United Nations, 1983. This lists general principles and details of 20 countries.

6 An example is support to political parties in host countries, which may be normal for local businesses. That intervention can occur in spite of company policy is evidenced by an incident recorded at the end of Chapter 9 (see: 'Gigantic Holdings AB – a staffing problem').

7 These meetings were widely reported back in 1984. See *The Economist*, 28 January p. 69, 26 May pp. 75–6, 24 November p. 84, *Dun's Business Month*, February pp. 72–4, *Multinational Business* (no.1, pp. 31–2).

8   This lobby is mentioned in Chapter 11 where its strength is seen partly to depend on the corporate structure. An example of how the balance of power can change is given among the examples at the end of this chapter (see 'Speizeprov AG: influencing subsidiary policy'); internal disputes within government over transfer pricing are mentioned below. Notes on the view of organization and strategy taken in this paragraph are to be found in Chapters 3 and 11.

9   This case, in which 17 electrical components' manufacturers were prosecuted for conspiracy, made history because a number of senior executives received prison sentences for their part; their companies were fined as well. See Blair, J.M., *Economic Concentration*, Harcourt, Brace, Jovanovich, 1972, pp. 576–87.

10   For a brief summary see: Cheesewright, P., 'What happened when an industrial giant fell foul of community law', *Europe 1984*, October 1984, p. 13.

11   Transfer of technology is discussed in Chapter 3 and research and development in Chapter 10. For the Canadian experience see Britton, J.N.H. and Gilmour, J.M., *The Weakest Link*, Science Council of Canada, 1978. Pressure on foreign companies was relaxed after the 1984 election.

12   See *Multinationals and Industrial Strategy*, Science Council of Canada 1980; see also Rugman, A.M., 'World Product Mandates: Theory and Practice', paper read at a colloquium at Queen's University, Kingston, Ontario, 27 May 1981.

13   Studies of the opportunities and problems involved in attracting foreign investment to areas of unemployment have been carried out in a number of countries. See, for example, Hood, N. and Young, S., *European Development Strategies of US owned manufacturing companies located in Scotland*, Her Majesty's Stationery Office, 1980.

14   For further information on transfer pricing see Chapter 7 notes 4 and 5.

15   For a review of the subject see Pearce, R.D., 'Overseas production and exporting performance: an empirical note', University of Reading Department of Economics, Discussion Paper no. 64, 1982.

16   Salehizadeh, M., *Regulations of Foreign Direct Investment by Host Countries*, University of South Carolina, 1983.

Chapter 16 International organizations

1   See: *Measures Strengthening the Negotiating Capacity of Governments in their Relations with Transnational Corporations*, United Nations, 1983. See also: Grosse, R., 'The Andean Foreign Investment Code's impact on Multinational Corporations,' *Journal of International Business Studies*, winter 1983, pp. 121–33.

2   This is called the Vredeling proposal, named after the Commissioner who sponsored it in 1980. The Council regulation on the European Economic Interest Grouping is no.2137/85 of 25 July 1985. See *Official Journal of the European Communities* no.L 199/1 (1985). For a commentary see 'A new instrument for cooperation between community companies in different member states: The European Economic Interest Grouping,' *Europe document*, no.1367, 2 August 1985.

3   For a fuller account see 'Harmonization of banking legislation in the European Community' *Weekly Bulletin*, Kredietbank of Brussel 6 December 1985.

4   For an up-to-date summary see: *European Competition Policy*, Commission for the European Communities, 1985. This is one of a series of leaflets obtainable free from Community offices. Examples of the workings of the policy can be found in *Europe 1984*, October 1984, p. 13 (the IBM case) and *Europe 1985*, January–February 1985, p. 24 (the case of Five European chemicals firms).

5   ECU = European Currency Unit. (1 ECU was equal to US$1.32797 in mid-1995. In 1991 it was made up of the following amounts of currency added together:
DM 0.6242 (Germany)
FF1.332 (France)
£0.08784 (Britain)
Lire 151.8 (Italy)
FL0.2198 (Netherlands)
BF3.431(Belgium)
LUF0.13(Luxembourg)
DKr0.1976 (Denmark)
Irish£0.008552 (Ireland)
ESC1.393 (Portugal)
DR1.44 (Greece)
Pes6.885 (Spain)
These figures were frozen at Maastricht although they do not take account of the latest members. An announcement is expected soon (1995).

6   See Blackwell, M., 'Lomé III: the search for greater effectiveness', *Finance and Development*,September 1985, pp. 31–34.

7   An unusually restrictive role is described later in this chapter (16.6). Readers having access to libraries that possess the publications of OECD will find them among the most up-to-date and reliable sources of information on the world economy. The report mentioned in the text is *Costs and Benefits of Protection*, OECD, 1985.

8   OPEC produces extensive documentation on energy supply and demand both in annual reports and monthly bulletins.

9   See *World Development Report 1994*, the World Bank's Annual Report.

10 For a detailed study of the Asian Development Bank see: Chan, R.M.L., *Asian Development Bank: Its Role as a Regional Development Bank* (Unpublished M.Sc. thesis, University of Manchester Institute of Science and Technology, 1984). See also 'Guidelines for Procurement under Asian Development Banks Loans' (first published by the Bank in 1981 and reprinted since).

11 The development of new instruments, already mentioned in Chapter 13, is highlighted in the World Bank's reports.

12 For information on GATT (WTO), see the organization's annual reports.

13 See 'Swiss try to protect a vested trade interest' *Financial Times*, 1 August 1985. For the following sentence in the text, see the OECD report mentioned in note 8.

14 For an account of the work of UNCTAD see its annual reports to the General Assembly of the United Nations or its periodical: *Trade and Development*.

15 For a full account see: Blanpain, R., *The Badger Case and the OECD Guidelines for Multinational Enterprise*, The Netherlands: Kluwer, 1977. The OECD code has been published by each of the member governments. See, for example, *International Investment: Guidelines for Multinational Enterprises*, Her Majesty's Stationery Office, 1976. A general review of codes of conduct can be found in Missouris, S.G., 'Codes of conduct facing multinational corporations', ch. 28 of Walter and Murray (1982).

16 The United Nations code has been the subject of a series of documents. See especially *Transnational Corporations: Issues involved in the formulation of a code of conduct*, United Nations, 1976; *Commission on Transnational Corporations: report on the special session 7–18 March and 9–21 May 1983*, United Nations, 1983; this document prints the code of conduct as agreed at the time, further documents have since

become available); Hanson, P., 'A new approach to the code negotiations', *CTC Reporter* no.20, Autumn 1985, pp. 15–19. Little has been heard of it lately (1995).

Chapter 17 International management: the future

1   See, for instance 'Country Profile: Pakistan', *OPEC Bulletin*, February 1985, pp. 27–37, where the use of solar-generated electricity in that country is described, as well as biogas from animal waste.

2   See: *House of Lords: Report from the Select Committee on Overseas Trade*, Her Majesty's Stationery Office, 1985.

3   The theory of the *communicative society* was put forward by Professor Tom Stonier (see Stonier 1983, see also Brooke 1990, ch. 1.2).

4   For a review of the possibilities of telecommuting see: Macrae, N., *The 2024 Report: A Concise History of the Future 1974–2024*, Sedgwick and Jackson, 1985.

5   Quoted from The *New York Times* by The *Guardian*, 3 December 1985.

6   For this passage I am indebted to Professor Sylvain Plasschaert who also contributed to Chapter 8.

7   A review of the future prospects for the European Union can be found in *The New Europe*, Euromonitor 1991.

Bibliography

This is a selected list of recent works. More specialized publications can be found in the chapter references and reading lists.

*For those wishing to build up a small collection of books on the subject, those marked with an asterisk are specially recommended.

Briggs, P. *International Trade and Payments*, Oxford: Blackwell 1994.

Brooke, M.Z., *Centralization and Autonomy*, Holt, Rinehart and Winston 1984.

Brooke, M.Z. and van Beusekom, M., *International Corporate Planning*, Pitman 1979.

Brooke, M.Z. (ed), *International Financial Management Handbook*, Macmillan 1990.

Brooke, M.Z. and Remmers, H.L., *The Strategy of Multinational Enterprise*, 2nd edn. Pitman 1978.

Brooke, M.Z. and Skilbeck, J.M., *Licensing*, Aldershot (UK): Gower 1994.

Buckley, P.J. and Brooke, M.Z., *International Business Studies: An Overview*, Blackwell (Oxford) 1991.

Buckley, P.J. and Casson, M., *The Future of the Multinational Enterprise*, Macmillan 1976.

*Buckley, P.J. and Casson, M., *The Economic Theory of the Multinational Enterprise*, Macmillan 1985.

Buckley, P.J. and Casson, M., *Future of the Multinational Enterprise*, 2nd edition Macmillan (Basingstoke) 1991.

Buckley, P.J. and Clegg, J., *Multination Enterprises in Less Developed Countries*, Macmillan (Basingstoke) 1991.

Casson, M., *Alternatives to the Multinational Company*, Macmillan 1979.

Casson, M., *The Growth of International Business*, Allen and Unwin, 1983.

Casson, M., *Multinational Corporations*, Elgar (Aldershot) 1990.

*Caves, R.E., *Multinational Enterprise and Economic Analysis*, Cambridge University Press 1983.

Channon, D.F. and Jalland, M., *Multinational Strategic Planning*, MacMillan 1978.

Choi, F.D.S. and Mueller, G.G., *Handbook of International Accounting*, new edn., Prentice-Hall 1992.

Clarke, I.M., *The Spatial Organization of Multinational Corporations*, Croom Helm 1985.

Czinkota, M.R., and others *The Global Marketing Imperative*, Lincolnwood (Ill) NTC Business Books 1995.

*Daniels, John D. and Radebaugh, Lee H., *International Business: Environments and Operations*, 7th edn., Addison-Wesley, 1995.

Davis, S.M., *Managing and Organizing Multinational Corporations*, Pergamon 1979.

*Dunning, J.H., (ed.), *International Production and the Multinational Enterprise*, Allen and Unwin 1981.

*Eiteman, D.K. and Stonehill, A.I., *Multinational Business Finance*, 5th edn., Addison-Wesley 1989.

Enderwick, P. (ed.), *Multinational Service Industries*, Croom Helm 1986.

Farmer, R.N. and Richman, B.M., *International Business*, 2nd edn., Cedarwood Press 1976.

*Fayerweather, J., *International Business Strategy and Administration*, 2nd edn., Ballinger 1982.

Goldberg, W.H., *Governments and Multinationals*, Oelgeschlager, Gunn and Hain 1983.

*Grub, P.D. and others, (eds.), *The Multinational Enterprise in Transition*, 2nd edn., Darwin 1984.

Håkansson, H., *International Marketing and Purchasing of Industrial Goods*, Wiley 1982.

Hofstede, G., *Cultures' Consequences*, Sage Publications 1984.

*Hood, N. and Young, S., *The Economics of Multinational Enterprise*, Longman 1979.
*Hutton, John, *The World of the International Manager*, Philip Allan 1988.
Kouladis, N., *Law Relating to Overseas Trade*, Oxford: Blackwell 1994.
Lall, S., *Multinational Corporation*, Macmillan 1983.
Lall, S., *The New Multinationals*, Wiley 1983.
Liston, D. and Reeves, N., *Business Studies, Languages and Overseas Trade*, Macdonald and Evans, 1985.
Murray, R. (ed.), *Multinationals beyond the Market: Intra-firm trade and the control of transfer-pricing*, Harvester, 1981.
*North-South: *A Program for Survival*, Pan Books and MIT Press 1980, (The Brandt Report).
Otterbeck, L., (ed.), *The Management of Headquarters-Subsidiary Relationships in Multinational Corporations*, Gower 1985.
*Piercy, N., *Export Strategy: Markets and Competition*, Allen and Unwin 1982.
*Poynter, T.A., *Multinational Enterprises and Government Intervention*, Croom Helm 1985.
Robinson, R.D., *International Business Policy*, Greenwood 1982.
*Robinson, R.D., *Internationalization of Business*, The Dryden Press 1984.
*Robock, S.H. and Simmonds, K., *International Business and Multinational Enterprise*, 4thd edn. Irwin 1989.
Rutenberg, D., *Multinational Management*, Little Brown 1982.
Schmithoff, C.M., *Export Trade: Law and Practice of International Trade*, 9th edn. Stevens 1990.
Sherlock, J., *International Physical Distribution*, Oxford: Blackwell 1994.
Spencer, J., *International Marketing*, Oxford: Blackwell 1994.
Stonier, T., *The Wealth of Information: A Profile of the Past-Industrial Society*, Methuen/Thames 1983.
Stopford, J.M. and Turner, L., *Britain and the Multinationals*, Wiley 1985.
Taylor, M.J. and Thrift, N.J., (eds.), *The Geography of Multinationals*, Croom Helm 1982.
Terpstra, V., *International Marketing*, 5th edn., The Dryden Press 1991.
Tsurumi, Y., *Multinational Management: Business Strategy and Government Policy*, 2nd edn. Ballinger 1984.
*Turner, Louis and Hodges, Michael, *Global Shakeout: World Market Competition and the Challenges for Business and Government*, Century Business 1992. This is an exceptionally interesting book, strongly recommended.
Vernon, R. and Wells, L.T., *Manager in the International Economy*, 4th edn., Prentice-Hall 1981.
Wainwright, K., *Marketing*, Oxford: Blackwell 1994.
*Walter, I. and Murray, T., *Handbook of International Business*, 2nd edn. Wiley 1988.
Wells, L.T., *Third World Multinationals*, MIT Press 1983.

A series of articles on recent research into international business as reflected in articles in the *Journal* can be found in the *Journal of International Business Studies*, 25.4, fourth quarter 1994.

Index